MW01224021

GLOBALIZATION AND INDIGENOUS PEOPLES IN ASIA

GLOBALIZATION AND INDIGENOUS PEOPLES IN ASIA

CHANGING THE LOCAL–GLOBAL INTERFACE

Editors

❧

Dev Nathan
Govind Kelkar
Pierre Walter

SAGE Publications
New Delhi ❧ Thousand Oaks ❧ London

First published in 2004 by

Sage Publications India Pvt. Ltd
B-42, Panchsheel Enclave
New Delhi 110 017

Sage Publications Inc.
2455 Teller Road
Thousand Oaks, California 91320

Sage Publications Ltd
1 Oliver's Yard, 55 City Road
London EC1Y 1SP

Published by Tejeshwar Singh for Sage Publications India Pvt Ltd, typeset in 9.5/11.5 Leewood BK BT at Excellent Laser Typesetters, Delhi and printed at Chaman Enterprises, New Delhi.

Library of Congress Cataloging-in-Publication Data

Globalization and indigenous peoples in Asia: changing the local–global interface/editors, Dev Nathan, Govind Kelkar, Pierre Walter.
    p. cm.
Includes bibliographical references and index.
    1. Sustainable development—Social aspects—Asia. 2. Economic development—Social aspects—Asia. 3. Indigenous peoples—Asia—Economic conditions. 4. Globalization—Economic aspects. I. Nathan, Dev. II. Kelkar, Govind, 1939—III. Walter, Pierre (Pierre Gilbert)

HC415.E5G66   306.3'089—dc22   2004   2004009690

ISBN: 0–7619–3253–4 (Hb)   81–7829–388–9 (India–Hb)

Sage Production Team: Larissa Sayers, Radha Dev Raj and Santosh Rawat

For
Krishna Raj
in memory of shared thoughts

Contents

SECTION 2
MARKETS AND CIVLIZATIONAL CHANGE

FOREWORD

China has, for a long time, been the fastest growing economy in the world. India, too in recent years, has managed fairly high rates of economic growth. Yet, both countries have regions of intense poverty, regions whose conditions have been little relieved by overall national growth. These regions are those inhabited by the indigenous peoples, called minority nationalities in China and Scheduled Tribes in India.

The indigenous peoples, at the same time, provide valuable environmental services to the national, regional and global economies. As this book points out in detail with case studies from India and China, the indigenous peoples are asked to bear the costs of providing environmental services, the best example being the logging bans in both countries in order to improve flood control in the plains, without, however, there being any positive link between provision of these environmental services and their own livelihoods. This book makes a persuasive case for setting up compensation mechanisms to enable indigenous people to benefit from the provision of environmental services, in place of the current system of extracting these services through state regulation. Such a measure would link improved livelihoods of indigenous peoples with enhanced provision of environmental services at the national, regional and global levels.

Setting up compensation mechanisms for the provision of environmental services inevitably means increasing the scope of market mechanisms. While pointing out the possible benefits from an increased scope for market mechanisms, the book also bring out various negativities involved in the process and discusses possible ways of dealing with them. The measures proposed in this book, for instance, continued non-market access to critical livelihood resources, land and forests, and new combinations of private and public decision making, go some way towards enabling market-based decentralization to be designed in a manner that protects the interests of the indigenous peoples.

Over the 1990s the International Fund for Agricultural Development (IFAD) has concentrated its work on poverty reduction among indigenous peoples of Asia. It is this concern which led IFAD to fund a research project on Creating Space for Local Forest Management in Asia. As part of the overall Centre for International Forestry Research (CIFOR) research project, the Asian Institute of Technology (AIT), Bangkok, Thailand, carried out the studies, many of which are published here. Although the case studies are of China and India, with one on Nepal, the analysis and lessons learned have a much wider relevance.

As the world comes to grips with the problems that need to be tackled in achieving the Millennium Development Goals the link between reducing the poverty of indigenous peoples and increasing the supply of globally needed environmental services (carbon sequestration, regulation of hydrological flows, etc.) looms large in the attention of policy-makers. This book is an important contribution to the designing of policies for the enhancment of the supply of environmental services and for the use of markets in a manner that contributes to the development of the indigenous peoples of Asia.

March 2004
Rome

Phrang Roy
Assistant President
International Fund for Agricultural
Development (IFAD)

Acknowledgements

Most of the papers in this book (all except those by Nathan and Shrestha and Nathan and Jodha) were funded by the International Fund for Agricultural Development (IFAD), Rome. They were carried out at the Gender and Development Studies Center of the Asian Institute of Technology (AIT), as part of the research project Creating Space for Local Forest Management, carried out by the Centre for International Forestry Research (CIFOR), Bogor, Indonesia. In China our collaborating institution was the Institute of Ethnology of the Yunnan Academy of Social Sciences, Kunming, China. Due to space limitations it has not been possible to include all of the case studies, in particular the studies by Prof. Guo Dalie, former Director of the Institute of Ethnology, Dr. K. S. Singh, former Director-General of the Anthropological Survey of India, and Samar Bosu-Mullick of Ranchi. The editors acknowledge the contributions of these scholars to the overall research project, without implicating them in the actual analyses of different papers.

The paper by Nathan and Shrestha was carried out under the IFAD–UNIFEM Gender Mainstreaming Programme in Asia; while Jodha worked on the paper (Nathan and Jodha) as part of a project on Globalization and Mountain Communities, financed by the MacArthur Foundation at International Centre for Mountain Area Development (ICIMOD), Kathmandu, Nepal.

Earlier versions of many of the papers were published in the *Economic and Political Weekly*. The papers on environmental services (Nathan; Kumar; Wang Qinghua; and Yu Xiaogang) were published together as a special section of the *Economic and Political Weekly*, 28 July 2001, vol. 36, no. 30; while the concluding paper (Nathan and Kelkar) was published in the *Economic and Political Weekly*, 17–23 May 2003, vol. 38, no. 20. The paper by Nongbri was also published in *Economic and Political Weekly*, 3 August 2001, vol. 36, no. 31. Some of the papers were discussed at various workshops at Bangkok,

Thailand; Kunming, China; Shillong and New Delhi, India; and Victoria, Canada among other places.

A collection like this incurs debts to a large number of people: Phrang Roy and Ganesh Thapa at IFAD, Rome, Italy; Prof. Gajendra Singh, who was co-principal investigator of the research project; and various members of the staff of Gender and Development Studies, Emilyn Madayag, Emilyn Mission, Agnes Pardillia and Yee Yee Swe, for their administrative support at various stages of the research project; at the Asian Institute of Technology (AIT), Bangkok, Thailand, Yu Xiaogang, who not only contributed some of the case studies, but played a key role in coordinating the Chinese studies; Prof. Guo Dalie, former Director of the Institute of Ethnology, Kunming, China who has been a constant source of support and encouragement for our work on China; the other coordinators of the CIFOR research project—Lini Wollenberg, David Edmonds, Madhu Sarin, Neera Singh, Liu Dachang and Antonio Contreras; Sadhna Jha, Krishna Kakad, Vandana Khurana and Lora Prabhu, at the IFAD–UNIFEM Gender Mainstreaming Programme in Asia, New Delhi, India; Krishna Raj and Padma Prakash, at the *Economic and Political Weekly*, for their work in editing some of the papers and for permission to reproduce them here; numerous participants at the various workshops who commented on the papers; a reviewer who gave us comments to help improve the manuscript; and Omita Goyal, Mimi Chowdury, our editors at Sage Publications, along with Larissa Sayers and the rest of the Sage production team, who saw this book through its various stages of publication.

Our thanks to all the institutions for helping carry out the research studies and for the publication of this book. Needless to say, the institutions involved are not responsible for the analyses and opinions in the papers, which remain the responsibility of the authors' alone.

INTRODUCTION

Dev Nathan and Govind Kelkar

Indigenous peoples are faced with two processes that are profoundly influencing their ways of living and their livelihoods: the role of their resources in providing environmental services and the civilizational change of privatization with the generalization of market systems. These two processes form the subject matter of this book.

The indigenous peoples of Asia are generally embedded within various states. Their territories, with forests and mineral resources, have historically been important for extracting minerals and timber and other forest products from which the indigenous peoples have gained little but which have been used for accumulation by the states, both colonial states and their successors. Currently, there is great global concern over the necessity of 'preserving' the forests to meet various needs for environmental services, e.g., absorption of greenhouse gases and the regulation of hydrological flows. Two major Asian states, China and India, have both imposed 'logging bans' in an attempt to extract the necessary flood protection services from the uplands. In areas of community-owned and privately-owned forests this imposes great costs in terms of livelihood options.

Breaking the resource exclusion policies of the states and acknowledging the rights of the indigenous peoples over the forest resources they have historically managed is a way of reversing the current marginalization of the indigenous peoples in both the states within which they are, and from global actions. Sale of environmental services through the introduction of markets for these services, rather than their forced extraction by state fiat, will signal a redistribution of resources within globalization and give the indigenous peoples an increased stake in the provision of needed global public goods.

At the same time, the indigenous societies and economies, under the impact of the generalization of market processes, are undergoing changes in their economic and social system that mark a civilizational change from a system based on stability to one based on accumulation. The new norms of production increase productivity, provide an advanced mode of self-activity and also provide improved well-being to many, but they come at the price of loss of guaranteed access to productive resources, the decline of traditional social welfare systems and the spread of commoditization. Such a transition, however, need not be a surrender to *laissez faire* or neo-liberal policies, but can deal with the negativities, including increasing masculine domination. New forms of community and continued non-market access to critical productive resources, like land and forests, would allow for a greater spread of the benefits of globalization.

Consequently, how to simultaneously deal with the marginality (exclusion) of indigenous peoples in global flows and with the *laissez faire*, nowadays called neo-liberal, privatization of indigenous peoples' economies, in order to craft a more equal and democratic alternative, both globally and locally, are important issues in the context of globalization.

In the rest of the introduction, we will set out the background to the discussion in the book.

GLOBAL PUBLIC GOODS

A recent United Nations Development Programme (UNDP)-sponsored study identified six global problems that require urgent attention: the challenges of global warming; growing international inequality; crisis-prone financial markets; emergence of new drug-resistant disease strains; rapid loss of biodiversity; and genetic engineering (Inge Kaul, Isabelle Grunberg and Marc Stern 1999).

To this list we should add an additional problem, which figured quite prominently at the Johannesburg Conference on Sustainable Development, 2000: providing clean and safe water. Further there are additional elements in the question of inequality. Inequality is no longer just a matter of international inequality, i.e., of inequality between nations. There is also the factor of inequality within nations—of regions within nations (or within multinational states); and of inequality within communities—i.e., of gender and class inequality.

Of these seven global problems requiring urgent attention, four are concerned with hill-forest regions and the indigenous peoples, either as the locus of the problem (inequality) or as pivotal actors who are suppliers (climate control, preservation of biodiversity and provision of clean and safe water).

The global environmental discourse of decline and the rescue of the environment has resulted in global conventions and treaties relating to the conservation of biodiversity, desertification, forest policies and climate change—all of which focus on the protection of 'global commons'. Having destroyed their own forests, plains communities and their states want to 'reconstruct nature as an ideal cultural form' (Castells 2000: 508) in the forests, ignoring the livelihood needs of indigenous peoples. They tend to restrict indigenous people from harnessing their livelihood opportunities. Adequate concern for, or understanding of, either the fragile areas or their inhabitants, who depend on such 'global commons', is lacking.

Further, global discourse informs and acts through state policy, which, often in tandem international finance, fashions programmes for 'protected areas', preservation of 'biodiversity hotspots', for halting deforestation and the like. State policy is informed by the global discourse and financed by international financial instruments, whether as multilateral finance for protected areas, for reforestation through Joint Forest Management (JFM) or through so-called debt for nature swaps.

If the livelihoods of the indigenous peoples were earlier historically ignored in extracting timber and other forest products for the purposes of first colonial and then national accumulation, they are thus still largely ignored in current global-cum-national environmental systems for increasing supply of needed global environmental goods. State management of forests has neither preserved natural capital, nor provided adequate livelihood sources for the indigenous people dependent on forests.

In the face of this failure, the attempted solution, as in various Joint Forest Management (JFM) experiments in India, is to institute village-level controls over access to forests. But in these exercises of 'joint' management it has been seen that the forest departments' agendas of timber extraction dominate the management system, with little benefit to the local communities (Edmunds and Wollenberg 2003). The record of Community Forest Management (CFM) in Nepal, for instance, is somewhat better. Yet there too the forest department agenda of setting aside areas of forest for regeneration of timber, holds sway, with restrictions that go against the poorest, usually single women.

On the whole, the indigenous peoples of Asia, and elsewhere, have been called upon to deliver the needed supplies of environmental services on the basis of governmental fiat or policy regulations, e.g., the logging bans currently in force in China and India, without any attention to the impact on their livelihoods. Thus, the current process of globalization increases the risk of further marginalization, disempowerment and also desperation unless it is specifically adapted to these areas.

Recent international instruments, including the Global Environment Fund (GEF), the Kyoto Protocol and the Clean Development Mechanism (CDM) have, however, begun the process of establishing international markets for some of the global environmental services that indigenous peoples can provide. One of the aims of this book is to urge the furthering of this trend as also making it more general.

INDIGENOUS PEOPLES

It is estimated that about 70 per cent of the worlds more than 250 million indigenous peoples live in Asia (Singh and Jabbi 1996). The indigenous peoples are known by different names: 'hill tribes' in Thailand; 'ethnic minorities' in Vietnam; 'minority nationalities' in China; 'Scheduled Tribes' in India; and 'cultural communities' in the Philippines. Geographically they live in the upland-forest regions. The social features that distinguish them from the lowland populations include a strong emphasis on kinship and clan structures and ethnicity bonds and a strong sense of identity as well as the higher position of women in these societies. Whereas the lowland societies have for long been patriarchal, gender relations among the forest dwellers and the highlanders are more gender-positive, ranging from matrifocal and matrilineal systems and various forms of transition to patriliny. Often subject to the overlordship of state systems, these indigenous peoples have, however, largely remained outside of these states. Economically, they have been outside systems of accumulation, carrying on a combination of swidden and terraced agriculture along with the gathering of forest products.

In this book the term 'indigenous people' is used along with forest communities, mountain peoples, and so on. It is true that in Asia the people of the hill and mountain forest areas are largely indigenous peoples, though there are mountain peoples who are not indigenous (migrants from the plains, or those who have formed states, e.g., the Hindus in Nepal) and there are indigenous peoples who do not live in the hill and forest areas, like the so-called plains' tribals of Assam. Therefore, while these are not identical terms, we broadly use the term indigenous peoples to refer to the upland, forest-dwelling peoples of Asia.

The incidence of poverty is very high among these people. For example, out of the ten regions of India with the highest incidence of poverty four are inhabited by indigenous peoples (known as 'Scheduled Tribes'), although they constitute only about 10 per cent of the population. In 1993–94, when slightly less than 40 per cent of all Indians were below the poverty line, the proportion was 54 per cent for the Scheduled Tribes (IFAD 1999a). The tribals of India accounted for only about 8 per cent of the total population, but for 40 per cent of the internally displaced population, another major characteristic of poverty. The literacy rate was only 24 per cent for the Scheduled Tribes, compared to 52 per cent for the country as a whole. Among the rural tribals, the literacy rate for women was only 13 per cent and the gross enrolment rate for girls among the Scheduled Tribes as a whole was only 27 per cent, as compared to 46 per cent for the general population. Tribal children also exhibited higher rates of malnutrition (Dreze and Srinivasan 1996).

In Vietnam, the incidence of poverty among the ethnic minorities—mostly indigenous peoples—ranges from 66 per cent to 100 per cent, far higher than the national average of 51 per cent (Hooke et al. 1999); per capita incomes are only USD 100 per annum, against USD 290 (almost three times as much) for the country as a whole. In China, the average life expectancy in the Yunnan province, which is dominated by indigenous peoples, is five years less than that of China as a whole (UNDP 1998). In the Wulin mountain area of China, where indigenous peoples comprise 80 per cent of the population, the per capita income was CNY 521 in 1996, compared to CNY 1,792 and CNY 1,277 for the rest of the provinces of Hunan and Guizhou (IFAD 1998) within which the Wulin Mountains are situated. In the area covered by an IFAD-funded project in Simao, cash incomes were about 50 per cent lower than those in the areas of other IFAD projects (which are all in poor, but Han, regions) in China, and grain availability was well below the national poverty line of 200 kg per capita (IFAD 1993). The higher incidence of poverty among indigenous peoples and their displacement by mega-projects is not unique to Asia. This situation also exists in Central and South America (van Genugten and Perez-Bustillo 2001).

Though the above figures show a higher incidence of poverty among the indigenous people than the rest of the population, they still understates the extent of poverty among them (Papola 2001). The calorie requirement for existence or for any activity in the uplands, where they largely live, is higher than in the lowlands. The uplands also require a larger consumption basket for survival, as there are higher housing and shelter needs, including space heating. Finally, prices in the uplands are generally higher than in the lowlands.

All of this leads to a higher incidence of poverty than is revealed by conventional measures that use a uniform income/consumption standard. By conventional, uniform standards the incidence of poverty in the lowlands, hills and mountains of Nepal is more or less the same at a little above 40 per cent. But calculations done by Papola (2001) using different standards for the three zones, shows increased poverty in the hills to about 50 per cent and in the mountains to 60 per cent. Indigenous people's areas are in remote mountains and also relatively inaccessible hill-forest regions. They have a higher proportion of poor, with high levels of morbidity and mortality among women. They are vulnerable to both market and natural shocks and thus deserve special attention for food security and livelihood problems.

Indigenous peoples are subject to displacement as their economic territories are submerged by dam projects or taken over for mining schemes. They constitute the majority of the ever-growing 'environmental refugees'. In Bangladesh, more than 50 per cent of a total of 1.2 million tribals live in the Chittagong Hill Tracts, and their lives have been severely disrupted in the recent past (IFAD 1999b). For example, the construction of the Kaptai Hydroelectric Project rendered some 100,000 of them homeless and submerged about 54,000 acres, equivalent to 40 per cent of the land suitable for intensive cultivation. Some of the displaced families who had settled in the lower hills were displaced again after 1975 by programmes for the resettlement of persons from the lowlands.

One group of increasingly marginalized peoples are the forest dwellers living on the outer islands and in the hilly areas of Indonesia and the Philippines and throughout the hinterland of Southeast and South Asia. Most of them combine swidden and terraced rainfed cultivation with the gathering of forest products. A second group of marginalized peoples are the highlanders or mountain dwellers of the Himalayas and the surrounding ranges that rely even more on gathering and animal husbandry. Although it is true that their isolation has, to some extent, buffered them from the Asian crisis, theirs is a situation of persistent and rising crisis.

THE MARGINALITY OF THE INDIGENOUS PEOPLES

As will be discussed in detail later in this book, the largely subsistence-oriented economic systems of the indigenous peoples are being brought under the sway of commodity forms of production with the resultant disruption of the processes of original accumulation, both economically and socially. During this process they, however, still remain marginal to the national economies of which they are part.

Available evidence shows that the indigenous peoples are being increasingly displaced from land ownership, as in the Thane district of Maharashtra or in Tripura in India. This means that they will eventually belong to the classes of landless and marginal farmers (Munshi 1997; Das Gupta 1997). Areas where the tribals still dominate land ownership, namely the hill forest regions, are those marked by a substantial lack of infrastructure. Some of these areas have been opened up essentially to extract timber, minerals, non-timber forest products (NTFPs) and other natural resources, but these investments have enabled the advance of non-tribal populations into the area and the tribals are losing their best lands.

What little development assistance the upland populations have received has—until recently—been guided by the primary concerns of the lowlands and the mainstream societies. The conventional industrial and agrarian sectors rarely flourish in the hills and mountains due to strong comparative disadvantages (e.g., in terms of production costs). The uplands do have attractive assets but, as seen above, past efforts to exploit their comparative advantages have tended to dispossess the local populations. Environmental services like controlled hydrological flows or carbon sequestration and the preservation of biodiversity are taken from them without any compensation. The current process of globalization in the context of weak property rights of the indigenous peoples enhances the risks of further marginalization.

Indigenous people are marginal to the growing national and global networks of capital in a number of ways. First, they are national minorities and hence politically marginal. Second, economically, they have a small role to play in '...labour markets (as workers), capital markets (as investors), commodity markets (as consumers) or even in debt markets (as tax payers paying for bonds)' (Lutz and Nonini 1999: 100). They are marginal even as far as their world-views and cultures are concerned, usually being dismissed as 'primitive'. Even in South East and East Asia the fast growth and poverty reduction of the 1980s and the first half of the 1990s largely bypassed them. They participated in fast growth only as the lowest rungs of the migrant working class, often as 'illegal' immigrants. With the onset of the Asian crisis, even these meager earnings were depleted as jobs disappeared and wages fell.

Policies for the indigenous peoples have so far been framed mainly with a view to the benefits that can be extracted for the outside economies. What the states covet from the hill-forest areas are the resources, like timber and minerals, which they extract from the local economies. Whenever deemed necessary for the national interest, be it for irrigation or for power supply, the indigenous peoples have been displaced to make way for dams, with most of them losing their livelihoods. In most cases the indigenous peoples do not own the forest and mineral resources of their economies. Consequently, revenues from mines and forests accrue to the economies of the lowlands. At best, the indigenous peoples get low wages at the bottom of the working class. In cases where the indigenous people do have some form of ownership rights over the forest and mineral resources, they have often been forced, in the name of national interest, to submit to policies that are not in their interests. For instance, both China and India have instituted logging bans that have seriously affected the incomes of those indigenous people who did have some ownership rights over forests. In many countries of Asia, the resources of the indigenous peoples have so far not been managed in ways that promote local accumulation and development. This is the essence of the marginality of indigenous peoples to the national states of which they are part.

VIOLATION OF THE HUMAN RIGHTS OF INDIGENOUS PEOPLES

To many indigenous peoples, marginalization and poverty are very much linked to their being deprived of the capabilities needed to lead the kind of lives they value, something closely linked to the issue of basic human rights. This is an aspect of human existence that is often opposed as a 'luxury' in a poor country on the grounds that the need to provide basic human necessities like food and shelter is more important than other human rights like freedom of speech, equality before the law and justice. Yet the poor, themselves, often rank human rights very high on their scale of values. The United Nations (UN) Working Group on Indigenous Populations points out that the indigenous peoples have been deprived of human rights and fundamental freedoms, thereby affecting their right to development 'according to their own needs and interests' (1993). There also exist extreme forms of exploitation by officials, traders and contractors.

The extended process of state intrusion into forest areas that characterized the colonial and even the post-colonial periods brought about a far-reaching change in the ownership and management of the forests in many countries. In India and the Philippines, this took place during the respective British and Spanish colonial regimes; and in China, it came about with the extension of central state rule over outlying frontier regions. In India and the Philippines in particular, the indigenous people had rights of collection or use granted by the state, but not having ownership or even recognized tenure, they became, at best, interlopers on their own lands or worse, lawbreakers because their daily actions, whether of gathering, conversion to agriculture or other uses, became criminal acts on 'state' property.

It is no wonder that forest departments have traditionally had not only administrative but also police and judicial powers. In India, the 1865 Forest Act initiated legal discrimination against forest dwellers (who are by and large indigenous peoples) by giving forest officials the right to arrest them without warrant, and also the power to levy penalties. This elimination of the separation of police and judiciary reduced the forest dwellers to the status of second-class citizens without the civil rights to due process of law. The separation of powers between the administration, judiciary and the police, that provides some scope for protection from abuse of their rights, is not available to forest dwellers. A basic civil right that other citizens, the plains dwellers, have is denied to them (Singh 1986: 14). The forest departments in the rest of Asia are modelled on the Indian system introduced by the British (which itself was based on the German system) in that extensive police and judicial powers are given to forest officials. In some countries like Thailand, the situation is even worse in that most indigenous peoples are not even recognized as citizens.

Can the lack of human rights, of the civil rights that citizens of modern states take for granted, have an effect on human development as noted by the UN Working Group mentioned above? The deprivation of forest dwellers of their basic human rights does have an impact on their human—more specifically their economic development. Because of their extensive and unbridled powers, the forest officials can declare as 'illegal acts' even the simplest use of the forests as a source of livelihood (e.g., selling fuel wood). At every step, forest dwellers live in fear of having to pay fines levied by forest officials. The essential relationship between the two sides is marked by almost daily coercion by all-powerful officials and the absence of accepted tenure or ownership rights for the forest dwellers. At the economic level, this means that governments—through the forest officials—confiscate a portion of the forest dwellers' already meager incomes. In Thailand, the lack of citizenship makes the forest dwellers subject to further extraction, as they need to get official permission to move out of their districts. This is both costly and laborious.

Deprivation of human rights can have serious consequences by retarding human development. Human rights, especially due process of law with separation of powers, are important in themselves as aspects of governance and modern human existence.

The transformation of indigenous peoples into people with secure tenurial rights marks an important change in their relation to the state. This process calls for a total change in the nature of the forest departments. In Nepal, the Forestry Service is in the process of being transformed from its earlier police nature to that of a technical, extension service, much like the agriculture departments. However, old habits die hard and the 1993 Nepal Forest Act still contains clauses that give forest officials the right to arrest without warrant and to settle fines of up to Rs 10,000. Further, recent by-laws proposed by the government seek to curtail the powers of forest user groups and increase the management role of forest officials.

The Panchayat Extension to Scheduled Areas (PESA) in India, the Ancestral Domains Act in the Philippines and other similar legislation, are important steps in recognizing the tenurial or property rights of forest dwellers. These are important prerequisites for the transformation of their status, from interlopers or squatters to that of full citizens and owners. Such transformation is not only a matter of recognizing property or tenurial rights, but also one of revoking, once and for all, the police and judicial powers of forest department officials. Without this correction, decentralization and devolution of power will be considerably less than what it seems or claims to be.

VIOLENCE AND CONFLICT

The extreme forms of exploitation and violation of civil rights that exist in areas such as Northeast India, the Chattisgarh and Jharkhand states of India and the Cordilleras of the Philippines have turned these areas into places of long-standing insurgency. Another reason that has led to rising violence in the forest areas is encroachment by migrants who are taking over the land of the indigenous peoples. Some governments sponsored some of these movements, like the Indonesian 'transmigration' policy of supporting the resettling of peoples from the crowded island of Java to the outlying islands populated by the indigenous peoples, as a means of reducing pressure for land reform on the plains.[1] Experience has shown that such migration schemes, whether in small numbers as in the Chittagong Hill Tracts and most other hill-forest regions, or on a large scale as attempted in Indonesia's 'transmigration' scheme, have resulted in heavy conflict over resource use. This intense conflict underlies the endemic ethnic violence in these areas. In Indonesia, as the central state power has weakened after the fall of the dictatorial Suharto regime there has been a resurgence of ethnic violence directed at driving out these 'transmigrated' settlers.

There have been attempts to resolve some of these insurgencies by holding 'peace talks', but these can yield results only if they deal with the fundamental socio-economic conditions of extreme exploitation and resource exclusion that underlie the insurgencies. Failing to do so, they have failed to resolve the causes of the violence. The formation of separate provinces or states as done in India has given some scope for the development of social classes among the marginalized ethnic groups. However, various issues relating to political, social and economic exclusion remain unresolved.

Indigenous communities, embedded within larger states, are subject to a process of 'resource exclusion' (Jodha 2002). The states claim the chief natural resources, like forests and minerals, as 'national property' and exclude the local communities from their productive use. Even if the indigenous people's ownership of the resources is not disputed, as in most of Northeast India, the ability to use these resources for livelihood purposes is denied through instruments like the Indian Supreme Court judgment instituting a 'logging ban'. In trying to establish the local community's rights over these resources a frequently deployed political weapon is that of 'identity politics'.

The rise of 'identity politics' has been put forward by Mary Kaldor (2001) as the prime factor behind the 'new wars' that accompany the current phase of globalization. Underlying this identity politics, however, is the attempted primary accumulation of capital, an accumulation that is being restricted or thwarted by the existing states' policy of resource exclusion. As an expression of primary accumulation, identity politics does not look like an irrational reaction to the supposedly progressive cosmopolitanism of the classical anti-colonial struggles. But not all identity politics have as their economic base,

---

[1] See Colchester and Lohman (1993). For analyses showing the connection between the lack of land reforms in the plains and the pressures for clearing forestland.

primary accumulation. The Basque struggle in Spain–France is clearly not a question of primary accumulation, since the Basque have had a capitalist class and a well-developed capitalist industry much before the rest of Spain. But the concentration of insurgencies across Northeast India, the central Indian forest areas (Chattisgarh, Jharkhand and Dandakarnya), the Himalaya–Hindukush region, the Chittagong Hill Tracts of Bangladesh, along with the indigenous people's areas in the Philippines and Indonesia, and the struggles in Malaysia, all show that in Asia there is a connection between identity politics, resource exclusion and primary accumulation.

The rise of this intense conflict underlies the endemic 'identity' violence in these areas. Wars within nations have replaced wars between nations as the main form of warfare in the contemporary world. During 1987–97, more than 85 per cent of conflicts were fought within national borders, overwhelmingly in poor countries: 14 in Asia, 14 in Africa and one in Europe (World Bank 2000).

At one level, the cost of fighting wars diverts public spending from productive activities. But these direct costs are not the only economic consequences. Contracts become difficult to enforce and property rights insecure. The suppression of civil rights associated with civil war reduces the efficiency of public expenditure (Collier 1999). Taken together, these factors mean that civil war reduces the GDP, with per capita output falling by about 2 per cent relative to what it would have been without civil war. This is because of the gradual loss of capital stock due to destruction, dis-saving and flight of capital, as well as emigration of highly skilled workers. Different sectors of the economy are differently affected. 'The sector intensive in capital and transactions (manufacturing) and the sectors which supply capital (construction) and transactions (transport, distribution and finance) contract more rapidly than GDP as a whole. The sector with the opposite characteristics (arable subsistence agriculture) expands relative to GDP' (ibid.). In the indigenous people's areas that we are dealing with, it is a question of retardation, rather than contraction, of sectors like manufacturing and an over-dependence on subsistence agriculture.

At a more general level, civil war promotes speculative trading activities at the expense of production. The dividing line between political opposition and banditry becomes increasingly blurred on both sides—the regular armed forces and those opposing them—and both individuals and groups take to earning in whatever manner they can. This results in the growth of an 'economy of pillage' (Lutz and Nonini 1999).

Overall in the 'new wars' civilian casualties by far outnumber military casualties. 'At the turn of the century, the ratio of civilian to military casualties in wars was 8:1. Today, this has been almost exactly reversed; in the wars of the 1990s, the ratio of military to civilian casualties is approximately 1:8' (Kaldor 2001: 9).

In these 'new wars' (*ibid*.) the frequent aim is the destruction of civilian life. Torture and terror on civilian populations are part of the methods of the 'new wars' aimed at 'meaning-destroying effects' (Lutz and Nonini 1999: 98). There is a gendered effect of the war process, which shores up gender orders in crisis. The new masculinities are defined by male participation in violence (*ibid*.: 101).

Peace, however, cannot be simply the absence of conflict or the elimination of fear of physical violence. That would be a 'negative' and insecure peace. To be 'positive', peace must eliminate the structures that support unequal capability fulfillment within or between countries (Brock-Utne 1989) and redress the wrongs done to all those involved in unequal power, including gender relations. Rather than a return to the *status quo*, a positive peace must include the elimination of unequal power and development relations.

The elimination of unequal power and development relations might be achieved under two conditions. The first is that of regions with varying degrees of autonomy within the nation state, the second that of independent countries. The indigenous peoples' movements have articulated both of these aspirations. There is a regional difference in this, with the Latin American movements largely opting for forms of autonomy, while some, though not all, Asian indigenous peoples' movements have favoured the demand for independence. Where the central state has been considerably weakened, as is the case of Indonesia after the Asian crisis, some regions, like East Timor with substantial support from the international community, have successfully broken away to form independent states. In most cases, as in India or China, there are degrees of autonomy gained by provincial or lower-level administrative units of indigenous peoples.

The formation of separate states may resolve some issues of devolution of revenues but not that of property rights of the indigenous peoples. This is seen in the instance of Jharkhand, where the Jharkhand government is continuing the earlier Bihar policy of replacing what little community management of forests there is, as in the *khuntkatti* areas, with the so-called Joint Forest Management (JFM), financed by the World Bank, forcing the state into the process (Sanjay Bosu-Mullick, personal communication). This retrograde process is occurring even in Uttaranchal, where the *van panchayats* are also being supplanted by World Bank-financed JFM institutions (Sarin 2003). A resolution of indigenous people's rights to their ancestral resources is something without which no lasting peace can be brought about in the various uplands.

In sum the national (or, rather most often, the multinational) state does not represent the appropriate institution for the development aspirations of the indigenous peoples. The centralizing aspects of these states deprive the indigenous peoples of control over their resources and downgrade their own forms of cultural existence and development. One person's imagined community is another person's prison (Appadurai 1996).

In this situation, linking up economically and culturally with distant powers, even if they are the dominant global powers, might seem an alternative to the forced linking up with the immediate power, whether it is India, China, or Indonesia. Adopting English as the medium of education and as the official language, as has been done by many indigenous people's states in Northeast India, and Western rock music as against the music of the Hindi film, seem less oppressive routes to modernity. With globalization they may have the advantage of allowing the indigenous peoples to more quickly tap into the new circuits of production and jobs.

The combination of identity struggles to overcome resource exclusion with primary accumulation complicates the picture of primary accumulation. But, along with the other poor, women are the main losers in these identity wars. War strengthens masculine domination, the new masculinities and the exclusion of women from economic resources. Further, the 'economy of pillage' carries over into the peace period. Those who led the armed insurgency during the identity war, now dominate the political and bureaucratic processes. This domination can be deployed to accumulate resources—witness the massive land grab of non-village land in Mizoram, a state formed as a result of a long-standing insurgency, where the insurgents subsequently took over the local state system after the peace agreement.

The accession to state power of the former militants only accelerates the process of civilizational change—the shift from what Marx called 'simple reproduction' to accumulation, the separation of access to productive forces from membership of the community and the denial of traditional forms of reciprocity. All these together constitute what is called the 'primary accumulation of capital'—the stamping of the commodity form on social relations including relations of production. Whether in conjunction with political position (village headmen or area chiefs) or not, violence or the ability to deploy violence, an age-old masculine monopoly, plays a role in local accumulation of productive resources.

The civilizational change, perhaps like any process of change, is a contradictory process. It liberates human productive capabilities and can help increase incomes while also increasing alienation. The first experience of modernity is adventure but then turns into routine, to use Marshall Berman's terms (1982). It can change the current terms of exchange between the indigenous peoples and the external world, both the national and global economies. But it also creates new forms of exclusion and poverty within indigenous communities. If this civilizational change were left to the current dominant 'neo-liberal' or more classically called *laissez faire* doctrine, the resulting structures would be much more unequal and undemocratic. Crafting more democratic alternatives in globalization is an important task, one that the various contributors in this book set out to do.

OVERVIEW OF THE BOOK

There are two forms of interaction of the global with the local—the vernacularization or localization of the global, which has been the central concern of a number of works (e.g., Appadurai 1996); and the globalization of the local. Our concern is more with the second, which is globalization of the local.

This book examines the connections and contradictions between global flows and management of local places. Starting with the area of ecosystem services, it goes on to consider traditional products like NTFPs, other commodities like ethnic tourism and former domestic, cultural products. Though global policy may be formulated in various international fora, like the Rio or Johannesburg Conferences, or the Kyoto Protocol, these global polices are then implemented through national states. Of course, global pressures are felt through the market. Thus, the two instruments of external or global intervention considered are state policy and the market.

The case studies are from the uplands of South Asia (India and Nepal) and East Asia (China). Some of the papers, however, also use material from other uplands of the Himalaya–Hindukush region and Southeast Asia.

For the case studies of local management of environmental service functions of forests, since the objective was to see the manner in which these functions were understood and integrated in local management, those regions of India and China were chosen which have systems of continuing community ownership of forests, as against state-owned forests. Thus, Northeast India and Yunnan are the focus of this study. The *Mundari-Khuntkatti* (MK) areas of Jharkhand also qualified as an area of community ownership, consequent upon a right extracted by the Birsa Munda-led rebellion at the end of the nineteenth century. The *van panchayats* of Uttaranchal in Himalayan India are also an area of community rights over forest. But here the nature of the Chipko Movement, led by women, for local management of forests is very well known. Forest communities in peninsular India, living in state-owned forests, were left out for this book, as they do not have ownership rights over the forests, though the argument of the book is certainly that they should be given some kind of ownership rights over forests.

Similarly for studying the effects of the market on existing communal formations, we excluded those forest areas of China (i.e., all those outside Western Yunnan) where forests were already privatized by state-sponsored household allocation. In Western Yunnan, communities which were under the overlordship of the Chinese state prior to 1949 but had still largely continued with their indigenous social and economic systems, reinstated forms of community ownership of forests in the post-1978 reform scenario. There were suitable areas, like Northeast India, to study the effects of the extension of markets, largely through the trade in timber and other forest products and more recently through tourism, on forms of community management.

Tourism is one of the prominent sectors that develops with globalization. The effects of tourism were studied by Kelkar in one case study and Walter in another in different parts of Yunnan, China.

The first section of the book deals with environmental services and argues that:

1. Forests are being increasingly viewed by external authorities (the state, international bodies) for the flows of ecosystem services (carbon sequestration, flood protection) they can provide.
2. These services are being taken from the forest dwellers free of any charge.
3. The provision of these services imposes various livelihood costs on the forest dwellers which are disregarded by external authorities.
4. A system of property rights (with some restrictions) would give forest communities an incentive to provide these global flows of ecosystem services, and enable them to better integrate the

supply of these services with their other uses of the forest. Anthropological, distributional and economic efficiency arguments are discussed for granting property rights to indigenous people to supply environmental services as commodities.

5. The demand for adequate property rights is an articulation of the forest communities' desire to end the resource exclusion that is at the base of their current marginal status.

Further, it is not only environmental services, but also indigenous peoples' cultural products and knowledge (of medicinal plants and herbs) that are being extracted from them free of charge. This free extraction or extraction which only takes into account the costs of extraction, imposes all other costs on the indigenous peoples and is at the heart of their unequal exchange with the rest of the world. In the second chapter, Nathan argues for the proper allocation of property rights, and the commoditization of various indigenous peoples' products, as an important measure to both increase global flows of these products, while improving livelihoods in the local places, as also to improve the sustainability of the flows of these commodities.

Case studies of indigenous peoples' management of community forests in India (Sanjay Kumar) and China (Wang Qinghua) show the extent of indigenous peoples' knowledge of the local environmental services provided by forests, and the manner in which their management takes account of these environmental service functions. On the other hand, state extraction of water as an environmental product in China is shown in the case study (Yu Xiaogang) to have adverse livelihood consequences for the local people, while transferring all the benefits to those in towns and to the areas irrigated. Similarly state management of forests through the Indian Supreme Court's ban on logging has had very negative consequences for both local livelihoods and forest condition in the privately-owned forests of Meghalaya (Tiplut Nongbri). As against the general impoverishment associated with timber extraction, on the other hand, the devolution of timber incomes and related tax revenues to local communities and governments in China has led to substantial livelihood benefits in China. In the specific case study of Lijiang the new sector of tourism that now contributes a large and growing share of local income, has been largely built on accumulation from local forest incomes and revenues (Dev Nathan and Yu Xiaogang).

Some aspects of localization have been discussed in various papers: the localization of natural resource management decisions so as to take account of local provision of various environmental services and non-traded goods; and the use of income incentives and price signals to allow local regulation of flows of global environmental services. What the above means is a change in the nature of existing national regulatory and management agencies, like the forest departments, to one of extension and facilitation, more akin to what agricultural departments, for instance, do. We have also discussed issues relating to the localization of revenues and the reinvestment of local savings. Of course, stressing the reinvestment of local savings does not rule out the role of international public money to support provision of global environmental public goods (like biodiversity conservation, reduction of global warming, regulation of hydrological flows and so on) at levels beyond those which are forthcoming from straightforward income and price incentives.

Since we are considering a system of property rights (at private and community levels) with marketable services, it is also necessary to understand the contradictions that emerge from such a system. The experience of indigenous management systems, initially designed for systems of production mainly for self-consumption, as they confront the market demand for higher flows of their products is analyzed in the concluding chapter.

The main conclusions of the second section are that:

1. The intervention of market forces has initiated or strengthened the formation of private property from earlier forms of communal or collective management, which were inadequate for the new purposes of production for the market and accumulation.
2. Privatization or enclosure of the commons has enabled investment and the development of production.
3. The market reduces inefficiency in resource use, and enables an intensification of resource use beyond that brought about by local demand for self-consumption.
4. The formation of private property, as it to be expected, has gone hand in hand with the rise of class inequalities and patriarchy, particularly the loss of assured access to land.
5. New forms of distribution of land and other productive resources, private–public interaction and public human welfare systems, however, can alter the shape of privatization from the *laissez faire* or 'neo-liberal' way of leaving it all to the market. More equal forms of gender relations, less unequal development and human welfare systems can be built along with privatization.

An example is studied from Nepal (Nathan and Shreshta) of such an attempt to build an alternative to 'neo-liberal' market allocation of productive resources by handing over dedicated patches of community forest to the poor, largely women.

The final two papers (Nathan and N. S. Jodha; Nathan and Govind Kelkar) sum up the manner in which indigenous peoples can respond to the market opportunities of globalization, its consequences and ways of fashioning an alternative to 'neo-liberal' globalization, through dealing with externalities, non-market access to land and critical natural resources, and education, and new forms of pubic–private interaction.

The conclusion of the book (spelled out in the chapter on civilizational change) is that along with acknowledging the property rights of indigenous peoples, instead of a *laissez faire* doctrine of leaving everything else to the market, we need specific interventions in property rights, gender relations, new welfare systems to recreate community, and public decision-making, in order to create a more democratic alternative to neo-liberal globalization. Both the global structure in which indigenous people's rights are denied and the structures within indigenous communities need to be addressed. Such alternative projects, however, to be achievable in a globalizing world need to look beyond national boundaries and to create global alliances to support them.

Changes in gender relations subsequent to the growth of tourism in Lijiang, China are the focus of the essay by Kelkar. But, overall, while most of the essays pay some attention to the formation of patriarchy and the challenges to it in the process of civilizational change, this important process of social change is not subject to a full analysis. The reason being simply that that is the subject of another book,[2] that largely grew out of the same research projects.

A task not taken up in this book is to go into the whole debate for and against globalization, that would require a book by itself. This book attempts to understand the ways in which the local of the indigenous people interacts with the global—in order to be able to change the terms of that interaction. Such a goal is modest, but is needed in order to craft better (more equal, and democratic) alternatives within globalization.

---

[2] See Govind Kelkar, Dev Nathan and Pierre Walter. eds. *Gender Relations in Forest Societies in Asia: Patriarchy at Odds.* New Delhi, Thousand Oaks, London: Sage Publications, 2003.

One of the terms often used in this book is 'localization'—there is reference to the localization of decisions concerning resource use and supply of environmental services, localization of accumulation, and so on. Localization, however has come to mean many things. In particular a very restrictive, meaning has been given by Colin Hines's slogan *Protect the Local, Globally* (Hines 2000). Since Hines' notion of localization is gaining currency in some environmental circles, in the rest of this Introduction we will put forward our differences with this notion of localization.

Not Isolation—But Changing the Terms of Local–Global Interaction

In Hines' localization, carried out within regional locations, there will be the minimizing of long distance trade to those goods whose 'output is not available in many parts of the world' (*ibid*.: 242), e.g., some cash crops, like coffee, tea and bananas, minerals and certain location specific luxury items like scotch whisky. This is a picture of world trade as it used to exist in the age of innocence, i.e., the world before trade in staples. Chinese silk, and Indian spices were the best examples of this trade, with South American precious metals (gold and silver) and African slaves later added to the list.

Hines comes to the proposition of the necessity of protecting local production of anything and everything from the point that 'the reduction of product or service miles (distance from provider to consumer) is an environmental goal' (*ibid*.: 28), presumably because there is an understating of transport costs, due to low energy prices. An increase in energy costs (*ibid*.: 30) will to some extent induce reduction of product or service miles. But, over and above such an effect of increasing energy costs Hines argues for 'positive discrimination in favour of the local' (*ibid*.: 28). Irrespective of differences in costs of production in different locations, anything that can be produced locally, should be protected against competition from low cost production elsewhere.

That energy costs are understated is a perfectly understandable proposition. This is so even for renewable energy sources, like fuel wood and other biomass. Other environmental services and products are also underpriced, or even given a zero price. That is why this book argues in favour of accepting the ownership rights of forest communities over the forests they use and manage. The removal of such subsidies, the costs of which are borne by those who are globally among the poorest communities, is a necessary, if not sufficient, step in changing the manner of use of these resources.

But the privileging of local production, over and above any such reduction in product or service miles, would have two very serious consequences for the world economy and the poorest within it. The first is the substantial loss in productivity by the duplication of inefficient and below scale production in many localities. More important is the second consequence—the loss of markets for low cost producers in the developing world. At a time when developing countries are trying to break down the barriers to increasing their exports of, say, garments to the Euro-American and Japanese economies, the localization of garment manufacturing will be a death blow to millions of workers in the developing economies. The current global downturn has already had a serious impact on the jobs of hundreds of thousands of, for instance, Bangladeshi women. For these women the admittedly low paid jobs in the garment industry, represent not only a substantial additional means of sustenance for their families, but also embody their increased dignity and self-worth as they move out of the stultifying restrictions of domestic patriarchy into what is a real, if partial and limited, advance into wage employment.

For millions of such workers around the world, the export markets for lower-level manufactures has been the means of meeting basic needs for themselves and their families. It is not, as Hines contends, a drain of resources from 'meeting the basic needs of the poor majority in those countries' (Hines 2000: 244). What is ignored in this characterization is the very real role of export markets for mass consumer goods in breaking out of a low-income and high-unemployment situation. In diversifying local production the barrier of the existing market is very real. Export markets come in as a way of getting around this constraint, with subsequent rounds of multiplier effects on local income and production. In the situation of the uplands, with their history of organic but low productivity (per capita/per annum) agriculture, export markets for organic products can be a real source of higher value realization. Cutting off the possibility of such export markets will only make it even more difficult for these economies to break out of the existing cycle of low production and high unemployment.

What are the social objectives of the localization proposed by Hines? There are two that stand out. The first is reversing the threat of relocation of whole industries 'ranging from low-tech to high-tech, from sandals to software' (*ibid*.: 243). Against the real loss to workers from the developed world, we must also place the real gains to workers from the developing world. A global perspective is only possible if workers everywhere count for as much. In which case relocation is not a loss of jobs, as it seems from the perspective of, say Europe. But relocation is a shifting of jobs from the developed to the developing capitalist countries. Given the desperate poverty of, say, Bangladeshi women, is there any global gain in the relocation of the garment industry to provide them with employment? If we give the movement out of dire poverty (and out of the strictest forms of domestic patriarchy) greater weight than a similar income improvement for workers in developed countries, then there is a global welfare gain in such relocation. One cannot be a globalist in outlook and argue against relocation that benefits the poorest sections of the global working class. Even within the neo-classical tradition there is the Bergsonian approach that gives differential weights to the poor on the ground that their marginal utility of money (income) is higher than it is for the rich. By any count a policy of opposing relocation of industries 'ranging from low-tech to high-tech, from sandals to software' would lead to real welfare losses for the poorest in the world and of the global working class. What is required from a globalist perspective is that in the developed countries measures are instituted to handle the social disruption of such relocation, through moving into new sectors, forms of social insurance, etc.

The other social objective that Hines' relocation is supposed to achieve is even more controversial. Relocation would [deal with or reduce] 'the domestic implications for Organisation for Economic Co-operation and Development (OECD) countries of the increased movement of people displaced by globalization's economic failures and its concomitant adverse environmental effects' (Hines 2000: 33). Such a concern with 'domestic implications for OECD countries of increased movement of peoples' is something quite widespread in Europe, affecting even otherwise more liberal societies, like Norway and Sweden.

In the first place such movements of displaced peoples is concentrated among those regions where industrial relocation has not taken place, e.g., in Africa, Kurdistan, etc. Areas of relocation, for instance Malaysia and Thailand, have themselves become destinations for migrants from other countries. So, to the extent that relocation of industry takes place it in fact reduces migration, and thus the 'domestic consequences for OECD countries of increased movement of people.'

The second point is whether one should oppose such increased movement of people. It can certainly be argued that the right to migrate in search of better living and other opportunities is a human right. What is needed is to improve the terms on which people can migrate. That depends very much on the condition of the economy from which they migrate and the capabilities they have developed before they migrate.

Finally, the regional localism that Hines advocates only sets the stage for inter-regional competition. Fortresses are set up in order to make one group immune to attack in order to be able to launch attacks on others. Such a defensive insulation is not meant to achieve isolation but immunity from retaliation. Similarly in trade matters too, the history of blocs has been the preparation for intensification of trade wars, leading at some stage, to actual wars. The type of regional localism proposed by Hines would only increase such global competition and sow the seeds of wars. Of course, such preparations are in fact being made, whether it is to unite the Americas in a vast trade bloc, to advance the Euro as a world currency or the halting moves to bring East and Southeast Asia into a regional bloc.

Consequently what we advocate is not isolation but changing the terms on which the local interacts with the global. Secure property rights in the resources, forests, etc. that the indigenous peoples' manage, and the concomitant right to sell the environmental goods and services deriving from the management of these resources. This is a measure that would change the terms on which the local (of Asian indigenous peoples) interacts with the global. The consequences of such market interaction, instead of the existing state policy of forced extraction of these environmental goods and services, has been explored in a number of papers in this book. The transformation of formerly communal into individual properties, the loss of earlier social welfare systems, class differentiation and the anomie caused by loss of one's norms, have also been explored in the papers dealing with market processes. Along with the costs there are also the benefits, both unevenly distributed.

How to simultaneously deal with the marginality (exclusion) of indigenous peoples in global flows and with the neo-liberal evolution of indigenous peoples' economies, in order to craft a more equal and democratic alternative, both globally and locally, is the agenda of this book.

36 ❦ Dev Nathan and Govind Kelkar

44

4444

Appadurai, Arjun. *Modernity At Large*. New Delhi: Oxford University Press, 1996.
Berman, Marshall. *All That Is Solid Melts Into Air: The Experience of Modernity*. New York and London: Penguin Books, 1982.
Brock-Utne, Birgit. *Feminist Perspective on Peace and Peace Education*. New York: Pergamon Press, 1989.
Castells, Manuel. *The Rise of the Network Society*. 2nd ed. London: Blackwell Publishers, 2000.
Colchester, Marcus and Larry Lohman. eds. *The Struggle for Land and the Fate of the Forests*. London: The World Rainforest Movement with the Ecologist and Zed Books, 1993.
Collier, Paul. 'On the Economic Consequences of Civil War.' *Oxford Economic Papers 51* (1999): 168–83.
Das Gupta, Malabika. 'From Tribe to Caste: The Mogs of Tripura.' In *From Tribe to Caste*, edited by Dev Nathan. Shimla: Indian Institute of Advanced Study (IIAS), 1997.
Dreze, Jean and P. V. Srinivasan. 'Poverty in India: Regional Estimates, 1987–88.' Working paper, Institute of Economic Growth, New Delhi, 1996.
Edmunds, David and Eva Wollenberg, eds. *Local Forest Management: The Impacts of Devolution Policies*. London: Earthscan, 2003.
Hines, Colin. *Localization: A Global Manifesto*. London: Earthscan Press, 2000.
Hooke, Gus, Peter Warr, Barry Shaw, Adam Fforde and Caroline Bassard. 'Agriculture in Times of Crisis: Impacts in South-east Asia of the Economic Crisis.' A report commissioned by the Australian Agency for International Development (Ausaid), from Hassall and Associates International, Canberra, 1999.
International Fund for Agricultural Development (*or IFAD*). *Yunnan-Simao Minorities Area Agricultural Development Project: Appraisal Report*, Rome, 1993.
——————. *Wulin Minority Area Integrated Agricultural Development Project: Formulation Report*. Vol. 1. Rome, 1998.
——————. *India: Country Strategic Opportunities Paper*. Rome, 1999a.
——————. *Bangladesh: Country Strategic Opportunities Paper*. Rome, 1999b.
Jodha, N. S. 'Policies for Sustainable Mountain Development: An Indicative Framework and Evidence.' Paper presented at the Asia High Summit, International Centre for Integrated Mountain Development (ICIMOD), Kathmandu, 2002.
Kaldor, Mary. *New and Old Wars: Organized Violence in a Global Era*. Stanford: Stanford University Press, 2001.
Kaul, Inge, Isabelle Grunberg and Marc Stern, eds. *Global Public Goods*. New York: Oxford University Press, 1999.
Lutz, Catherine and Donald Nonini. 'The Economics of Violence (and Vice Versa).' In *Anthropological Theory Today*, edited by Henrietta Moore. Oxford: Polity Press, 1999.
Munshi, Indra. 'The Warlis: From Shifting Cultivators to Peasants and Labourers.' In *From Tribe to Caste*, edited by Dev Nathan. Shimla: IIAS, 1997.
Papola, T. S. 'Poverty in the Mountains.' Kathmandu: ICIMOD, 2001.
Sarin, Madhu. 'Empowerment and Disempowerment of Forest Women in Uttarakhand, India.' In *Gender Relations in Forest Societies in Asia: Patriarchy*

at Odds, edited by Govind Kelkar, Dev Nathan and Pierre Walter. New Delhi, Thousand Oaks, London: Sage Publications, 2003.

Singh, A. and M. Jabbi. *Status of Tribals in India*. New Delhi: Har-Anand Publications, 1996.

Singh, Chhatrapati. *Common Property and Common Poverty: India's Forests, Forest Dwellers and the Law*. New Delhi: Oxford University Press, 1986.

United Nations Development Programme (UNDP). *Human Development Report*. New York: Oxford University Press, 1998.

UN Working Group on Indigenous Populations. *Draft Declaration*. Geneva, 1993.

van Genugten, Willem and Camilo Perez-Bustillo. *The Poverty of Rights: Human Rights and the Eradication of Poverty*. London and New York: Zed Books, 2001.

World Bank. *World Development Report*. Washington D.C., 2000.

SECTION 1

ENVIRONMENTAL SERVICES AND FOREST MANAGEMENT

1

ENVIRONMENTAL SERVICES AND THE CASE FOR LOCAL FOREST MANAGEMENT

Dev Nathan

INTRODUCTION

For a long time, forests, as seen from the viewpoint of states and forest departments, meant timber. More recently, the importance of Non-Timber Forest Products (NTFPs), on which forest communities rely for a large part of their cash income and self-consumed products, have become an integral part of the discussion on forests. 'The importance attached to NTFPs has possibly changed forever the way forest values and their development potential are assessed' (Wollenberg 1998). But forests are not only timber and NTFP; they also provide environmental services. Carbon sequestration is one of the global environmental services that forests provide. Disastrous floods in the lower Yangtze and Ganges–Brahmaputra basins have drawn attention to the role of forests in preventing large-scale flooding at the regional level.

Over and above these global and regional environmental services, forests are important in providing local environmental services to the economy of forest communities, who are for the most part indigenous peoples. In this chapter we argue that the fall in the provision of these local environmental services is the form in which the external costs of the state or other external agency conducted logging is internalized by the indigenous peoples. This accounts in large part for the drain from the forest-based economy resulting in lowered productivity and a loss of productive potential of the indigenous people. The effects of the fall in productivity, however, are not equally distributed across genders. Women bear a disproportionate share of the resulting higher burden.

External evaluations by forest departments, inevitably focus on what external agencies want from the forest, which is largely timber and to an extent NTFPs, and thus suffer from being partial or even one-sided. Local communities, on the other hand, can balance the benefits and costs accruing to the local economy from changes in the use of forest resources as a whole. Their management of forests is based on local knowledge of environmental interactions, local knowledge that is not available to external authorities, and can be used by such communities to protect locally critical natural resources.

By arguing in favour of establishing forest communities' property rights over forests, this chapter supports the establishment of markets for the regional and global environmental services provided by forests. Such markets, while they would not be a solution to all the problems associated with an inadequate supply of these environmental services, would help to increase the supply of these services by providing forest communities with some incentive for their production.

EXTERNALITIES IN LOGGING:
LOCAL ENVIRONMENTAL SERVICES

Timber has been treated as an isolated resource, one which does not interact with the rest of the economy of the indigenous peoples. To the extent that there has been any discussion of the costs of timber extraction, it has concentrated on the difference between 'cost of extraction' and full costs, which would also include the 'cost of regeneration' (that is, the cost of planting, tending and otherwise bringing a plantation to the mature extraction stage). But this is based on a mistaken notion of costless extraction, which assumes that there are no further effects on the economic activities of the forest communities. Costless extraction, even when the cost of regeneration is included, is the economic equivalent of the legal doctrine of *terra nullius*; lands vacant or empty of people.

Selective logging in tropical forests need not per se lead to deforestation. But there are numerous effects which lead at least to the 'degeneration' of the forest, defined as 'temporary or permanent deterioration in the density of structure of vegetation cover or its species composition' (Grainger 1993: 46). This affects the provision of local environmental services. 'Though local, these impacts are not trivial' (Fisher and Hanemann 1997: 508).

How should we view these 'local environmental impacts'? At the level of environmental analysis they are environmental impacts, but at an economic level they are costs. In the first place, as Grainger points out (1993: 39), while it is an over-generalization to assume that most nutrients in tropical forests are stored in the vegetation rather than in the soil, it is nevertheless necessary 'to maintain a continuous vegetation to sustain the fertility of the land as a whole'. Similarly Gradwohl and Greenberg state that the chief problem with logging is the loss of nutrients once the trees are cut since, in tropical forests, the soil is relatively poor, with most of the nutrients stored in the vegetation (quoted in Fisher and Hanemann 1997: 509). The loss of vegetation due to logging means that the immediate and future fertility of the soil is affected: there is that much less of nutrients to be transferred to crops, thus reducing yield. Yield is further affected by the loss of biodiversity that accompanies logging. And over time, 'clearing or logging forest exposes soil to erosion and to four other forms of degradation: fertility depletion, compaction, laterization and landslides' (Grainger 1993: 155).

A more important and immediate effect of logging is that it affects the collection of NTFPs. Some timber trees, such as *sal* (*shorea robusta*), themselves yield many non-timber products. Further, during logging, trees that are not commercially valuable as timber are also affected. Overall many forest products became unavailable or their availability is reduced—bushmeat, fruits, oils, sweeteners, resins, tannins, fibres, construction materials, a wide range of medicinal products, saleable products such as skins, feathers and live animals and also wood fuel. Recent studies have shown that the capitalized value of the income derived from such NTFPs which can be extracted sustainably, may greatly exceed that of timber harvests (Peters, Gentry and Mendelsohn 1989, quoted in Repetto 1997: 471).

The overall reduction in tree density reduces the harvest of these NTFPs, which have traditionally been an important part of the economy of the indigenous peoples. As the income (whether that directly consumed or through exchange) from NTFPs falls, indigenous peoples are forced to migrate as cheap labour (for example, in brick fields) for long periods of the year. They are in effect 'environmental refugees', forced to migrate permanently or seasonally by the deterioration of the productive potential of their economy. In the Jharkhand region of India, whole families migrate in about January, after having completed the round of post-harvest festivals, returning only in late June, in time to begin land preparations for the next crop. The more deforested areas and land-poor families experience greater migration. Single women, without land but having access to forests as members of the community, are also disproportionately more affected by the loss of forest cover. The reduction in NTFPs can also lead to an increased dependence on agriculture. This would lead to the expansion of agriculture into areas and soils that are not suited to agriculture, further reducing productivity.

Recently Costanza et al. (1998) have brought together a wide range of work on environmental services provided by 'natural capital'. Some of the environmental services are global (gas and climate regulation by the absorption of carbon dioxide and other greenhouse gases), while some are regional (water regulation and supply). Many of the environmental services are wholly or partly local. Some of these local environmental services are—erosion control, soil formation, nutrient cycling, pollination, biological control, food production, raw materials, genetic resources, recreation and cultural services. The effect of deforestation is then felt in the reduction of these local environmental services provided by forests.

The effect on the productivity of agriculture, the loss of potential production, the loss of forest products and the greater labour required at a given level of production are the costs that the indigenous people bear for logging and they are not compensated for these costs.

Who Pays the External Costs?

Environmental analysis points out that there is a difference between the price of timber and its full cost. But our question is: who pays the difference? Who pays the external costs, or where are these costs internalized? Environmental analysis points to the overuse of depletable resources as being a cost for future generations. This is an externality forced on the future. Our concern, however, is with the present costs.

One strand of analysis, eco-feminism, holds that capitalism involves a colonization of nature, as also of women. Following the analysis of Carolyn Merchant (1980), Mies et al. (1988) drew attention to the degradation of both nature and women as necessary aspects of capitalist accumulation. In a more recent analysis, Mellor (quoted in O'Hara 1997: 130) held, '...women and the natural world are both treated as externalities by western dualist economics...'

Nature (forests in this case), however, is not empty of human beings. The forests as we know them, are the result of the interaction of humans with nature. And, as seen earlier, it is the forest communities who pay for the externalities in the use of logging for capital accumulation. While we can talk of the negative effects of logging on nature, can we talk of the costs borne by nature? Costs, losses of income, or of productive potential, are necessarily borne by human agents. Eco-feminist analyses do at times recognize the role of 'economically and environmentally exploited peoples' (Mellor, quoted in O'Hara 1997: 147). But the consistent thread running through eco-feminist analysis is that women alone and nature are the two victims of capitalism.

It is not just nature and women that are involved in the externalization of some costs; it is also the indigenous peoples, women and men, who are the forest dwellers, and who pay the cost in terms of loss of income and productive potential.

Those who analyze who pays for the difference, conclude that the losers are the national economies of the developing world. Massarrat (1997) points out, 'Whereas the consequences of cost externalisation made a positive difference in the industrialised nations through lower costs for the use of natural resources and higher growth rates, the raw material owners of the south registered a minus due to the decreased income' (ibid.: 33). In fact, as the examples of the Southeast Asian countries show, within the raw material producing countries, logging has been a means of national accumulation too. The rate of this accumulation has certainly been lower than it would have been had the price of timber been higher. But what is important is that even the capital accumulation that did take place in the raw material producing countries has not been in the economies of the indigenous peoples. A more recent contribution combining environmental economics with a world systems approach, identifies the separate environmental conditions and the drain from one region to another (Hornborg 1998). Thus, it gets away from treating the territory of a state as being equal to the environmental economy. With this approach the drain can take place not only to the established metropolitan centers, but also to the emerging ones within the former Third World.

The earlier analysis, by A. K. Roy and the Jharkhand movement in India, of regions of the indigenous peoples as 'internal colonies' also stressed this relation of drain from the indigenous peoples' economies to those of the states within which they are encompassed (Sengupta 1977). But the drain was identified with the income from logging, and extraction of minerals and revenue from these economies. Here, we are extending the notion of drain to the somewhat neglected dimensions of local environmental services that are so crucial to the economies of the indigenous peoples.

Some environmental analysis does take into account the loss of income in the form of subsidy paid by forest communities. When the social costs of production are higher than private costs, there is a subsidy on the basis of non-valuation of environmental resources, which are production resources for the indigenous people. This subsidy,

> ... is paid not by the general public via taxation but by some of the most disadvantaged members of society: the sharecropper, the small landholder, or tenant farmer, the forest dweller and so on. The subsidy is hidden from public scrutiny; that is why nobody talks of it. But it is there. It is real (Dasgupta and Maler 1990: 112).

Costanza et al. (1998) bring together material from a number of studies to calculate the value of environmental services. For tropical forests they get a total value of US$ 2007 per hectare. Subtracting from this the amounts that can be identified as due to non-local environmental services, we get a figure of US$ 1766 per hectare (see Table 1.1). They emphasize that their figures are underestimates.

Table 1.1
Value of Annual Local Ecosystem Services of Tropical Forests (US$ per hectare)

Erosion control	245
Soil formation	10
Nutrient cycling	922
Waste treatment	87
Food production	32
Raw material	315
Genetic resources	41
Recreation	112
Cultural	2
Total	**1766**

Source: Costanza et al., 1998, Table 2.

This would be a minimum value of the local ecosystem services of tropical forests and represents the loss the forest communities suffer from a hectare of deforestation. Only a part of this accrues elsewhere as income from logging. That would be the part of US$ 315 due to timber, along with other raw materials like fuel wood or fodder. Even if the state claims all of the value of timber, what is left out of account is the US$ 1451 that is an uncompensated loss to the local economy.

OFFSETTING FACTORS

The above values of local environmental services are marginal values. It would be difficult to assume that marginal values of services lost are equal to average values as the effect of deforestation would increase with its extent. Average values being lower than marginal values, the amount of the drain would be lower than the figures above would suggest.

The impact of the loss of environmental services would vary with the distance of the community's agricultural area from the forest. The closer the forest that is logged the more would be the impact on the local economy; while the impact would fall if the forest were further away. Consistent with this, our field observations in Yunnan, China and Jharkhand and Bastar, India, showed that communities were more concerned about preserving the state of forests that were closest to their villages and less concerned about those that were somewhat far away.

To an extent the effect of the loss of environmental services would be less if the resulting income were used to develop other avenues of investment and income. Livelihoods would change, but the overall effect would not necessarily be negative if the resulting incomes accrued and were accumulated locally. Most often, however, logging incomes accrue as profits to outside companies or as revenue to central governments. In China, however, a large part of logging income accrues to local governments and local companies that have invested their income locally. Local accumulation of this type would obviously reduce the extent of drain. What logging would amount to in such cases would be the use of timber income to build up other productive potential, as analysed in Nathan and Yu Xiaogang (this volume). But the above is more true of China than of other Asian countries, where as a rule the revenue goes to central governments and the profits to outside companies.

Logging can often employ local labour. If wages are merely equal to the cost of production of labour, then wage employment does not represent a net addition to local income. But this is rarely the case. Nowadays wages include more than the cost of production of labour. The extra income over the cost of production is a net addition to the local economy. The effect of loss of environmental services can thus be offset to the extent that local labour is employed in logging and is paid at wage rates above the cost of production or reproduction of labour, as it is sometimes called.

The above-mentioned offsetting factors need to be taken into account in a full analysis of the problem. But they do not negate the main argument of this paper: that the external costs of logging are paid by the indigenous people in the form of loss of environmental services (including NTFP production) that forests provide. What these offsetting factors show is that it may be possible to design locally-managed logging policies as part of an overall local forest management system, which would take into account the interaction of livelihoods and changes in them. Recently attention has been drawn to sustainable timber production by local communities, e.g., by the Native Americans in the USA and on the *ejidos* (village communal farmland) in Mexico (IES 1995). This could integrate timber production into an overall forest management system.

GENDER DISTRIBUTION OF COSTS

The costs of lower productivity of agriculture, longer distances walked and more hours spent in collecting forest products are not borne equally by men and women in the indigenous communities. In swidden, cutting of trees and clearing of land is primarily a male task. This actually becomes easier with logging, since the biggest timber trees would have been cut. Besides reducing labour time in clearing land, logging also reduces the potential for hunting; further reducing the time that men work. Again, while women are not the only gatherers, they perform the bulk of the labour of gathering of NTFPs. Fuel collection, in particular, is largely a woman's job. Selective logging would initially reduce the time required for collecting fuel wood, as there would be a lot of residue. But as deforestation proceeds there would be an increase in the hours that women have to spend in various daily tasks.

The income effect of logging and forest degradation falls on the whole community, though it would also be unequally distributed. But the labour effect of increased working hours, in particular, largely falls on women, including young girls. Among indigenous peoples too, as in the mainstream patriarchal communities, what stands out is the long working day put in by women and the comparative leisure of men. In fact if hunter-gatherers are the 'original affluent society', as Marshall Sahlins (1972) characterized them, there too men seem to have had a greater share of leisure than women.

HISTORICAL DEVELOPMENT OF THE PROBLEM

Why are forests logged on the basis of price based on cost of extraction? In a commodity economy, or one dominated by the commodity categories, that which has no owner has no price. The forests were made legally empty of people and turned into *terra nullius* by the denial of ownership rights to the indigenous people. This question needs to be looked into in terms of, first, the notion of 'empty forests', second, the forms of labour and related tenurial questions with regard to forests, and, third, the relation between tenurial questions and ownership and prices of products and services.

It is now commonly recognized that historically forests are, and were, not empty over long periods. They have been inhabited by humans for a long period of history, certainly from before the formation of states in the plains; and various forms of management and labour are involved in their development and care. Forests are neither 'empty', nor simply 'just there'. They are populated by the indigenous peoples who have been the 'keepers of the forest'.

The people in the forests, the indigenous peoples, certainly knew that the forests were not empty of people. Now,

> ...ecologists are...very cautious about labelling forest as either 'virgin'—that which has never been disturbed by human beings—or 'primary'—which may have been disturbed long ago but has since undergone a process of succession through different types of 'secondary' forest before regaining the structure and species composition characteristic of the climax ecosystem, a process that can take a thousand years or more. This caution derives from the findings of archaeological remains in various areas of what were previously thought to be primary forest, and the realization that human settlement in the forests of West Africa and Central America in particular has a long history (Grainger 1993: 47).

Even in the case of the Amazon rain forest, increasing evidence shows that virtually no part of it has been unaffected by human activity over the last several millennia. For India, the archaeologists Misra and Nagar note,

> In fact, barring the alluvial plains of the Ganga valley, the narrow western coastal strip and the southern part of Tamil Nadu, where stone—early man's primary raw material for technology—was not available, almost the entire country was colonised by hunting–gathering

peoples of the Lower Palaeolithic period, at least half-a-million years
ago (Misra and Nagar 1997).

It is then no wonder that as against the empty forests idea, the
ecologist Mabberley notes, 'most forests are probably 'disturbed' but
some are more disturbed than others' (1992, quoted in Grainger 1993:
48). While the biologists Redford and Stearman say, 'In this light there
may be no such thing as "virgin forest"' (Grainger 1993: 253). The
forests, as we know them, are products of human labour in interaction
with natural resources.

Recognizing this means a change in the manner in which both
'nature' and 'culture' are conceptualized. The orthodox anthropological approach is to recognize the historical quality of human works by
attributing them to projects of cultural construction that are opposed
to, and superimposed upon, an ahistorical nature. The environment,
however, is being continually shaped by human labour, and is not
something fixed, against the background of which human labour
takes place. An adequate basis for forest management policy must
start from the recognition that 'enfolded within persons are the histories of their environmental relations; enfolded within the environment are the histories of the activities of persons' (Ingold 1987: 51).

The dichotomization of nature and culture as concepts has its
counterpart in the operational dichotomization of forest and farm,
and in the social dichotomization of 'civilized' and 'barbarian'. In the
settled cultivation of the state systems, the field or farm and village
is seized from the forest and the forest is continually held back. In
fact in the tropics the site of an abandoned village would, over time,
return to grass and shrub and then eventually to secondary and
primary forest. Consequently farm or field is an operational category
of settled cultivation opposed to forest.

By contrast in the swidden cultivation of hill-forest dwellers there
is no such absolute opposition between farm and forest. One is
transformed into the other. Forest is cleared to create farm, and farm
is left fallow to create forest. The transformation of one category into
the other represents a form of thinking different from dichotomous
thinking, which sets up one category in absolute opposition to the
other.

At the same time the village, or the area seized and held from the
forest, is the abode of the civilized; while outside, the forest, is the
abode of not just the uncivilized but also of evil spirits.

An important factor in the contempt of the 'civilized' states for the
'uncivilized' forest-dwellers lay in the idea that the forest-dwellers

merely use nature and do not produce, they only extract for consumption and do not perform any labour, which is the factor that differentiates human beings from other animals.

FORMS OF LABOUR

While the labour contribution in preparing agricultural land is recognized and property rights accepted as flowing from it, the same is not the case with forests used for gathering. The forests are supposedly a 'gift of nature'—unproduced, involving no cost of production. The indigenous people appear to only 'use' the forest's resources, and not to 'manage' it, and therefore are not thought to have any claim over it or at best to only have a claim to collect 'minor forest produce'.

To see how wrong this notion is, we here consider the example from West Kalimantan, Indonesia. 'While mature forests in the Balai area are largely confined to the hilltops too steep to cultivate, much of the area appears wooded.... The Tara'n distinguish three principal types of managed forest vegetation...*tembawang, tanah adat* and *tanah usaha*' (Padoch 1995: 35). The types of forests are, respectively, former house sites, forests preserved by customary law and not cleared in living memory and enterprise plots.

The three types of managed forests differ in the way they were created and also in their subsequent management.

> Like many similar sites in other tropical areas all are managed quite casually, with occasional slash-weeding as the most important task.... Weeding, although frequently done to enhance the ease of harvest, nonetheless has the effect of specifically removing undesirable species and promoting useful ones. Casual management, such as removing vines or other competing plants near an economic plant—when and if it is noticed—may also play an important role in traditional management systems' (*ibid.*: 35).

Even the area of forest that has not been cleared in living memory (*tanah adat*) is also managed. Fruit trees, and other desirable species are grown among the naturally occurring trees and other trees are removed. The brush is selectively cleared, particularly before time for harvesting fruit. Thus, what might appear as 'primary forest' is also to some extent created by human labour and management.

Padoch mentions two reasons why this traditional forest management is 'invisible'. The first is the 'apparent casualness of management' (one might add, like women's work in the home garden). The second factor is the 'appearance of the forest.... The plantings are not even-aged, not evenly spaced and appear haphazard. The most important factor in invisibility is doubtlessly that the traditional stands are extremely diverse. Spontaneous vegetation is not only tolerated but encouraged in plots' (Padoch 1995: 37).

This extract stresses the point that the forests are managed by the indigenous people who live in them. Many other studies of forests, for instance in the book *Farmers in the Forest* (Kunstadter et al., 1978), also make the same point about other indigenous peoples.

More recently, Wiersum (1997: 11) identified three stages in the evolution of management practices: controlled utilization (controlled procurement of wild tree-products); purposeful regeneration (cultivation of wild trees); and domestication (production of domesticated trees). The forests, as we know them, are the product of long human–nature interaction, involving various forms of management and labour by the indigenous peoples.

Thus, not only agriculturists and industrialists but also hunters and gatherers manipulate and manage the environment in various ways, in order for the environment to reproduce the characteristics they desire. The ways in which gatherer–hunters manage the environment, a management that did not start only with agriculture and the domestication of plants and animals, has been ignored by policy-makers and also by anthropologists and other researchers. In an overemphasis on the 'tools' of production, the technologies of managing the environment by the almost-universal practice of employing fire to influence the distribution and productivity of plants and animals, have been given little attention, as pointed out in Henry T. Lewis excellent article 'A Parable of Fire' (1991).

Since in one way or another the contribution of labour is seen as providing a justification for property rights (though not the only one, as the existence of non-producing owners testifies) it is important that notions of what constitutes labour (or conscious intervention in the environment) be broadened to include not only the agriculturist or commercial notions of labour (and possession) but also those relevant to hunters and gatherers. Ethnocentric notions of what is or is not labour are behind the idea that hunters–gatherers (or even swiddeners) do not 'properly' use the resources; or, that they do not produce, but merely appropriate from nature, more in the nature of animals, than of conscious human beings.

In opposition to this view, Ingold emphasizes the essential humanity of hunter–gatherer production and consumption. Staring from Marx's description of the labour process he redefines the essence of production of subsistence as '*the subjection of an extractive process to intentional control*' (Ingold 1987: 105, emphasis in original). It is the intentionality of the human agent that distinguishes gathering from foraging and hunting from predation, with the second of each pair of terms being the environmental relation and the first the social relation.

Nevertheless, is the acknowledgment of both labour and the intentionality of the human agent sufficient to establish the case for the tenurial rights of forest-communities?

TENURE

Tenure is a social relation that recognizes claims over resources. The manner in which resources are used to appropriate what is desired from them, will vary from one type of production to another. For hunters and trappers what matters are particular points or paths. Points and paths are one-dimensional. The resulting right is over animals that cross the line (*ibid.*: 151). On the other hand, gatherers require an area and not just a point. Swidden or slash-and-burn agriculture is spatial, but, like gathering, it too is occasional. In fact, many indigenous communities recognize individuals' claims over swidden land only when it is actually under cultivation. A plot left uncultivated for, say, three years (as among the Khasi of Meghalaya, India) would revert back to the community. In permanent agriculture plots of land are continuously used, or at least used within short intervals of less than a year. Thus, the application of 'useful labour' is generally accepted as being required in order for an individual to acquire tenure.

The first point about tenure is that it entails an act of communication about possession (Rose 1994: 14). Communication is relative to the audience concerned. What is perfectly obvious to an indigenous community may not communicate anything to outsiders. Those looking for written land records would not find any such evidence. Thus, when colonial bureaucrats enquired about indigenous tenure among the Munda of Jharkhand, India, they were told that their *sasandiri*, or megalith memorials, were the markers of village lands.

The second point is that the nature of labour (or useful labour) varies from one type of production to another, as we have discussed earlier. In this respect too it is necessary to overcome ethnocentricity in order to acknowledge the nature of indigenous tenure.

Some types of labour, such as hunting may only relate possession to lines, and not to the spaces around them. Would it therefore be sufficient to acknowledge only the rights of possession over one-dimensional lines but not the spaces around them? While individuals or groups may have specific rights only over particular lines and points, the community of the indigenous peoples has what can only be called collective tenure over the entire country (Ingold 1987: 157). This, then, negates the idea that, for instance, Australia was a vacant land (*terra nullius*) before the coming of British colonizers.

The combination of individual with collective tenure continues into agriculturist indigenous communities too. As mentioned above, in swidden systems it is common for individual tenure to relate only to the periods when the plot is actually under cultivation. Fallowing for a period of, say, three years makes the plot revert, not to *terra nullius*, but to collective tenure. The plot remains part of the collective village land. Thus, the third point is that indigenous communities combine forms of community with individual tenure.

Most current forest-dwelling communities in Asia carry on a combination of gathering, hunting and agriculture. The relevant area that they utilize, both for production and other social purposes, is then a combination of forest and agricultural plots. While acknowledging (a) all forms of self-conscious production activity as forms of labour; (b) the intermittent nature of all production activity as such; and (c) the existence of a combination of collective and individual tenure, one needs to map out the relevant area for tenurial consideration.

In the 1990s there were some advances in acknowledging tenurial rights of forest communities. The advances were limited, some even merely symbolic, but nevertheless they were advances. The legislation in the Philippines on 'Ancestral domain' recognizes the existence of areas over which indigenous peoples can claim tenure. There are many weaknesses in this law. Again, the 73rd Amendment to the Indian Constitution recognizes the *gram sabha* (village assembly) as owning the NTFPs and having a right to manage all the natural resources, which must include the forest, which it conventionally uses. This constitutional amendment has many lacunae and has barely been implemented. But it also represents a step toward or an advance in recognizing indigenous people's rights. Similarly the Australian *Mabo v. Queensland* judgement at least repudiates the concept of Australia being an empty land prior to British colonization (see Hill 1995; and Povinelli 1999).

The resource locale is worked into the development history of the group or community. The ways of using the resource have surely changed over history and continue to change even now. But there is a connection between the group and the locale, with each being part of the other's history. At present when attention is being drawn to ways in which forest communities can acquire stakes in developing the resources on which they rely for a livelihood, it is useful to recognize the importance of linking group and locale.

ENVIRONMENTAL SERVICES AS PUBLIC GOODS

Another way to approach the problem of supply of environmental services is to look on them as public goods, particularly so in the case of biodiversity and climate change. These are public goods in the sense that their consumption is non-rivalrous and non-excludable. If climate change occurs it affects the whole globe (though not in a uniform manner) and the benefits of slowing it down also accrue across the whole globe, and no one can be excluded from its benefits. Similarly, the consumption of the benefit of climate change by one person does not reduce its consumption by another person, that is, its consumption is non-rivalrous.

Water is not a public good in the same manner as the others. Its consumption is rivalrous, and one person's consumption decreases another person's ability to consume it. The manner of supplying water, through piped systems or more so the modern industrial system of bottled water, make it possible to exclude those who do not pay for its use. But in some senses, not water itself but the control of water flows is a public good. Floods affect all persons in the path of the floodwaters, though not equally. Again, the benefits of flood protection accrue to all concerned persons—they can neither be excluded nor does flood protection used by one person reduce the flood protection to another person. Water quality is also a public good. Water, water quality and the control of water flows are, therefore, unlike climate change, not pure public goods. Even biodiversity can be made excludable, through systems of intellectual property rights and related laws.

Whether pure or impure public goods, the problem with regard to the supply of these public goods is that their supply is insufficient: insufficient on the basis of standards that are now becoming globally established. An equivalent way of stating the problem is that the supply of the corresponding negative public goods (or bads) is too high.

The supply of the above-mentioned public goods is different from that of other public goods, like security or the rule of law. The latter are produced by the government or public sector, with the supply being determined by a national political process. But climate change, biodiversity and water are all goods the supply of which are the result of a myriad decisions of producers and consumers, including individuals, corporations and governments, throughout the world. Their production is, therefore, carried on in a decentralized manner.

The extent of biodiversity depends on the decisions of farmers and gatherers regarding the types of crops to grow or the plant products to gather. In these decisions they respond to the market and to their own non-market needs (use values). A change from swidden to, for instance, wet rice cultivation in terraces would inevitably reduce the extent of biodiversity conserved, as varieties of dry rice that are no longer cultivated would go out of existence. Thus, biodiversity is produced privately, as is, for instance, the extent of tree cover and the nature of tree cover in forests subject to collection for human use.

Thus, what distinguishes these public goods, like biodiversity and climate change, from the well known public goods like security or the rule of law, is that their production is private, not public. These are privately produced public goods.

Since individuals produce these public goods, they decide on their production on the basis of market conditions and overall livelihood situations (for individuals/households) or commercial conditions (for enterprises/corporations). These private decisions do not take into account the externalities of these decisions, for example, the effect on biodiversity or tree cover. The paradox of isolation in individual decisions comes into play—collectively a group may choose a certain level of supply of a particular good (tree cover or diversity of species), but the sum of individual decisions may not add up to that collective preference.

PRODUCTION BY STATE DECREE

The usual solution to this problem has been for the state to decide on the level of supply of the public good. This can then be secured through state decree by, say, controlling land use systems. In the late 1990s the response of the Central Government in China and the Supreme Court in India was precisely this; to order a certain type of land use pattern—banning or severely controlling decisions on logging in the uplands, in order to increase the supply of environmental goods to the lowlands. In most countries there are bans on carrying on agricultural activities on lands whose slope is greater than 15 degrees. Through such command and control methods the required level of production of environmental goods is sought to be assured.

Before we go on to consider the other possible options, we should point out that the experience with such command and control approaches for supply of privately produced public goods has not been very good especially in situations where it is not possible for the state to police and check on the implementation of those decisions. Such commands can work in certain cases, as in the case of switching from leaded to unleaded gasoline for private transport and from diesel to natural gas for public transport in cities in India, particularly since the use of these products (unleaded gasoline and natural gas) can be assured at the limited number of supply points. But in situations where the supply points are not limited (for example, use of wood fuel or of other tree products in forest areas) it would be very expensive to attempt successful systems of control over the use of these products. This has been the experience in particular with forest resources.

The inability of the state to control use of the forests by the forest-dwellers has turned the forests into open access resources or unregulated commons, quickly subject to degradation. Control over logging, in the absence of other livelihood options, which is the usual case, leads to high levels of extraction of lower-value products, for example, for wood for fuel rather than as timber. Analyses of the effects of the logging ban in India are given in Nathan (this volume) and Nongbri (this volume); while the experience of China is analysed in Nathan and Yu Xiaogang (this volume). The failure of these high cost systems of controlling forest use or, in other words, the inefficiency of the resulting economic system, has led to attempts to incorporate communities into the management of forests, through either so-called Joint Forest Management (JFM), which, however, has been nothing more than a disguised way of continuing the Forest Departments' agendas, or through Community Forest Management (CFM) schemes. For an analysis of the limitations of the attempts to institute various forms of 'joint' forest management schemes in Asia see Edmunds et al. (2003).

The failure of centralized systems of command to control land use is also due to the fact that centralized administrations do not possess information about eco-system interactions that are available to local communities, in a gendered distribution depending on the local division of labour and its strictness. This local knowledge of eco-system interactions is often of the rule of thumb variety, unformalized and not subject to appropriation by central authorities.

In addition to the failure of the centralized decision systems to implement their decisions or even to arrive at correct decisions, we should also add the high human cost of these attempts in terms of their negative impact on the livelihoods of the forest-dwellers. The logging bans in China and India in the late 1990s both had serious recessionary effects on the local economies, increasing poverty and leading, among other things, to increased school dropout rates and increased entry of young girls and women into the commercial sex trade.

What this shows is that in the production of some environmental services, like biodiversity and tree cover, the livelihoods of tens of millions of poor producers are involved. Both justice and economic efficiency require that rather than command and control approaches with negative impacts on the livelihoods of the poor, we try to change the nature of the incentive system facing these small producers so that they modify their livelihood systems in ways that produce more of the needed environmental products and services.

There have been two approaches to changing incentive systems faced by private producers in order to increase the supply of environmental goods that society desires. One is through a system of taxes to discourage forms of production that produce environmental negatives, or subsidies to encourage forms of production of the environmental positives. This is the approach first formulated by Pigou (1920). The second approach, following from Coase's analysis (1960), is to award or create property rights and concomitant markets where they did not earlier exist.

We have mentioned both the high costs and the ineffectiveness of the state command approach to increasing supply of privately produced environmental goods. Either of the last two approaches—taxes and subsidies or property rights and markets—would cost less than the command approach (Heal 1999: 225). Further by enabling local decisions that utilize local knowledge not available higher up in the hierarchy, the decentralized decision systems are even likely to be more effective in producing more of the desired environmental products and services.

A system of taxes and subsidies would require an administrative structure with recurrent costs to implement it, along with the possibilities of its misuse through mis-reporting and concealing facts. With the pressures on budgets due to globalization it would be difficult for states to introduce yet another system of subsidies and taxes. Even if the subsidies are paid out of the taxes, there would be a large centrally financed administrative burden involved in the procedure. The creation of property rights and markets, on the other hand, will spread most of the costs among the myriad producers and consumers and thus be less of a burden on national budgets.

Further the formulation and working of a system of taxes and subsidies depends on the political strengths of various parties to the deal. Forest/mountain communities are, by and large, economically and politically marginal to the national economies of which they are part. Defined as not having property rights over the resources they use, they are legal interlopers on their own land. Often they do not have recourse to the same legal safeguards as other citizens of the countries. All of these factors substantially increase the possibility that the forest peoples would have very little bargaining power to influence the terms of the deal.

Bargaining in the absence of property, does not give the non-owner much with which to bargain. Without ownership of the oil, OPEC could not have changed the terms of the oil trade, a change that benefited not only the OPEC countries but also the whole world by increasing the push for fuel-efficient vehicles.

PROPERTY RIGHTS AND MARKETS

The alternative approach, based on Coase's analysis, starts from a recognition of the reciprocal nature of the problem. While administrative measures, like the logging ban, place the blame squarely on one pole of the relationship, viz., the mountain peoples of the uplands, it is necessary to see, as Coase insisted, the reciprocal nature of the problem. What has to be decided is if the gain in the plains from preventing logging is greater than the loss that would be suffered in the hills as a result of stopping the logging. This also points to the relevant type of cost to be considered—it is not the cost of the action or abatement as such, but the opportunity cost of such action or abatement. 'It seems to me preferable to use the opportunity cost concept and to approach these problems by comparing the value of the product yielded by factors in alternative uses or by alternative arrangement' [Coase 2001 (1960): 51)].

When we consider the opportunity cost of alternative arrangements, in terms of income gained or income foregone, then we necessarily have to take into consideration the fact that the marginal utility of income goes down as income goes up. An equal amount of income would have a higher marginal utility in a poor (developing) country as compared to a rich (developed) country. Such differences would also exist as between poor (rainfed uplands) and rich (irrigated plains) regions within a country.

In a series of papers, Chichilnisky and Heal (2000) developed the consequences of Coase's argument that the relevant cost concept is opportunity cost, with the additional rider that the marginal utility of income varies as between developed and developing countries. The cost of ensuring a certain supply of environmental services of products is not its direct cost but its cost in terms of consumption or income foregone. For the same technology applied to secure the required environmental product, US$ 1 of consumption foregone in a developed country is not equal to US$ 1 of consumption foregone in a developing country.

This argument can be extended to an intra-country analysis. This is particularly important in upland–lowland relations in countries across Asia, where there is generally a lower per capita income and a higher incidence of poverty in the uplands as compared to the lowlands.[1]

We can apply this analysis to the case of logging in the uplands and the control of water flows (flood control) in the lowlands. We start from the proposition that income in the uplands is lower than in the lowlands, thus giving a higher marginal utility of income in the uplands. How should the costs of flood control be distributed between the uplands and lowlands? One way is that attempted by the central authorities in China and India, which is to put all of the onus of the problem on the uplands and institute a logging ban as was done. This ignores the reciprocal nature of the problem.

So far, on the whole, the mountain communities of Asia have been called upon to deliver the needed supplies of environmental services on the basis of governmental fiat or policy regulations, like with the logging ban currently in force in China and India. Having destroyed their own forests, plains communities and their states want to 'reconstruct nature as an ideal cultural form' (Castells 2000: 508) in the mountains, ignoring the livelihood needs of mountain communities. What is proposed over here is that price or other compensation systems should be used to bring forth the needed supplies of these environmental services and products. This would link improved

---

[1] For a detailed assessment of poverty in the uplands and lowlands of Asia see IFAD (2002). Also see Papola (2001) for the argument that conventional poverty figures, assuming a uniform consumption requirement irrespective of geographical and climatic conditions, understates the extent of poverty in the uplands. For accounts of the much greater incidence of poverty among indigenous peoples than the rest of the population in Latin America see the papers in van Genugten and Perez-Bustillo, 2001.

livelihoods of the mountain communities with enhanced and better quality supplies of needed environmental services. The supply of these environmental services depends on maintenance of asset quality. This is in contrast to the situation with regard to supplies of timber or NTFPs, which can quite easily and often does deplete the resource.

In the Coase analysis it does not matter who has the property right. Either, the lowlands could have the right over the environmental services of the uplands and the upland communities would then have to pay the lowlands for the right to use the forests. This in a sense is the approach of governments that enforce logging bans and other forms of land use control in the uplands, with the payment being made to state officials who have to be bribed in order to continue agricultural and other economic activities in the uplands. Or, the upland communities could have the rights over the forests and other upland resources and lowland communities/farmers would have to pay for the environmental services (e.g., water, in quantity and quality, and with control over the flows) provided by the uplands.

Either distribution of property rights, in the Coase analysis, gives an equivalent solution. But with the analysis of Chichilnisky and Heal we can now see that this holds true only in the limiting case where incomes or amounts of the private good are equal as between uplands and lowlands, so that the marginal utility of income would be the same in both cases, thus equalizing the opportunity costs of the interventions. Or, even if such an equal per capita income did not initially exist, it is brought about by lump sum transfers of the type preferred by economists to solve distribution problems, but which do not work in practice.

In the actually existing case of unequal incomes between the uplands and lowlands the Coase equivalence between property rights to any one of the parties would not hold. With lower incomes in the uplands, it would be necessary to allocate more or all of the property rights to the uplands in order to arrive at an efficient solution.

Looking at the opportunity cost of the flood control measures, a unit of consumption foregone in the uplands has a higher marginal utility than a unit of consumption foregone in the lowlands. Consequently, instead of penalizing the uplands to make them provide the needed public good, the approach should be to compensate them for providing the same. The upland peoples can be given property rights over the environmental products and services they provide and should be able to sell these to the lowlands. The environmental services could be separately valued, as is being done in Costa Rica—US$ 10 per hectare of forest for water, US$ 5 per hectare for biodiversity and so on. The payment could be through specific agreements between watershed communities and those to whom they supply water, as has been the case with the upland cantons and the urban power companies in Switzerland, or between the Catskill Mountains and New York City.

A distribution of property rights in assets that were so far free from any property considerations must mean a redistribution of income. But a condition where property rights in the asset do not exist is itself one with certain distributional consequences. The lowlands, in the case that we are analyzing, get the benefits of the upland communities' maintenance of forests free of any cost. But this maintenance of forests is not costless for the uplands. It means income and investment foregone. By bringing in the reciprocal nature of the problem, this opportunity cost can be compared with the opportunity cost to the lowlands of the payments made to the uplands for the provision of these services. Two distributions can now be compared, rather than attention being focused on only one side. This analysis has the merit of bringing distributional questions into the structure of the problem itself.

Measures for the creation of property rights where none previously existed are measures of explicit redistribution of assets. The creation of property rights in environmental products and services is an asset redistribution that increases the efficiency of the economy in producing environmental public goods. The redistribution (transfer from state to community and/or private assets) or creation of assets, as argued by Bowles and Gintis (1998), would link income with labour and investment in producing the necessary environmental public goods for sale. This is an egalitarian or equality enhancing measure that is asset and not income based. It is likely to be both more just and also increase productivity, since the measure increases the asset value of the mountains, rather than their extractive value. The reform of the system of providing for these environmental services, as a reform would certainly qualify as a Rawls improvement under his so-called Difference Principle with its focus on producing 'the greatest benefit of the least advantaged' (Rawls 1971: 90), given that in all national economies the mountain peoples as such are the least advantaged. From having had their forests managed by state fiat and paying a subsidy for the provision of forest products and services to the world, they would be able to graduate to getting some returns for managing their productive assets to meet global environmental public good needs.

LOCAL KNOWLEDGE AND ITS GENDER SPECIFICITY

Many aspects of the environmental services provided by forests or particular trees are known only to the local communities. This knowledge has very probably been gathered over centuries. A lot of this knowledge is not formalized, but based on rule of thumb methods and broad approximations. These are the types of knowledge that it is difficult for modern, bureaucratic organizations, like forest departments with their single-valued functions, to deal with. But this local knowledge of the forest communities is indispensable to developing higher productivity-based, multiple-use forest systems, based on the ecosystem rather than single product management. Community management, or local forest management, rather than management by forest departments, can best harness this knowledge for effective forest management.

Local knowledge is based on labour in the transformation of nature. To the extent that there is a gender-based division of labour, to that extent there would be gender-specific local knowledge. Given that women do most of the labour of gathering, women would have more of the knowledge of various plant substances and their uses. Similarly the types of trees that are best for fuel, their regeneration and harvesting are matters that women would tend to know more about than men. Possibly more important is women's knowledge of multi-tier, multi-crop cultivation both in swiddens and in the home garden. Men, on the other hand, know more about timber trees, which are their province in most forest-based societies. Men, who are traditional healers would also tend to have a monopoly over certain kinds of specialized medical knowledge regarding local forest resources.

The case study by Wang Qinghua (see chapter 3 in this book) bears out the point made in many other studies—that local knowledge is often gender specific. Rocheleau (1987) and Madhu Sarin (1996) are among many who make the point about the gender-specific nature of local knowledge. Thus, an adequate management system not only has to be local, but also gender-sensitive in its design. It is common for traditional village councils, including those in matrilineal societies, to exclude women. Besides the question of different interests, such men-only village councils would ignore a good part of the community's local knowledge. Given that women-specific knowledge is not trivial, on the contrary, it is an important component of local knowledge, a local forest management system that excluded women would not be efficient in its use of forest resources.

The local knowledge of the forest-communities includes important aspects of the ecosystem services provided by forests. They are aware of the relationships between forest cover, water and moisture retention and nutrient recycling. The studies by Wang Qinghua (Chapter 3) and Sanjay Kumar (Chapter 2) give details of indigenous or local knowledge about ecosystem service functions of forest and the consequences of changes in forest cover on the provision of these services. This local knowledge is crucial for a holistic management of forests, not just as timber or even timber plus NTFPs, but also including ecosystem services. The effects of different forest cover and compositions on these ecosystem services provide signals about the condition of the forests. Decision-making in distant centers ignores these ecosystem services. This disembedding of decision-making means that little attention is paid to feedback signals from local ecosystems (Hansson and Wackernagel 1999: 204). It is only when regional or global ecosystem services are affected (e.g., disastrous flooding in the Chinese or Indian plains) that the distant centres pay attention to local conditions and react, as they did in the late 1990s, by banning all logging.

On the other hand, the embedding of forest management decisions in local communities, in the relevant local contexts, would enable these various local ecosystem services to be taken into account in local forest management decisions. Wang Qinghua (Chapter 3) shows that the Hani of Yunnan, China, value the water providing service of forests. The tops of the mountains are virtually zones of exclusion for extractive activities because of their importance in providing water for the Hani's terraced agricultural system. Even when these forests are state forests, and thus usually subject to destructive extraction of timber, etc., by the local community, the Hani, preserve these forests. The value of the environmental service, provision of water is so high that they do not even cut timber illegally (a practice that used to be quite widespread in other forests in China). Given the Hani's understanding of the importance of forests in their agricultural system, the importance of forests is irrespective of the kind of tenurial system in existence. This is perhaps an extreme case of the environmental service function of forests overriding any other function, to the extent that even tenure does not matter. The many instances of community-initiated forest protection in Orissa (Singh 2003), even in formally state-owned forests, also reflects the importance of local environmental service functions of forests.

On the other hand Sanjay Kumar points to the importance of tenure in the manner in which environmental service functions are integrated into local management decisions. In community-owned forests (the so-called *Mundari Khuntkatti* system) Munda understanding of the water and nutrient cycling functions of forests, is integrated into forest management decisions. Forests are protected from logging so as to allow for satisfactory provision of these services. On the other hand, where the forest is state-owned, and the local community has no control over logging and other forest use decisions, the villagers try to increase their area of agricultural land.

There may be a few cases, like that of the Hani, where the environmental functions of forests are so critical and override all other forest uses, that the form of forest tenure makes no difference to whether people protect the forests or not, they will always protect the forests. But this is a limiting case of 'critical natural resources' that are essential to the existence of an agriculturist-cum-gathering community. More likely is a situation where there is a trade-off between different types of forest use. In these cases, local forest management, based on community ownership of the forest, and public decisions in this case, can take account of local environmental services. Being based on local knowledge and on various tacit relations between elements of the ecosystem, it would not be possible for a disembodied, that is, non-local management system, to capture these relations in forest use planning. In particular, all of the things that are locally valued would not be amenable to reduction to monetary measurement. Thus, a process of public decision-making would be necessary to arrive at the level at which these local public goods should be maintained.

The neglect of the provision of local environmental services in a situation of private ownership and in the absence of a good system of (local) public government, is seen in numerous examples from the mountain and hill regions. In Meghalaya both timber and coal are privately owned. The extraction of the first led to the neglect of the role of forests in provision of water and other local needs. In the case of coal, its extraction by unregulated private enterprise has led to a landscape dotted with holes in the ground. In the Swat region of Pakistan, hotels have mushroomed to meet the needs of a booming tourist industry, but without any regard for the capacity of the local arrangements to meet water and sanitation needs.

On the other hand, there are also examples of good local regulation of such extractive activities. In one hill county of Yunnan, the economy has benefited from the sale of local sand to glass factories in Kunming. But the extraction is governed by rules about the filling of holes, etc., quite in contrast to the case of coal in Meghalaya. Similarly, in the case of timber too, collective village-owned forest has been logged in Yunnan with due regard to the needs of the concerned villages for various ecological goods, like pine needles for animal sties and so on.

The provision of such environmental services is not something to be left to the market. It is a matter of public decision-making, to be arrived at through a deliberative process. How well this is done, depends very much on the quality of local pubic decision-making. In this matter, it is not the market and its signals, but local public decision-making, an explicitly political process involving various interests and claims, that decides the provision of such environmental services.

But signals from the outside would largely be in the manner of prices of ecosystem services and commodities that are demanded on the external markets. These signals could be combined with the non-monetized and 'rule of thumb' valuation of local ecosystem services in taking management decisions at the local level.

There is an asymmetry here between external (that is, regional or global) and local signals. The external signals are based on the demands for the various products and services provided by the forest communities. Such demands are easily translatable into price terms and can thus be easily and unambiguously transmitted to the local unit. On the other hand, the valuation of local ecosystem services and the understanding of the effects of various management decisions (for instance, of selective logging of particular species, or logging at distant or near areas, etc.) are *tacit* kinds of knowledge, which cannot easily, or not at all, be codified for transmission to external agents. The volume of information about local trees, plants and various ecosystem relationships would be very vast for each local management unit. If at all they could be codified, it would be very expensive. On the other hand, the signals from the external world can be more easily transmitted through the price system. Of course, market prices are not perfect vehicles for transmission of signals of external requirements, particularly in the case of public goods.

But what we are arguing for is not a decision on the extent of provision of external environmental services on the basis of some market valuation process, whether cost-benefit analysis or contingent valuation (what would you pay if...?). As in the case of national public goods, like security of person (and property), the decision on the level of provision of these environmental services would necessarily be a political one. Similarly too at regional and global levels, whether through some form of 'global process bargaining (see Keohane and Ostrom 1995) or some other UN-centered political process, bargaining and global power play would determine the levels of needed supply of these goods and services. The Kyoto Protocol and the current US Government's refusal to stand by those commitments, testify to both the possibilities and the role of power in these political decisions.

It is at the next level of transmitting such global, regional or national political decisions, on the needed level of supplies of environmental goods from forest communities, that we are arguing for the use of price and other compensation systems, particularly since, as argued above, these are privately-produced public goods.

Local forest management has the merit that decisions concerning use and regeneration of the forest resource would be made by those affected by the decision. This is a factor that promotes efficiency of resource use. At the same time local forest management would also vest control of the forest in a well-defined group—another condition for socially efficient resource use.

LOCAL FOREST MANAGEMENT: A WAY TO INTERNALIZE COSTS

The land use situation that results from state decisions and local contestation and resistance to the same, will, in general, be an inefficient solution. It is not likely to be the preferred solution either from the point of view of livelihoods or from that of forest conditions. To take the case of Lashi Lake, Yunnan, China, the desired level of water supply to the town can be achieved by allowing the watershed community to sell the water, and adjusting overall land use decisions to this factor. The land use decision will depend on the relative prices of water and livestock and the yield per hectare of water and livestock. When the price of water is zero, as at present, the conversion to pasture will be higher than with any positive price of water. Both for local livelihoods and for the supply of environmental services there will be a preferred solution if communities are allowed to sell these services and markets allowed to set their prices. Of course, there will be a transfer of incomes from the towns to the countryside which itself is a desirable outcome. This transfer may not be from the town-communities themselves, but from the tourists—to the extent that the town-communities are able to pass on the additional cost to the tourists.

If all types of income from the forest were to be handled by the same group, then local negotiations could settle the differences between different groups' valuation of resources. Such differences could be on the basis of class (agriculturist and non-agriculturist forest producers) or gender (women and men). The forms of local forest management, whether simple community management, management by user groups or by households, or some combination of the above, are not discussed in this paper. Here we more or less identify local forest management with a broadly defined community management, modified to take into account the existence of different interest groups, women and men, non-agriculturists and agriculturists, within the community. Another issue for subsequent consideration is the identification of the appropriate community for local forest management.

While analytical attention has been focussed on the allocational effects of underpricing of forest products, we here wish to emphasize their income effects, recognizing that productive potential lost is likely to be greater than productivity-related actual income loss. Given that indigenous peoples, the forest-communities, are among the poorest in Asia, the sustainable betterment of their livelihoods needs to be the central concern in designing forest property and management systems.

Correcting prices, through taxes that would cover the 'costs of regeneration' and even the imputed value of environmental services lost, may remove distortions in timber use, but need not change the income relation. Taxes collected by the state will be used to benefit those who dominate the state. The indigenous peoples are poor seconds to the commercial and industrial interests. As we saw above in relation to Indonesia, the regeneration tax collected by the Indonesian government goes to subsidize industrial timber plantations. Such price corrections through taxes need not and do not have any income effect on the indigenous people, do not reduce the drain they face through logging. In order to make an impact on the poverty of the indigenous people, it would be necessary to act on their property rights. Further, a property reform would have the additional advantage of being a straight-forward measure, which would not increase, rather would reduce, bureaucratic presence and burdens.

Property rights, however, are not just a single rights, but a bundle of rights. In India's Northeast, the Naga and Garo clans, have the right to their trees and forest products; but they are restricted in their right to sell these products. They are only allowed to sell them to licensed, monoposonist buyers. This restricts village-gate prices below what would be obtainable with full selling rights. The same restriction applies in China, with a similar lowering of prices that farmers can get (Liu Dachang 2003).

Thus, property rights should include, (a) right to manage the forests, (b) right to use and sell its products and (c) right to residual income and its disposal. Management, again, also includes a number of functions, including land-use planning, choice of species, choice of silvicultural technology, and so on.

'Increasingly foresters are beginning to think in terms of managing ecosystems rather than managing a few valuable timber species.... Re-orienting management emphasis to multiple-use, non-timber forest production will help maximise both social and environmental benefits' (Ravindranath, Gadgil and Campbell 1996: 306). What kind of agency can better carry out such multiple-use management, the forest department or the local community?

From an economic point of view, for all external agents, whether the state or industrial interests, the forest represents to them only that which they can get from it, the value of timber and related government. The use value and income value that the forest communities gain from it cannot enter into the valuation of an external agent. But they are part of the valuation by the forest communities themselves. Accepting the right of forest communities to manage their forest would enable them to bring their multi-dimensional valuation into play and also take account of what are now externalities and, therefore, disregarded. Since both income and costs would accrue to the local community, a reform of the property and management system would not only increase the income the forest communities gain from the forest but also lead to a more all-round and sustainable system of forest management.

References and Select Bibliography

Bowles, Samuel and Herbert Gintis. *Recasting Egalitarianism: New Rules for Communities, States and Markets.* Edited by Erik Olin Wright. London and New York: Verso, 1998.

Broad, Robin. 'The Political Economy of Natural Resources: Case Studies of the Indonesia and Philippines Forest Sectors.' *The Journal of Developing Areas* 29, no. 3 (1995): 317–40.

Castells, Manuel. *The Rise of the Network Society.* Oxford and New York: Blackwell, 2000.

Chichilnisky, Graciela and Geoffrey Heal. 'Who Should Abate Carbon Emissions? An International Viewpoint'. *Environmental Markets: Equity and Efficiency,* edited by Graciela Chichilnisky and Geoffrey Heal. New York: Columbia University Press, 2000.

Coase, Ronald. 'The Problem of Social Cost'. *Journal of Law and Economics,* The Law School, University of Chicago, no. 3, 1960. Reprinted in *Environmental*

Economics, edited by Ulaganathan Sankar. New Delhi: Oxford University Press, 2001.

Costanza, R. et al. 'The Value of the World's Ecosystem Services and Natural Capital,' *Environmental Economics* 25, no. 1 (1998). Reprinted from *Nature* 387 (15 May 1997): 253–59.

Dasgupta, Partha. 'The Environment as a Commodity.' *Working Papers*. Helsinki: World Institute for Development Economics Research (WIDER), 1989.

Dasgupta, Partha and Karl-Goran Maler. 'The Environment and Emerging Development Issues.' *Proceedings of the World Bank Annual Conference on Development Economics*. Washington D.C.: World Bank, 1990.

Edmunds, David and Eva Wollenberg. 'Alliances in Multiple Stakeholder Negotiations.' Manuscript, 2000.

Edmunds, David et al. 'Conclusion'. In *Local Forest Management: The Impacts of Devolution Policies*, edited by David Edmunds and Eva Wollenberg. London: Earthscan, 2003.

Food and Agriculture Organization of the United Nations (FAO). *State of the World's Forests 1997*, Rome, 1997.

Fearnside, Philip. 'Environmental Services as a Strategy for Sustainable Development in Rural Amazonia.' *Environmental Economics* 20 (1997): 53–70.

Fisher, Anthony C. and Michael Hanemann. 'Valuation of Tropical Forests'. In *The Environment and Emerging Development Issues*, Vol. 2, edited by Partha Dasgupta and Karl-Goran Maler. Oxford: Clarendon Press, 1997.

Flint, R. 'Biological Diversity and Developing Countries.' In *Environmental Economics*, edited by Anil Markandaya and Julie Richardson. London: Earthscan Publications, 1992.

Grainger, Alan. *Controlling Tropical Deforestation*. London: Earthscan Publications, 1993.

Guha, Ramachandra. 'Forestry in Pre-British India.' In *Economy and Political Weekly* (1983): 44–46.

Hansson, C. B. and M. Wackernagel. 'Rediscovering Place and Accounting Space: How to Re-embed the Human Economy.' *Environmental Economics* (1999): 29, 203–13.

Harkness, James. 'Recent Trends in Forestry and Conservation of Biodiversity in China.' *China Quarterly*, no. 156 (December 1998). London: The School of Oriental and African Studies (SOAS).

Heal, Geoffrey. 'New Strategies for the Provision of Global Public Goods: Learning from International Environment Challenges'. In *Global Public Goods: International Environment Challenges*, edited by Inge Kaul, Isabelle Grunberg and Marc A. Stern. New York: United Nations development Programme (UNDP) and Oxford University Press, 1999.

Hill, Ronald. 'Blackfellas and Whitefellas: Aboriginal Land Rights, the *Mabo* Decision and the Meaning of Land.' *Human Rights Quarterly* 17 (1995): 303–22.

Hornborg, Alf. 'Towards an Environmental Theory of Unequal Exchange: Articulating World System Theory and Environmental Economics.' *Environmental Economics* 25, no. 1 (1998).

Hurst, Philip. *Rainforest Politics: Environmental Destruction in South-east Asia*, Kuala Lumpur: S. Abdul Majeed & Co., 1990.

Ingold, Tim. *The Appropriation of Nature, Essays on Human Ecology and Social Relations*. Iowa: University of Iowa Press, 1987.

Institute for Environmental Studies (IES). 'Case Studies of Community-Based Forestry Enterprises in the Americas.' Paper presented at the Symposium 'Forestry in the Americas: Community-Based Management and Sustainability', University of Wisconsin Madison, Wisconsin, 3–4 February 1995'.

International Fund for Agricultural Development (IFAD). 'Assessment of Rural Poverty: Asia and the Pacific'. Rome: IFAD, 2002.

Jeffrey, Roger and Nandini Sundar. A New Moral Economy for India's Forests? New Delhi: Sage Publications, 1999.

Kelkar, Govind and Dev Nathan. Gender and Tribe. New Delhi: Kali for Women, 1991, and London: Zed Press, 1991.

Keohane, Robert O. and Elinor Ostrom, eds. Local Commons and Global Interdependence: Heterogeneity and Cooperation in Two Domains. London, Thousand Oaks and New Delhi: Sage Publications, 1995.

Kunstadter, P., E. C. Chapman and S. Sabshri, eds. Farmers in the Forest. Honolulu: University Press of Hawaii, 1978.

Lewis, Henry T. 'A Parable of Fire: Hunter-Gatherers in Canada and Australia'. In Traditional Ecological Knowledge: A Collection of Essays, edited by Robert E. Johannes. Gland, Switzerland: World Conservation Union (IUCN), 1991: 9–16.

Liu Dachang. 'Tenure and Management of Non-state Forests in China since 1950: A Historical Review.' Environmental History, 6, no. 2 (April 2001).

—————. 'Devolution in China'. In Local Forest Management: The Impacts of Devolution Policies, edited by David Edmunds and Eva Wollenberg. London: Earthscan, 2003.

Mabberley, D. J. Tropical Rain Forest Ecology, 1992. Cited in Controlling Tropical Deforestation, by Alan Grainger. London: Earthscan, 1993.

Massarratt, Mohssen. 'Sustainability through Cost Internalisation: Theoretical Rudiments for the Analysis and Reform of Global Structures.' Environmental Economics 22 (1997): 29–39.

Merchant, Carolyn. The Death of Nature: Women, Ecology and the Scientific Revolution. San Francisco: Harper Row, 1980.

Mies, Maria, Veronika Bennholdt-Thomsen and Caludia von Werlhof. Women: The Last Colony. New Delhi: Kali for Women, 1988 and London: Zed Press, 1988.

Misra, V. N. and Malti Nagar. 'From Tribe to Caste: An Ethnoarchaeological Perspective'. In From Tribe to Caste, edited by Dev Nathan. Shimla: Indian Institute of Advanced Study, 1997.

Nathan, Dev. 'Timber in Meghalaya'. Economic and Political Weekly, Mumbai, May 1999.

Novellino, Dario. An Assessment of El Nino, La Nina and the Asian Crisis in the Province of Palawan. Rome: International Fund for Agricultural Development (IFAD), 1999.

O'Hara, S, U., 'Toward a Sustaining Production Theory.' Environmental Economics 20, no. 2 (1997).

O'Neill, John. 'Markets and the Environment: The Solution Is the Problem,' in Economic and Political Weekly (26 May 2001): 1865–73.

Padoch, Christine. 'Creating the Forest: Dayak Resource Management in Kalimantan'. In Society and Non-Timber Forests in Tropical Asia, edited by Jefferson Fox. Honolulu: East-West Center, 1995.

Papola, T. S. 'Poverty in Mountain Areas'. Kathmandu: ICIMOD, 2001.

Poffenberger, Mark and Betsy McGean, eds. *Village Voices, Forest Choices*. New Delhi: Oxford University Press, 1996.

Polanyi, Karl. *The Great Transformation*. Boston: Beacon Press, 1944.

Povinelli, Elizabeth A. 'Settler Modernity and the Quest for an Indigenous Tradition.' *Public Culture* 11, no. 1 (1999). Duke University Press.

Ravindranath, N. H., Madhav Gadgil and Jeff Campbell. 'Environmental Stabilization and Community Needs: Managing India's Forest by Objectives'. In *Village Vioces, Forest Choices*, edited by Mark Poffenberger and Betsy McGean. New Delhi: Oxford University Press, 1996.

Rawls, John. *A Theory of Justice*. Cambridge, MA: Harvard University Press, 1971.

Rocheleau, Dianne. 'Women, Trees and Tenure: Implications for Agroforestry Research and Development.' in *Land, Trees and Tenure*, edited by John B. Raintree, Nairobi: International Center for Research in Agroforestry (ICRAF) and Madison, the Land Tenure Center, 1987.

Repetto, Robert. 'Macro-economic Policies and Deforestation.' *The Environment and Emerging Development Issues*, Vol. 2, edited by Partha Dasgupta and Karl-Goran Maler. Oxford: Clarendon Press, 1997.

Roemer, John. 'The Limits of Private-property-based Egalitarianism.' In *Recasting Egalitarianism: New Rules for Communities, States and Markets* by Samuel Bowles and Herbet Gintis, edited by Erik Olin Wright. London and New York: Verso, 1998.

Rose, Carol M. *Property and Persuasion: Essays on the History, Theory, and Rhetoric of Ownership*. Boulder: Westview Press, 1994.

Sahlins, Marshall. *Stone Age Economics*. Chicago: University of Chicago Press, 1972.

Sarin, Madhu. *Who Is Gaining? Who Is Losing? Gender and Equity Concerns in Joint Forest Management*. New Delhi: Society for Promotion of Wasteland Development, 1996.

Sengupta, Nirmal. ed. *The Fourth World*. New Delhi: Sterling Publishers, 1972.

Singh, Neera. 'Community Forestry in Orissa'. In *Local Forest Management: The Impacts of Devolution Policies*, edited by David Edmunds and Eva Wollenberg. London: Earthscan, 2003.

Smith, Joyotee, Kalemani Mulongoy, Reidar Persson and Jeffrey Sayer. *Harnessing Carbon Market for Tropical Forest Conservation: Towards A More Realistic Assessment*. Bogor: Centre for International Forestry Research (CIFOR), 1999.

van Genugten, Willem and Camillo Perez-Bustillo. *The Poverty of Rights: Human Rights and the Eradication of Poverty*. London and New York: Zed Book, 2001.

Wiersum, K. F. 'Indigenous Exploitation and Management of Tropical Forest Resources: An Evolutionary Continuum in Forest-people Interactions.' *Agriculture, Ecosystems and Environment* (1997): 63, 1–16.

Wilson, Charlie, Pedro Moura Costa and Marc Stuart. *Transfer Payments for Environmental Services to Local Communities: A Local-Regional Approach*. Rome: IFAD, FAO and the International Union for Conservation of Nature and Natural Resources (IUCN), 1999.

Wollenberg, Eva. 'Methods for Assessing the Conservation and Development of Forest Products: What We Know and What We Have Yet to Learn.' In *Incomes from the Forest*, edited by Eva Wollenberg and Andrew Ingles. Bogor: CIFOR and IUCN, 1998.

2

INDIGENOUS COMMUNITIES' KNOWLEDGE OF LOCAL ECOLOGICAL SERVICES*

Sanjay Kumar

INTRODUCTION

It is common knowledge that forests are intricately connected to the livelihoods of rural people: they provide timber, Non-Timber Forest Products (NTFPs), and a host of non-forestry services—climate control, water recharge, storm protection, fertility and nutrient balance, etc.—that are commonly called *ecological services*. Despite this knowledge, sustainable timber production has remained central to the scientific management of forests for centuries. In recent decades, as a result of the alleged virtues of 'decentralization'[1] in sustainable natural resource management, and the consequent establishment of new local institutions such as 'Joint Management of Government

* The author wishes to thank Stuart Corbridge and Dev Nathan for intellectual stimulation and constant encouragement. The support of Alpa Shah in revising the text, and Usha Kiran Horo in assisting the collection of field data is gratefully acknowledged.
   [1] Four forms of decentralization are recognized in the current development debate. They are: *political* (also called *devolution*), for example, a *gram panchayat* in India; *administrative* (also called *de-concentration*), for example, a Local Health or Education Authority; *integrated*, such as multipurpose institutions, for example, a district or regional council; and *sectoral*, such as a single purpose institution, for example, a village forest committee. Most of the decentralization efforts in natural resource management fall into the last category. For a full description of forms of decentralization, please see Eriksen et al. (1999).

Forests' (JFM) in India and similar forms of participatory forest management elsewhere,[2] there is much talk of the inclusion of NTFP
management in the mainstream of forest development discourse
(see Mitchell et al. 1999, for a discussion on the NTFPs of Bihar and
Orissa). A discussion about *ecological services*, however, remains
marginal to the debate. The main reason for this considered ignorance
by sylviculturist, forest managers, international forestry institutions[3]
and donors[4] appears to be the difficulty of measuring ecological
services, both conceptually and empirically. Insofar as the concept of
'ecological service economics' in forest management decisions has
gained ground, it has been as a consequence of the publication of its
rough estimates for the earth-biome by Costanza et al. (1998).[5] Studies that describe the local ecological services provided by a forest, or
which link them to the livelihoods of the village community are rare.
This essay is an attempt to broaden the list of services available at
the local level, and to strengthen such views in forestry management
science.

This essay is concerned with local ecological services in the eastern India plateau region, whose indigenous communities, similar to
their counterparts in other parts of the world, are the bearers of
extensive local ecological knowledge that revolves around the forests
of the area. This knowledge could be an extremely useful tool not only

---

[2] Participatory forest management has not only been initiated in countries with
a narrow natural resource base, for example, those of South and Southeast Asia
and Africa (Kothari 1998) where forest to population ratio is quite low, but also
in countries with a high forest to population ratio, for example, Canada (Hall 1997),
the United States of America (Danks 1996) and Australia (Buchy and Hoverman
1999).

[3] See for example, the International Tropical Timber Organisation. 'Criteria and
Indicators for Sustainable Management of Natural Tropical Forests.' 1998. (website:
http/www.itto.org/)

[4] For example, 'sustainable livelihoods' is the core-theme of development
assistance by agencies like Department for International Development (DFID) of
the UK government and the United Nations Development Programme (UNDP) for
the removal of rural poverty. Similarly, 'social capital' formation is central to the
recent development debate in the World Bank. Ecological services are crucial to
both sustainable livelihoods and social capital formation in the rural communities
living in and around forests. But, none of the recent programmes of these agencies
has an explicitly designed component for local ecological service provision strengthening.

[5] The authors estimate that the average value of ecological services of the
biosphere is USD 33 trillion (10^{12}) per year whereas the global gross national
product is around USD18 trillion per year.

in involving them in forest management and development programmes, but in improving their general economic condition and ensuring the long term sustainability of forest management in the area. It can reasonably be argued that *local ecological services* are the 'missing link' in designing plans for successful decentralization and the sustainable management of forests. A first step in this direction is to acknowledge that such indigenous knowledge exists and is useful, and then to understand this knowledge, and show that it can be incorporated into forest management systems. This essay seeks first to list the types and the extent of *local ecological services* provided by forests in the eastern India plateau region, and in doing so it fills a critical gap in the knowledge of natural resource management. It then proceeds to analyze the differences in perceptions about the *local ecological service*s and attendant practices within communities that are dependent on forests under two contrasting land-tenure regimes, namely community forests and state forests. Our aim is to understand the kind of institutions that can be developed and owned by local users for sustainable management of forests. In this essay we suggest that:

1. The field realities of natural resource management are often at odds with the popular assumption that there always exists a simple and linear correlation between indigenous communities and forest conservation; and that

2. forest management policies and practices need to be more sensitive to the changing community–nature relationship and to the internal dynamics of indigenous communities.

This essay is organized as follows. In the following section titled Background, information on the study area and the methodology of the field study is outlined. The next section summarizes the main field observations and offers reasons for the unique sylvic-ecological systems prevalent in the area with a view to their use in future policy-making and planning. The essay concludes with a brief note suggesting how to proceed in the direction of policy implementation in respect of *local ecological service*s.

Background

The data that forms the basis of this essay comes mainly from three villages, namely Katwa, Karudih and Hesadih situated in the eastern plateau region of India, a region that is home to both one of the best *sal (Shorea robusta)* forests in the world and the most populous indigenous communities of the Munda and Santhal tribes. The study area provides a unique opportunity to compare two different forestry institutions as it has both community-owned forests and state-owned forests occurring in neighbouring villages. The first two villages of this study are under *Mundari-Khuntkatti* (MK) land tenure,[6] and contain community-owned and managed (in short, MK-forests) forests. The third village, Hesadih, is a non-MK village whose state-owned forests are managed by the state forest department under the broad principles of JFM. It also has small patches of private forest alongside the boundaries of state forests. Administratively, the villages are part of Bandgaon block in West Singhbhum district of the new state of Jharkhand.

Almost 50 per cent of the geographical area of Bandgaon block is classified as forest in the revenue records. But according to present estimates only 20 per cent of it contains good forests with a crown cover of 40 per cent or more. The rest of the forests of this area have degraded or are in the process of degrading to a shrub and bush covered 'barren' land, which is used by the villagers for a very low level of subsistence farming on private holdings. The region was very well forested until about three decades ago, but since then it has experienced extensive forest loss that is continuing till date in the form of fresh clearing and encroachment on the forests, including the government reserve forests.[7]

Semi-structured interviews with a stratified sample of 10 households in each village in proportion to the socio-economic classes of the village population, and group discussions in the general body meeting of the villages have provided the data for this essay. The main objective of these interviews was to explore indigenous knowledge of the *local ecological services* that the forests of this area provide to the communities. The knowledge we sought to explore did not only represent 'know-how' (which is actually 'technical knowledge'), but was also centred around the understanding of 'cultural knowledge'—

---

[6] *Mundari-Khuntkatti* is a unique type of land tenure guaranteed by the Chota-Nagpur Tenancy Act of 1908. It allows a *munda* (headman of a village, who is in the direct lineage of the original founders of the village) to own and maintain village wastelands (including forests) for the exclusive use of the village community.

[7] According to a very rough official estimate, more than 50,000 acres of valuable government forest in Singhbhum alone has been under fresh encroachment since 1979.

the knowledge that produces and reproduces the understanding and identity of the members of the indigenous communities where 'technical knowledge' is linked to 'non-technical knowledge' in a mix of cultural, ecological and sociological knowledge. The knowledge we were interested in thus goes far beyond the 'indigenous technical know-how' and becomes 'rural people's knowledge' (RPK).

Given the time frame and the resources available for this study no quantitative measurement of ecological parameters such as infiltration, run off, sediment load, humus formation, nutrient-cycle, etc., could be undertaken. However, the study highlights broad trends, and thus it will serve as a useful baseline for future quantitative research work.

FIELD OBSERVATIONS AND DISCUSSIONS

For self-governance to be successful, key users must develop knowledge of the spatial extent of the resource, including accurate knowledge of its boundaries and the internal microenvironments (Ostrom 1999). That is so with the men of the MK-villages but not with the women. One reason why women are not so aware of the forest boundary is found in the following statement of Subasi Mundu (a female respondent of Karudih village):

> Unless it is useful why should one roam through the whole of the forest? My needs are fulfiled from only the lower portion [the valley portion] of the forest. I am able to collect the required quantity of firewood, mushrooms, etc., for my own bonafide use while I collect chew-stick and leaves for daily use from the nearby forest. So why should I go farther?

The knowledge about the legal administrative nature of MK-forests is weak, in fact it is almost absent, among the female members of the interviewed households.[8] The scanty knowledge of the legal–

---

[8] Munda society is male dominated. Village level decisions are taken by all-male bodies. Inheritance does not pass to female members of a household. One example will suffice. The village headman (*munda*) of Hesadih village has three daughters, but no son. As a *munda*, he owns large chunks of farmland. Despite being a village headman, however, he has to tolerate the usual comments of even a recent settler (*raiyat*) in the village, for example, 'The day you die I will take possession of all your [the *munda*'s] land'.

administrative nature of the MK forest system amongst women respondents is attributable to the fact that many of them have come
from parental villages that have only government owned, insignificant
or degraded forests. Therefore, their dependence on forests has not
been so great and as a result their knowledge has not developed to
the same extent as many original MK-residents.

For example, in Subasi Mundu's parental village of Gourbera there
are only a few *palas* (*Butea monosperma*) and *ber* (*Zizyphus mauritiana*)
trees left in the village commons/ revenue wastelands. She was also
not aware of the legal type of the *sal* forest of Karudih village, where
she now lived, or where the demarcation line between the *raiyat*
(private) *sal* forests and the MK-*sal* forests was located. These observations once again support the argument that although the eco-
feminist ideas of a 'special link' between women and nature has been
very significant in raising awareness of gender–environment issues,
a deeper understanding of the local complexities of political ecology
and socio-cultural realities influencing the use of forest resources is
essential to involve women in forest management (Jewitt and Kumar
2000).

Forests and Air Quality

The role of forests in the maintenance of the gaseous cycle of the
earth's atmosphere is one of their most important functions. Although
this effect is global, the proximate local population of developing
countries remains more prone to deforestation-related changes in the
local gaseous cycle because of poor adherence to environmental
standards as compared to developed countries of the North. Forest
degradation and clearing has taken many forms in the study area,
including large scale firewood extraction, politically motivated felling
of trees in the Jharkhand Andolan[9] that are then left to decompose
at the site (temporary clearing), and the clearing of forests for farming
and encroachment (permanent clearing). There is a remarkable difference in the level of degradation and of the perception and quality
of local ecological service changes between MK and non-MK villages.
Large scale extraction of firewood and small timber continues in our

---

[9] The Jharkhand Andolan (agitation) for separate statehood started as the self-
assertion of indigenous communities in the 1970s. State-owned forests, mainly
the Reserve Forests, became the main target of the opposition during the period
of agitation.

non-MK study village, although a rudimentary form of JFM in this village has prevented permanent clearing of forests for encroachment to become as apparent in Hesadih as it is in the adjoining non-MK villages. Forest degradation and clearing causes a decrease in the amount of carbon held per unit of area of forest. Also the distinction between 'temporary' and 'permanent' clearing is important because these two processes release different amounts of carbon into the atmosphere. Some of the carbon released with temporary clearing is again accumulated on the land with re-growth of fallow forests. Permanent clearing, for agriculture or otherwise, does not lead to re-accumulation of carbon. It represents a transformation from a carbon-rich to a carbon-poor regime entailing a permanent loss of carbon to the atmosphere that acts as a potent contributor to global pollution and warming. The amount of carbon released into the atmosphere due to forest degradation/clearing also varies with the type of forests (see Table 2.1). Much of the forests that were cleared in the Jharkhand Andolan were mature stands, and obviously they held much more carbon than swidden fallow or degraded forests. According to one estimate, the tropical closed forests of Asia hold between 135 to 250 tonnes of carbon per hectare in their vegetation and 100 tons of carbon per hectare in the soil. For the open forest these figures are 40 to 60 tons and 50 tons respectively (Houghton 1993). Loss of carbon from the soils of cleared and degraded forest lands is directly manifested in the drastically reduced mushroom yields on these lands, and in this form at least the effects of forest degradation are well understood by the local villagers.

Table 2.1

Indicative Percentages of Initial Carbon Stocks Lost to the Atmosphere from Vegetation and from the Soil when Tropical Forests are Converted to Different Kinds of Land Use

Land Use	Carbon Content Loss in Vegetation (%)	Carbon Content Loss in Soil (%)
Cultivated land	90–100	25
Pasture	90–100	12
Degraded crop lands and pasture	60–90	12–25
Shifting cultivation	60	10
Plantations	30–50	–
Degraded forests	25–50	–
Logging	10–50	–
Extractive reserves	0	0

Source: Houghton 1993: p. 30.

Despite lower levels of forest conservation in non-MK-villages, the general awareness regarding the contribution of forest degradation to global warming is quite high. How forest degradation is linked to carbon release and global warming is not known even to the literate villagers, but all villagers appreciate the fact that the forest is crucial for clean air. In the absence of such clean air they might suffer from various respiratory ailments like tuberculosis, asthma, whooping cough, etc., and some villagers point to the high incidence of these diseases in Chakradharpur and Karaikela (nearby towns whose peripheral forests have almost completely disappeared in the last three decades) as evidence of this proposition. Rather than worrying about the global warming effect of forest degradation, people of this area have a strong awareness of trees as controllers of pollution through their capacity to filter 'unclean' air. Villagers appreciate that the trees with larger leaves and dense and shiny foliage, for example, sal (Shorea robusta), pipul (Ficus religiosa), jamun (Syzium cumuni), kusum (Schliechera oleosa), palas (Butea monosperma), etc., are efficient air-cleaners. While all the villagers knew of these qualities of the specific tree species, only MK-villagers were aware of the actual regeneration status of these species in the forests. The presence of a strong and robust local governance institution in the MK-villages has also meant that their inhabitants are able to interact more closely and frequently with their environment and enhance their local ecological knowledge in the process. This iterative learning process is reflected in the villagers' knowledge—that the anti-pollution efficient trees, for example, pipul, jamun, kusum, palas, etc., have become less prevalent in the last two or three decades—and their conscious efforts to protect the new trees of these species from fire, trampling, cutting and grazing. The same degree of awareness of the regeneration status of different species is not present in Hesadih, which once again points to the necessity of a strong and compatible institution of local governance that can quickly respond to match the local capabilities and needs for the sustainable management of forests (Ostrom 1999).

Influence on Water-Regimes

Most literate villagers of the study area acknowledge that, through their influence on the hydrologic cycle, forests affect the water resources of catchment areas both quantitatively and qualitatively. They also appreciate that the role of forests in hydrology cannot be considered in isolation: their influence depends on the soil and climate conditions; on the precipitation regime and the amount of precipitation; as well as on the evaporating capacity of the air. Similarly, and despite insufficient experimental data, the idea that forests improve our water resources and climate has also taken possession of many non-local forest managers. The fact remains that on the one hand important advances in forest hydrology during the past 25 years have improved our knowledge of the field, even while it is true that contradictory results and difficulties in the measurement of certain variables make interpretations of how forests exactly influence water resources uncertain and contested. Nevertheless, the positive relationship between forests and ground water levels is common knowledge amongst policy planners and government functionaries at all levels. Therefore, the Central Government's Technology Mission on Drinking Water that provided for the installation of drinking water hand pumps in selected villages of the Chota Nagpur districts during the 1990s emphasized the need for good forest cover for efficient ground water recharge. A forest regeneration plan in the area where hand pumps were to be installed (though it later remained un-implemented) was, therefore, made an integral component at the planning stage of this mission.

Despite some indirect experimental evidence that forests considerably increase precipitation (upto18 per cent) at the regional level, no conclusive connection has yet been made between forests and precipitation under different combinations of topographic and geographic variables (Guehl n.d.). Indeed, there is no record of any previous study of the climatic effects of the tropical *sal* forest region, characterized by numerous forest stands separated by small patches of forest, which is a common spatial design not only in the study area but in much of South Asia. The villagers of the study area, however, believe that it is only because of their forested neighbourhood that they receive more, as much as 25–50 per cent more, rainfall than their deforested neighbours near towns like Chakrdharpur and Chaibasa, or in areas with denuded vegetation. Villagers vividly recall how their region escaped the fury of a drought that gripped almost the entire plains region and deforested areas of West Singhbhum district in 1998. Elderly villagers readily recall, that because of continuing deforestation, the area is receiving less precipitation than before, which is causing the moisture in the ground to dry up well before the end of January, whereas two to three decades ago the subsoil moisture used to persist until late March. This has a telling effect on *rabi* (the winter crop) cultivation, the productivity of which has fallen considerably in recent years.

In addition to lower amounts of precipitation, the indiscriminate fires during the summer season in the forested hills of non-MK areas[10] are causing much desiccation and exposure of the soil, and this in turn causes erosion and degradation of the nearby private farmlands. Forest fires are known to cause an upto 20 fold increase in the sediment load of the nearby streams, which indicates why the subsoil moisture and vegetal status of the slopes of MK and non-MK-villages, especially in the summer season, differ so remarkably, and why re-generation of native forest species has been replaced by invaders like the hardy *Lantana camara* bush—a plant despised by the farmers of the area—on the slopes of non-MK-villages.

The Hydrologic Cycle of Forests

The rain that falls on forest covers is designated for diverse fates. Part of it is intercepted by the various vegetal layers of the forest ecosys-tem—main stand, understorey, shrub layer, herbaceous layer, and litter (Clarey and Ffolliott 1969). The rest reaches the ground either directly or as throughfall or even stemflow. Part of the water that reaches the ground drains off the surface, and the remaining part is infiltrated in the soil, where, depending on the characteristics of inclination, structure and texture, it can circulate by subsurface flow (Freeze 1972). The most important part of the hydrologic cycle is the surplus water, which then percolates and feeds the groundwater and the streams.

The interception of rain by the forest cover represents a major component of the influence forests exert on the water cycle. Although no quantitative study has been carried out thus far in the study area, by comparison with the data available for other types of forests (Goodell 1963; Leonard 1961; Avery and Fritschen 1971; Collings 1966), and empirical observations in the study area, one can say that the interception is in the range of 15–20 per cent.

As regards the infiltration and the water-holding capacities of different species, the villagers were unanimous in their choice. The following scale (see Table 2.2) has been constructed on the basis of the household interviews, which is not inconsistent with the scale

---

[10] Burning of forest floor ash in the summer season, both for collection of *mahua* (*Madhuca indica*) flowers and production of leaf, is quite common in the state-owned forest areas, especially in the Protected Forests. To the contrary, there is almost a complete ban on putting forests to fire for any reason in the MK-villages.

prepared by scientific forest managers (Forest Department, Government of Bihar 1996).

Table 2.2

Water Infiltration Capacity (WIC) of Different Trees as Perceived by Villagers

Name of Tree (Latin Name)	Vernacular Name	WIC
Shorea robusta	Sal	*****
Ficus bengalensis	Bar	*****
Ficus religiosa	Peepul	*****
Bamboo clumps	Baans	*****
Mangifera indica	Aam	****
Artocarpus heterophyllus	Kathal	****
Syzigium cumuni	Jamun	****
Schliechera oleosa	Kusum	***
Butea monosperma	Palas	**
Pongamia pinnata	Karanj	**
Zizyphus jujuba	Ber	*

Note: The number of stars against the name of each tree species represents its water infiltration capacity (WIC).

In the forested watersheds, the interception of precipitation generally decreases with the intensity of the rainfall. The run off situation becomes worse when large areas of forests, similar in extent to the study area, are degraded (Garczynski 1980). The vicious cycle of soil moisture loss due to high run off and forest degradation continues with increased intensity in the non-MK portion of the study area. In this manner a substantial portion of rainwater is washed away rather than being infiltrated into the soil to increase the subsoil moisture and aid forest regeneration/agriculture in the post rainy period. As a result, even hill slopes with a gentle incline in non-MK-areas bear a stunted look during dry summer months. In contrast, at places only 50 meters apart in MK-areas, at the hill base/valley the soil is thick and moist and the vegetation dense. Heavy run off and soil erosion during persistent heavy rains during July–August and the October elephant rains (*hathia* rains) is now common, more so in the non-MK area. These facts are known to the villagers very well, so they cherish the month of August when a prolonged spell of low intensity rainfall facilitates slow run off from the forested hills and fills their lowland (*don*) paddy fields with the right amount of water[11] loaded with high concentrations of forest nutrients.

---

[11] Water about 3–4 inches deep during that period is considered very good for paddy productivity. Water in excess of this will cause overflowing that harms the

Interception increases with growing age and density of the forest stands. For example, in beech, the annual interception reaches 20 per cent at the age of 50 and increases to 25 per cent at 120 years; in the case of the larger crowned Douglas Fir interception is already very high (35 per cent) in 15 year old stands (Guehl n.d.). Similarly, clear-cutting and slash burning increases the amount of sediment in the streams and nutrients in the soil (Kimmins and Feller 1976), especially increasing the amount of bicarbonates and calcium and the pH of the soil. That is why clear-cutting and slash and burn agriculture is still preferred by marginal farmers of non-MK villages in the study area for short term gains although they know that in the long term it is not going to help their agriculture. No published figures for the interceptive capacity of *sal* forests of the study area is available, however, the moisture from forests to the lowland paddy farms flows for much longer duration in the MK-villages than in the non-MK-village, which is perhaps the result of larger diameter *sal* stands of higher density in these villages. For the same reason, the traditional drinking water facilities, *Chuan* and *Danri* that lie within the natural drainage line of the area remain serviceable for a longer period in the MK-villages.

In regions characterized by frequent fog, earlier experiments have indicated that forests are able to condensate by 30 to 50 per cent more than the open land (Guehl n.d.). That is why Hesadih, which is not as yet completely denuded, remains moist for comparatively longer periods in the post rainy period than do similar villages in the deforested valleys near Chakradharpur. The villagers also well appreciate this fact.

Apart from fog, the formation of dew is observed during the night when the temperature of the air drops below the temperature of the dew point. The degree of dew formation is certainly higher in village areas having better quality forests. Forests and the adjacent farmlands profit from dew if the condensed water comes from the atmospheric air mass, but, in many cases, the dew appears to originate at least partly from the water of the nearby rivers and streams. The contribution of dew to the total moisture content, however small, is quite beneficial to the *rabi* (winter) crops but not to the most important industry of the area, namely *lac*. Dew kills *lac* insects (*Laccifer lacca*), and thus the income of the farmers. In the villagers' opinion, cultivation of *lac* is more productive and secure in Karudih village where

---

farms in two ways: first, the field bunds are damaged; and second, the nutrient/fertiliser of that field is washed away.

the *lac* growing area of the village is quite distant from the village forest. In, Hesadih village, which is situated on a riverbank in a valley basin, and which has interspersed forest plots and farms, there is much more dew formation and resultant death of *lac* insects during the crucial propagation period in October–November.

Aquatic Food and Forests

Together the surface run off and the subsurface flow from the forested uplands and hills in the study area contribute to a network of meandering *nalas* (small streams) locally called *gara* that feed the perennial river that finally meets the river South-Koel. All these *gara* though termed perennial do not have water all the year round but are at least wet. In part the stream may become subterranean, and in places the *nalas* form themselves into quiet pools. These pools, locally called *dahs,* are important for the local villagers as they harbour populations of fish and tortoise. In the summer these pools also act as waterholes for the wildlife of the area.

These water bodies are important not only for the hydrologic cycle and the irrigation of farms, but also for a wide variety of important aquatic food, for example, fish, crab, oyster, etc., obtained from them. The common fish (*haku* or *hai* in Mundari) in the rivers and streams of the area are: *chingri, telpia, choruka, pothi, getu, budu* (surface floating fish), and, *garai, singhi* and *mongri,* which prefer marshy sites in and near the paddy fields. The *choruka* and *pothi* varieties of fish are also common in the slow flowing water of the terraced paddy fields. Together with oyster, crab and tortoise, fish is an important dietary supplement during the lean rainy season, so it is customary for the whole village to gather and organize fish catches twice or thrice a year between the flowering and harvest of the paddy crop. Groups of two or three (males only) use ordinary buckets to catch 1–1.5 kilograms of fish in the 2–3 hour exercise. Deforestation, and forest degradation in the study area in general has caused both reduced amounts of water-flow and silting resulting in diminution of water-pools both in size and duration. The effect is more pronounced in and near the non-MK-village of Hesadih, which has experienced severe forest degradation in the recent past. The washed up silt, leaf and other debris from the deforested hill slopes tends to accumulate and fill the clefts and crevices in the moist rocky sides of the perennial pools, which once acted as an ideal hibernating and breeding ground for the fish, crab and tortoise. Study respondents fondly recall, more so in the non-MK-village Hesadih, how they used to collect 6–7 *bhars* (a *bhar* being a shoulder-load weighing about of 15–20 kilograms) of fish in one night during the communal *Hai-Karkum*[12] festival. Reduced pool size and duration has adversely affected both the size and number of common fish and other aquatic animals, which is a strong disincentive to organizing village fish catches, leading to further thinning of social capital in these villages. For example, only six or seven households out of 35 households in Pahantola hamlet of Gengira village now take part in a fish catch and that too when they are sitting idle in the paddy flowering season.

A similar reduction has not occurred in the crab (*katkom* or *karkum* in Mundari) population, which mainly inhabits the wet rice fields rather than the adjacent rivers/streams. Every year the villagers organize up to 12 catches during the paddy transplantation season as before, but the volume of the catch has severely declined since it is difficult to find big-sized crabs as in earlier times. As expected the catch is larger in the paddy fields near the forests, because the tall paddy tillers of the shaded areas provide a better niche, both nutritionally and physically, for the crab population. In open rice fields away from the forests the catch is quite poor: only four or five crabs per trip. Similarly, the 1–1.5 kilograms body weight tortoise population has now been completely replaced by a population that has a maximum bodyweight of 0.25 kilograms.

Oysters (*ghonghi* in Mundari) are also common in the wet rice fields of the *don* (lowland), but they are harvested by individual families 3–4 times a year during July–August. Each paddy field will yield about 1–1.5 kilogram in successive harvests. A family would harvest 3–4 kilogram oyster in each trip, which is more than sufficient for a day's meal. White ant (*deemak*) hills and red ants (*chunta, demta*)[13] are also more common in the uplands near the streams where moisture is available throughout the season. Together these food items constitute an important protein supplement, as the villagers of this area do not consume any milk.

---

[12] *Hai-Karkum* day is observed a day before the *Sarhul* festival (*Sarhul* is observed to commemorate the flowering of the *sal* trees). *Hai* means fish and *Karkum* crab in the local Mundari dialect. On this day all the male members of the village assemble to catch fish in the nearby river/stream. Fishing carries on throughout the night. To store the fish catch, as many large leaves as these are participating households are spread on the riverbank. After each round, the fish catch is distributed equally, and each household's share is put on the respective leaf.

[13] *Demta* (red ant) is so important to the study area that one of the high Munda clans is named after it.

In terms of the relationship between the type of forest and the quality and quantity of aquatic food, bamboo forests are considered the best. Leaf litter from bamboo forests, according to the knowledge of villagers, is a very good growth promoter, especially for fish and tortoise. Residents of Hesadih recall with a sense of agony how the depletion of the bamboo forests in their neighbourhood[14] caused a reduction in the size and number of tortoise in the nearby Hirni river.

Drinking Water Sources and Forests

Apart from *gara* there is a network of slender channels, called *lors*, that drain excess rain water off the forested hill slopes down to the *gara*. These are generally steep and rocky, and dry up shortly after the rainy season. Some stagnant pools, small in size, are seen here and there at flatter intervals. These pools are an important source of drinking water for the villagers, as near to these pools or the subterranean water channels or on the edges of the adjacent farms, people dig/refine traditional water sources, locally called *danri* or *chuan*. Villagers have an intimate knowledge of the subterranean water movement and they have dug these traditional *danri* or *chuan* within the line of movement of the subterranean water, but in the villagers' memory the duration for which these pools/subterranean streams now remain moist has decreased considerably. In the non-MK-village of Hesadih, where forest degradation is severe, these traditional water sources are now completely dry by January–February each year, whereas 20–30 years ago when the area was forested they used to dry up only towards the end of May. Deforestation has caused permanent drying of a number of water sources in the forests adjoining Hesadih village. It has also impacted upon the handpumps drilled under various government programmes in the area, rendering them dry and non-functional. Traditional water sources still remain very important to the local villagers in the wake of the large-scale failure of the mechanical handpumps. Literate villagers appreciate the importance of safe drinking water drawn from handpumps, but most of them prefer the *'sweet'* taste of water from the traditional sources that are fed by ever flowing water from the forests (in contrast to the handpump water, which is drawn from a stagnant source). Villagers' choice of a *danri* or *chuan* location is also dictated by an intricate knowledge of

[14] The vast bamboo forests of the area experienced gregarious flowering in the late 1960s. Thereafter, natural regeneration of bamboo from the fallen seeds failed to establish because of a host of biotic and sylvicultural factors.

the subterranean water flow of the area in order to make the water source serviceable in the hot and dry months of May and June, which once again brings to the fore the need for such indigenous knowledge to be recorded and blended with contemporary forest management science.

The Influence of Forests/Trees on Water Quality

The influence of the forests on the water quality of streams and rivers is difficult to define as other factors are involved as well, especially the soil type and atmospheric inputs. However, it seems that, compared to grassland and other broad-leaved forest species, *sal* produce a more acidifying litter and, through their persisting and usually more important foliar surfaces, constitute a more efficient sink for atmospheric pollutants (in particular nitrogen and sulphur). In this context it has to be underlined that forests sequestrate the nitrogen inputs in their biomass and that forest strips along rivers and streams obviously reduce the nitrate content of alluvial layers.

The villagers of the study area are also aware of the effects of forests on water quality. The common concept is that the water of streams passing through well stocked forest is *mota* (thick), nevertheless sweet as compared to the *patla* (thin) and brackish water of streams and rivulets passing through open or non-forested areas. They say that the water of Ranchi city is *patla* as it does not pass through forests. This concept of *mota* and *patla* water is especially important to the housewives because of the vast difference in cooking times of rice and lentils in these two types of water.

As regards trees that are considered important for improving water quality, *jamun* is the choicest species. The fruits of *jamun* not only purify water but give it the required sweetness. Thus, it is common to see *jamun* trees near the traditional water sources, e.g., the *Samuel Danri* in Karudih village. The villagers, however, caution that the trees/forests should not be so near to the water source that the leaves falling from the trees make the water source dirty.

Water Regime Planning

One of the most important empirical observations of some of the respondents is about the moisture status of the area. This also has important policy implications. One key observation is that despite no appreciable decrease in rainfall, the moisture regime of the area, that is so important for agriculture both in the *kharif* (for upland crops) and *rabi* (for low and medium land crops) season, has significantly deteriorated because of degrading forests and their vegetation. Similarly, the water levels of the wells of the area has gone down considerably, and these days the situation sharply deteriorates during the dry summer months. Consideration of rainfall data only in the formulation of renewable natural resource and farming systems development programmes is thus not enough. The pre-project surveys and the meteorological observation stations must provide for measurement and monitoring of moisture status of the area as an important indicator.

Villagers are also well aware of the fact that the rain in its early spell brings a lot of disease, especially of the gastro-intestinal variety. As a prophylactic measure, therefore, the villagers take a dose of *sal* seed powder[15] in the pre-monsoon period.

Forests, Farming Livelihoods and Nutrition

Farming in the study area is closely linked to forests. Not only are the farms directly dependant upon forests for the incoming soil moisture and leaf litter nutrients, but certain wild animals from the forests also help maintain the sustained productivity of the farmlands by protecting the crops from pests and disease.

Forests continue to be the most important source of farm fertilization in the area. As such, existence of better quality forests is crucial here to the maintenance of farmland productivity. Rural people's knowledge of the nature and extent of moisture and nutrient flow from the forests is very rich. Historically, the oldest and the most productive farms are those which fall within the direct line of moisture and nutrient flow from the forests. A quick survey indicates that the rich and the influential in the villages of this area, for example, the *munda* (administrative head of the village) and the *pahan* (village priest) *khunt* (lineage) and their kith and kin, possess a larger proportion of the farms near to the forests. This in itself explains the importance of forests to farming in this area.

The main input from forests to farms is through the decomposed leaf litter of forest floors from which essential nutrients gradually leach into the nearby fields during the rainy season. Traditional small *bunds* (raised soil barriers) between the forests and the adjacent farms

---

[15] The *sal* seed is boiled and washed in running water for about 24 hours, then boiled again and dried and powdered to be used as prophylactic dose of anti-gastroenteric medicine.

are commonly constructed by the farmers to let the rain water pond towards the forest side and to facilitate the slow release of both moisture and nutrients from forests to farms on a continued and long term basis. External irrigation and fertilization is, therefore, not required at all in farms that are situated up to a distance of about 150 metres from the fringe of an average stocked forest. This means a saving of the price of 600 kilograms per acre (or 1.5 metric tonnes per hectare) of the precious cowdung manure and upto 30 labour-hours for dung collection and its application. The cowdung manure thus saved is used up on the farms that are distant from the forests. In contrast, a degraded forest is able to fertilize and moisturize the farms upto only 30–50 meters distance, highlighting the stark difference in the nutritional status of farms in MK- and non-MK-villages. In the non-MK-village of Hesadih not only is a larger area of forest required to fertilize a unit area of farm, but the number of farmers benefiting from forest nutrients has come down to just three or four. Other farmers in this village have either to purchase costly chemical fertilizer, or be content with cowdung fertilizer which is becoming increasingly difficult to find. This is in stark contrast to the situation 20–25 years ago when forests were better and about 50–60 per cent of the farms in this village were being fertilized with forest nutrients.

Tables 2.3 and 2.4[16] explain how the farmers of this area value the nutrients from forests:

Table 2.3
Comparison of the Productivity of Various Crops on Forest Fertilized Farms and Other Farms

Crop	Forest Fertilized Farms		Other Farms (Fertilized with Cowdung Manure/ Inorganic Fertlizers)		Remarks
	Distance from Forest Fringe (metres)	Pro- ductivity (quintals per hectare)	Distance from Forest Fringe (metres)	Pro- ductivity (quintals per hectare)	
Lowland Paddy	Up to 150m	20q	>200m	24q	The nutrient effect of forest fertilizer is offset by the shade (light and wind) effect on the forest fringe farms.

(contd.)

---

[16] Figures are based on the empirical knowledge of our study respondents.

Table 2.3 contd.

Crop	Forest Fertilized Farms		Other Farms (Fertilized with Cowdung Manure/ Inorganic Fertlizers)		Remarks
	Distance from Forest Fringe (metres)	Pro- ductivity (quintals per hectare)	Distance from Forest Fringe (metres)	Pro- ductivity (quintals per hectare)	
Flatland Paddy (IR-36 variety)[17]	Up to 250m	24q	500m	26.5q	Same as above
Potato	Up to 100m	25q	>200m	20q	The size also of the potato grown in the forest fringe farms is bigger. In addition, distant farms need artificial irrigation which is a costly affair. In forest fringe farms the productivity is in the ratio of 1:5 (seed to crop).
Khesari/ Batura[18]	Up to 150m	5q	>200m	3.5q	No need to plough the forest fringe paddy farms before these lentil inter crops are sown (because of the high residual moisture). The lentil crop is hoed naturally when the paddy is harvested.
Mustard	Up to 200m	5q	>200m	5q	Production is similar in both type of farms.
Tisi[19]	Up to 150m	1q	>200m	0.8q	—
Masur[20]	Up to 200m	2.5q	>200m	1.75q	—

---

[17] A high yielding variety developed by the Indian Agriculture Research Institute, Pusa that is quite popular in the area.

[18] Coarse varieties of lentil.

[19] *Linum*, an oilseed crop. Its oil is preferred to mustard oil because of its sweet taste when fresh.

[20] Red gram—a highly proteinaceous lentil.

Table 2.4

Quantity of Cowdung Fertilizer Required to Compensate for the Absence of
Nutrients from Forests on Farms about 750m away from the Forest Fringe

Crop	Quantity of Cowdung Fertilizer (kilograms/hectare)
Paddy	1500
Mustard	500
Red Gram	500
Potato	875
Tisi	500
Khesari/Batura	375

Elderly villagers opine that food crops grown with leaf litter nutrition from the forests are healthier and better. For example, they say that the rice grown now, with the application of chemical fertilizer, tastes less sweet and turns sour within 8–10 hours of cooking. When stored, its nutritive value considerably decreases within a year, whereas rice grown on forest fertilized farms remains firm and nutritive for up to 3–4 years in storage. They think that this may be one of the reasons why they (and their family members) are not as healthy as their predecessors used to be. They also attribute the early attack of *banki*, an insect pest, on their paddy crop to increased use of chemical fertilizers. In their opinion, a paddy crop of the traditional variety, fertilized with forest nutrients, has the least chance of attack from pests.

As regards forest species that are considered important for farm fertilization, bamboo is the choicest type. In the pre-1969 days our non-MK study village of Hesadih had well stocked bamboo forests in its neighbourhood. Elderly respondents of this village fondly recall the productivity of their farms and stream fertilized with the decomposed leaf litter, locally called *gaad*, from the bamboo forests. The severe drought of 1969, and the gregarious flowering of bamboo in the following season coupled with increasing alienation of local people as regards the government forests in their neighbourhood resulted in a complete failure of bamboo to regenerate by fallen seeds in that area. Villagers in both MK- as well as non-MK-villages are aware that even now the small farms in Hesadih village that are fertilized from the little remaining bamboo forests near the village are not only more fertile and productive, but the best variety of paddy can only be grown there. *Sal* tree leaf litter occupies the second place in terms of nutritional efficiency after bamboo. Other broadleaf indigenous species are grouped together at the third place. Strangely, our village interviews do not support the otherwise popular notion that local forest popu-lation opposes exotic tree species like teak, acacia and eucalyptus for the fear that their leaves degrade farm soils. Villagers feel that their leaves too are important fertilizers, though not as good as other broadleaved indigenous species. They do, however, admit that these exotic species consume much more water so they promote a xero-phytic condition that is not good for the nearby upland crops.

All respondents, especially the literate and the elderly, contend that increased application of pesticides and chemical fertilizers by farmers to compensate for the loss of forest nutrients has negatively affected the availability of fish, crab, tortoise and oyster in the wet rice fields. Besides, the crops grown with these chemical pesticides quickly loose their natural flavour and nutrition whereas the use of natural and traditional pesticides like, the branches of *barango* and *bhelwa* trees and *sabai* grass[21] do not have any such side effects.

In the opinion of many villagers, the fertilization of their farms with forest nutrients is directly related to the size of the resident popula-tion of earthworms. In farms away from the forests, the population of earthworms is quite small. It may be because the earthworms prefer leaf litter, abundantly available near forests, as food. It is a common belief in the area that frequent sighting of earthworms and oysters on farms is positively correlated to the productivity of the site. Some elderly villagers also opine that reduction in the popu-lation of earthworms is linked to deforestation and global warming. For example, they were able to clearly recall that the sighting of earthworms was negligible in July–August this year (the preceding summer was actually very hot), so they already expected a bad har-vest (an expectation which indeed came true despite initial good signs).

Forests and Choice of Farm-Crops

A farm that has recently been cleared of forest vegetation or upland farms on the fringe of forests are the preferred sites for growing tuber crops like potato, sweet potato, radish and turnip, especially potato, due to higher content of phosphorus that continuously leaches in from the nearby forests. The acreage of potato cultivation in the area is increasing as it is a profitable cash crop. Inspired by the farmers

---

[21] *Barango* and *bhelwa* trees and *sabai* grass are common in the forests of this area.

of the adjacent Ranchi district, and as a response to declining rice yields, some farmers of this area have started leasing their forest-fringe farms/private forests for potato cultivation to outsiders, although this practice has not as yet acquired menacing proportions. In addition to receiving a rent, farmer owners are also encouraged because their uneven uplands are levelled by the potato leaseholder. This has serious ecological repercussions as it encourages farmers to clear their private holdings of forest/tree vegetation. This trend is easily discernible in the non-MK area, including to some extent in Hesadih village. In the MK-study villages no farmer has so far leased or cleared land for potato cultivation. How far this contrasting response to diversification of farming livelihoods is because of environmental awareness is not clear, but the MK-villages have more opportunity to diversify because of the proximity of these villages to the main weekly market and *lac* processing industries of the region, and retention of soil moisture on the uplands for longer duration in the winter and early summer season that is far more suitable to vegetable cultivation than in the non-MK-villages.[22]

In the opinion of the elderly villagers, the increasing cultivation of potato is adversely affecting wild tuber production (due to the loss of forest area to potato farming) and consumption (due to people getting used to sweeter tasting potato). This change in food habits is not without adverse environmental effects: the wild tubers, namely *Kukai,* *Harad-bo* (*genthi-kand*) and *Buru-sanga* (various species of the genus *Dioscorea*)[23] are not only an important carbohydrate supplement without the environmental externality associated with modern day agriculture, but act as important prophylactic/curative measure for various gastro-intestinal ailments. In terms of social equity too, the decreasing production and consumption of wild tuber means more hardship for the landless and the poor for whom it is both a diet staple in a deficit season and a source of handsome income (the local price being Rs 15–20 per kilogram).

---

[22] Please also see Baker, 2000 for a comprehensive account of farming livelihood diversification by the men and women of Gambia in response to recurrent drought.

[23] *Kukai* (also known as forest pear), *Harad-bo* and *Buru-sanga* are all very tasty, palatable, easily digestible and nutritive. They are boiled just like potato, except for *Harad-bo* which requires washing in running water for 24 hours, before boiling to remove its initial bitter taste, and eaten as staple food. Whereas *Kukai* is available during the October–November period, *Harad-bo* is common during September–November and *Buru-sanga* during November–December.

As with tuber crops, the productivity of leafy vegetables[24] and mushrooms[25] has appreciably decreased in the non-MK-villages (both in forest as well as on non-forest land), which poses a serious question of malnutrition of the population, especially the poor. Reduced availability of leafy vegetables and mushrooms also means that more vegetated lands will need to be converted into farmlands to compensate for the loss of wild sources of protein, carbohydrate and minerals.

Forests and Agricultural Labour

Paddy is the most important crop of the area. In addition to providing much-required nutrients to rice fields, forests also help farmers to undertake larger rice acreage with available family labour in the busy *kharif* season when labour is in short supply. Paddy grown on farms near the forests quickly grows tall because of the shade effect of the forest trees, and then it has a tendency to fall down during strong winds. The farmers have responded to the shade effects by sowing their forest-fringe farms quite late in August (contrary to the broadcast sowing of upland paddy in June–July, and transplant of lowland paddy on distant farms in early-mid July), and thus they are able to spread their family labour resources efficiently for undertaking larger areas of rice cultivation during the otherwise very busy *kharif* season.

Forests and Farm-Soil Erosion

Most upland farms are situated on the lower side of the forested hill slopes. The traditional *bund* between the forest and the adjacent farmland prevents the rainwater from gushing into the farms, thereby arresting soil erosion. Also the presence of a thick leaf-litter and humus on the ground due to good forest cover means good infiltration of the rain water that ponds along these bunds. This water is then slowly released along with forest leaf litter nutrients into the farms

---

[24] At least 13 different types of leaves and flower species are used as vegetables in this area. Many of them possess medicinal properties (e.g., *Beng-sag* is a good cure for jaundice). Some of them, e.g., *Saru-sag*, are essential culinary items during marriage festivities.

[25] At least 15 different types of mushroom and puffball species are collected and used in this area. Each mushroom/puffball type is available in a definite season and in a definite succession between June and October. Thus the availability of mushrooms/puffballs as an important protein source to the household nutrition requirement is ensured for a 5-month period between June and October.

to provide long term moisture and nutrients for the success of both the *kharif* and *rabi* crops. In the non-MK-villages, however, a disturbing trend of removing this *bund* is slowly gaining ground. This is done in order to obliterate any boundary mark between the government forests and private holdings, so that expansion/encroachment into the government forests becomes easier. Farmers do so despite the risk of a higher rate of erosion and loss of nutrients due to the gushing rainwater. Part of the river side paddy fields in Hesadih village are, thus, completely eroded, and no crop can be grown productively there. Their owners are aware of the severity of the problem, but short term gains from the sale of timber/firewood illegally extracted from the encroached forests and a long term prospect of regularization of encroachment are strong disincentives to these poor and marginal farmers against thinking of a sustainable future. The absence of a strong village institution in the non-MK-village Hesadih makes it easier for the individual farmers to take and implement such private decisions. The vestigial institutions of the *munda* and the JFM in this village are not able to specify rights and duties for its participants because of which they are not able to get 'out of the trap' and organize for public action. Hesadih village, thus, truly exemplifies the 'second level of dilemma' of common property resource management (Ostrom 1999).

All villagers agree that deforestation has one positive effect: the washed away soil from the adjacent deforested hills will be deposited on the lower fields, so that the gross area of the highly prized *don (wet rice)* farmland will increase. Despite this knowledge, the MK-villagers (and for that matter, the non-MK-villagers also agree during discussions) are not ready to clear forest lands because of the risk to long term fertility of their farms. The similarity of the MK and non-MK population—in terms of social and economic variables—adds to the puzzle: as to why the two populations act so differently despite similar level of understanding. Is it only because of the difference in land-tenure systems in these two sets of villages? The answer to this question is not easy to come by, and that is why it requires a deeper and independent enquiry. A possible line of enquiry could unravel the role of the communal institution in providing repeated opportunities for 'learning' interactions between diverse stakeholders, which in turn could facilitate positive changes in the actors that leads to better understanding of the forest, authority, interpretation of rules, etc.,—all of which together increase the amount of trust and reciprocity variables in the social capital production function of that village.

Pest Management

As indicated in the previous paragraphs some of the forest trees and grass provide useful pest protection services to the farmers. In addition to vegetative pesticides (the most important of which is *Karanj, Pongamia pinnanta*, oil cake and leaf extract), some of the jungle birds also provide this service. It is common practice in this area for farmers to fix a *bhelwa* (washerman's nut tree) stick in their fields to allow jungle birds like *dhenchuan* and *kerketta* to perch and prey on insects, pests and rodents that are otherwise deleterious to the paddy crop. The population of the *dhenchua* bird, which lives only in the forests, however, is declining fast because of forest degradation, especially in Hesadih village whose respondents were able to clearly distinguish this trend. Farmers also believe that many insect pests, for example *chaiya* and *banki*, spread with storms, so the forests indirectly save the crops from the spread of those pests.

Storm Protection

Villagers are aware that the forests are crucial for protecting their standing crops from storm damage. But they are also conscious of the fact that the nearness of their farms to forests leads to the increased height of their paddy tillers that are more prone to damage in stormy conditions. Farmers in all the study villages felt that an appropriate distance between farm and forest is necessary to reap the full benefit of moisture and nutrients leaching from the forests. The knowledge of shade-effect reflects in a conscious absence of efforts by villagers to plant trees on or near their farms. As an adaptive strategy though they will usually plant small size shrubs, for example, *sindwar* (*Vitex negundo*), and small trees, for example, *karanj* (*Pongamia pinnata*) on the slopy uplands as a measure to bind soil and protect the sharp edges of the field below. The choice of *sindwar* and *karanj* as soil binder once again reflects the depth of the indigenous ecological knowledge of these communities. As a visible distinction, no tree is planted on the *bund* of wet rice fields, although the need for soil binding and run off protection is much pronounced at many sites on these fields. Villagers' answers in this regard did not appear convincing, and varied from 'thick roots of the trees make soil of the *bund* porous, so the *bund* gets easily damaged' to 'because of tree roots it is easier for rodents to burrow in the *bunds* and cause damage to the crop', which suggests an internal conflict in their present understanding of the nature, risk assessment and prevailing customs in the area.

Nevertheless, the differential treatment of lowland and upland farm-bunds with respect to planting of trees and shrubs also demonstrates local people's knowledge and perceptions of soil erosion under different land conditions.

Cultural Beliefs about Forests

Forests are integral to the 'cosmovision' of indigenous communities of the study area (Parajuli 2000), which manifests in a direct relationship between cultural events and beliefs with trees or forests. For example, *Sarhul*, one of the important festivals of the forest population across the eastern India plateau is observed to mark the flowering of *sal* trees in April–May. No person can bring any flower to the home for consumption, or otherwise, before *Sarhul* as it is believed that this will invite a deadly snakebite. The custom unconsciously keeps the flowers unharmed until pollination and seed setting is over in most tree species of the area. The sacred groves of the villages (*sarna*) also serve as a weather forecasting station during the *Sarhul* festival worship. On the day of *Sarhul* the village priest (*pahan*) takes a water filled pitcher to the grove and keeps it there overnight after the usual prayers to the *bonga*. If the water level in the pitcher recedes, the *pahan* forecasts that the rainfall is not going to be adequate this year and the farmers plan their agriculture accordingly. Conversely, an undisturbed water level means a good rainfall year is in the offing and an increase in water level means heavier rainfall than usual. The ritual does have some scientific validity. Obviously, April and May (when the *Sarhul* festival is observed) are the months when humidity starts building up in the atmosphere. Pre-monsoon showers and monsoon rains follow in the next months. Clearly, less humidity during April–May would mean delayed or less cloud formation depicted by a lowering of the water level in the sacred pitcher.

Other festivals of importance are:

- *Karama* [in which the *karam* (*Adina cordifolia*) tree is worshipped],
- *Van-Puja* (forest prayer—in the month of May, to propitiate the wild animal god),
- *Rog-Har* (disease eradication prayer, observed during the summer months, performed at a particular place having a specific type of vegetation; for example, the *Rog-Har* place in Hesadih village is called *loa-ikir* which is encircled with *loa* (*Ficus glomerata*) trees; in Katwa village it is *sarjom-ikir* which is encircled by *sal* trees, etc.),

- *Bishu-Shikar* (the community wild-animal hunt in which the game, however small, has to be shared equally between all households of the participating villages), etc.

Most people believe that the trees should be protected because it propitiates the rain god and brings rainfall by stopping clouds, as mountains do when causing orographic rainfall. Elderly people also believe that the big trees should be conserved because the cuckoo bird sings for rain and it likes to rest on these big trees. Ancestral spirits also come and rest on these trees particularly those in the sacred grove (*sarna*). The fear of retribution, that they will be punished by the gods (*bonga*) if they cut or harm the *sarna* trees, is common amongst all age groups and classes.

The local knowledge and management of forest/tree resources for cultural/religious purposes is set within the complex social framework of the area. Conservation of tree resources through the propagation of cultural and religious beliefs can best be understood in the context of control by the rural elite, namely the *pahan* who was the most venerated person of Munda society in pre-British days. The *pahan*'s high position in this society, even today, is strengthened by the ecological arguments for these religious and cultural rituals. At the same time, these rituals serve as a potent tool that keeps outsiders/immigrants from ever using the village's natural resources as it is argued that it will displease the *bonga*.

Redoing Forest Management

Estate forest management has historically been based on the principle of 'management by simplification'. In the zeal to simplify things, the Forest Department (FD) first demarcated the forests thereby making them a separate entity from the adjoining farms and habitations. In this process the FD excluded the 'people'. In its second step, the FD introduced the system of management by working plans that was based on the knowledge gained from European forestry. The management plans oversimplified things by prescribing 'conversion to a uniform system' in order to maximize the ease of logging, harvesting and transport operations (see Scott 1998: chapter 1, for a more general discussion). Being decadal or bi-decadal plans of operation, they also suffered from a kind of rigidity that was undesirable in view of the limited knowledge of the effects of different sylvicultural systems on the regeneration of species in the area. In this whole process of simplification, the one aspect that suffered the most was the ecological relationship between the forest and its surrounding habitation. Once this local ecological link was completely broken, the degradation of forests continued at a faster pace. The decades of 1980s and 1990s have sought to reverse this process after experimenting with different forms of people's participation regimes in the 1990s, especially since the 1992 Rio Declarations. Despite the emphases attached to development of farm forestry and Non-Timber Forest Products (NTFPs) during these two decades, forest degradation could not be reversed. The forestry community has only recently begun to realize that *local ecological services* are the crucial 'missing link' to forest restoration. But, our knowledge of these services is at a rudimentary stage. Much effort will be needed before a policy of sustainable forest management based on multiple objectives of timber and non-timber forest production, and local and distant ecological services provision is introduced. The first task, of course, will be to collate the rural people's knowledge with the existing systematic forestry management literature, in the manner we call 'action research'. The second task will be to build an appropriate institutional framework in which the findings of the action research are replicated on a larger scale.

It is not necessary to reiterate here that the group whose fate both present and future is most directly linked to the fate of the forest and the land is the indigenous community. Yet the exigencies of survival in government owned forest areas seem to subvert the best efforts of the elderly and literate forest households to ensure ecological stability of these forests. In these villages aspects of the traditional society have broken down because there was no resource in the village which could have facilitated the central role of the traditional leaders, *munda* and *pahan*, and subsequently traditional natural resource management systems in such villages too have become dysfunctional.[26] In addition, there is an emerging section of the forest people, in both types of villages (having community owned or government owned forests) who have broken their links with the land and have adopted the life styles and aspirations of middle-class urban Indians in white-collar

---

[26] On the other hand, in the Mundari-Khuntkatti villages the *munda* and the *pahan* were able to maintain their leadership role because forests in these villages are communal property and their management required regular village level meetings under the chairmanship of the *munda*. This process in turn allows the traditional resource management systems to be strictly adhered to.

jobs. These two processes are important to our understanding of the relationship between forest culture and nature. There is a great deal of literature today that celebrates the conservationist values of 'indigenous knowledge'. Some of this literature, especially what we call 'ethnobotany', tends to have an extremely instrumentalist view of forest culture and seeks to appropriate forest knowledge for pursuing the agenda of the state or their own establishments.[27] While it is all very well to give due recognition to cultural practices and beliefs that have been systematically ignored or rejected as 'primitive' and 'unscientific' in the past, it is also important to situate this knowledge within the larger context of the changing forest reality. That is, before defending 'indigenous ecological knowledge' we must also speak of restoring the rights of the indigenous community over the forests. This is by no means an easy move because, in a differentiated indigenous community, squeezed by the state and the market, some economically vulnerable households may continue to practice a profession that is antithetical to the goal of forest conservation but gainful to them in the short term. It will, therefore, be crucial to recover or establish anew the value of *local ecological services* as an explicit output of forest management and not as something which occurs 'naturally' or which can be taken for granted.

REFERENCES

Avery, C. C. and L. J. Fritschen. Hydrologic and Energy Budgets of Stocked and Non-Stocked Douglas-fir Sites as Calculated by Meteorological Methods. Research Completion Report for A-0320WASH for July 1969–July 1971. Seattle, WA: College of Forest Resources, University of Washington, 1971.

Baker, K. 'Ecological Possibilities and Political Constraints: Adjustments of Farming to Protracted Drought by Women and Men in the Western Division of The Gambia'. In *Political Ecology: Science, Myth and Power*, edited by P. Stott and S. Sullivan. London: Arnold, 2000: 157, 178.

Buchy, M. and S. Hoverman. Understanding Public Participation in Forest Planning in Australia: How Can We Learn From Each Other? Forestry Occasional Paper 99.2. Canberra: Australian National University, 1999.

---

[27] Five large research grants have been obtained during 1998–2000 by different institutions in Ranchi district to prepare ethnobotanical literature of the district. These studies, however, are being carried out in isolation of each other and are tending to become mostly redundant. None of the data banks, thus being prepared, is being discussed with the communities feeding these literatures, and obviously the communities are not getting any benefit from these research projects.

102 ❦ Sanjay Kumar

Clarey, W. P. and P. F. Ffolliott. 'Water Holding Capacity of Ponderosa Pine Forest Floor Layers'. *Journal of Soil and Water Conservation* 24, no. 1 (1969): 2.

Collings, M. R. 'Throughfall for Summer Thunderstorms in a Juniper and Pinyon Woodland Cibecue Ridge, Arizona'. Geological Survey Professional Paper 485-B. Washington D.C.: U.S. Government Printing Office, 1966: 13.

Costanza, R., R. d'Arge, R. de Groot, S. Farber, M. Grasso, B. Hannon, K. Limburg, S. Naeem, R. V. O'Neill, J. Paruelo, R. G. Raskin, P. Sulten and M. van den Belt. 'The Value of the World's Ecosystem Services and Natural Capital.' *Ecological Economics* 25 (1998): 3–15. Reprinted from *Nature* 387 (May 1997): 253–60.

Danks, C. Developing Institutions for Community Forestry in Northern California, ODI Rural Development Forestry Network, Network Paper 20a. London: Overseas Development Institute, 1996.

Eriksen, S. S., J. Naustdalslid and A. Schou. *Decentralisation from Above: A Study of Local Government in Botswana, Ghana, Tanzania and Zimbabwe.* Oslo: Nerwegian Institute for Urban and Regional Research (NIBR), PLUSS series, 1999: 4–99.

Forest Department, Government of Bihar. *Vanropan Padhati* (in Hindi). Ranchi: Forest Department, Government of Bihar, 1996.

Freeze, R. A. 'Role of Subsurface Flow in Generating Surface Runoff. 2. Upstream Source Areas'. *Water Resources Research* 8, no. 5 (1972): 1272–83.

Garczynski, F. 'Effects of Percentage Forest Cover on the Hydrological Regime in Three Regions of the USA'. Proceedings of the Helsinki Symposium of the International Association of Hydrological Sciences, 23–26 June, 1980.

Goodell, B. C. 'A Reappraisal of Precipitation Interception by Plants and Attendant Water Loss'. *Journal of Soil and Water Conservation* 18, no. 6 (1963): 231–34.

Guehl, J. (undated). 'Forests and Water: Relations between Forest and Ecosystems and Water Resources'. *IUFRO Occasional Paper no. 9*. Vienna: International Union of Forest Research Organizations.

Hall, J. E. 'Canada's Model Forest Program: A Participatory Approach to Sustainable Forest Management in Canada'. *Commonwealth Forestry Review* 76, no. 4 (1997): 261–63.

Houghton, R. A. 'The Role of the World's Forest in Global Warming'. In *The Future of World Forests: Their Use and Conservation*, edited by Ramkrishna and Woodwell. Dehradun, India: Natraj Publishers, 1993.

Jewitt, S. and S. Kumar. 'A Political Ecology of Forest Management: Gender and Silvicultural Knowledge in the Jharkhand, India'. In *Political Ecology: Science, Myth and Power*, edited by P. Stott, and S. Sullivan. London: Arnold, 2000: 91–116.

Kimmins, J. P. and M. C. Feller. 'Effect of Clearcutting and Broadcast Slashburning on Nutrient Budgets, Stream Water Chemistry and Productivity in Western Canada'. *Proceedings 16th IUFRO World Congress, Division I:186–97*, 1976.

Kothari, A. 'Community-based Conservation: Issues and Prospects'. pp. 25–27. In *Communities and Conservation: Natural Resource Management in South and Central Asia*, edited by A. Kothari, N. Pathak, R.V. Anuradha, and B. Taneja. New Delhi: Sage Publications, 1998.

Leonard, R. E. 'Interception of Precipitation by Northern Hardwoods'. USDA For. Serv. Station Paper No. 159, Northeastern Forest Experiment Station, Upper Darby, PA, 1961: 16.

Mitchell, C. P., S. E. Corbridge, S. Jewitt, A. K. Mahapatra and S. Kumar. 1999. *Availability, Consumption, Marketing and Management of Non-Timber Forest Products in Eastern India*. Research completion report for the UK Department for International Development (DFID), Renewable Natural Resources Research Strategy (RNRRS) Programme, 1999.

Ostrom, E. 1999. Self-Governance and Forest Resources. *CIFOR Occasional Paper no. 20.*

Parajuli, P. 'No Nature Apart: Adivasi Cosmovision and Ecological Discourses in Jharkhand, India'. In *Planting A Tree: Natural Landscapes and Cultural Politics*, edited by Phil Arnold and Ann Gold. London: Ashgate Publishers, 2000: chapter 5.

Scott, J. *Seeing Like a State: How Certain Schemes to Improve the Human Condition Have Failed*. New Haven: Yale University Press, 1998.

3

Local Environmental Services

Forest Management and Terraced Agriculture, a Case Study of the Hani of the Ailao Mountains, Yunnan, China

Wang Qinghua

Introduction

This essay is a study of the impact of a forest management system on the provision of environmental services to the local economy. To understand this interaction we have chosen a village of the Hani, among the Ailao Mountains in southeast Yunnan, China. The Hani of this area are famous for their terraced agriculture. What is not so well known is that this terraced agriculture depends on an elaborate management and engineering system, linking the forests and the agricultural fields. This essay elucidates this point, and looks at the connection between the local importance of the environmental services provided by the forests and the local attitude to forests, which reflects the importance of forests as providers of environmental services. The Hani have a saying, 'Without the forest there can be no Hani'. This seems a curious attitude for a people with a livelihood system that is not based on swidden cultivation, where forest and farm are directly related and transformed into each other, but on terraced agriculture. It is the importance of forests in providing water for the terraces, the lifeblood of the Hani, that explains what otherwise looks like their curious reluctance to cut trees even from state-owned forests, a reluctance that is in sharp contrast to the usual practice in other parts of China, even, other parts of Yunnan. In looking at indigenous (local) knowledge we find a clear difference between women's and men's knowledge in many areas of human interaction with the forests. But, of course, given men's domination of community-level functioning, there is a disregard of women's knowledge in community decisions on forest management.

After briefly describing the geographical setting of the study village, this essay will discuss the role of forests in providing various environmental services. This is largely based on discussions with villagers and, to an extent, local technical officials. This local knowledge and the gender differences therein are then looked into. The changes in forest tenure and their effects on forest condition and provision of environmental goods and services are then taken up for analysis. The essay ends with a brief account of what the local people think is needed, both in the sphere of forest management and in other forest interventions, to improve forest condition and increase the supply of environmental goods and services.

GEOGRAPHY AND FORESTS

The fieldwork, on which this essay is based, was conducted in the village of Dayutang (Big Fish Pond) in the Ailao Mountains of Yunnan. The village is similar to other Hani villages in this region: it is a small-scale settlement located in the middle of the mountains with terraced agriculture that is dependent on the flow of water down the mountainside. But this flow of water is not just a natural flow; it has been enhanced by a combination of engineering and forest management methods, utilizing the topography of the area. The village, like other Hani villages in the region, has a three-level structure ranging from 800 to 2,500 metres: alpine forest at the top of the mountain; village settlement in between at about 1,800 metres; and terraced paddy fields at the bottom.

More or less corresponding to the three levels are differences in climate and vegetation. At the foot of the mountains it is hot and humid, there are few trees and the slopes are mainly covered with grass. In the middle zone, there are clearly distinguishable hot and cold seasons. It is usually misty in winter and hot and humid in summer. In this zone there are both firs and broadleaf trees. The top zone is cool and humid, and the trees here change from verdant broadleaf trees to alpine, evergreen, bryophyte trees and brushwood.

FORESTS AND ENVIRONMENTAL SERVICES

To the Hani the forest forms the basis of their survival. In their language the forest is called *pu-ma-e-bo*, which means 'forest is the home', indicating that the forest is their home. This idea of the forests as the basis of existence has persisted in spite of the transition from swidden to terraced agriculture. At some time in the past, the Hani migrated southward along two routes. As they moved south, the westerly migration learnt terraced agriculture from the communities with whom they came into contact along the way. By contrast, the easterly migration, which continued into northern Thailand (where they are known as the Akha), did not come into contact with terraced agriculture and continue their swidden practice even today. But both groups of Hani use the same term *pu-ma-e-bo* for the forest, and both continue to regard the forest as the foundation of their existence.

Usually the transition from swidden to terraced agriculture brings with it an entire change in nomenclature and even in attitudes to the forest. Swidden forest is transformed into farm, and it reverts back to forest after a while. Thus, the two are not opposed categories, one is transformed into the other. Terraced agriculture, on the other hand, is created by permanently eliminating the forest from agriculture, and the forest and the terraced field become two opposed, dichotomous categories. The Hani's terraced fields and the forests are spatially quite separate, being located at the foot and at the top of the mountains respectively. But in the Hani language and in their attitude to the forest we do not find any such dichotomy. Is this merely a relic of a past relation? Or, is the continuation of this attitude due to the important role of the forests in providing the environmental services that are critical to the practice of terraced agriculture? A look at the way in which the contemporary Hani understand the role of the forests in providing these environmental services inclines one to the idea that it is this important role of the forests that accounts for the continuation of their attitude to the forests.

WATER PROVIDED BY THE FOREST

As mentioned above, there is a vertical distribution of microclimate and vegetation types in the village of Dayutang, as in the rest of the Eastern Guanyin Mountains.[1] Owing to the sharp difference in altitude

---

[1] Guanyin (Goddess of Mercy) Mountains is another name by which Ailao Mountains are known in Yuanyang County. The mountain is further divided into

and the effects of the maritime monsoon from the south, the top of the mountain is covered with mist and fog, and experiences plentiful precipitation. The first water function of the mountain-top forest is to trap this rain and release it downward to the valley. Water that evaporates from the river valleys and rises as mist or fog is also captured by the trees, on which it condenses and then drips down to the lower areas. This happens mostly during the monsoon season. But the water that infiltrates the ground continues to seep down throughout the year to feed numerous ponds and streams. The forest acts as a natural green dam. Thus, the Hani have a saying about this water-conserving function of the forest, 'The water can reach [only] as high as the forest'. They understand that without the forests on top of the mountains, water vapour would not be trapped and come back into their ecosystem. Local water and forest technicians estimate that the water-source forests in the Guanyin Mountains as a whole can store more than 20 million cubic metres of water, making Yuanyang County (in which Dayutang is located) a place with abundant water resources.

The local people understand that the alpine forests on the mountain-tops carry out various water harvesting functions. The forests trap rainwater and water vapour that evaporates from the valley. Further they recognize that the infiltration of rainwater into the ground is higher with a good forest floor cover. As such, they neither allow the removal of the leaf litter in the alpine forests, nor do they allow logging; only collection of dead branches or small branches and twigs is permitted. They know the trees break the force of the rain, and that a good layer of litter and forest cover does the same thereby reducing soil erosion.

All of the above local knowledge, it may be noted, is reasonably in accord with current scientific knowledge. For instance, scientists know that the 'protective value of tree cover lies, not so much in the ability of the tree canopy to break the force of the rain, but, rather, in developing and maintaining a litter layer' (Bruijnzeel 1990: 118); and that the infiltration capacities of forest soils are higher than those of bare soils (ibid.: 12). This is knowledge on which the Hani have, over the centuries, based their forest management systems, which allowed only very low intensity interventions in the alpine forest on the mountain-tops.

If the natural functioning of the forest system traps the water, it is human engineering that brings this water down to the settlements

---

Western Guanyin and Eastern Guanyin Mountains. Dayutang Village is located on the northern slope of Eastern Guanyin Mountains.

and terraces. To this end, the Hani have dug channels, which look like belts winding through the mountains. Some of the channels are dozens of kilometres long, traversing the neighbouring counties. They are all directly connected to the water sources—the ponds, creeks and streams—in the alpine forests, ensuring that the terraced fields receive water throughout the year. These ditches also capture spring water seeping from the mountains and the forest. During the monsoon season, rainwater fills these ditches and flows into the fields. Otherwise it is the water trapped and released by the forest that is carried to the fields all the year round.

Soil Formation and Nutrient Recycling

There are many processes of soil formation. But we are concerned here only with those processes centred on the forest. In the process of exuberant biological accumulation, leaves and decomposing tree stems release carbon dioxide and some organic acids, which eventually lead to biochemical reactions in the soil. At the same time, the roots of trees change the composition and elements of microbes in the soil, promoting and balancing some biochemical processes. The physical penetration of roots enhances the formation of the structure of the soil in formerly hard rock. After the remains of dead forest organic matter (plants and animals) are absorbed into the soil, the soil is enriched with a large amount of organic materials.

The accumulation and circulation of nutrients is, on the one hand, a natural process and, on the other hand, an artificial process created by the use of water by humans. In the high alpine forest, there is little human interaction in the process of soil formation, which takes place in a natural cycle of formation and development, with its nutrient content being accumulated, depleted and replaced. At the opposite end, in the 'wastelands', where the vegetation has been destroyed by human activity, the accumulation of soil is on the decline, and erosion on the rise. With an imbalance in the circulation of nutrients (more being taken out than are put back) the land is increasingly infertile.

In terraced agriculture, where there is a high level of human interaction with the natural process of soil formation, the natural ecology is transformed into an agro-ecology. In this transformation, water stored by, and brought down from, the forest plays a crucial role. The Hani understand that the water flowing down from the forest, brings with it a large accumulation of humus. Since local people usually graze their livestock in this forest, water from the forest also washes down animal manure. In this way the forest-based water enhances the organic content of the soil.

The combination of leaves, stems and humus contributes to the recycling of nutrients in the agro-ecological system. With an abundance of organic matter available, the Hani do not use much inorganic fertilizer. Our field investigations (corroborated by the local agriculture office) showed that only about 0.4 kilograms of inorganic fertilizer is used per *mu*.[2] This is due to the recycling of nutrients within the ecosystem, largely from the forests to the fields.

SIMILARITY WITH OTHER TERRACED SYSTEMS

It would seem that the terraced agriculture systems of certain other communities, like the Angami Naga and Apatani in India, also have a similarly close relation between forest cover and the provision of water and nutrients for the terraces (Dev Nathan, personal communication). The spatial arrangement of forest, settlement and terraces takes the same vertical order. Forest cover at the top of the hills regulates the flow of water brought down through channels. Soil formation and nutrient recycling are again both dependent on forests.

These terraced systems all favour maintenance of forest cover on the crowns of the hills. On the other hand, the easterly Hani who remained swiddeners are not similarly reluctant to convert forests on hilltops into fields. The Hani who have not converted to terraced agriculture (as in Xishuangbanna Yunnan, China and in Thailand) convert hilltop forest into swidden fields. For them too the forest is *pu-ma-e-bo* (meaning 'forest is the home') but in another way. For the Hani who are swiddeners, the forest is the provider of a livelihood through its conversion into agriculture, but for the Hani who practice terraced agriculture, the forest is the provider of water, soil and nutrients as inputs into the terraces.

At one level it could be argued that with the higher per area productivity of terraced agriculture, it is possible for these communities to set aside some portion of forest, that is then kept free of any form of cultivation. But at another level what our investigation of Hani indigenous knowledge shows is that this setting aside of forest also results from the dependence of terraced agriculture on the water, soil and nutrient supplying functions of forests. Without such setting aside of forests, terraced agriculture would itself collapse.

---

[2] *Mu* is a Chinese measure of land area—5 *mu* is roughly equal to 1 hectare.

The understanding of the connection between the forests and terraced agriculture is an important component of the indigenous knowledge of the Hani and other similar communities. This is different from the usual analysis of terraced agriculture, which stresses the permanent conversion of field into forest as the characteristic that differentiates it from periodic conversion of forest into farm and vice versa in swidden (see the analyses in Croll and Parkin 1992). The Hani, on the other hand, stress the dependence of permanent terraced agriculture on forests. The Hani call the mountain forest *Guanyin* or 'Mother', and the water from the mountain 'milk of the Mother', meaning that without the forest there would be no life.

OTHER PRODUCTS AND SERVICES

Besides the water and soil environmental service functions (which are really what lead the Hani to say that the forest is the home) the forests also provide a number of Non-Timber Forest Products (NTFPs) and aesthetic/recreational services. Since these products and services are quite well known we will not spend much time discussing them. The Hani do not have special gardens for growing vegetables, and depend on the forest for most of their vegetables. Many tubers and mushrooms are also collected from the forest. There are over 100 species of tubers, roots, leafs and flowers which are edible.

The Hani raise livestock, mainly cattle for ploughing the terraces, and pigs. Cattle are left to graze in the forests, except during the ploughing season and in winter, when they are stall-fed. Apart from corn and rice bran, the fodder for pigs is mainly from the forest—leaves from trees and plants like taro and wild buckwheat, and many other kinds of plants that have only Hani names.

The Hani use quite a lot of firewood in their daily lives. Every house has a fire pit, and will often consume over 20 kilograms of firewood a day. A lot of this is collected from the forests. Earlier they used to cut branches, besides collecting fallen tree branches, but all in a manner that did not lead to deforestation. But with the forest being declared a 'Nature Reserve' there are further restrictions on what they can collect from the forests. This has forced them to turn to other sources of fuel supply—agricultural residues and wood from trees grown on private land.

These private lands are actually poor quality terraces that were cut in the 'Learn from Dazhai' movement in the early 1970s, which saw a massive conversion of hills into terraces, even where terraced cultivation was not viable because of the soil being too sandy, etc. With the distribution of these terraces as private land in the 'Household Responsibility System' after 1978, multi-purpose trees were planted on these lands. These trees are now a source of firewood.

But the overall supply of firewood is a problem. As pointed out above, agricultural residues are also being used as fuel. This means that a portion of the organic material is not being recycled into the ecosystem, either as animal feed or as stubble in the fields. Over time, the withdrawal of these nutrients from the ecosystem will affect soil fertility and have to be compensated by the use of purchased fertilizers.

GENDER DISTRIBUTION OF KNOWLEDGE AND RESPONSIBILITY

Local or indigenous knowledge is not an indivisible whole. It is acquired through labour, the interaction with natural processes to produce the means of subsistence, etc. In line with the division of labour between the genders there is also a corresponding distribution of local knowledge.

The Hani say, 'Women do not plough, and men do not carry firewood'. The prohibition against women ploughing is, of course, part of the culture of plough agriculture. But the injunction against men carrying firewood is carried over from the swidden system of earlier times. In areas where the Hani still carry on swidden agriculture (e.g., in Xishuangbanna Yunnan, China) women normally return from the swidden fields laden with firewood, and vegetables (besides spinning thread as they walk back), while men usually come back emptyhanded. They carry largely symbolic hunting rifles. The Hani of the Ailao Mountains, who have changed to terraced agriculture, continue with the same prohibition against men collecting firewood.

As one would expect, it is the Hani women who are the main collectors of wild plants and have a correspondingly good understanding of the usage, taste, properties and functions of each kind of edible plant. Similarly, given their almost sole responsibility for looking after the animals, it is the women who are knowledgeable about the wild plants used as fodder.

Despite being the repositories of important parts of local knowledge regarding the use of forest resources, women are not involved in community-level management of these forests. For example, women are not involved in the traditional selection of a 'dragon head' (leading family) to be responsible for the care of the sacred grove or 'dragon tree forest'. Such exclusion from traditional, community management roles carries over into contemporary village councils. The effects of such exclusion of women from community councils on the efficiency of forest management or on production remains to be investigated.

FOREST MANAGEMENT

It can be said that everything concerning the survival of the Hani rests with the natural ecological functions and services of the forest of the Ailao Mountains. Every Hani knows that without the forest, there would be no water, and without water, there would be no terraced fields; without the terraced fields, there would be no survival for the Hani; without the forest, there would be no plants and animals, and no vegetables or meat. The forest is thus, the lifeblood of the Hani People. From time immemorial, no matter what dynasties, governments or forest policies took shape, the Hani's worship of the forests, and their perception of the necessity of protecting it, could not be shaken.

Prior to the 1950s, the Ailao Mountains on the southern bank of the Yuan River were under the feudal system. The forestland belonged to the *tutsi* (chief), who also held the rights to divide, use, buy and sell and control the forestland, which had never been allocated to the villagers. However, to meet the needs of the terraced fields and livelihood, the 'dragon tree forest' (sacred grove of trees) near the villages, scenic forests and the water-source forests at the top of the mountains were owned and managed communally by the local communities.

To preserve the forest, a kind of spontaneous mode of management of the forest developed, which encompassed: (*a*) village regulations for the management of the forest; (*b*) education on forest preservation; and (*c*) designating the forests as sacred.

Traditionally, there have been special watchmen in every Hani village, and every headsman was responsible for the preservation of the forest. No cutting of the 'dragon tree forest' community forest, scenic forest or water-resource forest was allowed. Very severe punishments were imposed for breaking these restrictions—the offenders usually had to plant trees, sweep the village, construct roads, etc. While men could enter the 'dragon tree forests' for ritual purposes, women were not allowed to enter them.

Every village made its own regulations to supervize the management of forests. These regulations continue even today. The following rules are taken from the village of Dayutang:

1. No one is allowed to cut trees, collect firewood, reclaim land, graze animals or light fires in the 'dragon tree forest' or the forest near the village. If any cutting occurs or if a fire is started, the offender must sacrifice cattle and pigs to the gods, and hold a one-day feast for all the villagers as a punishment.
2. For other forests under the administration of the village, if the villagers need timber for house construction they can cut down a certain number of trees, on the approval of the village committee. A fine is imposed if they cut more trees than allowed.
3. No village family can 'exceed its boundary' to reclaim land, cut timber, collect firewood, cut weeds or engage in any other activities as a sideline. Those who break these rules are heavily fined and all the forest products collected are confiscated.
4. Every household takes turns to act as the 'dragon head' or guard responsible for the preservation of the water-source forests, which no one is allowed to cut. The guards are empowered to punish those who break the rules by asking them to 'sacrifice pigs and chickens to the dragon'. As mentioned earlier, women cannot be chosen as guards.
5. Specially valued plants like the Chinese catalpa, nanmu (*Phoebe nanmu*), etc., cannot be felled. Earlier the chief or *tutsi* had sole rights over these precious plants.

The special watchmen and village regulations have played an effective role in the preservation of forests over a long period of time.

SOCIALIZATION OF THE UNDERSTANDING OF FORESTS AND EDUCATION ON THE PRESERVATION OF THE FORESTS

For the Hani the forest has always been an important cultural theme. In their ancient traditions and history, the forest has always been the refuge and shelter of the Hani, and has been a provider of food and other necessities. After terraced agriculture was developed among the Hani, the forest was closely associated with the mountains and rivers, farming seasons, climatic changes and the terraced fields, and this close association was incorporated into legends, stories, poems, ballads, proverbs, children's songs, etc., which served to educate the local people, particularly those of the younger generation. This cultural inheritance and education, passed down from one generation to the next, has developed a species of 'forest complex' in the hearts of the Hani, to the extent that all of them have a very deep reverence for, and feelings towards, the forests.

Many local activities of the Hani have enhanced the processes by which they have socialized an understanding of the forests. For instance, as soon as a Hani baby is born, the parents will usually plant three young trees near the forest at the foot of the village, the placenta is buried beneath the trees and they are watered with the water used to wash the baby. The trees grow as the baby grows, and when there are more children, more trees are planted, making a forest. Such activities strongly emphasize the relationship between forest and people.

SACRALIZATION OF THE FOREST

The worship of plants has long been a part of the Hani system of beliefs. There is a patch of dense oak forest (called *la-bai-la-ba* in the Hani language) near every Hani village in the Ailao Mountains. Palm trees, bamboo and firs can be found close to Hani villages, which are all symbols of life and are regarded as the guardians of the village. They believe that without such trees near the villages, the dead can never be transformed into spirits, and those who are still alive might immediately die. When they offer sacrifices to the gods, they often collect perfectly shaped leaves, which are then placed in ceramic jars and decoct into thick juice which is then offered to the gods and ancestors. This worship of the trees has played a role in the preservation of the forest in an imperceptible manner. With a deepening of the understanding of the natural ecological system of the Ailao Mountains and the construction of the ecological system of the terraced farms which fits rather well into the natural ecological system, the relationship between the Hani and the forest and the water use of the terraced fields is more clearly exhibited. The grand scale and the solemn atmosphere of the annual occasion of the 'sacrifice to the divine tree' calls forth in the people a feeling of veneration.

The Hani wish that the sacred trees will live forever with them. 'Tree worship songs', often contain lines such as the following: 'Ever since our mothers gave birth to us, the sacred trees have been protecting us. The sacred trees at the boundary of the Hani villages can never be separated from us for even a single day.' They also list the names of various kinds of plants, especially trees, to form a 'family tree', and the idea that 'the gods plant the trees by themselves' is reinforced in order to designate the trees sacred.

These religious ideas strengthen the people's veneration of the forest, and this has played a significant role in the preservation of the forest. No Hani will touch a single branch of the trees in the 'dragon tree forest'.

EVOLUTION OF FOREST TENURE AND MANAGEMENT

Since the 1950s, the Hani in Dayutang and the entire area of the Ailao Mountains have been ushered into a socialistic society through peaceful negotiation and land reform. The forested land is thus controlled by the state, but community forests and private forests were also established. The community forests are the original 'dragon tree forests', village forests and water-source forests, while the private forests are the small patches of forest near, or at the back, or in the front of Hani houses.

After the People's Commune movement in 1958, all forestland was brought under the administration of the communes. Individual households in each village took turns in looking after the forest. Those who cut down the trees were severely punished according to village regulations. These rules continued more or less as before. In the next readjustment of the rural system, the forests were divided into state-owned forests, community forests and private forests. However, soon after in 1966, the private forests were again brought under the control of the agricultural production cooperatives. A forest station at the commune level was set up and special persons were assigned to take care of the forests. This system lasted until 1982.

From 1958 to 1982, although there were many changes in the organization of the forests, the management methods were still primarily traditional ones, which had been passed down for hundreds of years. However, two political movements during this period caused great damage to the forests in this area.

The first was the Great Leap Forward in 1958, when people all over the country, including those in the Ailao Mountains, were encouraged to cut down trees to make iron and steel. Many forests were clear-cut, and were terribly degraded. The second was the Learn From Dazhai movement in 1972, when trees were cut down to make fields, and forests were once again greatly damaged.

During these two political movements, the traditional practices of the Hani for managing the forests were regarded as superstitious and were thus eliminated. Sacred trees and sacred groves were also cut. As a result of these two movements, according to the statistics of Yuanyang County, forest cover declined from 56 per cent in 1957 to 20.8 per cent in 1982. The destruction to the forest led to great disorder in the ecological functions and service networks, which eventually led to frequent flooding. For instance, in May 1974, there were flash floods in Dayutang that damaged six water channels and 695 mu of fields. In August 1976, flash floods once again damaged 65 big and small water channels, 486 mu of terraced fields, four sheds, one classroom in the school, and one house. Further damage included, six wells, thirteen high-tension poles, 30 mu of bamboo forest, four small bridges and 3 kilometres of paved road, in addition two people were killed.

The destruction of the forest also made it difficult to secure drinking water for both human beings and livestock, and caused a shortage of water in the terraced fields. Landslides and mudslides also occurred in some places. For example, in July 1989, mudslides occurred on the western side of the Guanyin Mountains, destroying or damaging 171 houses, 36 sheds, seven bridges and tunnels, one 75 kilowatt power plant, over 2000 mu of forests and 2686.5 mu of terraced fields. Further, nine persons were killed, seven were seriously injured, and a number of animals perished. In September 1989, there was a landslide at the headquarters of Yuanyang county, and more than Yuan 100 million was spent on relocating the people living there.

CONTEMPORARY FOREST POLICIES AND REFORESTATION

By the end of 1982, the new forest policies of stabilizing the rights to the forests, and fixing the division of household forest, had been implemented all over Yunnan Province, including Dayutang village. The original 'dragon tree', scenic and water-source forests are more or less the present community forests. The household forests are again more or less those that were part of the homestead and areas nearby, where fruit trees are grown.

The land turned into terraces during the Learn from Dazhai movement is not suitable for cultivation, since it is too dry. These plots have been either allocated to individual households or contracted on lease. On many of these terraces families have planted shueidenghua, which is useful in that it retains water. In this manner, much of the land cut into terraces has been returned to forest.

Some of this barren or waste land has been leased to individuals or groups of individuals. On this land, from which income is needed to pay the lease, families and other groups have planted Chinese fir. One group of nine families has leased about 75 hectares of land and planted 200,000 Chinese fir trees. Families have also begun to plant Chinese fir on land near their homesteads, where they can keep watch over them.

CRITICAL NATURAL CAPITAL

The important forests on the hilltops, that comprise the sacred 'dragon tree forests', and water-source forests have changed in status over time. Before 1950 these community forests were managed by the village. After that they became state forests. More recently they have been classified as 'Nature Reserves'. In one way or the other, since 1950 they have been state forests. During two periods of strong central policy direction, the Great Leap Forward and the Learn from Dazhai Movement, these forests were damaged with negative effects on the ecological services that they provided. Since then, however, even though they remain as some sort of state forest, there is no clear tendency to use them for private gain.

This is in contrast which what one finds in many other parts of China, where there has been a tendency to 'eat the state forest' and preserve that which belongs to the household or the community. The Hani village of Manmo (which does not have an irrigated terraced agricultural system) in Xishuangbanna, Yunnan has done just that. It has preserved one side of the hill which belongs to the village and from which it gains income as a tourist attraction. At the same time, its swidden and wood fuel needs have been transferred to the other side of the hill, which is part of the state reserve forest (see Pierre Walter's essay in this volume). In fact, in the case of Manmo it is the front of the hill that functions as critical natural capital, since their booming tourist business depends on it.

As mentioned earlier, the declaration of Dayutang's forest as part of the 'Nature Reserve' has affected the villagers' ability to use this forest for even low impact wood-fuel collection. The burden of supplying fuel has been shifted to private trees and agricultural residues. The villagers state that this creates many problems for them. In spite of this, they have not changed their attitude towards protecting the 'Nature Reserve' forest.

The reason for this non-invasive relationship of the village with the state forest may be found in its essential role in sustaining the terraced agriculture, which is the basis of the village economy. In more formal terms, one may state that for Hani terraced agriculture, the mountain-top forests constitute the 'critical natural capital' on which their existence depends. This is reflected both in their old sayings and in their current practice. Irrespective of the tenurial status of this critical forest, the Hani of Dayutang do not degrade it for immediate livelihood purposes. The criticality of this component of natural capital overrides any issues of tenurial status. Whether as traditional sacred forest, village-owned community forest or state-owned 'Nature Reserve', the role of this forest as critical natural capital has dictated the way in which the village has related to it. This changed only when strong central policy dictated the transformation of the forests to other purposes (iron and steel manufacture or terraces). But after each such disaster, when the village was allowed to revert back to low impact uses of the forest, its role as critical natural capital was reasserted.

REFERENCES

Bruijnzeel, L. A. *Hydrology of Moist Tropical Forests and Effects of Conversion: A State of Knowledge Review*. Humid Tropics Programme of the International Hydrological Programme of UNESCO, Paris and Vrije Universiteit Amsterdam (Free University Amsterdam), 1990.

Croll, Elizabeth and David Parkin, eds. *Bush Base: Forest Farm*. London: Routledge, 1992.

4

Conflict in Resource Management of Ecosystem Services

Water in the Lashi Watershed, Lijiang, Yunnan, China

Yu Xiaogang

Introduction

Lashi watershed is 8 kilometres away from Lijiang town, famous as a World Cultural Heritage site and now the most popular tourist destination in southwest China. The basin-shaped valley is surrounded by mountains with an elevation ranging from 2500 to 3840 metres. Lashi is an integrated watershed, clearly marked out by a basin, which drains water from the hill-forests into Lashi lake, which is also home to a large number of rare migratory birds in winter.

The watershed has a population of just over 18,000 people in about 3250 households. The economy is a combination of agriculture (wet rice and dry crops, like wheat and maize in the valley and potatoes and buckwheat in the uplands), a growing horticulture in former dry land croplands, along with lake fishing and animal husbandry. Until the 1998 logging ban, timber provided a substantial part of cash incomes, particularly for those in the uplands. The main Non-Timber Forest Products (NTFPs) are many varieties of mushrooms, including the high-priced *songrong* (*mashtake* in Japanese). Overall per capita income (1998) is just above the poverty line, but 10 per cent of the valley and 90 per cent of the hill-dwellers are below the poverty line. The

Naxi, who live in the valley, account for 94 per cent of the population, while the Yi in the hills are just 6 per cent.

In the period of socialist construction, since Lashi was close to Lijiang, it was logged quite extensively. Over the 1980s and 1990s, with forestry devolution, there was household logging and conversion of forest into agricultural lands. The growth in the demand for timber in the 1980s and 1990s spurred the growth of logging. The Naxi, better placed in the lowlands, with access to more resources (labour and animals), carried out logging that may be termed 'medium scale' (non-mechanized). The Yi, on the other hand, were restricted to artisanal logging. While the former therefore benefitted more from logging, they also benefitted from the use of water in their paddy fields and fruit orchards, and even from taking so-called degraded lands on lease for fruit tree cultivation.

Some of the income from logging was used by the better-off Naxi to change their livelihood system, with more income now derived from fruits and cash crops. The effect, however, has been to turn the formerly slack winter season into another busy season for the women, who use this non-agricultural season to collect firewood and pine needles from the forest. Men, on the other hand, still relax and visit each other in the winter.

The forests, however, are important not only for their timber, but even more so for their water supply and flood-control functions. The forests trap and release water over time into the lake in the valley. Besides supplying water that is used to irrigate the paddy fields in the valley, the lake also supplies water to Lijiang town. Concentrated logging in some areas, led to a marked deterioration in the water supply and regulation function of the forests. There was accelerated silting of the lake bottom. Runoff during the rainy season increased, leading to the flooding of fields. Additionally, there was a shortage of water in the dry season. This along with a deterioration in the quality of water in the lake led to a fall in bird populations wintering on the lake.

In order to deal with the problems faced in the provision of external ecosystem services (i.e., those ecosystem services supplied to the external world, outside the Lashi watershed), the provincial government initiated three resource management programmes: the Wetland Nature Reserve (1998), the Water Transfer Project (1994) and the Ban on Logging (1998). All these resource management projects have had serious repercussions on the local population. There has been a loss of income from logging; water supply requirements keep the water levels of the lake such that flooding occurs in an area of cropland;

and fishing has been affected by the Wetland Nature Reserve policies. While the very success in improving the quality of water supply has increased the lake's attraction to migratory birds, this has had a negative local effect in that there are more crop losses to these birds.

The benefits, from these resource management projects, on the other hand, flow more to the external world. The biodiversity benefit of an improved habitat for migratory birds is global; and increased water is supplied to Lijiang town free of charge. The likely future flood-control benefits of the logging ban will be to an extent local, but also more for the plains of China.

With the area's per capita income just above the poverty level, and with most of the upland Yi well below the poverty line, it is necessary to question whether the commoditization of forest-based, ecosystem services (rather, goods, chiefly water) supplied to the external world will not better meet the twin objectives of: (a) securing the desired supply of goods like water that can be privatized, and of increasing the supply of goods like 'Wetland Nature Reserve' that are essentially public goods; and (b) improving the livelihoods of the local people. It is also necessary to ask whether it is possible to combine the marketing of services (goods) that forests provide, with 'low impact' extractive activities, rather than the current ban on logging? All of this has implications for whether the interests of external stakeholders (regional, national or global) are better met through prescriptions that violate local forest management and take these services free of charge, or through more sustainable ways of local forest management in combination with the commoditization of services provided to external users.

Forests, Local Ecosystem Services and Livelihoods

Over time the Naxi and Yi have developed a system of land-use based on five different elevation zones, from the mountain-tops down to the valley and lake. While the Yi use the top three zones, the Naxi rely on the bottom two zones. This brief description of the different zones and their functions is based on discussions with the local residents. The relationships between the forests and ecosystem services mentioned in what follows is largely based on these local discussions, i.e., they form part of the indigenous knowledge of the forests and ecosystem services, and the effect of human intervention, viz., labour, in transforming the extent and nature of these ecosystem services.

Following C. F. Jordan (1985, in L. A. Bruijnzeel 1990: 3) we identify three levels of human intervention, viz., low, intermediate and high. The first category includes small-scale and short-lived events such as natural tree falls and small clearings. The second includes selective logging, forest fires and shifting cultivation. High intensity interventions are those like forest clearing and conversion to pasture, extractive tree crops, forest plantations or permanent annual crop cultivation.

The top 200 (or so) metres of the local ecosystem is covered with thick, dark coniferous forest, of *Abies forrestii* and *Picca likianggensias.* The trees are old and very valuable as timber. The soil has a thick layer of leaf cover, other organic matter and humus. The thick forest on top of the mountains has two functions. First, it helps trap some of the moisture released into the atmosphere by evapotranspiration, and through mist and dew returns this moisture to the area. Second, the thick cover of leaves and other organic matter prevents rainwater from flowing downwards. This increases both infiltration of rainwater into the ground, to be later released down in the streams and into the lake; and reduces the surface runoff, restricting both soil erosion on the mountain-tops and flooding in the valley down below.

In this mountain-top zone there are some grassy patches or pastures. These, however, do not seem to have been created by human clearing and burning of trees. Local people say that these grass patches have always existed. They know that trees cannot grow on these patches because there is only a thin soil layer with a deposit of limestone rock below.

The Yi men herd their livestock (horses, cattle, goats and sheep) in these pastures in the summer, camping for weeks together on the heights. Along with the hunting and medicinal herb gathering they carry out while camping, this is low intensity intervention in the forest system. There was some logging in this zone in the 1980s and 1990s, but it was not very substantial and was restricted to old, high quality trees. Access continues to be a problem. Being some distance from the villages, there is no removal of branches and leaves for use lower down.

The next 400 metres has a mixed mossy forest with coniferous and broadleaf trees and bush of arrow bamboo (*Sinarumdinaria nitida*) and rhododendrons. The dominant tree species include oak (*Quercus pannosa, Quercus longispica*), Huanshan pine (*Pinus armandi*), and highland willow (*Salix sp.*). The forest soil is classified as dark brown forest soil, rich in humus and organic matter, with a deep soil layer and high fertility. From this zone, the Yi collect firewood, fodder and herbal medicines. In the past, this zone was the principal hunting venue. There are many sloping grasslands scattered in the forest, serving as ideal grazing land for herding in spring and autumn.

The forest in this zone performs an important function in conserving water-sources, and most Yi water-source forests are in fact distributed in this zone. These are called 'village spirit forests'. Once a year, men conduct rituals and sacrifice some animals in these 'village spirit forests'. Women are not allowed to participate in these rituals. The 'village spirit forests' are quite far from the settlements, and there is no extraction of any kind from these forests.

The next zone of 400 metres is a highly biodiversified zone, covered with a mixed forest of coniferous and broadleaf trees. Dominant species are Yunnan pine (*Pinus yunnanensis*), Huanshan pine (*Pinus armandi*), highland pine (*P. densata*), hemlock (*Tsuga dumosa, T. forrestii*), Lijiang fir (*Picea Likiangensis*), highland oak (*Q. longispica*), yellow leaf black oak (*Q. pannosa*), etc. The bushwood species are arrow bamboo, Yunnan azalea, low oak (*Q. monimotricha*), etc. The soil is brown forest soil. The topsoil is highly fertile and covered with thick leaves and semi-decomposed organic matter. The forest land is also an important water reservoir for the lowlands. The pastureland in this zone is used by the Yi for herding in winter and spring. This zone is ecologically suitable to cold-resistant crops. The Yi have reclaimed about 200 hectares of sloping land to grow potatoes, buckwheat, oats and kidney beans. This zone suffers from soil erosion.

The Yi have mostly made their settlements in this zone, and this is associated with the various uses of the forest that are possible in this zone. First, it provides fertile brown forest soil; second, the cool climate is suitable for the growth of cold-resistant and cash crops; third, the high biodiversity in this zone can provide the Yi with multiple natural products and ecological services, which include firewood, fodder, herbal medicines and wild animals. They can also cultivate plants at this altitude, although the yield is less than in lower elevations. Fourth, drinking water for people and animals is assured at some points thanks to the protection of the water-source forest at higher elevations. Fifth, the numerous grasslands, bushes, open forest and shifting cultivation lands are favourable places for herding animals in winter and spring.

The Yi have traditionally maintained various patches of forest— village-protection forest, soil-conservation forest, scenic forest, water-source forest and 'village spirit forest'—and the like around their villages. These culturally significant conservation zones are even now strictly protected. Within a patch of forest near the village, every family has its own 'ancestor spirit forest'. Here too, men conduct the ritual ceremonies, but women also take part in them. This forest is also very thick, like the 'village spirit forest'. But from the 'ancestor spirit forest', dead and fallen branches are collected, unlike in the case of the 'village spirit forest', from which, nothing is extracted. The 'ancestor spirit forest' is protected from domestic animals, and some households plant bushes of Chinese pepper and green prickly shrub (for oil and as medicine) around the home garden or cultivated land to prevent soil erosion and the entry of animals.

The Yi also understand that a higher tree cover increases moisture in the soil. Tree cover helps keep the temperatures lower at night. This in turn means that more of the moisture in the atmosphere condenses as dew and frost.

The Yi have large home gardens, fenced to keep animals out, as has been mentioned previously. Potatoes, vegetables and fruit trees are planted in the home gardens. As is to be expected, Yi women perform virtually all of the labour in the home gardens. Yi women also perform 70–80 per cent of crop labour and 90 per cent of woodfuel gathering. Besides the occasional hunting, men are responsible for logging and grazing livestock, which often requires them to be away in the forests for weeks on end.

The main NTFP collected is mushrooms. The mushrooms that grow on the upper slopes are not of very good quality. The high-priced *songrong* (or *mashtake*) mushroom grows only in the foothills, in the Naxi area. The Yi have taken to extracting mushrooms for sale in this middle zone only in the 1990s.

The government has long been trying to get the Yi to give up sloping land cultivation and take to terracing, which is expected to prevent soil erosion and conserve water, soil and fertility. However, the Yi have not done so. They argue that the heavy local rainfall in summer, would cause the artificially-built terraced fields to be destroyed by floods. Further, waterlogging could destroy the potato crop, which is their staple food. From the perspective of soil formation, the matrix of soil formation is from the aggregation of the scrap and residue of various rocks from the mountain-tops. They also understand that the massive surgical movements of soil involved in the cutting of terraces will cause large-scale landslides.

The Yi normally use a shallow ploughing method on sloping land in order to minimize soil erosion. Though this sloping land cultivation is more suitable than artificial terraces for these lands, the Yi have also been learning improved cultivation techniques from other highlanders. Agro-forestry and the planting of cash trees and bushes along contour lines have now become common practices.

In the top three elevation zones, the Yi interventions in the forest range from the very minimal (right at the top) to low intensity at the third level of their settlements.

The zone from 2500 to 2800 metres above sea level is covered primarily with Yunnan pine forest (*P. yunnanensis*), highland pine forest (*P. densata*), a mixed forest of pine and oak, and small patches of semi-moist evergreen broadleaf forest and highland katus forest. Beneath the vegetation of dominant pine trees there is a red soil which varies from neutral to slightly alkaline. The soil contains less organic matter, due to the lowland Naxi practice of gathering pine needles for manure from this zone. The forest here provides firewood, timber, fodder, organic manure and small forest products for the Naxi people. The *songrong* mushroom (*mashtake*) is from the mixed forest of pine and oak.

The heavy extraction of various kinds of organic matter (pine needles, branches, mushrooms and other NTFPs) means that the leaf cover is low in the forested areas. As a result, surface runoff is very high, since the infiltration capacity of the forest floor is low. With heavy rains there are often flash floods. The soil also has a low organic content, and fertilization is needed. Soil erosion too is a serious concern.

The last zone is the valley area which amounts to 50 square kilometres apart from the wetland area. The soil is primarily alluvial and paddy soil. The alluvial soil is mainly distributed around Nanyao Natural village and Jiyu Administration village at the lower reaches of mountain streams. The matrix of soil formation for the alluvial soil is sediments of river, fluvial and glacial residues, and it is of quite high fertility. Because of long-term cultivation, it is very adaptable to agriculture, which can secure high and stable yields. To sustain land resources and increase income from the land, the Naxi have developed agro-forestry and inter-cropping patterns. The paddy soil is distributed in farmland around the Lashi Wetland Protection Zone.

The two zones inhabited by the Naxi are the sites of high intensity interventions—forest clearing and conversion to annual cropping, and more recently fruit tree plantations. They have also been the sites of intensive logging. In the 1950s and 1960s, the area of the foothills on one side of the lake was clear-cut for timber, appropriated by the state. This clear-cutting has had a continuing impact on the lake, with soil erosion in the foothills and sedimentation of the lake bottom being the result.

The Lashi valley area has favourable agricultural conditions and land resources, yet floods and droughts have become rampant due to changes in forest-use and soil erosion. In Nanyao and Jiyu villages the farmers frequently suffer from floods and droughts. At the same time sedimentation in the Lashi lake is increasing. Because of the reduced depth of the lake, the surface area of water in the rainy season has been increasing, causing regular flooding.

WATER AS A FOREST ECOSYSTEM PRODUCT

In the discussion that follows we focus on water, and ignore other ecosystem services. The formation of soil and the control of soil erosion, both of which were mentioned in the earlier description of forest-provided ecosystem services, are not discussed further. The reason being that though these are important ecosystem services, they are largely local in nature. Their benefits are confined to the watershed community, or more correctly, communities. Water, on the other hand, besides having important local uses, is also exported by the watershed system to the neighbouring town of Lijiang. It is this export of water, and the implications of various forest management systems in its export, upon which we wish to concentrate our analysis.

Forests, as discussed above, play two main roles in the provision of water as an ecosystem service. Though water is more correctly described as a good, being a physical product, we follow the convention of Costanza et al. (1998), in using the term 'ecosystem services' to include 'goods' like water. The water related function can be split into three functions: water regulation; water supply; and disturbance regulation (*Ibid.*: 5). The first relates to the regulation of hydrological flows, as in the provision of water for irrigation or to towns. The second is that of water supply, meaning the storage and retention of water and its subsequent provisioning by watersheds. The third is the function of flood control.

In the case of the Lashi forest-based ecosystem (or watershed) all three water related functions are of relevance. The forests play an important role in the retention of water. On the mountain-tops dense forests increase the local retention of water that would otherwise be lost through evapotranspiration. The water is supplied both to local irrigated cultivation, of rice and fruits, and to the nearby town of Lijiang. The thickness of the leaf cover on the forest floor increases the infiltration of water into the soil and groundwater areas, to be subsequently released through springs and other channels into the lake. The same infiltration reduces surface runoff, thus controlling floods in the locality.

Besides the above, the forests also seem to play a role in waste treatment, as the quality of water in the lake is reported to have deteriorated with the loss of forest cover in the 1980s and 1990s. Both the surface area of water in the dry winter season and the quality of water affect the ability of the lake to attract migratory birds in winter. Thus, the state of the forests affects biodiversity in the lake, as well as its recreational and tourist potential. After 1994, the surface area of the lake has increased, along with its biodiversity potential.

The above are some of the water-related ecosystem services produced in the Lashi watershed area. They can be divided into two types of services. The first are local ecosystem services, like the provision of water for irrigation, moisture retention in the soil and control of floods. The second are of a regional nature, involving the watershed in an export relation with the outside world. Of course, there is also a third kind of ecosystem service, the conservation of biodiversity, that is global in nature.

Water from the Lashi lake is supplied outside for irrigation of about 4,000 hectares of paddy land in the Lijiang valley. This supply has been going on since 1994. Water supply to Lijiang town is more recent, having begun only in the spring of 1999. The water supplied to Lijiang town, via underground and overhead channels, is altogether 10.78 million cubic metres of water during the dry season. This means an uninterrupted flow of water at the rate of 1 cubic metre per second for four months.

Lijiang old town has a unique system of canals running parallel to the streets. These canals supply water for household needs and also help keep the town fresh and clean. Water is acclaimed as the soul of the town. It is a major part of the town's attraction (the other being its old, wooden architecture) as a tourist site. The canal system and architecture together are what qualifies the town as a UNESCO World Cultural Heritage site.

During the last decade there has been a shortage of water every alternate year in Lijiang. The water shortage usually lasted for a month in February—March, which is also one of the peak tourist seasons, coinciding with the Chinese New Year. In this period of water shortage the old town used to become quite smelly, as the old drainage system depended on water flow. In 1983–84 there was a prolonged period of water shortage, extending to some 17 months.

Talking to various persons in the tourist business and to officials in the town, it is estimated that a shortage of water would cause a fall of about 20 per cent in the 2 million tourists it attracts each year. Tourism brings in an annual income of Yuan 1 billion (or about

USD 125 million at the current rate of Yuan 8 to USD 1). A fall of 20 per cent, i.e., USD 30 million, in income from tourism would be an economic disaster for the county, which has already been badly hit by the Chinese government's ban on logging.

We will now look at changes in forest tenure and their effect on the provision of these local and regional ecosystem services.

CHANGES IN FOREST TENURE, FOREST USE AND EFFECTS

Before Liberation in 1949, the forests were under the control of the He, a clan of Naxi that first settled the area. Those who came in subsequently were given or had to buy agricultural land and even plots for graves, but the forest as such remained under the He. When the Yi migrated into the area in the 1920s and 1930s they were given lands in distant forests in the uplands, in order that they might look after the extensive forests.

After Liberation, the state took over most of forests in Lijiang—state forest accounted for 82 per cent of total forest area in the county. But the Lashi lake forests continued as village collective forests. However, this does not seem to have made much difference to the state's use of the Lashi forest for its timber requirements. Since Lashi lake is very close to Lijiang town it was one of the areas to attract early attention for logging.

The logging in the 1950s and 1960s involved clear-cutting in the Naxi village of Runanhua, the village most easily accessible by road. This clear-cutting in a large area of about 1,000 hectares was to have serious repercussions on the condition of the lake. The Naxi village of Nanyao, on the side of the lake farther away from Lijiang, was not connected by a good road to Lijiang. Thus, it did not attract the same attention for logging.

There was no logging for external supply in the uplands during this period. The difficulty of access inhibited any logging, other than for local house construction. But in the 1970s, before the initiation of devolution policies, the administrative district ordered the Yi Western village to fell a certain quantity of trees. The village committee had to comply with the order and organized young and strong men to go up the mountains and work for about 6 months cutting trees. But when the time came to transport them, it became apparent that there was no way these logs could be transported down the mountains. As a result, about 80 per cent of the logs were simply left to rot on the mountain slopes.

In the 1960s and 1970s the state took timber for government construction projects by simple order. The villagers were paid some logging and transportation costs (at very low rates); no payment was made for the timber, although these were supposed to be village collective forests. As a consequence of the state officials' requisitioning of timber, with hardly any payment, it was not clear who was to look after the management of the forests. At the same time, local demand for timber was limited to house building, of which there was not a great need.

There were two aspects to the devolution of the 1980s. The first was the return of or reaffirmation of village collective forests, and the second was the allocation of forests to individual households. In the Lashi lake area there were no state-owned forests, so it was only a reaffirmation of collective village rights over forests. Some village forests, for instance, the forest of Nanyao village, where the Naxi, He clan retained importance, did not distribute any forests to households. But other villages, for instance, the Yi Western village, did allocate some part of their forest as household forest.

Within the category of household forest there were two types. One was the household holding, on which the household had the right to change the land-use system. Household holding forest land could be converted into agricultural land. On the second type of household contract holding, there was no right to change the land-use. Trees could be cut, but the land could not be converted to agricultural use.

But in all categories of devolved forest, whether of the village collective or households, trade in timber remained tightly controlled. Logging required permits from the Forest Bureau. For a long time, timber, whether from collective or household forests, could only be sold to the forest companies owned by the Forest Bureau. In principle these regulations restricted the lower levels' management rights over the forest. But in practice what it meant was that individuals had to pay officials down the line in order to carry on logging and trade in timber, thereby increasing the transactions cost of timber and effectively reducing the income from timber below its existing market price.

The Lashi lake area never had a logging quota from the Forest Bureau. As a result, all logging in this area was strictly illegal. Given the close proximity to Lijiang and the increase in timber prices over the 1980s and 1990s, there was, however, a fair amount of logging. This was particularly true when timber was in high demand following the earthquake which destroyed a good part of the old town of Lijiang in 1996.

In terms of the effects of devolution on forest-use there were four major events. First, the household holdings of the Yi were rapidly clear-cut and converted into agricultural land. The desire to increase the holdings of agricultural land was the main factor in this clear-cutting on household holdings. In other types of contract holding forest land where land-use conversion was not permitted, the Yi did fell trees, but it was not clear-cutting, as it would have been had timber income been the main motivation. Nowadays these clear-cut plots have been converted to agro-forestry or fruit orchards with vegetable inter-crops.

The second event was the continuation of the Nanyao forests as village collective forests. As mentioned earlier, the He clan continued to be important in this village. The persons leading the village had changed from the landlords to the former poor peasants of the clan. But the clan as a whole retained its importance in the local political and administrative structure and also had an internal solidarity. The clan was thus able to exert its influence in maintaining the Nanyao forests as village collective forests.

The Nanyao forests were important in protecting the water sources and streams for drinking water as well as irrigation. Providing this important public good of river protection, the loss of which would lead to increased sedimentation of the lake, these forests were not suitable for private management. With private management the individual returns of income from timber would be much larger than the private share of the resulting loss of the ecosystem service of controlling erosion and sedimentation.

But with a general atmosphere of private accumulation, and with the growing demand for timber from the town of Lijiang, private logging could not be prevented in the village collective forests. Accepting the inevitability of such logging, the village leadership tried to control it, by specifying that only household labour could be used in cutting and transporting logs. This too was violated by villagers, many of whom brought in relatives from other villages to increase the ranks of 'household labour'. Those who had more money could use the money to bring in more relatives (who had to be housed and fed besides being paid some kind of wage) and organize transport of logs to the market in the town. Some bought seven or eight horses and donkeys to transport logs down from the forests. Those who had more money and labour benefitted more from the breakdown of collective norms.

In 1989 the local government became strict about illegal logging. Timber, not logged under logging permits was seized. Village administrations were asked to employ forest guards and improve protection measures.

The third event was the privatization of the mushroom forests. Songrong (or mashtake) mushroom has very high value because of the demand from Japan. This mushroom grows in mixed forests (pine plus oak) in the foothills. In Nanyao village this area was retained as village collective forests. But as recounted above, the collective norms broke down and there was considerable, unplanned cutting of trees. This affected the growth of songrong mushrooms. In 1997, collection rights of songrong mushroom were leased by auction. After this the user's group improved its management of songrong growing and collection.

Jizi village, on the other end of the valley from Nanyao, however, distributed the forest among individual households. With this there was better care of the forest, timber harvesting was less and people paid attention to increasing the production of the valuable mushrooms.

After the collapse of the Japanese market (since the Japanese switched their import demand to Bhutan, where songrong mushrooms are cheaper) local prices fell. But domestic demand kept up the price of songrong at about Yuan 300 per kilogram, as against the earlier price of Yuan 700 or 800 per kilogram.

What this shows is that if other uses of the forest, e.g., for NTFPs, are more valuable than timber, and depend on the extent of forest cover and the diversity of species (mixed rather than monocrop forests) then under individual management, forests could be managed so as to maintain required forest cover and diversity.

The fourth event was the privatization of so-called wastelands. A forest was common to both the Naxi and the Yi village. This forest at the foot of the hills was in a degraded condition, after having been subjected to uncontrolled household logging, and it remained a degraded grazing area. In 1996 there was a new wave of devolution to lease out degraded land on long-term contract.

Although considered a wasteland, this land did yield some fodder and fuelwood, both of which were mainly collected by the Yi. In order to 'rehabilitate' this degraded land, it was decided to lease it out to the highest bidder for raising fruit trees. Obviously it was only the better off Naxi, with the capacity to mobilize capital for the planting and tending of fruit trees, who could bid for leases. Four families secured leases, and land which formerly yielded products to the poorer Yi could no longer be used by them.

In the uplands some felling of trees by the Yi continued throughout the period. But given the difficulty of access, the felling was not very substantial. As pointed out earlier, all this logging was strictly illegal. But it continued and was even tolerated by village and township authorities, since it was the most important source of cash for the Yi, who were almost all below the poverty line. In the process, some of the Yi, better able to mobilize money and labour, benefitted more than others and did accumulate some wealth, and built elaborate new houses and so on.

The Yi Western village allotted each family timber to construct new houses. The village allowed villagers to cut trees not only from their household and contract holdings, but also from the village forests. Each family was allowed to cut about 10 to 15 trees a year.

In contrast, the Yi Eastern village did not have any such rule or restriction on its village forestland. This forest was shared with a Naxi village. Neither the Yi nor the Naxi village, could, individually or collectively, establish an effective management system over this forest. In effect, it became an open access area in which anybody could fell trees. The stronger, young men could work about 100–50 days per year in logging, getting cash income of about Yuan 3,000 per year. Since the logging was strictly illegal, various amounts had to be paid to officials along the way. Organizing transport to the market was also expensive. Consequently, most Yi men ended up working for wages, employed by a local contractor who had or could acquire the capital to organize the whole process.

Another factor affecting forest cover was the continued use of wood as fuel. In the fishery village of Xinrong on the shores of Lashi lake, there was a project to develop biogas as a woodfuel substitute in some 200 households. But there was no other direct family investment in fuel systems that saved labour. The labour of collecting wood for fuel, as well as pine needles for organic manure, was carried out by women, both among the Naxi and the Yi. With increased agricultural activities in the wet season, this labour was concentrated in the slack season, the winter months, when the usual agricultural labour was not required. As a result, the slack winter season also became a busy season for women. Men, who valued their own leisure more than they did women's leisure, continued to enjoy winter as a slack season, spending most of the time in chatting and visiting friends and relatives. Women, on the other hand, were the household labourers. Although Naxi women have traditionally played the major role in the management of household incomes, there was also an increase in their labour burden.

A change in the provision of woodfuel is noticeable only in those lowland villages and among those Naxi families who have developed dry season cultivation or fruit tree plantations, as in the fishing village. These families have taken to the biogas system, since there is now a year-round need for women's labour in various field and animal care activities.

What were the effects of these changes in forest use on the provision of ecosystem services?

Provision of Ecosystem Services

Clear-cutting by the state for its construction projects, by the Yi to clear land for agriculture, and uncontrolled household felling by the Naxi were all high intensity activities that had a substantial effect on the provision of various ecosystem services. We will concentrate on the situation with regard to the provision of water, both in quantity and quality.

The streams running down from clear-cut areas visibly reduce the area of the lake bottom. Sediment has shrunk the area at points where the two main streams enter the lake. The winter and spring flows in the streams are now much reduced from what they were in the 1950s. As a result, there is less water available for irrigating the winter and spring crops, while, at the same time, the demand for such water has increased. Villagers thus have to carefully watch all through the day and night to make sure that they get their share of water. This takes 40 to 60 days' labour, with both men and women taking part.

Along with the reduced flow of water in winter and spring, there is an increased flow in summer, because of the lowered water infiltration and absorption capacity of the reduced forest cover. This leads to flash floods when there are heavy rains. Every villager is expected to participate in flood protection labour. Every year, however, there is damage to crops, land, houses and bridges. This amounts to at least Yuan 200,000 in Nanyao village, for example. Nowadays, flooding is the most important issue in the village. While the rich of the village benefitted more from the open access logging, it is the poor, who did not benefit as much from the logging, and are not so well equipped to withstand floods, who bear more of the cost of increased flooding.

These local environmental effects were taken into account in local forest management decisions; which is exactly what a disembedded, external agency would not be able to do. In 1999 the money acquired from leasing the rights to collect *songrong* mushroom, totalling about Yuan 12,000, was used to strengthen the river bank, digging the river bed to increase depth, and also used to improve the forest, through the planting of saplings.

The ecological system in Lashi watershed offers a wealth of water to the local people. The government invested in and constructed a trans-watershed water supply project to establish a water supply of 18.28 million cubic metres of water each year to Lijiang valley to irrigate 65,000 mu[1] of land and provide 10.78 million cubic metres of water each year to urban residents of the ancient town, maintaining the image and attraction of the World Cultural Heritage site for tourism development. The project includes blocking the natural drainage routes into the Yangtze river lower down, a 3 kilometre long mountain tunnel, 8 kilometre long elevated water channels and a large dam. The entire project is now complete and the Lashi wetlands have as a consequence been converted into an intensively human-controlled lake, under the administration of the Hydraulic and Electricity Bureau of Lijiang County.

As a result of the project, a large area of land traditionally cultivated in winter now remains submerged. In 1999 there was flooding beyond the designated lake area, which itself submerges some traditional agricultural lands. The direct loss in 1999 was about Yuan 1.16 million (USD 170,000) due to crop losses. The county government attributed this flooding to a natural disaster. But it was actually a result of a management decision by the Hydraulic and Electricity Bureau. Anticipating that there would be low rainfall, the lake area was kept larger than normal. But when there was fairly normal rainfall after all, extensive flooding occurred. It was ironic that the Hydraulic and Electricity Bureau reported in its year-end work summary in the local newspaper that 'because of its successful work, all reservoirs and lakes are at full storage. Therefore irrigation water for agriculture is guaranteed for the year 2000'.

For the wetland's wildlife habitat function, the Provincial Wetland Nature Reserve, protecting 57 species of water birds, was established in 1998. The establishment of the Lashi Wetland Nature Reserve has created some difficulties for the local people. On the one hand, increasing migratory birds destroy local people's agricultural crops, on the other, local people's traditional waterfowl hunting activities are banned. Furthermore, a new management rule has enforced a 3-month fishing ban from April to June when fish spawn.

The trans-watershed water supply project is designed to benefit urban residents who have developed the tourist economy in the last decade, and downstream agricultural areas which have developed vegetable production bases for urban consumption. Downstream

[1] Mu is a Chinese measure of land area—5 mu is roughly equal to 1 hectare.

people enjoy the water free of charge, while the upstream people suffer large losses from flooding. The villagers have lost their traditional farmland, to the tune of, about 3 *mu* per person, as the government took over these lands. The compensation (a one-time amount of Yuan 810 per *mu*, to be given in four installments, not necessarily in cash but through benefits, a subsidy for establishing biogas plants) and the increased lake surface for fishery cannot make up for the losses.

The Nature Reserve was established suddenly without consulting the traditional wetland resource users. Local people are getting marginalized, since every decision that affects them is made by outside centers. Are there more challenges waiting for them? Forests and wetlands have great value for local people. There is both a current labour input and an accumulation of past labour in the stock of these resources and the services and products they provide. What local people need is to be able to sustainably use these valuable resources for their desired development.

CONTESTATION AND NEGOTIATION

How did the local people react to decisions about the unpaid withdrawal of water and the logging ban? The logging ban means that timber trees do not have direct value, while the free extraction of water means that the indirect value of trees is also considerably reduced, being only equal to that of the local ecosystem services.

The objective of the logging ban was to enhance the water regulating capacity of forests. Even earlier when the Lashi lake area did not have any logging quotas, logging took place. The local administration also sympathized with the upland Yi's need to cut trees as that was a major source of cash income for paying school fees, etc. But with the logging ban it became difficult to continue such informal (or illegal) trade. From various parts of China there are reports that forest-dwelling people have switched to selling logs as low-value fuelwood, which is not controlled, rather than high-value timber, which is controlled. More trees will have to be cut to get the same income (say, for paying school fees) than in the case of timber.

There can be yet another tendency for a change in land-use to grazing. Particularly for the upland Yi, livestock has remained the main source of cash incomes. Though the present slump in meat prices has retarded this tendency, Yi farmers expressed an interest in increasing their livestock holdings. Any micro-credit programme is likely to be used for this purpose. The increase in livestock holdings would have a drastic effect on forest condition, as grazing lands would be increased at the cost of tree cover. If the objective of central, provincial and county government policy is to increase the provision of ecosystem services, in the form of water supply and flood protection, the increase of livestock holdings in the hills might have the opposite effect.

There are also examples of overt forms of struggle to change decisions imposed by external centres. External is relative and would change with the context. There are instances of struggle of upland Yi to establish their rights against encroachment by lowland Naxi, and by villages in the watershed against the external centres that withdrew water.

STRUGGLE OF YI AGAINST NAXI ENCROACHMENT

With devolution the Naxi tried to go back to the pre-Liberation situation when they alone had ownership of the forests and the Yi were invited settlers without any ownership rights over the forest. But in the 1983 devolution of forests, some were handed over to Yi villages. Despite this, the stronger Naxi tried to cut trees in Yi forests. Yi villages had to struggle in different ways to secure their claims to forests allotted to them.

In the upper part of No. 2 village, for example, there is a good 20 hectare patch of guardian pine forest. This is the forest that is located above and around the village. It protects the village from the hazards of wind, upland flooding and soil erosion. With devolution, the Yi decided not to divide this amongst households, but to manage it collectively, since it was important for the village.

The pine forest has been very nicely tended and has become quite prominent in the surrounding area. Unfortunately, the good quality of its trees attracted Naxi farmers who cut them down. The Yi had their village guards, but they could not stop the more economically and politically powerful Naxi from carrying out logging. Realizing that they were not strong enough to protect the forests on their own, the Yi mobilized the administrative village office to issue a certificate stating that the forest in question was a protected forest (guardian forest) and that any logging or cutting of trees was forbidden. They then got this document attested by the township government and forestry bureau. With this they were empowered to stop logging by the lowland Naxi.

Another Yi village (No. 5 village) was contracted a large forest of 12,000 *mu* in 1983. This forest faced logging threats from the people of the neighbouring township and also from Naxi within the same administrative village. It was particularly difficult to stop the local Naxi from carrying on their logging activities. They claimed that since this was administrative village forest, and since they belonged to the same administrative village, they too had a right to the forest. They came with numerous horses and mules and carried on logging. This posed a great threat to the Yi village, since it led to soil erosion that had the potential to cause landslides. Unable to stop the more powerful Naxi from logging, the Yi village came up with a stratagem to stop the threat of logging. They let it be known that their village was no longer suitable for habitation and that they would move to another spot. A group of young men cleared over 20 *mu* of sloping land, directly above the Naxi village. In the rainy season, mud poured into the Naxi village. With this counter-threat to their own village, the Naxi soon came to an agreement to respect Yi rights over their forest and stop logging there.

The success of the Yi in No. 2 village in preventing the Naxi from another township from logging in their village forest is attributed to the support they received from the Naxi on their side. However, the Yi in No. 5 village could not stop the Naxi from within their own administrative village from logging because they were not powerful enough. Instead of direct confrontation they cleverly solved the problem by manoeuvers and counter-threats.

Another case in Shuizhakou village (a small Naxi village), shows that even where the power centre involved is external, the township in this case, local villages, could use various methods to change actions that they opposed.

Shuizhakou is located by the side of the Jizi dam. The village contracted forest is the drinking water source for thousands of residents in the downstream Tai'an township, including the township government and several government offices. In 1994, some farmers from Tai'an village went to this forest to cut trees. Shuizhakou village complained to the township and Tai'an village committee, but the logging was not stopped. Shuizhakou village then cut the water supply to the downstream township. This action resulted in a severe water problem for hundreds of households and the township government offices. The township government issued many orders but they were in vain. The cutting off of the water supply lasted for 45 days. Finally, the township government and the heads of several villages had to go Shuizhakou village, beg the forgiveness of the villagers and guarantee that the illegal logging would never be repeated. After that Shuizhakou village resumed the water supply.

This is a successful case of forest protection, more significant since it shows that upland marginal groups do have ways of changing decisions. They can be decision-making centres for allocating ecological services.

EMBEDDING DECISION-MAKING

An important part of decisions, for example, extent of water to be provided to external centres, protection of the bird sanctuaries and bans on logging, that have an impact on forest management are made in external centres (provincial, prefecture and country governments). These decisions are handed down to the township administration and local people, and those staying within the township have to implement them. Thus, they have to take these externally made decisions on their forest resource use as given and then work within the confines set by those decisions.

Of course, as we saw above, local administrations and people are not entirely powerless in their relations with the external world. They are able to contest and negotiate these decisions, and change them to a certain extent. More important, however, is the fact that local people's livelihood systems, responding to the options available to them, may develop in directions that are actually harmful from the point of view of the external stakeholders. In response to a ban on logging, in order to increase the ecosystem services (water) provided free of any charge to the external world, local people may develop and are developing livestock rearing, which may over the medium-term be harmful to forest regeneration.

What these experiences show is that different criteria are adopted in cost-benefit analyses of the economic activities (which cause ecological degradation) by people and organizations with different social status or power. Villages take note of local ecological effects (like soil erosion, water retention, flooding, loss of agricultural land and crops) while external decision makers take account of only their costs (in establishing and running water transport structures). A better system of decision-making would combine both sets of costs.

A system of embedded decision-making, that is, embedded in the local community and local relations (Hansson and Wackernagel 1999), could better combine both sets of costs and benefits. Costs and benefits that are external to the local community would be reflected in prices of commodities bought (water) and sold (water transport system). It would have the advantage of combining these factors with local effects (both positive and negative) which are otherwise neglected in externally located decision-making.

Further, the different decisions, both local and external, have different consequences on different sections of the local community. Lowlanders are affected by the loss of agricultural land and crops. Uplanders are affected by the loss of income from logging. Women are affected by the increase in the labour they have to perform. In this essay we have demonstrated how the strong and powerful within the community of the township (Naxi vs Yi and men vs women) try to use logging or the growth of new economic activities to their advantage. But here too there is clear struggle between those differentially affected.

The current system of management on external order violates two important requirements of democratic economic decision-making. The first violation is of the principle that those who bear the consequences (costs) of resource (forest and lake) management decisions should be the ones to make them. The second is that of local decision-making as a component of economic democracy. China has radically decentralized in the economic sphere. But this radical decentralization stops short of the forest areas. Even before the recent management decisions (water withdrawal, conversion into bird sanctuaries and logging bans) village ownership of the forest was not translated into a right to trade—logging permits were required. Thus, economic decentralization has been more restricted in the forests than in the plains, where there are no similar restrictions on trading agricultural outputs.

A better system than management by external order would be to give the local people a stake in the sustainable use of the forests and the watershed services through the sale of ecosystem services, specifically water. With such rights they could balance the income from the sale of water for irrigation and to the downstream townships, against their direct and indirect costs, and their benefits, in cash and kind, in goods and ecosystems services, from other forms of forest land use.

REFERENCES

Costanza, R., R. d'Agre, R. de Groot, S. Faber, M. Grasso, B. Hannon, K. Limburg, S. Naeem, R, W. O'Neill, J. Parueto, R. G. Raskin and P. Sutton. 'The Value of the World's Ecosystem Services and Natural Capital'. *Environmental Economics* 25, no. 1 (1998). Reprinted from *Nature* 387 (15 May 1997): 253–59.

Hansson, C.B. and M. Wackernagel. 'Rediscovering Place and Accounting Space: How to Re-embed the Human Economy.' *Environmental Economics* 29 (1999): 203–13.

Jordan, C. F. *Nutrient Cycling in Tropical Forest Ecosystem*. New York: J. Wiley, 1985. Quoted in, *Hydrology of Moist Tropical Forests and Effects of Conversion: A State of Knowledge Review*, by L. A. Bruijnzeel. Amsterdam Free University and UNESCO, 1990.

5

IMPACT OF THE STATE LOGGING BAN IN MEGHALAYA, INDIA

Tiplut Nongbri

INTRODUCTION

On 12 December 1996 the Supreme Court of India passed its historic judgement on the civil writ petition No. 202, 1995, filed by T. N. Godavarman Thirumulpad against the Union of India and others, with respect to the cutting of trees in Jammu and Kashmir and Tamil Nadu. Later, taking cognizance of the extensive deforestation in the region, the case was extended to include the Northeast states, including Meghalaya. While the judgement is a major victory for environmentalists and wildlife lovers in the cities, it came as a bolt from the blue for the poor forest-dwellers and the indigenous communities of Northeast India.

To conserve the country's declining forests, the court laced its judgement with an interim order banning the felling of trees and all wood-based activities in the concerned states. The order also directed all state governments to constitute within one month an Expert Committee to identify all forests irrespective of class or ownership; all saw mills, veneer or plywood industries operating in the state; and to assess the sustainability of the forests *qua* timber needs. Till these requirements are complied with, the felling of trees in and removal of timber from the region stood suspended except for those required for defence or other 'Government purposes'.

Seven years have gone by since the historic judgement was passed by the Indian Supreme Court, but the ban has yet to be removed.[1] For the tribal populations of the Northeast, the ban and its continuing operation has generated untold misery. For a number of families it has brought about a sudden termination of their only source of livelihood.

The seriousness of the matter comes into sharp focus in the state of Meghalaya where a blanket ban on the felling of trees, on all common as well as privately grown forests, has been imposed following the Supreme Court order. Interestingly, the state government on its part consistently maintains that the determination of forest and forestland will be difficult in Meghalaya because the management of all areas outside the reserved forests vests with the Autonomous District Councils (ADCs).[2] Moreover, due to the inability to carry out a cadastral survey of the land, proper records of forest do not exist in the state. 'As such, whether or not a private plantation is on any area which is not 'forest' will not be easily determinable'.[3]

It is not within the scope of this essay to comment on the correctness or otherwise of the Supreme Court's interpretation of the Sixth

---

[1] While the ban itself has yet to be lifted, the Supreme Court in response to petitions filed by various state governments, land and forest owners associations and Autonomous District Councils (ADCs) in the region has allowed the state governments, vide its order dated 15 January 1998, to remove and dispose of the felled timber lying at various sites in the state. The quick disposal of the timber has, however, been seriously affected by the stringent conditions laid down by the court. The order made it mandatory that the disposal of the felled timber would commence only after the *Principal Chief Conservator of Forests certifies that inventorization of all felled timber in the state is completed*. Also, the disposal of timber should be carried out through the agency of the state government only, according to specified rules and procedures, and not directly by the owners. As a result of difficulties encountered in complying with these stringent measures, in many states considerable quantities of cut timber continue to lie in a state of decay.

[2] The state of Meghalaya comprises three distinct regions with separate ADCs for each region. These are the Khasi Hills, Jaintia Hills and Garo Hills Autonomous District Councils. While the Khasi and Jaintia people are of common ethnic stock and social and cultural background, the Garos are ethnically different. However, except for a slight variation in their land tenure system, the people of the three regions share a close similarity with each other both in terms of the affinity that they have toward the forests, and its importance in their social and economic life.

[3] Quoted in 'Note about the Hon'ble Supreme Court's Orders in the Writ Petition (Civil) No. 202 of 1995 T. N. Godavarman Thirumulpad vrs The Union of India and Others and Writ Petition (Civil) No. 171/1995—and their Implications' (Govt. of Meghalaya not dated). Interviews conducted on some ex- and present legislators, members of ADCs and officials also yielded the same response on the issue.

Schedule; this is a matter of deliberation for lawyers and jurists. But what is of interest to us is its exemption of private forest or *Ri Kynti* from the regulatory powers of the ADC. This raises the question why the same exemption is not followed in the implementation of the 1996 Supreme Court order. This question assumes significance when we view it against the land tenure system prevailing in the state and the importance of the forests to the tribal economy.

Traditional Land and Forest Tenure System

Traditionally, both in the Khasi and Jaintia Hills, land and forests were governed according to customary laws and practices. Although some changes have occurred in the pattern of landholding, the principle of transmission of rights remains largely the same. In the conception of the Khasi, land belonged to the people and not to the state or its rulers who were merely administrative heads with no territorial powers. Indeed, in ideal terms land is believed to belong to the community with families enjoying only occupancy rights. However, long years of occupation of a particular piece of land may convert occupancy rights into ownership rights. Thus, in terms of ownership, two classes of land can be identified in the Khasi–Jaintia society: *Ri Raid* (common or community land) and *Ri Kynti* (private land).

Ri Kynti refers to land that is under the effective control of the holder, who enjoys proprietary, heritable and transferable rights over it. This includes any part of community land that was acquired by the original settler through jungle clearing, fencing or other forms of improvement on it, or which was bestowed upon the family or clan in lieu of services rendered to the community. *Ri Raid,* on the other hand, refers to that class of land, which is under the control of the community and over which members have only rights of use and occupancy but no proprietary rights. As such, ideally speaking, *Ri Raid* cannot be transferred to an heir or leased or sold off, and, if a person leaves the land unoccupied for three consecutive years it reverts to the community. This, however, does not always happen in practice. Where the occupant has made permanent improvements on the land, in the course of time, his/her family usually becomes the de facto owners of it.

This fluidity in the system has given a peculiar turn to the pattern of landholding in Khasi–Jaintia society. In the majority of cases, land is in the hands of families and clans who exercised exclusive rights over it. Given that land (this includes forest) is the most important productive resource, families who occupy a plot are not always ready to leave it but rather use their labour power and the capital at their command to plant crops and trees, and in the process gain individual rights over it. This process has not only led to a considerable decline in the availability of common land but also changes the very character of forests in the region. Both in the Khasi and Jaintia Hills, forests are not mere jungle lying out in the wild, untouched and uncared for by humans. Except for those forests located in the very remote parts of the region most of the forests are of secondary growth, cared for and nurtured by local people. Investigations show that, apart from fencing and the maintenance of fire lines around the forest area, removal of dead wood, thinning and the lopping of unwanted leaves and branches are regular functions of forest owners in many parts of the hills.

Significantly, long years of interaction with the forests have equipped the rural folk with a deep knowledge of conservation skills and techniques which they put to effective use in the management of their natural resource. This fact is clearly demonstrated by the systematic manner in which the ancient Khasi classifed their land to optimize resource utilization and control. Indeed, it would be no exaggeration to say that the land tenure system that prevails in the Khasi and Jaintia Hills is unique. In addition to the two broad classes of land mentioned earlier, the Land Reforms Commission (LRC), set up by the Government of Meghalaya in March 1973, identified more than 35 categories of land and forests in the Khasi Hills alone.

The sheer variety of land types and modes of management reflected in the classification suggests not only the complexity of the system but also the ingenious manner in which this vital resource is put to use. Each category clearly indicates the manner of its origin, the specific purpose and the intended beneficiaries for whom the land/forest in question is meant.[4] What is also significant about the classification is the lack of clear-cut separation between land and forests. This, however, does not imply that the Khasi see no difference between these two vital elements. In fact, in their cognitive map land (Ka khyndew) and forest (Ka khlaw) are conceptually and terminologically distinct. But as trees invariably grow on land and land is reclaimed from forests, on the empirical plane the distinction between the two often gets blurred.

---

[4] For a keen observer this classification is an important source of information, which throws valuable light not only on the pattern of resource utilization and control but also the economic and political history of the region.

FOREST CLASSIFICATION BY THE STATE

With the establishment of state control over forests, new classes of forests have emerged. The process, which began in the colonial period, has brought large tracts of forest under the direct control of the state, through a system of reservation. It is interesting to see how in its attempt to streamline the management and control of forests, entrusted to it by the Sixth Schedule, the Khasi Hills Autonomous District Council has tried to integrate the two systems by classifying forests in the district under the following heads:

1. *Private Forests:* these are forests belonging to an individual (or clan) which have been grown or inherited by him (or them) in recognized private lands.
2. *Ri Law Sumar:* these are forests belonging to an individual, clan or joint clans which are grown by or inherited by him (or them) in village or common *raj* land.
3. *Ri Law Lyngdoh, Law Kyntang, Law Niam:* these are forests set apart for religious purposes and hitherto managed or controlled by the *lyngdoh* or other person or persons to whom the religious ceremonies for the particular locality or village or villages are entrusted.
4. *Law Adong and Law Shnong:* these are village forests hitherto reserved by the villagers for conserving water etc., for the use of the villages and managed by the *sirdar* or headman of the village with the help of the village *durbar*.
5. *Raid Forests:* these are forests looked after by the heads of the *Raid* and under the management of the local administrative head.
6. *Protected Forests:* these are forests already declared protected for the growth of trees for the benefit of the local inhabitants and also forests that may be so declared by rules under the Autonomous District Councils Act.
7. *Green Block:* these are forests belonging to individual families or clans and *raj* lands already declared as 'Green Block' by the Government because of their aesthetic beauty and water supply functions to the town of Shillong and its suburbs and also forests that may be so declared under the Autonomous District Councils Act.
8. *District Council Reserve Forests:* these are forests that may be so declared by the Executive Committee under the Autonomous District Councils Act or the rules made thereunder.

9. *Unclassed Forests*: these are forests hitherto known as Unclassed State Forests before the commencement of the Constitution of India; they are directly managed and controlled by the state government of Meghalaya including any other forest(s) not falling under any of the above classification.

According to the classification outlined above there seems to be no fundamental difference between private forest and *Ri Law Sumar* from private plantations as defined by the 1996 Supreme Court order. Both are owned and managed by the people, save that according to the Sixth Schedule the former is subject to the regulatory powers of the ADC. Since the tribal economy is integrally linked up with the forests, which constitutes more than two-thirds of the land area in the region, the effect on their lives is far-reaching. A close look at their system of production will bring out this fact.

FORESTS AND PEOPLE'S LIVELIHOOD

For the indigenous communities, the state's forests have been an important source of livelihoods, providing them not only with fuel, fodder and timber but also food, fruit and medicine. For thousands of years the tribal people have lived on things gathered from forests. And with sharp insights, gained through close and sustained interactions with nature, learnt to adapt new modes of production to their forest life. *Jhum,* that is, slash and burn or shifting cultivation and horticultural plantations are two examples of this adaptation, where the tribes efficiently use the basic skills of agriculture to grow food crops and fruit plants on their forest lands.

While this mode of production continues to be the primary source of livelihood for a large number of rural families, it is usually complemented with income derived from the sale of minor forest produce. Interviews with shifting cultivators in the Ri Bhoi and West Khasi Hills districts revealed their high dependence on the latter to augment their meagre means. While shifting cultivation ensures them a wide variety of crops necessary to meet their basic nutritional needs through the different seasons,[5] minor forest produce provides them with regular, albeit sparse, income for the purchase of meat, fish and groceries.

---

[5] Some of the important crops grown by shifting cultivation are maize, millet, job's tears, potatoes, gourd, pumpkin, beans, peas, tomatoes, chillies and green leafy vegetables.

Significantly, a large number of those who collect minor forest produce are women, who in the course of the day's work gather various types of herbs, roots, fruits and fungi.[6] While a small part of the produce goes into the family kitchen to supplement the family diet, the rest finds its way into the local weekly market or is sold to proprietors of roadside shops and stalls, or small-time traders who cater to the urban consumer. To understand the importance of these natural resources to the economy of poor households, visitors to the state capital need only look at the roadside stalls and the lanes and bylanes of the central market (*Iewduh*) in Shillong which are flooded with these goods.

While the poor subsist on shifting cultivation and the bounty of the forests, landed farmers engaged in sedentary agriculture infuse stability into the family income by selling trees. Many farmers sell trees from their forests not only to buy seeds, fertilizers or to try out new crops but also to invest in houses or taxis. For many this has proved to be a ladder to a better future. A large number of people have experienced a remarkable change in their status, as they used the income derived from the sale of timber to educate their children or set them up in business. In fact, many of the leading families in most of the 25 odd villages I visited attributed their position to the benefits derived from the sale of timber. That the sale of timber has given these families a rare opportunity, which they would otherwise have found difficult to achieve, is evident from the fact that most of the children of these households, who have matriculated from some of the best institutions in the region, are also the first generation to have been educated.

At Puriang village, one of the women informants recounted many families in the village who had sent their children to be schooled in Shillong on the income derived from the lease of trees. Some had even sent them to New Delhi for a higher education. In Modymmai village, on the other hand, people used the income derived from the sale of trees to purchase paddy fields at Sung, a fertile stretch of land on the border of the Khasi and Jaintia hills, which is regarded as the rice bowl of the region. This is one of the few villages where substantial income

---

[6] Interestingly, many of the herbs have the prefix *ja* before their names, such as *jamyrdoh, jangew, jalyniar, jathang, ja ut, etc.* In Khasi, *ja* means rice, which is a staple food in the Northeastern region. According to local sources, when the British imposed an economic blockade on the Khasi Hills during the popular resistance against the inroad of colonialism in the 1830s the people sustained themselves on herbs and roots from the forests.

from forests is ploughed back into the land. Though some families did use their income to educate their children and to buy motor vehicles and houses in the town, almost all households in the village continue to engage in agriculture as their primary occupation.[7]

But while rural farmers have successfully integrated timber into their agricultural economy this has opened the door to non-tribal businessmen who lease forests on a contract basis from private landowners and sell the timber to urban consumers or transport it outside the state. Obviously catering to a large market and eager to gain maximum profits from the business, most forest-contractors resorted to clear-felling of the forests under lease. As a result, in no time at all, in many parts of the region signs of depletion of forests became apparent.

THE ROLE OF THE STATE IN DEFORESTATION

In order to have a realistic understanding of the problem, it is important to identify the different categories of forest users and the manner of their operation. This is important because while the imposition of the ban has severely affected the livelihoods of local communities, the Supreme Court has yet to take cognizance of the real exploiters of forests. There is ample evidence to suggest that it was the indiscriminate cutting of trees by outside contractors who catered to the national market that posed a threat to forests in the region. Central to this process is the commercialization of forests by the state. The process, which began with the extension of British rule, consolidated after Independence and found full expression in the 1970s, with major changes in the political arrangements in the region (exemplified by the reorganization of Assam) and the acceleration of the forces of modernization and development.

The imperative for development not only sanctioned the indiscriminate destruction of forests, but also converted them into a mine of raw materials for national industry. This fact is clearly borne out by the differential stand taken by the Supreme Court with respect to people's needs and the needs of industry. While the Supreme Court order has sought to impose severe restrictions on the cutting of trees by local communities, it has exempted contractors and companies that supply timber and/or wood to government departments and

---

[7] The *sirdar* of the village estimated the number of people engaged in agriculture at over 95 per cent.

industries. In Meghalaya alone three companies, Meghalaya Plywood, Timpack Private Ltd and Vishal Enterprise, have been exempted from the purview of the ban as these had ongoing contracts with the government-run ordnance factory, the currency press, and North-Eastern Coal Fields, respectively. Significantly, all three companies exempted from the order belong to non-tribal entrepreneurs. From the employment point of view, timber contractors were a boon to the rural economy, as many persons from landless families found ready jobs in their concern. As compared with wage labour in agriculture, wood cutters earned more than double the income. The average wage of wood cutters before the Supreme Court ban ranged between Rs150–200 per day.

Though a lot has already been said about the role of the state *qua* ADC in the management of forests, a closer look at the modality of its operation would not be out of place. In pursuance of the powers conferred by the Constitution, the three ADCs in the state each have their own forest departments headed by a Chief Forest Officer (CFO), and their own Acts and Rules, assent to which has been given by the Governor. In the Khasi and Jaintia Hills, forest operations are governed by the provisions of the United Khasi and Jaintia Hills Autonomous District (Management and Control of Forests) Act, 1958. The Act empowers the CFO or any other officer to call upon all local chiefs (*syiem, daloi, sirdar*, etc.) to provide a list of private forests and *Ri Law Sumar* within the area of their jurisdiction. The Act also prescribes that no timber or forest produce can be removed for the purpose of sale, trade or business in certain categories of forest without the written order of the ADC (Section 5). It also provides that no forest can be felled without the previous sanction of the ADC (Section 7).

Where felling is allowed, the law categorically states that no tree below 1.37 metre at breast height is permitted to be cut.[8] To ensure compliance with the provisions, the Act prescribes that no tree shall be felled unless a forest officer of the ADC has first marked the tree in accordance with the instructions of the CFO. After the tree is cut, it cannot be removed from the site unless it is piece-marked by the property hammer of the owner and accompanied by a certificate of origin (CO) granted to him/her by the ADC (as proof that revenue was paid). Further, no timber extracted from a private forest can be taken outside the jurisdiction of the ADC for sale, trade or business unless

---

[8] This specification was laid down by the Second Amendment, 1979, to the United Khasi and Jaintia Hills Autonomous District (Management and Control of Forests) Act.

it is first taken to the Revenue Station of the ADC for tax clearance and a transit pass (TP). Similar rules exist to regulate the management of other classes of forests.

The above account makes it clear that timber logging in Meghalaya is not an illegal activity, but an economic pursuit fully legitimized by the state. In a land-based economy, with little access to outside capital or alternative modes of employment, it is little wonder that people increasingly depend upon their natural endowments both to subsist and to improve their material condition. But having said that, it is important to note that as an economic activity, timber logging is the culmination of a series of changes that have occurred in this society, an important aspect of which is the commercialization of forests by the state.

Interestingly, the ADCs, which had been entrusted with the task of protecting the people's traditional rights to the forests, became part of the process that takes away their rights. Notwithstanding their diverse functions outlined above, it would be naïve to assume that they enjoy unbridled power in the management of forests. While the ADCs are the main functionaries in the day-to-day management of the forests, their ability to influence policies is circumscribed by their subordination to the state and central governments.

Adequate laws and rules exist to regulate sustainable use of forest. In fact, many people allege that the immense power that the state enjoys over the forests is responsible for the evils associated with timber logging. Timber is not only an important source of revenue for the government but also an important tool for bureaucrats and politicians to wield their influence over the people. While ordinary people largely operate within the rules, those with connections are able to bypass them. Indeed, sustainable use of the forests is not an alien concept to the Khasi. Much before the winds of change brought western ideas to the hills, ecological values were deeply etched in their practices. The planting of trees was already a common practice among the people. Besides, to minimize the destruction of forests, usually only mature trees were cut leaving the undersized ones untouched. This technique, known as *pom sud*, or selective felling, is widely practiced in the Mairang and Nongstoin Divisions of the West Khasi Hills District.

Though overuse of the forests in recent years cannot be disputed, an encouraging feature observable in Khasi–Jaintia society is the deep respect for nature embedded in their tradition. While consumerist and materialistic values have not left society untouched, tempting many people to exploit this natural resource as a shortcut to riches, local communities are increasingly coming forward to put a check to the indiscriminate use of the forests. Not only are they keeping a closer watch on activities in private forests, they are also maintaining tighter controls over common property resources. To cite a few examples, in Modymmai village, felling of trees in the village forest surrounding the Sung and those located at Lum Myrlang, Wah Mynser, Poh Soh Shieh and Lum Kyrpad has been forbidden for a number of years, except for bonafide village needs. In Mawpat, a village on the outskirts of Shillong, the village *durbar* prohibited the collection of fuel or the conduct of agricultural activities in the village reserved forest, a 44 hectare plot covered with rich pine, oak and schima species (*dieng ngan*) of trees. To foster a sense of collective responsibility, the village council made it mandatory that all adults in the village take part in the annual cleaning of the forest and contribute a minimum of Rs 10 per household towards its maintenance. In the Shella area bordering Bangladesh, many villages in the vicinity of Cherrapunjee have imposed a ban on shifting cultivation to preserve the fragile ecological balance of the region.

IMPACT OF THE LOGGING BAN ON LOCAL PEOPLE

The ban on timber and the consequent impoverishment experienced by the local population raises pertinent questions about their right to livelihood. In the tribal economies of Northeast India, forestry and agriculture are closely interlinked. Hence to restrict a farmer from the use of the forests is to infringe on his/her livelihood. The Supreme Court order, however, seems to have overlooked this vital point. In its eagerness to protect the environment, it has failed to perceive the effect its judgement would have on the people whose very survival depended upon open access to the forests. Given the material conditions within which the tribal economy is rooted what made the court decide the way it did? If we are to look for clues to this question in the historical process, facts suggest that the decision was neither a result of ignorance nor oversight, but is symptomatic of the state's attitude to the rights of indigenous people. Both the colonial and the postcolonial state have been extremely insensitive to the social, cultural and territorial rights of the indigenous people. The ideology of centralization, combined with Western materialist values and the craze for development, has given rise to policies and programmes that have led to the mass appropriation of tribal land and forests, and the destruction of their cultures and traditions. The Supreme Court order is but an extension of the exercise of draconian power by the state towards a region, which has thus far enjoyed relative autonomy and freedom.

The ban on timber has affected not only the forest owners and contractors who had a stake in the business, but, more seriously, thousands of farmers and woodcutters for whom the forests are the primary basis of their subsistence. In its affidavit submitted to the Supreme Court in May 1997 the Government of Meghalaya reported that in all 5,396 persons were employed in wood-based industry in the state. However, working out the number of the affected on the basis of families who essentially depend upon forests for their livelihood, Mr H. S. Lyngdoh, ex-Minister of Forest Government of Meghalaya, put the number at 231,980 persons. The worst affected, he observed, are those in West Khasi Hills District. The sheer abundance of forest and rough terrain in large parts of the district not only inhibits agriculture but also increases people's dependence on nature.[9]

A paper in the *Economic and Political Weekly* (Dev Nathan 2000) states that in 16 villages around Kymrod (West Khasi Hills) more than 85 per cent of families owned forests and sold timber. Data collected in the same area during the same period as Nathan's study reveal that the entire rural economy revolves around the forests. Forests are not only central to agriculture, but the income derived from them in turn feeds the market and other economic activities. As a result, consequent to the ban, over 500 food shops operating between Mawngap and Nongstoin were forced to close down due to a sharp fall in business. Given that most of these shops were run by local women, many of whom were the main earners of their (matrilineal) families, the effect on the households can well be imagined. To gain an idea of the magnitude of the problem, I furnish below some of the firsthand information collected from villages in the area.

According to the *sirdar* of Nongkhlaw, a village of 275 households immortalized for its role in Tirot Singh's[10] celebrated rebellion against David Scott in 1827, there has been a drastic slide in its economy since the imposition of the timber ban. This finds stark reflection in the

---

[9] In comparison with other districts in the region, such as the East Khasi Hills, Jaintia Hills or RiBhoi districts where agriculture has been extensively practiced, in many parts of the West Khasi Hills conditions are not conducive to agriculture.

[10] Tirot Singh was the Chief of Nongkhlaw who bravely fought against the British in the famous Nongkhlaw Rebellion (1827–32) that was set off by a conflict in which two English officers were killed over the construction of a road through the Khasi Hills in an attempt to link up Sylhet and Assam.

depression of wages, rising unemployment and the high incidence of dropouts from schools and colleges. An examination of the wage structure during the years 1996–99 shows that prior to 1996, the minimum wage in the village was Rs 60 per day, but in 1999, even the maximum wage barely crossed Rs 50 per day. Secondly, before 1996 there were about 20 trucks owned by different families in the village. Now only six trucks are left, as the rest have been sold off in distress. Similarly, two cloth shops, a goldsmith's shop, a tailor shop and a number of tea shops were forced to close down due to poor business. But the most discouraging trend is found in education. Before 1996, there were about 30 students from the village who attended college in Mairang and Shillong (located at 17 and 61 kilometres., respectively, from Nongkhlaw). In 1999, only two students were found pursuing a college education. The same trend is discernible in the schools. When the new English nursery school opened in 1996, 120 students registered for admission, but within two years the number of students on the rolls had fallen to less than 70, as parents had difficulty in meeting the expenses for books, fees and uniforms. That some of the students have been sucked into the labour market is evident from the fact that, whereas, previously child labour was almost an unknown phenomenon in the village, now it has become a regular feature.

Investigations into the banking sector corroborate the theory of the downward slide of the rural economy. A study of the deposit and withdrawal trends of some of the banks operating in the district shows a marked fall in the daily transaction of business. In one of the banks in Mairang Division, where more than 70 per cent of the population are engaged in agriculture (and timber sale prior to the ban), the number of frozen or inoperative accounts shot up from less than 100 in the last year before the ban (1995) to 300 in 1999. Interestingly, in terms of overall deposits during the year, the figure shows an increase by 12 crore rupees. A close examination of the reason, however, shows that this figure is made up of deposits by a few big investors engaged in government contracts. Among small-time investors the deposits have crashed heavily. Indeed, according to the branch manager who heads the bank, in the last two years, the number of fresh accounts has fallen from the usual 25–30 per month to hardly 5 per month. This dismal picture is indicative not only of the growing trend of rural poverty following the Supreme Court ban on timber, but also its differential effect on the rich and poor sections of the population.

Notwithstanding the green concerns that provided the ecological underpinning of the Supreme Court order, the decision banning the extraction of timber also seems to have boomeranged on the ecology. To escape starvation, in many parts of the hills, people have reverted to shifting cultivation, charcoal burning and even removing and selling the bark of trees, practices that are no less (if not more) destructive to the environment than the felling of trees. Though shifting cultivation per se is not injurious to the environment if carried out with prudence, the idea that the forests have no value since their timber cannot be sold has, however, made many throw ecological caution to the wind. But, what is most damaging is the descaling of trees. Many persons in the district are making their livelihood by peeling off the bark of the *jalawan* (*litsea glutinosa*) and other varieties of trees and selling them to non-tribal businessmen (Marwari businessmen) for a paltry Rs 2–6 per kilogram. The latter in turn sell the material to pharmaceutical firms in South India for making incense and medicines. The practice, which is akin to the removal and selling of the body parts of human beings, is not only ecologically destructive (the descaled tree gradually dries up and dies), but if not checked could immediately give rise to large-scale biopiracy.

Effect on Women

Hidden under the cloud of controversies generated by the Supreme Court order is its effect on women. Although logging is basically a masculine activity with women having little to do in its actual operations, paradoxically the effect of the ban falls more heavily on women. Where the men of the household are thrown out of work, the result has been an increase in women's already heavy responsibilities. Indeed, in many households, the ban on timber has not only imposed additional burdens on women to meet the economic needs of the family, but has also resulted in a manifold increase in their domestic chores. This fact was brought home by a group of women from Nongthliew village who desperately pleaded with a bus conductor at Mawmaram to allow them to board the bus with their empty kerosene cans for refilling at Mairang. With most forests in the vicinity privately owned by the better off families, women from poor households used to obtain their fuel from the branches discarded by timber loggers and the residue from the lone saw mill located in the village. However, with the implementation of the Supreme Court order, these sources of fuel had become inaccessible. Hence every week the women had to undertake the 22 kilometre trip from their village to Mairang with their plethora of cans to get kerosene for their kitchens. This has not only added to their work load, but it has also affected the quality of food their families eat, as to save kerosene, many households have been forced to reduce cooking time, the use of meat and the eating stews by switching to dry fish and chutneys as substitutes.

Driven by the economic crisis that afflicts their households, in some parts of the hills, women are increasingly pushed into road construction, a task they had previously avoided. Though given the nature of the job, and the easy availability of male labour, women workers rarely get a fair deal in these activities. Discussions with women working on the Mawnai road reveal that they are paid much less than men for the same kind of work. The dual wage structure is, however, just one side of the picture. As female construction workers often represent the poorest of the poor, with few options open to them for alternative employment, in many instances they have had to put up with coarse behaviour and sexual harassment from their male colleagues, many of whom happen to be non-tribals. The economic hardships caused by the ban have also threatened women's security in indirect ways. One telling effect of this is the increasing rate of crime and violence, which accentuates women's vulnerability. According to information given by the villagers, the incidence of both highway robberies and petty crime has registered a significant increase since the imposition of the timber ban.

Aside from the socio-economic effects outlined above, what is really detrimental to the interests of women is the concept of the working plan mooted by the Supreme Court, according to which forests can be used only in accordance with centrally approved plans prepared by the state government. This concept not only threatens women's traditional right to land and forests but also reinforces their marginalization from the management of their natural productive resource. To be sure, Meghalaya is the only state in the country where the matrilineal system of inheritance is still fairly strong. But though women are the legal custodians of the land and forests owned by the family, management of resources is primarily the men's responsibility. Yet, so long as the right to decide 'how', 'when' and in 'what' manner a forest was to be used rested with the family, women could wield their influence in the matter, albeit within limits. The introduction of the working plan concept marks the transfer of this right from the family to the state, and the formal erosion of women's right to property.

The policy also clearly marks the negation of the indigenous system of natural resource management and use, in which women play an important role. In the traditional system, though men are the managers of land and forests, as gatherers of food, fibre, fuel, fodder and in their active participation in shifting cultivation, women are a repository of vast knowledge and skills in resource use that are handed down the ages through successive female generations. Women are particularly knowledgable about seed varieties and storing techniques, skills which they put into effective use in their daily task of meeting the family's needs. However, the working plan concept not only ignores women's role in resource generation, which is no less significant than men's, it also intensifies men's control over women. Not only is the state highly patriarchal in orientation, but women's lack of education and their ignorance of bureaucratic rules and procedures effectively combines to increase their dependence on men. Experience in other domains of life shows that whenever women have had to interact with the state machinery, they have invariably had to fall back upon their brothers, husbands or sons in executing their affairs.

As a policy, the working plan reflects the growing bureaucratization of forest management and the centralization of control. Salient to this process is the assumption that the state is the best guardian of forests, and scientific forestry the best mode of conservation. Empirical evidence, however, belies this contention. An examination of successive forest policies through the decades indicates that the bottom line of scientific forestry is revenue generation rather than conservation for its own sake. As a concept, the working plan itself originated in the context of the commercial use of forests, though of course its purpose is to bring stability to forests by infusing ideas of sustainable use.

In Meghalaya, the preparation of the working plan is already under way (under the close scrutiny of the Union Ministry of Environment and Forests). However, women's marginal position in the state process puts a check on their ability to influence its content. What accounts for this situation is their historical isolation from the political process. Both among the Khasi and the Garo (another matrilineal tribe in the state), though descent and inheritance rights are transmitted through the mother, women are traditionally debarred from the system of administration and/or governance as this is primarily regarded as a man's domain. In recent years, women's isolation from the decision-making process has allowed the state not only to come up with policies that are highly detrimental to their interests, but also to propagate an ideology that perpetuates their subordination to men (Nongbri 2001). Given the state's bias against women and the commercial slant in the concept of the working plan, the prospects for women are far from encouraging.

Ecology, Community and the State

To conclude, it would not be far wrong to say that women in particular, and tribal and indigenous people in general, have been seriously affected by the Supreme Court order. But, while women experience the order in gender-specific ways, they cannot be completely disassociated from the problems that afflict the community as a whole. Central to this problem is the element of powerlessness that characterizes their lives. Though distinctions along the axes of age, class, status and gender may divide the indigenous community internally, collectively they share certain common elements that mark them off from the rest of the population. One can come up with an endless list, but critical among these are their economic and political subordination, and their marginalization from the structures of power and influence. Ironically, the high resource potential of their territory has added to their vulnerability as, in the majority of cases, this provides the material *raison d'etre* for their colonization (read exploitation). It is an established fact that areas inhabited by indigenous communities both in India and abroad are rich in minerals, water bodies and forests. While this has provided them with an important source of livelihood it has also attracted resource-hungry colonizers to their territories.

The case discussed above is but one of the trajectories of this process. As is clear from the account, though the Supreme Court order is concerned with the protection of forests, the real issues revolve round the use of resources, and the struggle for rights over these, between competing users. As is typical in conflicts over resources, who wins and who loses is not determined by (ecological) ethics but by the degree of power and influence one is able to wield. Thus in a struggle between unequals it is only logical that the powerful come up tops and the powerless are vanquished. The decimation of the tribes' rights to their land and forest, *despite centuries of their association with, and dependence upon, the resource* can be understood within this framework.

However, to add an epilogue to the process, it needs to be noted that the state's violation of the people's rights has not gone unchallenged. The Supreme Court order has snowballed into a major political issue, with the 'Durbar of the Rulers of Khasi States' comprising the *syiems, sirdars, wahdadars*, etc., demanding the scrapping of the Sixth Schedule as it has failed to protect the interests of the people. They would go back to the terms contained in the Instrument of Accession and Annexed Agreement for the administration of the Khasi states, questioning the authority of the ADC and demanding the restoration of the rights over land and forests to the Khasi states.

To come back to the Supreme Court order and its bureaucratic concept of the working plan, it may be noted that the issue can be more fully understood within the framework of the tribe's powerlessness and their subordinate position, vis à vis, the nation state. Though the Supreme Court order is concerned with the conservation of resources, in reality it is an expression of the dominant position enjoyed by the state and its ability to enforce what it considers ecologically appropriate policies. What lent credibility to the contention of the order is the fact that the people on whom the order is enforced are not devoid of ecological ideas to conserve their resources. Indeed, data from the Khasi Hills shows that the people have a deep respect for nature.

If we are to have a realistic understanding of the current process in Northeast India that centres around the Supreme Court order, we need to relate it to the twin, though ostensibly contradictory, elements of powerlessness and the high resource potential of the region. It is interesting to see how these two elements have worked in tandem to contribute to the vulnerability of the tribes. While the rich resource base has provided the material basis for the colonization of their territory, their powerlessness ensured their easy subjugation. What this suggests is that we cannot hope to comprehend the full significance of the order on the people of Northeast India without relating it to the material and political factors that inform their lives. Though the Supreme Court order is dictated by the ideology of resource conservation, in reality it is an expression of the dominant position enjoyed by the state and its ability to enforce what it considers ecologically appropriate policies. The appropriation of their resources by the state and the more advanced sections of the population, and the ruthless destruction of their cultures and tradition under the guise of development is a direct outcome of their political subordination.

REFERENCES

Nathan, Dev. 2000. 'Timber in Meghalaya.' *Economic and Political Weekly* 25, no. 4 (22–28 January 2000): 182–86.

Nongbri, Tiplut. 'Khasi Women and Matriliny: Transformations in Gender Relations.' In *Gender Relations in Forest Societies in Asia: Patriarchy at Odds*, edited by Govind Kelkar, Dev Nathan and Pierre Walter. New Delhi: Sage Publications.

SECTION 2

MARKETS AND
CIVILIZATIONAL CHANGE

6

Timber and Local Accumulation in China

Dev Nathan and Yu Xiaogang

Introduction

Capital flows, with capital regimes that are globally or even nationally open, are determined by comparative rates of profit. Consequently flows into Asia have largely been into urban, industrial and service sectors. Profit rates in agriculture, particularly in poor areas of rainfed agriculture and the hill-forest regions, are not high enough to attract outside investment. This is a big part of the problem. On the other hand, uncontrolled capital movements drain savings out of these areas which are then invested in areas of higher returns. This happens even in nationally-closed capital regimes.

How can this drain of savings, through the banking system, from rural to urban areas be reversed? It is necessary to investigate whether a system of regional/rural banks could help the process of local accumulation in poor areas. Banks in the early phases of capitalist development in the USA had only regional charters. They had to confine their operations to the state in which they were chartered. Similarly, there are regional banks in China.

In China, the 1980s phase of rapid growth was based on agriculture and other on-farm production (what the Chinese call sideline activities) which both reduced rural poverty and provided surpluses for industrial investment. But agriculture quickly comes up against the barrier of diminishing returns (in the absence of technological change) and capital is then diverted to other, more profitable investment activities. Where this investment in industry was made in the villages [as happened on a large-scale in the Township and Village Enterprises (TVEs) in China] it contributed to a relatively stable increase in local income.

One factor which made this possible was that the investment horizon was limited and local. The TVEs had to look at the most profitable investments in their own locality. At the same time, the markets in which they could sell their products were not necessarily local.

The combination of wide commodity markets with restricted, localized capital markets prevented the appearance of the phenomenon so widespread in India—where credit/deposit ratios are lower in the poorer areas and higher in the better off industrial and Green Revolution centres, leading to the flow of capital from poorer to better off areas. The Grameen Bank type of organizations have also partly replicated the same phenomenon of rural to urban capital flows. The investments by the NGOs in big office/commercial centres in Dhaka have come from income earned in the loan process to poor rural women.

At the same time it has been observed that where there are sizeable local savings (as in the women's Self Help Groups in Maharashtra or Tamil Nadu, India) the groups often have no reasonable investments that can be undertaken. This points to the necessity of paying attention to the complementary and prior public investments in infrastructure, education, etc., that are needed for local, private (whether by individuals or by groups) investments to take place.

Along with a system of regional (local) banks, there is need for devolution of government revenues from local natural resources, like forests or minerals. In state-owned forests, timber revenue and logging company income both go outside the forest economy. In the case of the Indian State of Bihar, a substantial part of which now lies in the newly formed State of Jharkhand, the State government has admitted that 60 per cent of its revenue used to come from this region. This revenue included not only that from forests but also from the coal and other mines in the region. The latter is likely to have been much more than the forest revenue. But forest revenue would still have been significant enough to constitute a direct drain from the local economy.

Government expenditure on the forest economy bears no necessary relation to the revenue earned from the region. Infrastructure spending in forest regions has usually been determined by considerations of facilitating extraction. More recently, at least partly as a result of the growing dissatisfaction of people in the forest areas expressed in various protest movements and insurgencies, and partly (in electoral systems) as a result of the need to get votes, there have been increases in social welfare infrastructure spending in these areas. But even now health and education infrastructure in these areas are usually much poorer than in the plains. Lower population density does make it more expensive to supply these facilities. But the political marginalization of these communities (even in electoral systems they are far outnumbered by the plains people to whom they are joined in common states) related to their being ethnically different, reinforces low government spending.

What does remain within the local economy is the wages earned by local labour, plus whatever is spent by forest department officials and logging companies on local supplies and materials. This is small compensation for what is extracted in timber revenues and logging company incomes, even without taking into account the external costs, in the form of a reduced supply of environmental services, that are borne by the local economy.

The combination of ethnic discrimination and geographic compactness has often led, as in India, Indonesia and Myanmar, to movements of forest-based communities for autonomy or separation. Besides, these regions, whether the Cordilleras in the Philippines, the Jharkhand and Dandakarnya regions in India or Northern Thailand, have also been the sites of peasant insurgencies. In pre-Liberation China, particularly during the Long March, the minority nationality peoples provided important support to the communist government.

While the peasant insurgencies articulated demands for ending or reducing exploitation by forest officials and traders or contractors, some of the ethnic movements identified themselves with a different relation to the forest and a different kind of forest policy. The extraction of forest revenue was considered the exploitation of the region as an 'internal colony'. In the case of Jharkhand, plantation policy of teak to replace the multiple use and multiple-species, natural *sal* forest was considered an attack on the culture and livelihood of the forest-dependent people. One of the slogans was 'Teak is India; Sal is Jharkhand'. Monoculture plantations were uprooted to oppose such an attack on livelihood and culture.

While the above details are given from various parts of India, there have been somewhat similar struggles in many other forest communities of Asia. Establishing community control over forest resources and opposition to extractive policies of the nation states is common to these movements. Many of these struggles of Asian indigenous peoples have often sought political self-determination, as against the politically more restricted objective of autonomy that characterizes the Latin American indigenous peoples' movements.

These movements have forced the attention of policy-makers to the problems of forest-dwellers suffering from extractive modes of relations, and subject to the enormous powers weilded by forest department officials, timber traders and other contractors. A combination of all these political factors and movements has led to the appearance and strengthening of administrative units (states, provinces, or at the lower levels, district councils) for regions of the forest-dwelling communities.

The result has been the formation of separate provinces in India, specifically in the Northeast, comprising the hill-forest dwellers. In other areas the movements for autonomy of the hill-forest regions still continue. Some of these regions, like Jharkhand and Chattisgarh, have become States. The Chinese government has had a long-standing policy of forming 'autonomous' regions (prefectures, counties or townships) for areas dominated by the ethnic minorities, referred to as minority nationalities.

The 'local' in local forest management usually refers to the village. But in this essay attention is drawn to the necessity of considering other levels of the local, as is the case in discussions of decentralization. This is particularly so when there is an ethnic homogeneity between the village and the higher levels of administration—district or prefecture/township/county and even province, as the case may be. For instance the Autonomous District Councils of the North Cachar (NC) Hills and Karbi Anglong Districts form relatively ethnically homogenous administrative units with ownership over the forests, though they form part of the state of Assam. But the Ukhrul district of Manipur, largely populated by the Tangkhul Naga, does not have similar powers. The states of Meghalaya, Mizoram and Nagaland, on the other hand, are states of relatively homogenous ethnic composition. Similarly Lijiang County or Xitoh Township in Yunnan Province, China, are both administrative units of minority nationalities.

In such cases, where there is an ethnic correspondence between the village and the higher administrative unit as will be shown in this essay, it is relevant to consider the supra-village administrative unit in discussions of local forest management. Of course, even within minority areas we need to consider the differential effects of local forest ownership and management between, say, the lowland Naxi and the upland Yi or Lisu in Lijiang, or between town and country even among the Khasi in Meghalaya, India.

TIMBER AND LOCAL ACCUMULATION IN CHINA

This essay is a study of the role of income from timber in local accumulation in China. The study is based on investigations in Lijiang County. The investigations were carried out in May 1999 largely in Laoshe and Xitoh Townships. The Naxi inhabit the villages located in the valleys, while the Yi and Lisu live in the upland villages investigated.

Lijiang County is highly forested, with a forest cover of about 55 per cent. These forests are either state-owned or collective (village)-owned and managed. The share of forest land distributed to households for household management is very small (less than 5 per cent) and restricted to the degraded areas near Lijiang town, in which investment was needed for regenerating tree cover.

The discussion of devolution of management from central to local forest management has usually been conducted with reference to non-state forests in China. For instance, Liu Dachang's (2001) review of devolution in China is explicitly about non-state forests. From the perspective of forest management, this may seem okay; since state forests are clearly centrally managed. But, when we want to analyze the impact on people's livelihoods and local accumulation, then it is not warranted to leave state forests completely out of the discussion. If timber revenue is devolved to accrue to local governments (county or township in the case of China), then the effects on people's livelihoods would be quite different from the usual case where timber revenue accrues to the central or provincial governments.

Timber income, both as revenue and as the profits of timber companies, has usually been a vehicle for accumulation outside the forest areas themselves. In China, however, there has been a divergence from the usual pattern. In the first place there are both state-owned forests and collective (village)-owned forests. The income from the sale of timber in the latter case goes to the villages. Second, the County or Township Forest Bureaus own the forest companies that carry out the logging, and, thus, that part of their income that is invested goes into local accumulation. Third, until 1993, the County and Township Forest Bureaus collected various funds and fees from the timber companies, and this became local income. Fourth, the local governments were paid a small 'village collection charge'. Fifth, after 1993, the state income collected as a tax on the volume of timber was devolved to local governments (i.e., county and township governments). Finally, the labour employed in logging was always local labour, which meant that logging wages accrued to local farmers/workers.

Thus, while logging was strictly controlled through the system of quotas, the income from timber nevertheless accrued locally. It was a large part of local government revenues, used for building infrastructure and for accumulation in other sectors. It also formed a substantial part of the cash income of the farmers. Consequently, when in late 1998, following the disastrous floods in southern China, the Chinese central government banned logging (in natural forests) there was an immediate recessionary effect on the economy of the forest-dominated townships of Lijiang County, like Xitoh Township.

Governments get another category of income, besides tax and related revenues. These governments own the companies that operated in the timber market. They are not as per the Chinese definition, 'state enterprises', which are owned by the central government. Initially these companies had monopsony rights in buying and selling timber. Later, other companies were also allowed to buy and sell timber from the collective-owned forests. When the central government found that this led to higher logging than the quotas given and probably accelerated deforestation; in 1996 the monopsony buying powers of these government-owned companies was restored. But some amount of collective-owned timber still finds its way to the privately-owned companies, even though they are legally forbidden from buying timber directly from the villages.

In Lijiang County, the Senlong Forest Products Company is part of the Senlong Group of Companies, which is owned by the Lijiang County government. It handled 90 per cent of timber sales in the county. After paying all taxes, company's net profit was available to the Lijiang County government for reinvestment as it saw fit. In 1997, the last year of full operation before the logging ban in late 1998, it made a net profit of Yuan 25 million. Earlier 70 per cent of its net profit would go to the county government; this changed to 60 per cent and then to 50 per cent. While the government, for infrastructure or other such non-investment activities, would use the amount paid to it, the profit remaining with it would be used for investment. But this amount too remained under the control of the county government, which owned the company. Basically the company's net profit could be used by the county government, in one way or another, for development and investment.

From the point of view of devolution, what is important is that this surplus was available for local accumulation. In contrast, where the companies operating the timber trade are either 'national' or 'multinational', the surplus would not necessarily be available for local accumulation. The national or multinational company would decide on the sphere and location of its investment on the basis of its comparison of likely profit rates nationally or globally. Local investment of surpluses from the timber trade is important in the context of the usual drain from the regions of the forest economy.

Of course, local accumulation can have many meanings, the implications of which would be different for livelihoods of those in villages and those in towns. Local investment in Lijiang County could be mainly in Lijiang town. The hotel industry that has come up in Lijiang town has been built mainly from timber surpluses. This though local to Lijiang County is still extractive from the villages of the county. At the same time, the development of Lijiang town as a growth centre has had a more beneficial impact on the economy of the county as a whole than, say, if the surpluses were to be reinvested in Beijing or even in Yunnan's provincial capital, Kunming, for that matter.

There would be backward (supply of agricultural and forest products, e.g., mushrooms) and forward linkages (development of 'eco-tourist' sites outside the town), besides the increased demand for labour in the town, to cater to the needs of tourists in Lijiang. There are backward linkages of the tourist industry to the villages, which supply agricultural and animal products, forest products like mushrooms and so on. But the largest share of the benefits from tourism goes to the businesses in the town and to regular workers in the same. This is monopolized by the urbanized Naxi. Only those who already have relatives in the town can easily go and take up jobs there. Since the Naxi are the main nationality in Lijiang town, it is mainly Naxis from the villages who are able to migrate into the town to take up new jobs that are created. The Yi or Lisu cannot as easily migrate to the town, and thus do not benefit as much as the Naxi from the growth in urban employment.

A counter-example of local accumulation that provides more benefits to the villages is the development of the bamboo board industry in Suinin County, Hunan Province. In this case there is substantial increase in the number of days worked and thus increased income in the villages and for the growers of bamboo. Another hill county in Yunnan was able to use its resource of sand, sold to glass factories in Kunming, to transform its agriculture and build up livestock production.

Because the accumulation is local, or in the hands of the local government, does it give the local people more scope to intervene in directing the accumulation or development process? Is it more likely that the local government will be more responsive to the needs or desires of the local population than distant governments? At one level it can be pointed out that it would be more feasible for local people to make their desires or grievances heard by local authorities, than by distant authorities. This is not to say that the dominant local interests will not influence the local government. But, since the local government has to live with the local people, it can be more susceptible to pressures from below.

Further, studies of China (e.g., Siu 1989; Oi 1989; and Nathan and Kelkar 1997)) have pointed out that there often is a close relationship between the cadre who run the local administration, and the people. The party–state apparatus is not monolithic in its operations. Farmers and others often do express their grievances and resentments in various ways, and the local party–state apparatus is forced to take these into account. For instance, in the Yi villages of Laoshe Township, the local administration deliberately allowed the Yi to cut and sell timber, even though the township did not have any logging quota. This was explained on the basis of the poverty of the Yi, and the fact that timber was the major source of cash income with which they could pay school fees and meet other cash expenses. Similarly, even after a village was prohibited from cutting timber, when its forest was declared part of a Nature Reserve, the local administration continued logging, since that was almost its only source of revenue (Harkness 1998). We are not here considering the ecological consequences of such decisions; that discussion will be taken up later. But what we wish to point out is that, where decisions are taken at local levels (village or township) rather than in distant capitals, there is more scope for local needs to impress themselves upon decision-makers and to be taken into account while implementing, if not while framing, policies. This is a positive gain from devolution of decision-making power to local government levels.

Village Income from Timber

In Yunnan as a whole and in Lijiang County too, forests are almost equally divided between state and collective ownership. Collective forests are owned by the administrative village, and have to be managed by the village administration. But the forest bureaus set their cutting quotas. Further, they cannot sell their timber on the open market, but only to the state-owned timber companies.

Village forests could be either collectively managed or allocated to individual households for household management. In Lijiang County virtually all village-owned forests are collectively managed. Only some village forests on seriously degraded land, and usually close to Lijiang town, were leased out to households for regenerating (invariably by planting fruit trees) forest cover. But in other parts of China there have been experiments with household management of forest patches. The functioning of household management of forests will be discussed later. In this section we deal with collective management of village forests, using the administrative village of Li Chiu in Xitoh Township as the main example.

Li Chiu village has about 18,000 mu[1] of collective forest and 20,000 mu of state forest, which is close to the county average of equal proportions of collective and state forest. The quota for logging was 3,000 cubic metres per year, which could be gathered from an area of 50 to 100 mu, i.e., not even 1 per cent of its forest area.

In terms of distribution of income, had the same timber been logged from state forest the village would have got the wage income and the forest resource fee, amounting to Yuan 150,000, or 20 per cent of gross income. In the case of the collective forests being logged, the village gets an additional Yuan 300,000, increasing the proportion of village income in gross income to 60 per cent.

The additional 40 per cent of gross income was used by the village to finance various development expenditures, like road construction, electrification and schools. For instance, a primary school student was given an annual stipend of Yuan 50, a middle school student Yuan 100, a high school student Yuan 200, and a university student Yuan 300. Besides this the village also undertook expenditure on the construction of improved school buildings and on paying a part of the salaries of 'locally-hired' teachers, as against the graduates of the teachers' colleges, who were fully paid by the county or township governments. Salaries of some village-level officials, like the heads of the natural villages, their accountants and All-China Women's Federation representatives were also paid out of logging income.

The income from logging formed the entire development fund of Li Chiu Administrative Village. This does not mean that there would not have been any development funds in the absence of logging income. But logging income enabled the village to use its own funds for development as a matter of right, without having to rely on allocations from higher government sources. This ability to use one's own resources as a right can be particularly important for upland villages, which tend to be politically marginal. It is highly unlikely that allocations from higher government levels would have amounted to

---

[1] A mu is a Chinese measure of land—5 mu is approximately 1 hectare.

the 40 per cent of gross timber income that the administrative village could get due to its ownership of the forests.

Wage Income

Logging involved the employment of local labour, which was organized into teams. The method of organization and payment was the same in state and collective forests. Wage rates over the late 1980s and 1990s had kept up with inflation—a wage of Yuan 4 per day in the late 1980s now translates into about 30 to 40 per day. Workers look at the net wage they earn, i.e., after the cost of food, lodging in the camps and even alcohol has been deducted. From a gross wage of Yuan 40 per day in 1998, Yuan 7 went to meet the cost of food (other than rice which they carried with them) and lodging and Yuan 3 for alcohol and other incidentals. The net wage was Yuan 30 per day. A healthy worker could manage about 100 days of work in a year, with a net income of Yuan 3,000. Most workers could get about Yuan 2,000 per year, while a few might get just Yuan 1,000 in a year. The net income from logging was normally more than that from other cash sources, including the sale of mushrooms or livestock. In a year of good mushroom prices (depending on Japanese export demand) a highly skilled woman could earn up to Yuan 3,000 in a season. But this was unusual, while a logging income of Yuan 3,000 was quite common.

Did the wage income represent a net addition to the local economy, or did it merely represent the money equivalent of energy spent in logging? If it merely represented the money equivalent of logging energy, then one would not expect any surplus that could be invested in other activities. But we saw that logging yielded a net wage income, after deducting direct, living costs, i.e., the cost of reproduction of wage labour. To these direct costs, we must add the value of rice that the loggers had taken with them, and other indirect costs—like possible increases in health expenses due to the intensive use of energy in logging labour. But even making an allowance for such additions, what is clear is that the logging wage yielded a net income over the cost of production of wage labour. What this shows, is that wage labour is a unique commodity in that its price (i.e., wages) is not governed by the cost of production, as is the case with other commodities.

The net income from logging wages was used for a number of transformations of the local economy at the household level. One of the changes in production that the logging wage made possible was the efficient use of high yielding varieties HYV (high yielding varieties) seeds. Prior to the development of logging in the mid-1980s, most farmers (in the valley-bottom Naxi villages) could not afford to buy the required fertilizer. After earning a logging income they were able to regularly buy fertilizer, which increased their rice yields. In the uplands, logging wage income enabled households to buy plastic sheets, which increased yields in corn, potato and other crops. Some of the wage income also went into investment in livestock, increasing the productive activities of the households. Some of the wage income, as must be expected, went into improving houses, and buying new equipment, like television sets. School expenses, which amounted to Yuan 200 per month for a middle school student and Yuan 300 per month for a high school student, were met from the logging income. Particularly for upland children, this enabled them to remain in school longer than they previously would.

EFFECTS ON GENDER RELATIONS

Logging is a masculine activity. And it became the main source of cash income in communities like the Naxi, where women have traditionally controlled the purse strings. Further, it meant the absence of men from the village for long periods of time. What was the impact of these two changes on gender relations?

Obviously, men while they were away did not need to check with their wives before spending money on themselves. On returning too, both women and men reported that men deducted their 'pocket money' (for cigarettes and alcohol) before handing over the rest of the money to their wives. But, what is important is that women still retained control over the rest of the money. Naxi women said that they needed to maintain this control, for men tended to spend the family money on non-essentials. The fact that men now earned the main cash income of the family made it easy for them to claim a part as their legitimate 'pocket money', but this does not seem to have overturned the existing control of women over the family income. At the same time, men remained 'heads' of the family, a function reinforced by the distribution of village income from logging (the village collection charges) to family heads and not to individual persons. Among the Lisu, where men have traditionally had control of the purse, the growth of logging only reinforced this role.

Women saw their role as having become more important, since they now had to perform some of the jobs that were formerly done by men. For instance, men were away during the crucial period when floods threatened the fields. The task of flood protection, then, had to be undertaken by women on their own. Further, logging led to an overall shortage of male labour in the area. A man and a woman, with the women leading the buffalo, now did the ploughing which was formerly done by teams of two men. Women reported that their confidence grew in taking up these new tasks.

While women reported that their confidence grew on taking up new tasks, this also meant an increase in women's already heavy burden of work. Among the Naxi, the route to economic prosperity is said to lie in acquiring a 'hard-working wife'. The increase in income did not lessen the women's burden. At the same time, men who often had little labour to perform, found themselves busy during the logging season. A traditional masculine task of cutting trees (and constructing houses) became the main source of cash income. This made the sharing of the labour burden between men and women somewhat more equal.

Logging provided an avenue for men to make a substantial contribution to the family cash income. Except for relatively small amounts spent on liquor and cigarettes (amounting to about 20 per cent of the money remaining after meeting food and board costs) the rest was handed over to the women to run the household. This was a big change from the traditional situation where men contributed relatively little to household cash.

But there was little change in the expectation from men and women and the socialization on the basis of accepted gender roles. Women still had the main responsibility of maintaining and sustaining the families. Particularly before marriage, young men were not expected to contribute to the family. Some young men who went to the towns to seek work did remit money home, or maintained younger siblings at school. But most young men did not contribute to their families; rather, they regularly asked for some money from their families, as mentioned by Naxi mothers in Xitoh Township. On the other hand, all young women who went to Lijiang or other towns to seek work, regularly remitted money to their families.

These expected gender roles that play such a strong role in socialization had their influence on children's continuation in school and higher education. Mosuo mothers stated that if they could not educate both children, they would decide on which child would continue education on the basis of grades. This seems like a very gender-neutral manner of deciding on the children's education. But given that boys and girls usually worked with the father or mother respectively in helping in household chores, and given that women's household chores were much more than those of men, it meant that girls had less time to devote to their studies or other forms of self-development, like play. Consequently, even on the basis of grades attained, boys invariably continue to study longer than girls do. The increased importance of men in cash earning activities and patrilocal marriage could only reinforce this bias in favour of boys' education.

Household Logging

While in Lijiang County, non-state forests remain collectively owned by the villages, in other parts of China forests have been allocated to households under the 'household responsibility system' introduced in the late 1970s and early 1980s. The following analysis is based on discussions in Tiantang Village in Suinin County, Hunan Province. In line with the allocation of agricultural land to households, forests were also similarly allocated. But households still needed to get timber-logging quotas from the forest bureaus. They had the right to manage and to get the income from authorized logging, but could not decide on the extent of logging.

The 'household responsibility system' in forests (as in agriculture) came after three decades of change in economic organization—the land reforms after Liberation, followed by the move to cooperatives, the organization of higher-level cooperatives in the Great Leap Forward, the later moves to communes, and the retreat from collectivization in the 'household responsibility system'. As one must expect, farmers were naturally suspicious of how long the new 'household responsibility system' and household rights would last. They responded by immediately cutting trees and harvesting timber on scales much higher than those authorized by the forest bureaus. This over-harvesting of timber, without any attention to sustainability, is not the result of the system of household allocation as such, but a consequence of uncertainty over the stability of the new policy. Such over-harvesting need not result if households are secure in their rights over their allotted forests. However, there could still be other factors leading to over-harvesting in a social sense. The sum of individual decisions might well lead to under-provision of environmental services.

Not all individuals in the village value the income from timber and environmental services in the same way. Those who have other sources of cash income, or whose livelihood is non-agricultural, value environmental services (e.g., the provision of water, or protection from floods) more; while those individuals without other sources of cash income might value the cash income from logging somewhat more. It is no accident that it was persons with other sources of income, like school teachers and village officials, who took the lead in pressing for the move from household to village collective forestry. The nego-tiation of such differences would involve local political processes.

There are some other problems in household forest management. The allocation of forests of differing qualities leads to equity prob-lems. Attempts to overcome such equity problems by allotting patches of different quality in different locations to each household increased the cost of managing diverse and far-flung locations. Further, the poorer households had problems in meeting transportation costs and in undertaking replanting.

The problems of household management were magnified where this was done in a strictly illegal manner. Where households did not actually have valid quotas for logging, overcoming the legal problems often meant that the income they got was not much more than the prevailing wage. In the Naxi village of Xitoh Township it was realized that the income from such household logging was in fact not more than the logging wages. But in the Western and Eastern Yi villages of Lashi Lake, Lijiang, Yunnan, where there was no logging or other such employment available, the logging income, even if no more than possible wages, was virtually the only available source of cash in-come.

Individual logging without individual ownership will certainly re-sult in 'competitive over-logging'. Each household will seek to imme-diately cut as much of the timber as possible, since what one household does not cut will be cut by another household. In the Naxi village of Xitoh Township when assurance that households would follow col-lective rules broke down, there was a very quick denudation of the village forest. Within a couple of months there was no forest left.

The Western and Eastern villages in Laoshe Township also prac-tised household logging in collective forests. If similar denudation did not result the reason lies in the difficult access; there is no road up to the villages. This makes it difficult to increase the scale of logging, in the way that was possible in the Naxi village of Xitoh Township,

EFFECTS OF THE LOGGING BAN

Following the disastrous floods of 1998 in central and southern China, the central government instituted a ban on all logging of 'natural forests' in the Upper Yangtze region. This ban had an immediate effect on both local governments and the people of the villages we had studied. The ban meant that the township governments, which from 1995 had been receiving all the taxes on timber, lost this source of revenue. The villages, which had been selling their collectively-owned timber, also lost this source of income. Both at the township and village levels there was a corresponding slowdown or even complete stoppage of development work. Forest bureaus also lost their main income. While the government paid employees' salaries, the forest bureaus had no funds with which to carry out fire or pest prevention measures.

As we saw above, wage income from logging, both on state- and collectively-owned forests, had become the main source of cash income, and even of overall income, in the upland villages. This wage income completely stopped. Households and villages that were formerly reasonably well off, experienced a sudden fall in income and consumption levels. This affected their ability to meet the cash expenses of bringing up their children. Agricultural production was also affected, as farmers were unable to buy as much fertilizer or plastic sheets as before.

During logging operations there was a big market for foodstuffs to feed the workers at the logging sites. This demand even drove prices in the logging areas higher than in the neighbouring towns. The fall in the demand from logging workers led to a fall in prices in the logging areas, which ceased to be higher than in neighbouring towns.

In order to meet the shortfalls in income, households were forced to adopt a number of coping strategies. One was to turn to other sources of cash income, which meant mining the existing natural resources even further. Mushroom collection increased, but coinciding with the overall deflation in China and exacerbated by the fall in Japanese demand for some varieties and the increase in local production, mushroom prices fell. In those upland villages (for example, in Xitoh and Laoshe Townships) men increased the sale of hunted animal skins. Goats too were sold to generate income to pay school fees, etc. Families also adopted measures to reduce consumption—men too reduced their consumption of alcohol and cigarettes. All this would have led to a withdrawal of some upland children from school; but some school teachers stepped in to contribute to the childrens' school expenses.

Besides gathering local forest products, the other option to earn cash was migration. Migration, however, is not an option for those who do not have relatives in the town, which means that non-Naxi minorities, like the Yi and Lisu, who were in fact more affected by the ban, were relatively less able to use this option. While young women went to work in restaurants and bars, it was not clear what jobs the young men were taking up in the towns. Further, while young men rarely seem to remit any money, young women do so regularly.

ENVIRONMENTAL SERVICES AND SUSTAINABILITY

The villages manage collective forests. Though the logging quota in collective forests too is set by the forest bureaus, the villages can decide on the distribution of the logging. The villages seem to decide on the distribution of logging taking two factors into consideration. First, they do not log in areas close to the village. The Lisu village, Xitoh Township, decided in 1994 that they would not carry out logging in a forest area of about 100 hectares, close to the village. This is the forest on which they relied for supplies of pine needles, which are used as bedding for animals and, when mixed with animal dung, becomes organic fertilizer for the fields. In other villages too, e.g., Western village in Laoshe Township, logging was not carried out near the village, because that was the area on which they relied for supplies of organic fertilizer.

In villages alongside the Yangtze river too farmers took steps to plant willow along the banks, both to prevent soil erosion and to create new agricultural land. Willow was not only useful in binding the soil but since its trunk was not very straight, it had little value as timber, which meant that it was less likely to be the target of illegal logging. Thus, an appreciation of the environmental services provided by trees, did inform tree management decisions of the villages.

The second factor was that villages did not undertake clear-felling, but only selective cutting. This again was on the understanding that deforestation resulting from clear-felling could cause flooding and soil erosion. This is in contrast to the state logging system, which was generally one of clear-felling.

One can see that logging was carried out in collective forests not with the single-minded concern of minimizing costs (as is likely to be the case in state forests), but with an eye to maintaining the supply of environmental services from the forests.

Further, the villagers also undertook various forms of labour in managing collective forests, which were not undertaken with the same intensity, or even not undertaken at all, in State forests. Labour in managing forests includes that involved in thinning, fire prevention and promoting regeneration. Particularly around the village, leaves and dry branches were regularly collected in order to prevent fires. Besides the guards and village officials who toured the forests at regular intervals, the herders keep a look out for fires, pest infestation and outsiders. The role of the herders seems quite crucial in this respect, since they are the ones who regularly cover most of the forest.

The quotas given to villages for logging from their collective forests were quite small. In the case of the Lisu village (Xitoh Township) the quota was not even 1 per cent of the village collective forest. With a 50-year regeneration cycle for pine and fir, this quota is quite easily sustainable, in terms of not reducing the extent of forest cover. Further, given that villages carried out selective rather than clear-cutting, the age composition of the forests would also not be uniform, as was the case in state forests with cost-minimizing clear-cutting.

Local Organizations in a Strong State

Policy, whether of the ownership of forests or agricultural land, is something decided centrally. But even in this situation there is considerable scope for 'localization' of policy. For instance, in China's 1978 reforms, along with agricultural land, forest land too was devolved upon households. But in virtually all of Lijiang County, where there were reasonably ethnically homogenous villages of indigenous peoples, the county government did not implement this policy. It was able to successfully argue that the traditions of the minority nationalities supported the collective management of forests. As a result almost all of Lijiang County away from the urban centres, retained collective ownership of village forests. There are considerable areas of collective forests in South China too. The status of state forests, of course, did not change in this reform process.

Another instance of localization of central policy directives is that of the response to the 1998 ban on logging in China. The ban was on logging in 'natural forests' but not on plantations. Local authorities promptly classified many forests as plantations. After this the central government then changed the order to apply to all forests, whether natural or planted.

There were instances, as in Suinin County, Hunan Province, where villages initially de-collectivized and then re-collectivized, after their negative experience in being unable to control the rate of logging. Going beyond forest villages there are the collective villages of Nanjie (Henan Province), Liuminying (Beijing) and Huaxi (Jiangsu Province) which all resisted various degrees of pressure from Beijing to fall in line with the central policy of the 'household responsibility system' (Nathan and Kelkar 1997). In all these cases of resistance to the central policy there was a degree of agreement between the cadre and the villages on the desirability of maintaining or re-establishing collective systems.

What such successful 'localization' of central policy required was a strong consensus in the villages on both goals and the institutions to achieve them. With this consensus the villages were able to subsequently establish norms, and sanctions for breaking norms, that enabled them to overcome 'free rider' problems, while providing incentives for work.

On the basis of consensus on goals and processes, there is also trust between cadres and the people. It is not that there is equality between all families. There are clear differences between some of the leading cadre families and the rest. But where there is inequality, this inequality is not so glaring. More important in maintaining trust is, perhaps, the fact that the poorest have also gained substantially. The poorest of the villagers have certainly gained a share of fairly comfortable living. But even the migrant workers, largely young women, have also shared in something more than they would have received in their villages of origin or even in other villages nearby.

Trust in the case of these collective Chinese villages is based on shared goals, consensus on processes, including norms and sanctions for breaking them, and, perhaps, most important of all, the fact that the poorest have shared substantially in the distribution of benefits. Meeting the Rawlsian condition of justice in development—that the poorest get a substantial share of the benefits—would seem to be a strong base for trust.

The concern of some cadres in seeing that the poorest got some cash income even led to cases where they knowingly overlooked violations of laws. No timber can be logged without a permit. But, in the upland villages of Lashe lake (near Lijiang Town), where the poorest Yi live, they did carry out some small-scale logging. The income from the sale of timber was their main source of cash income, with which they could pay school fees, etc. In a not uncommon complicity between cadre and villagers this illegal logging was allowed to continue, right until the time of the countrywide ban, when it became virtually impossible to transport any unauthorized timber.

Further, when fields of lakeshore villages (on the shores Lashi Lake, Lijiang) were flooded by the need to maintain high water levels for the bird sanctuary, local farmers refused to pay land revenues. The township administration did not press for these revenues, and was instead compensated by the county government for the loss. These forms of trust are necessary if local governments are to get the support of residents in undertaking development measures.

Thus, while decentralization of revenues helps local accumulation, it is likely to occur in ways that increasingly benefit the locally dominant community. This is part of the larger problem with decentralization. As Partha Dasgupta put it, the critical problem in decentralization is how to prevent the elite from monopolizing the benefits of it?

The poor will benefit from decentralization only to the extent that they mobilize and make their impression on the programmes and projects implemented. This itself is more likely in a situation where decisions are made locally, than where decisions are made in distant administrative centres. But wherever the decisions are made, the constituency of the poor will have to make its voice heard for pro-poor policies and projects to be adopted.

This too is more likely where decentralization is accompanied by democratization. Local democracy, particularly at the village level, need not be of the restricted representative type, where the role of the citizens is limited to periodic voting. Direct democracy can be used to take decisions, with implementation left to elected committees. Where the numbers of the poor are large and where they are well-organized, such downward accountability will make it increasingly possible for the poor to set their impress on local policies.

A measure of downward accountability can exist even in the absence of formal democracy, as in the Chinese villages. Studies (Siu 1989; Oi 1989; and Nathan and Kelkar 1997) have shown that there is often a close relationship between the cadre who run the local administration locally and the people. The party–state apparatus is not monolithic in its economic operations. Farmers and others do express their grievances and resentments in various ways and the local party–state apparatus is often forced to take these into account. Needless to say, there are also many villages in which the local administration acts quite high-handedly and disregards the views and needs of the villagers, or where such differences result in serious conflicts. The conditions in which one or the other siutation obtains need to be investigated.

DEMOCRACY AND SELF-CORRECTION

A consensus in favour of a programme or project, however, is not all that is needed. In any development there are always unintended effects, both positive and negative. For instance, the positive effect of women's micro-credit groups on their familial and social standing was, perhaps, an unintended effect of the scheme to provide credit to assetless families. Similarly, there are also inevitably unintended negative effects of changes. The failure of privatization of forests to meet local needs of forest-based environmental services may be an unintended, though inevitable, negative effect of the development of privatization.

Taking account of unintended consequences, both negative and positive, means that any course of development will also require changes along the way. We simply do not know enough (perhaps, we could never know enough) to adequately predict all that will happen. Changes along the way will then be necessary. These changes depend not just on the leadership of the village and its far-sightedness but, more importantly, on the ability of those negatively (and positively) affected to articulate their problems and needs.

A system of political organization that does not allow for the articulation of these problems and needs will fail to induce the necessary changes. Democracy, in allowing all groups and persons to put forward their views and opinions, their needs and demands, comes in as a powerful instrument to enable any administration or organization to introduce mid-course changes. Whatever its other intrinsic merits, democracy also has an instrumental role in continually fashioning and refashioning local policy. Of course, such fashioning and refashioning of local policy is itself a political process, one that is facilitated by democracy.

DIRECTIONS

Devolution policy covers not only the granting of rights to local communities as communities, but also to local governments. When timber revenues accrue entirely to the provincial or central governments, what is subsequently spent on local development needs (infrastructure, education, health, etc.) depends entirely on how much the provincial or central governments allocate for local development needs. On the other hand, when local governments have by law a share of the revenue they will have a clear amount of money that they can spend for local development. This distinction can be particularly important where there is an ethnic divide between the higher-level and local governments, which is often the case, with the higher-level governments being more representative of the dominant ethnic community, and the local governments being more representative of the minority indigenous peoples. Even if the local governments do not always start out as representative of minority interests, they can be more susceptible to pressure or the articulation of felt needs by the local communities.

Our study of Lijiang shows that timber revenue, when accruing locally (in this case to the county) can also be an important source of local accumulation—the extensive tourist industry infrastructure in Lijiang has been largely built from timber revenues. That capital remains local instead of merging into the general pool of capital in China, means that the capital will be invested in the locally, higher profit-earning sectors—which may not necessarily attract as much capital on the basis of a nationwide comparison of profit rates. Of course, in the case of tourism in Lijiang the fact that even foreign capital is being attracted to invest in it, means that profit rates are sufficiently high even on a China-wide scale. But the importance of timber income remaining local capital (as in the case of Xitoh Township) is that this capital can be accumulated locally, contributing to the local enhancement of production and labour absorption. At the same time, it should also be noted that the easy availability of timber revenues can lead to simple reliance on these easily-available revenues, without any attempt to develop timber-based or other industries.

Wage income in logging, where the wage is higher than the costs of reproduction of labour, can be a significant contributor to higher household income. This income can be used to both directly increase the level of well-being (through improvements in housing, purchase of television sets and the like) and to increase production possibilities and productivity (through investment in fertilizers, increased livestock, expenditure on education, etc.). How the two will be combined depends on how permanent the logging wage is taken to be, and also on the existing possibilities of investing in household production.

Logging is a quintessentially masculine activity and the income from logging accrues directly to men. While it did allow the men some additional scope of indulging in cigarettes and alcohol, women, who among the Naxi have traditionally managed the cash, continued to do so. Nevertheless, the growth of a male-dominated external activity, points the way to the continued confinement of Naxi women to a domestic role.

Villages managed their own forests more intensively, putting in more labour in cleaning, fire protection, etc., than state forests. At the same time they were also more mindful of the environmental services provided by forests and carried out logging as far away from the village as was possible, and, therefore, with the least effect on the provision of these services to the village. Logging, when managed by the village, could be integrated into overall forest use.

Though the villages had some form of ownership rights over their forests and could retain a substantial portion of the income from logging, this did not lead to the villages advancing into the market for lumber (sawn timber). They remained confined to selling timber and did not set up saw mills or other forest-based enterprises. Such enterprises remained the prerogative of the county forest bureaus. This showed the limitations of village enterprise, to being passive sellers of timber, for cutting which they received quotas. It also meant that the labour they performed remained restricted to artisanal logging of timber and did not extend into processing timber, leave alone the manufacture of end products. There was no movement up the value chain.

This not only points to the limitations of their emergence as 'social protagonists', to the extent possible within the dictates of the market system, but could also be a weakness in the approach to sustainability. As extractors, sustainability is limited to the factor of continued extraction. But were forest-based enterprises to be established the stake of the village (or community) in sustainability would be increased, since it would now also involve all the jobs and income that the community earns from the industry. Vertical integration of timber-based processes from extraction to processing and even manufacture of end products seems likely to increase the stakes in sustainable harvesting of timber, while also enhancing the social role of the villagers as entrepreneurs, managers and skilled workers.

REFERENCES

Harkness, James. 'Recent Trends in Forestry and Conservation of Biodiversity in China.' *China Quarterly*, no. 156 (December 1998), London: School of Oriental and African Studies (SOAs).

Liu Dachang. 'Tenure and Management of Non-State Forests in China since 1950: A Historical Review'. *Environmental History* 6, no. 2 (April 2001).

Nathan, Dev and Govind Kelkar. 'Collective Villages in the Chinese Market.' in *Economic and Political Weekly*, 20 and 27 May 1997.

Oi, Jean C. *State and Peasant in Contemporary China: The Political Economy of Village Government*. Berkeley: University of California Press, 1989.

Sen, A. K. 'Isolation, Assurance and the Social Rate of Discount.' In *Resources, Values and Development*. New Delhi, Oxford University Press, 1984.

Siu, Helen. *Agents and Victims in South China, Accomplices in Rural Revolution*. New Haven and London: Yale University Press, 1989.

7

NORTHEAST INDIA

MARKET AND THE TRANSITION FROM COMMUNAL TO PRIVATE PROPERTY

Dev Nathan

At the time of India's Independence in 1947 most of Northeast India was only loosely held under the British Empire. Unlike the rest of India, the British did not lay direct claim to the forests of this region. Over the past half century the central government of India has tried to bring the Northeast under the same regulatory forest management framework as the rest of India. But the forest laws of the rest of India have limited applicability to this region.[1] In fact one of the keys to understanding the situation in Northeast India is to realize that there is a clear difference between so-called policy and the situation that prevails on the ground.

What is important about the Northeast is that the state, whether in the form of the all-India or provincial states does not own much of the forest land. Unlike in the rest of India, forests owned by the

---

[1] In the case of Nagaland, for example, which falls under Article 371A of the Indian Constitution, which provides that, 'Notwithstanding anything in this Constitution—(a) No Act of Parliament in respect of (i) religious and social practices of the Nagas, (ii) Naga customary law and procedure, (iii) administration of civil and criminal justice involving decisions according to Naga Customary law (iv) ownership and transfer of land and its resources, shall apply to the State of Nagaland...' Similar provisions of Article 371G apply to Mizoram. The rest of the hill areas of the Northeast come under the Sixth Schedule of the Constitution, with Autonomous District Councils (ADCs).

state range from just 8 per cent to about 40 per cent of forest area. Thus, whether it is the all-India or the provincial states and their respective forest departments, they do not have any significant area in which they can directly implement their policy. Forests are largely owned by communities, clans or families. Of course, the states do have many indirect instruments, like control over transit and trade, and the effect of these instruments will be considered subsequently.

We distinguish between the state, whether all-India or provincial, and the instruments of local self-government. The village level institutions are in most cases a continuation in modified and restricted (restricted in the sense of excluding women) democratic form of earlier village ruling systems. The Autonomous District Councils (ADCs), though recent creations, also have a clear genealogy that harks back to the earlier chieftainships and represent an attempted democratization of the supra-village institutions of the communities. These supra-village institutions claim to have ownership or management rights over forests in their respective areas, but, as will be seen below, in most cases it is actually the village and its constituent families that have ownership and management rights over the forests.

The devolution of forest rights from the supra-village and from the community or clan to the family level has largely come about through the pressures emanating from the development of a market, in particular the market for timber and Non-Timber Forest Products (NTFPs). For timber this takes the form of enclosing of commons by members of the community itself. For NTFPs this takes the form of moving more valuable plants to farms, and leaving the commons to unregulated exploitation by the poorer sections of the community.

TIMBER MARKETS AND DISSOLUTION OF COMMUNITY/CLAN OWNERSHIP

Among the Khasi the growth of the timber trade was the main factor behind the large-scale privatization of forests. There was private (lineage or family) ownership of agricultural land. Swidden plots reverted back to village commons, and there were large areas of uncultivated village land which remained as village commons. There were also lands between villages that remained directly under the chiefs (*syiems*).

Before the growth of the timber trade claiming more land than a family could cultivate (i.e., all of its swidden plots) made sense only if there were landless families who could be settled as tenants and pay a rent to the landowner. The numbers of the landless before the 1960s, from all accounts, was not substantial. Further, even now rents are quite low, for instance. Rs 50 (less than USD 1.3) per family per year in the villages of the West Khasi Hills. The rent is more a nominal acknowledgment of ownership than an economic factor as a share of total income.

The growth of the timber trade, however, led to a new form of forest use. Timber could be sold or trees could be used to make charcoal. The ability to use the forest for these new purposes was not restricted by the extent of family labour available, but more by the amount of capital that a family could command. Those with political influence and economic connections, the headmen and their families, could register vast areas of inter-village and uncultivated village land as their own private land. But those with less influence and connections could also claim some parts of the forest land. In villages where the non-headman families could assert themselves, where there existed a stronger community relationship, there was a more or less equal distribution of forest lands among the families.

The influence of the growth of the timber trade on the privatization of forests can be seen in other cases too, for example, among the Tangkhul Nagas. But the growth of the timber trade did not necessarily lead to privatization in all cases. There are examples among the Tangkhul Nagas of the village decided to allot equal rights on harvested trees to each family, without allotting them the land itself.

Another way in which the growth of the timber trade led to privatization was through the growth of plantations. Most of the communities here (as also, for instance, the Rungus of Sabah, Malaysia) have a long history of accepting the rights of those who planted them, and their descendants, over planted trees. This was initially the case with regard to fruit trees. But the development of a plot as a plantation was inhibited by the cost of fencing the plot, which was needed because of the system of grazing of animals in the wild after the main harvest. With the introduction of high value timber trees into the mix in a plot, plantations became more valuable and thus able to cover the costs of fencing. There are clearly economies of scale in this process. The cost of fencing as a proportion of total costs would fall with the size of the plantation. This again points to the importance of the command over capital, and thus of external connections to banks and the bureaucracy, in determining the ability to set up plantations. This is exemplified by the situation in Mizoram, where plantations hundreds of hectares in size have been set up by the urbanized political and bureaucratic elite.

The development of new forms of land-use—either through the sale of trees as timber, or through the planting of timber trees—both related to the growth of the timber trade, can explain the privatization of forests among the Khasi, Mizo and Tangkhul Naga.

IMPACTS

As a result of the privatization of forest ownership, in the Khasi Hills there is a large class of farmers who own forests. In two groups comprising 24 villages in all, more than 80 per cent of the 2,100 families owned some forest land. Of course the distribution of ownership of forests is quite unequal, with the families of the headmen (sirdars) owning large tracts, while many small farmers have patches with only a few trees, and many have no forest land at all. There are also villages with no or hardly any landowners. The farmers pay rent to the absentee owners; they only have rights to crops, which they grow on rented land, but they do not have any rights over the forests.

While the use of agricultural land is related to family size, that of forest land is not. Only the biggest owners of forests, the headmen (sirdars), have their own hammer marks. The rest of the farmers transport their timber under the hammer marks of the big owners, certainly paying them something for this. The smallest forest owners used to sell just a few trees a year. After harvesting these trees they would go off to work as wage labourers in logging organized by the big forest owners (Chakravarty 2000). Wage labourers earned about Rs 100–150 per day (USD 2.5–4), which was higher than other rural wages.

Besides the owners of forests, there are also the timber traders or contractors as they are called. These are not necessarily from among the bigger forest owners. Often they were persons who had learnt the tricks of timber trading by working as employees of timber contractors. Many of the timber traders also subsequently became sawmill owners. The timber traders often earned the most, after the sawmill owners (Chakravarty 2000). Some of them were landless or marginal forest owners, but they earned more than the forest owners.

The last category of persons involved in logging in Meghalaya are the sawmill owners, who usually possess some forests of their own (or rather, manage forests that belong to their wives). They also take leases on other forests and buy timber from the market. In discussions with a group of seven sawmill owners from Mairang, what emerged was that the sawmill owners treat their wives' forests differently from those that they take on lease. The leased forests are clear-felled by the end of the contract period. Since the duration of the leases are just a few years, the period is too short for any possible investment in growing trees to pay off. Consequently the leased forests are quickly degraded. On the other hand, forests owned by their wives are looked after relatively well with care taken not to cut immature trees, and to carry out replanting, along with organizing the labour for thinning and other management of the forests.

The sawmill owners in Meghalaya, based on the discussions with the seven owners, were all either village leaders before they became sawmill owners, or subsequently became village leaders. As is to be expected, they are the persons with external contacts, those able to raise some capital from the Meghalaya Industrial Development Corporation (MIDC) or borrow from other sources. Further, from the discussions and looking at the extent of the knowledge of sawmill operations they exhibited, it would seem that the small sawmill owners are also the managers of their mills, rather than functioning as proxy (*benami*) owners for outside, pan-Indian capitalists, the ubiquitous Marwaris. It is the big sawmills, located in the industrial estates that seem to be owned in proxy.

EFFECTS ON THE LOCAL ECONOMY

Sale of timber has become part of the household economy of these farm families. The income has been used to improve houses, buy consumer durables like television sets, and also to invest in education. Those who can afford it send their children to residential schools in Shillong, and the way of meeting these heavy expenditures is through the sale of timber. Rather than undertake improvements in agriculture, timber sale, itself, seemed to be viewed as a stable source of cash income. The agricultural changes—like the planting of fruit trees on other permanent uses of the uplands—that one witnesses in Meghalaya are in areas other than those which have a high participation in timber sales.

The reliance on timber for cash incomes has led to changes in the way timber is sold. Initially, most sales were by lease of the forest for a fixed period. This had the disadvantage of all fixed-term leases, in that it led to clear-felling at the end of the lease period, and also that there was no investment by the contractor (i.e., the logger, often a sawmill owner) in planting trees. But over time people seemed to have learnt the value of regeneration and the possibility of sustainably increasing income, and this is seen in the growing trend to logging organized by and timber sold by the forest owners. Such owner-sellers were mindful of the necessity of regeneration. They had also begun undertaking management efforts to maximize the growth of Khasi pine, not through planting but through selective regeneration.

Methods of harvesting have also changed to become more sustainable. For instance, in the group of nine villages around Kymrod in the West Khasi Hills, the various village assemblies of men (*durbars*) passed a rule forbidding the lease of forest land to contractors, thus allowing only owner-managed cutting and sale. Some villages have regulations restricting burning (undertaken to increase pasture growth), careless cutting and slashing of undergrowth. But even where there is no such village rule regulating logging, there is still a growing trend towards owner-managed logging as against leasing to contractors.

In Nagaland in particular the timber boom of the 1990s led to the growing of timber trees on private plots all over the state. But in Mizoram where most village land is still commonly held, tree plantation has been taken up by settling common lands that are claimed by the state. This has resulted in large plantations of hundreds of hectares, set up by those with political and bureaucratic connections, who can raise the necessary capital.

The investment of labour and other resources in increasing timber growth is more visible in the fully private plots. On the other hand, in village-owned forests of the Nagas in Manipur, where timber income was distributed among families, but land remained collective, there is no investment of labour or other resources in increasing tree productivity.

PROBLEMS WITH HOUSEHOLD LOGGING

There could be a recurring tendency to over-harvesting, in a local, social sense, in individual logging. The income from timber accrues to the individual. But the individual bears only a small part of the effects of logging in terms of environmental services that are foregone. The individual would, for instance, bear only a small part of the negative effect of over-harvesting on agricultural productivity. The sum of all individual decisions at the village level will then, result in a provision of environmental services lower than each individual would prefer. This is the 'irrationality' of individual market decisions, which A. K. Sen (1984) analyzes in the 'isolation paradox', leading in the case he analyzes to under-saving, and in this case to under-provision of environmental services. The only way a group of individuals can overcome this irrationality is by agreeing to a collective decision to decide on the extent of logging, or to state it in other terms, on the extent of provision of environmental services by setting aside areas that are not to be logged.

In Meghalaya there is a neglect of local environmental services as a result of household logging decisions. Important watershed areas, for instance, are not protected from logging.

There are additional problems of sustainability arising from rural–urban migration and the fragility of marriage, combined with men's lack of responsibility for children. The upper classes of the villages, who are the families with larger forest holdings, are also the ones who invest in urban areas, and whose families tend to migrate to the cities. At one level this transfer of rural surpluses to urban investment since it remains within the same ethnic political unit, is not a loss to the local economy. But at another level such transfer of timber income can also mean that the families involved in such migration may not be as concerned about the long-term sustainability of forest income.

In the Khasi family system, children belong to the mother's clan and are her responsibility. At the same time, marriage tends to be fragile (Mukhim 2000). While married to a woman the husband can take charge of timber operations. The fragility of marriage again means that he would not be so concerned about sustainability of the timber income, and may instead try to maximize his short-term income. Along with this the legalization of the notion of 'self-acquired' as against ancestral property makes it possible for men to accumulate and bequeath property as they wish.

These two factors exacerbate the problem of sustainability of timber income in household logging. In economic terms the discount rate on future earnings is increased, leading to logging beyond possible rates of regeneration.

BAMBOO

Bamboo occurs in Northeast India in either of two ways. One, as swidden fallow vegetation, where the swidden cycle is about six to eight years. Second, it is grown in home gardens and other similar privately-owned locations. Bamboo as a fallow vegetation is widespread in the Garo Hills, dominant in the North Cachar (NC) Hills of Assam and in Mizoram, and also in a group of villages around Khatarshnong (East Khasi Hills). Special varieties of bamboo as a cultivated crop exist in home gardens all over the region, but also in fields in some parts of the Ri Bhoi District.

Where bamboo is widespread as fallow vegetation there are still a number of systems of harvesting, each with different implications on the quality of the product. In the NC Hills the ADC claims the fallow vegetation bamboo as its own (in the name of Unclassed State Forests) and leases it to private companies for harvesting. What the local people, who as they point out manage the whole vegetation system, get is only the wages for cutting bamboo, along with some small amounts paid to the headmen of the respective villages, an amount which the headmen may or may not share with the rest of the villagers. Not only is the impact on livelihood low (being restricted to the wages that cutters earn) but there is also the tendency to over-harvest, for instance, particularly when the current lease is coming to a close. Further, the external company, only concerned with minimizing its cost of harvesting, also carries out bamboo cutting in areas that are otherwise prohibited—like the 50 metres on either side of the road, that are not supposed to be harvested, but which when harvested are a low cost option, involving minimal transport costs. Any ecological damage due to such harvesting along the roadside, in terms of formation of ridges or other soil erosion effects, are borne by the local people and do not figure in the calculations of the extracting company. Such leases are the most destructive form of extraction, as has also been seen in the case of timber.

In the Garo Hills, on the other hand, the villages have clearly defined ownership rights over the fallows and all vegetation within the village (or *akhing*) land. There are one or two examples of villages leasing out extraction rights to external companies, as in the village of Rengmin Rongbretgre in the West Garo Hills. As one would expect, this led to extraction of even immature, one-year old bamboos. After some years of such leasing to contractors, there is no longer sufficient bamboo to be attractive to a contractor. The village no longer has a rule to regulate extraction of bamboo. Anyone from the village can cut bamboo from anywhere on the village common lands, but there is not much bamboo left. While people got a higher per piece income by selling the bamboo and not just working on piece-rate wages, the bamboo available is just a year-old. If this bamboo were left in the ground, the price realization would increase. But in an unregulated commons situation, competition to harvest ensures that this does not occur.

In most of the other villages investigated in the West and East Garo Hills, plots are allocated to families for cutting bamboo. At times they are the same as their *jhum* plots. Such allocation of plots for cutting has the beneficial effect of immature bamboo not being harvested. It is only before the plot is again cultivated that even young bamboo are cut. Discussion with the villagers revealed that even after regularly harvesting bamboo there is still vegetation, including bamboo, for *jhum* cultivation and this cutting of bamboo has not had any effect on *jhum* productivity. In the NC Hills too it was said that harvesting of bamboo has not reduced *jhum* productivity.

But all the villages reported a fall in the availability of bamboo. In no village was there any report of discussions of what to do about the falling availability. In fact, when bamboo availability goes down what seems to happen is that the system of regulated commons, with plots for harvesting allocated to families, falls apart and there is then unregulated cutting of bamboo. It is likely that with a smaller amount of bamboo available, it is not worth the villagers' while to regulate the cutting of bamboo. More time has to be spent in cutting bamboo, since the density of clumps goes down. Only the poorer families in the villages continue to carry on cutting bamboo.

In contrast with the lack of replanting and the falling availability of common bamboo, is the situation of the more expensive varieties of bamboo. They are planted and tended in home gardens. Most often they are meant for the family's own use, but some are also sold. In the area near the Shillong airbase such varieties are cultivated not only in home gardens but also in fields.

Such movement of NTFPs into private lands is seen in some other cases—bay leaves (*tej patta*) and broom grass being the most prominent examples. Why is there this move towards privatization of production of higher value NTFPs, including highly priced bamboo, bay leaves and broom grass? This is part of a trend towards domestication/cultivation of those NTFPs for which there is higher market demand.

NTFPs: Problems of Unregulated Commons

Where the forests are privatized, as among the Khasi and Naga, what is privatized is the right to trees and to transform forests into agricultural land. The collection of NTFPs is not similarly privatized. What is wild, i.e., not planted, can be collected by anyone belonging to the relevant community, clan or village. The exceptions are some communities like the Gallong of Arunachal Pradesh, India, among whom the right to collect NTFPs or even hunt is restricted to the family that owns the particular plots on which the activity occurs.

Even with regard to what is planted, while local systems accept the right of the planter to the tree and its produce, though usually not to the land on which it is planted, the rights to the produce in particular have to be established through presence. Absentee planters would find it very difficult to have their rights to the produce of planted trees accepted by the community. The tree itself may not be cut down, but it would be harvested for its products.

Most communities also had rules or informal norms about the time when harvesting was to be carried out. Hunting was governed by regulations regarding the seasons in which it was allowed, taking into account the reproductive requirements of the animals concerned. The hunting of some animals was completely forbidden. For instance, in Arunachal Pradesh hunting the tiger or leopard was prohibited. Anyone found hunting these animals, even if it was a case of accidental trapping, had to undergo various forms of penance, which were both onerous (including ostracism for a long period of time) and expensive.

These rules of access and harvesting developed in a system of collection for self-consumption. Many community rules, as in Northeast India, also specify that any collection for sale is not allowed, or requires the prior permission of the clan or village. The harvesting of timber was allowed only for house construction, and even that often required prior permission from the clan or village.

At the low levels of harvesting characteristic of production for self-consumption, these access rules did not lead to any problems. Rates of extraction were possibly much below rates of regeneration. But it should be pointed out that it was not always so. In certain cases rates of collection often exceeded rates of regeneration. When this led to a serious decline in the availability of wild (i.e., uncultivated) products, the result was migration. In fact, one theory of migration of swidden communities attributes it to a decline in the availability of wild foods and products, rather than the depletion of agricultural fertility.

Two important factors intervene to upset this scenario, a large market and accessibility through road construction. The introduction of new technology was not so much in collection as in transport, linked to access. With these developments the collection and sale of NTFPs became one of the main, if not the only, source of cash with which to buy locally non-produced goods, whether cloth, implements, education or new forms of entertainment.

In region after region the story after the introduction of large-scale commerce is the same—the rapid or slow decrease in availability of the product and often its disappearance. A study of NTFPs in Northeast India points out,

> Many NTFP species, viz., Podophylum hexadrum, Coptis teeta, Aconitum sp., Barberis sp., Pirochiza korrora, Panax pseudoginseng, Aquilaria agalocha are threatened due to over exploitation. According to a conservation assessment and management plan workshop of WWF, 11 species of medicinal plants of north east are critically endangered and 3 are vulnerable (Tiwari 2000).

In Madhya Pradesh, Rauwulfia serpentina (*sarfaganda*) has disappeared from the forests while the availability of *chiraita* is rapidly falling. In both cases methods of extraction are at fault. In the case of *Rauwulfia serpentina*, the demand is for the roots, and this has led to the uprooting of the shrubs. In the case of *chiraita* the market is for the whole shrub. The traders due to competition among themselves try to secure supplies in October–November, which is prior to the flowering season. Thus, harvesting is carried out before flowering, affecting regeneration.

There are two factors at work here. The first is the over-extraction of the NTFP. This occurs even if tradition actually forbids the collection of NTFPs for sale. But in the absence of other avenues for earning income, extraction and sale of NTFPs is the only viable source of income. Thus, the rules prohibiting the extraction of NTFPs for sale break down in the face of the dual pressure of external market demand and the internal need for a cash income.

The rule that does largely remain in effect is that of restricting access to those who are members of the relevant community, clan or village. But since there is no effective regulation of rates of harvesting, the usual effect of competitive over-harvesting easily comes into play.

The second factor is that if the harvesting of NTFPs is to be sustainable, some measure of investment of labour and other resources is needed. A study of NTFP harvesting in the Amazon and Borneo points out, '...almost any form of resource harvest produces an impact on the structure and functions of tropical plant populations. If nothing is done to mitigate these impacts, continued harvesting will deplete the resource' (Peters 1994: 40). This is so irrespective of the rate of harvesting, though the process is accelerated by destructive harvesting, of the type brought about by competition.

The author goes on to point out,

> There are ways to exploit the non-timber resources produced by tropical plant populations with a minimum of ecological damage. Doing so,

however, requires management.... Although quite a bit more involved than simply picking up fruit or tapping rubber trees, these management procedures will produce a sustainable form of resource utilization (Peters 1994: 45).

Is it likely that the needed investment in labour and other resources will be forthcoming in the existing systems of NTFP access and collection? Where the investment of labour and other resources will result in an income that does not necessarily accrue to the person or group undertaking the investment, is such investment likely? Here again the logic of individual decision-making comes into play. The income will be shared among all members of the community, while the investment in labour and other resources is undertaken by one person or family. This will inevitably restrict the possibility of investment to maintain sustainability.

Thus, we have two processes leading to the depletion of NTFPs on common properties, even if access to the resource is limited to defined village residents. The first is competitive over-harvesting and the second is the paucity of investment in sustaining the productivity of the resource.

One response of families and communities to the above problems has been to bring the trees into the home garden or into privately-owned orchards carved out of the commons. A study of Meghalaya (Northeast India) also showed that most NTFPs sold in the market came from gardens and not from the forests as such. With the disappearance or very restricted availability of medicinal herbs, in Bastar, Madhya Pradesh, India, too most of what is sold as NTFPs is actually produced in the home garden or swiddens, and not in the forest as such. Valuable trees, such as tamarind and *mahua*, are in the swiddens, home gardens, orchards or otherwise within the settlements. What this shows is that with commercialization there is a clear tendency for common property systems to be privatized. As a review of worldwide NTFP studies points out, 'If any further generalization is possible, it is that the increased commercialization of NTFPs is likely to lead to a breakdown of common property systems and a trend towards individual private property' (Neumann and Hirsch 2000: 43).

The process of privatizing and domesticating an NTFP depends on the return from the NTFP. As one would expect, those NTFPs which yield a higher return are domesticated, while those with lower, including uncertain, returns are not domesticated. In this process there is a difference between regions depending on the trading system, which affects the returns from a particular product.

For instance, the trade in hill broom is free in the Khasi Hills but monopsonistic in the Garo Hills, both of which are in Meghalaya. With a higher return from the production of hill broom, it has become a regular field crop in the Khasi Hills, while it continues to grow and be collected from the wild in the Garo Hills. Similar is the case of some spices, like bay leaves (*tej patta*), which are grown along with broom grass in the Khasi Hills, but remain in the wild in the Garo Hills. In both these cases, of hill broom and bay leaves, the availability in the wild is declining in the Garo Hills, but its domestication has been retarded by the poor returns.

Other studies of NTFPs (Homma 1996; and Olsen in Neumann and Hirsch 2000) also conclude that 'if returns from collection of a species remain competitive over a period of time and availability decreases significantly the species is subjected to domestication and/or cultivation' (Olsen in Neumann and Hirsch 2000: 57). Through this process of domestication, the supply of the product can be increased and possibly at a lower cost. Such domestication may also mean conservation of natural resources by reducing pressure on stocks and any remaining primary forests (Homma 1996: 72 and 77).

Domestication and/or cultivation of NTFPs has ecological consequences on biodiversity, since it results in high population densities of the desired NTFP species and low biodiversity, an ecological condition which is conducive to larger-size, commercial harvesting. How to combine this dynamic with the public need for biodiversity is an ecological issue that needs to be investigated and addressed.

But what needs to be noted is that the ecological consequences are not just a function of the type of product but also, and even more importantly, that of the type of production and management system. NTFP cultivation by corporations would not have the same concerns and thus ecological consequences as NTFP, or for that matter, timber management by smallholders.

Corporate management of forests is oriented toward the intensive production of one or a very few species. Smallholders, as an analysis of Peruvian Amazon and Indonesian Borneo smallholders points out, may also run specialized operations. But,

> Among smallholders such specialisation does not, however, tend to result in quite the same single-species stands and single-purpose utilisation that characterises many industrial operations. Even the most timber-oriented of village specialists in the Peruvian Amazon, for instance, uses his or her managed forests for hunting, fishing, honey

production, and the collection of medicinal plants, ornamentals, fruits and firewood (Padoch and Pinedo-Vasquez 1996: 106).

The authors point to the difference in management approach between industrial corporations and smallholders, species exclusion in the first case and individual exclusion in the second. 'By managing individuals rather than species or life forms smallholders often maintain high plant diversity in their managed forests. Because of the richness of species composition, the structure of forests managed by smallholders is often very similar to that of natural forests' (Padoch and Pinedo-Vasquez 1996: 107).

This only reinforces the point that while NTFP processing may be partly industrialized, their cultivation should continue to be organized by smallholders. This has both positive welfare effects for the families concerned and can result in a less negative impact on biodiversity.

We should revert to the main point of this section—the failure of traditional management systems of NTFPs to cope with problems of regeneration and of maintaining the sustainability of the output. A change in the rules governing rates of harvesting is clearly needed, as also a system of incentives to allow for investment in enrichment planting and other forms of management to improve regeneration. The first can be done by marking trees to be harvested (or, not harvested as the case may be), or by specifying the block within which harvesting will be carried out in any period. These are the rules, as suggested in Peters (1994: 42). But more important than rules is the type of institution that can implement them.

In unregulated commons, where 'first come, first collect' rules operate, there is a strong incentive to harvest immature products before a competitor can do the same. The spontaneous solution of privatization, which would improve and maintain quality, has been mentioned above. But privatization works against those who do not have any land or who have less land. For instance, in Bastar, Madhya Pradesh, India and in Jharkhand, India too, access to common forests is important for the poorest, particularly for single women, widows or divorced women. Privatization is inevitably inequitable.

The other attempted solution, as in various Joint Forest Management (JFM) experiments in India, is to institute village-level controls over access to NTFPs. But with varying levels of dependence on forest products this is difficult to implement and also leads to inequity. The better off sections and those relying less on forest resources for income, very easily decide to set aside areas of forest for regeneration.

As pointed out by Madhu Sarin (1996) with regard to women who collect fuelwood for sale, such restrictions go against the poorest, usually single women.

A more viable solution to the problem might be to organize at the level of producer or user groups. Given that there are many alternate uses of forest resources, and many different types of users, this would not be easy to implement. But it has been tried out in two types of cases. The first, which is quite frequent in China, is the lease of the land to the highest bidder for developing orchards, with the condition that it cannot be used for agriculture. With this privatization of formerly common land, investment and regeneration can follow. But the poor are left out of this process of enclosure of the commons.

Another approach is to lease the degraded forest land, not to the highest bidder, but to the poorest sections of the village, those who depend on common lands more than others in the village. This has been tried out in at least one case, the International Fund for Agricultural Development (IFAD) project of 'Leasehold Forestry' in Nepal (Nathan and Shrestha, this volume).

Is it contrary to the nature of indigenous social organizations to suggest that investment activities be undertaken on a largely private nature? As pointed out earlier, indigenous social organizations have included elements of both communal and private property. It is possible, at least in theory, that the collective systems of managing labour could be developed or adapted. But the evolution over the past few decades, however, has been in the direction of strengthening the elements of private property, though in such a laissez faire manner that the more powerful have gained more.

DECLINE OF RECIPROCITY AND THE RISE OF CLASS-DIFFERENTIATION

A major factor that inhibited the rise of economic class-differentiation in Northeast India was the existence of forms of reciprocity that used up surpluses that occurred. Obligations to fellow clan families were not balanced. On the contrary, those who had more were obliged to provide more. Further social prestige was linked not to accumulation (as it now largely is) but to the extent to which a family provided for others.

One of the major forms of this unbalanced reciprocity was the famous 'feasting' or 'potlatch' of the Nagas. The families of the 'big men', the chiefs, village headmen and clan leaders engaged in not just feasting but competitive feasting. Social prestige depended on the lavishness of the feast. Such competitive feasting quickly liquidated any surpluses in the hands of the political elite.

The spread of Christianity marked the decline of feasting. In order to establish their own spiritual communion the Christian missionaries attacked feasting as a pagan practice. In a sense the Protestant (perhaps not just Protestant but more broadly Christian in the context of this transformation in the Northeast) ethic of hard work and saving replaced the earlier ethic of warfare and feasting. Christianity was then an important factor in the rise of accumulation and thus of class-differentiation in the Northeast.

Another factor of social relations that inhibited private accumulation was that of the belief about how families become rich. They were supposed to have acquired their riches through service to the serpent or other evil spirits. The jealousy and fear of such families was also translated into forms of social stigma, like that of being denounced as worshippers of the serpent spirit (u thlen) among the Khasi (Nongbri 2002: 4).

Such social action and stigma of accumulation have been considerably reduced in the contemporary situation. The growth of urban centres has allowed these well-to-do families a less cloistered atmosphere in which the effects of social stigma are not felt as much as they were in the village situation. At the same time, in tune with the rest, moneymaking has itself become respectable and the means don't matter very much. In Meghalaya, for instance, the sudden and large volume of central government spending on refugees from Bangladesh in 1971 was the first occasion for primary accumulation through looting of the public exchequer. Since then this has become acceptable, as it is in other parts of India too.

A second factor in reciprocity was labour obligations toward the community and the needy. For cutting a rice terrace, which could only be done by a better off family, the landowner had to provide a feast for all those who came to labour. This could have cost just as much as employing wage labour. But for a family that was sick and unable to carry out its agricultural operations, there were still obligations to help, even if the family could not provide any food, let alone a feast. In some communities (like the Apatani of Arunachal Pradesh) house building is still a communal activity. Those families who do not send a representative for the work have to pay a fine. Such reciprocity is unbalanced, since it benefits those who are needy. It is the traditional system of a clan- or village-based social safety net.

These safety nets are also changing. In particular, the extent of contribution is now limited to a certain equal amount, not depending on the capacity of the family. The Tangkhul Naga clans now collect an annual amount from each family. This is fixed per family and does not depend on family income or family size (which would also tend to vary with income). In Toloi village of Ukhrul district in Manipur, some of the clans use this annual collection to subsidize the shift from thatched to corrugated iron roofs. Of course it is the poorer families that would benefit from this clan fund. On the other hand, some labour help is skewed the other way. On social occasions clan members usually help the family that has guests. They help in fetching water and cutting firewood. In this mutual help, it is the poorer families that would help the better off families more, since it is the latter who are more likely to have more guests and thus need more labour help from other clan members.

At a community level, families also contribute to their respective churches. The required contribution seems to be fixed, irrespective of income (10 per cent of cash income in a number of cases). Over and above this required payment to the church, families may make extra contributions, especially on the occasion of feasts. But the important thing is that the required contribution is fixed as a proportion of cash income. Such a fixed rate of taxation, as any student of taxation knows, is regressive. The effect on the well-being of the poor is greater and they might have to cut back on needed consumption to part with 10 per cent of their income as compared to the rich, to whom 10 per cent of income may make little difference.

Among the Dimasa Cachari of the North Cachar Hills, Assam, where the level of accumulation is also quite low, there is a regular system of exchanging labour in fieldwork. Besides clan members, even neighbours, help the sick or infirm with labour. While among the Khasi and the Tangkhul Naga of Ukhrul district, Manipur, help is restricted to cash contributions in times of extreme need and some support during illnesses, there is a greater extent of cooperative labour among the Dimasa.

Among the Mizo, the old institutions of reciprocity have been replaced by modern ones of services provided free by the Young Mizo Association (YMA). This institution of which virtually all youth (and many who are no longer youth) are members, bears a similarity to the old youth dormitory, which among the warlike communities (like the Mizo and Naga) used to be village watchguards. Now the YMA helps with various social tasks, like carrying the sick to the road so that they can avail of transport to reach medical facilities, arranging funerals, and so on.

The changes in the systems of reciprocity have: (*a*) eliminated the disposal of surpluses through feasting, whether for prestige or forced redistribution; (*b*) reduced the unequal contributions of different families to the pools of socialized labour and resources; and (*c*) replaced labour with cash contributions reducing the onerousness of contributions for the better off. Thus, internal relations of exchange, of surpluses and labour, have been changed and no longer inhibit individual accumulation.

At the same time, while clan solidarity helps in times of extreme or sudden need, for example, in cases of serious illness, it cannot deal with problems of endemic lack of resources and income. The system of inheritance, for instance, among the Tangkhul Nagas (other Nagas too) is biased towards primogeniture. The oldest son receives most of the family land, while the younger sons may receive very little or even nothing at all. While this too helps accumulation by reducing partition of property, it also increases the scope for creating landlessness. Families of younger sons among the Naga, or older daughters among the Khasi, may end up being landless or near landless. And for those with little land, the limited alienability of land makes it possible for their lands to be bought by the better off persons in their clans or communities.

In this process of class-differentiation, the privatization of forests means that all livelihood resources become privatized. Membership of a community alone is no longer sufficient to ensure access to livelihood resources. Where class-differentiation has developed the most, among the Khasi, there are whole villages (e.g., near Riangdoh or Mawterang in the West Khasi Hills District) of rent-paying tenant farmers. One or two families own all the land in these villages. The cultivating families pay rent for the use of agricultural land. But they do not have any rights to the forests, particularly to timber. During the timber boom of the 1990s, until the Supreme Court order that imposed a logging ban, the men of these villages worked as labourers in logging. Tenant families do have the right to collect firewood and other NTFPs, which are basically for self-consumption, but timber harvesting is restricted to the landowners.

What this shows is that with privatization, membership of the community is separated from the right to livelihood. Even among the Dimasa Cachari or the Mizo a family cannot just go to any village and claim swidden cultivation rights. Shifting to a village other than the village to which a family belongs, requires the permission of the headman of the village, who has to consult the assembly of village male heads of families. But in the case of the Khasi it is not just permission that is required, the family has to pay the landowner rent to acquire the right to clear forest or bush for cultivation.

GENDER RELATIONS

Concomitant with, though not necessarily a consequence of, privatization and class-differentiation there have been a number of changes in gender relations. For example, among the Khasi, women's status has depended on their ownership of, and claims upon, ancestral property. But the registration of former community-owned forest as private lands does not constitute ancestral property. It comes under what is now called 'self-acquired' property, the right to inherit which the men were able to legislate on the basis of different principles. Where, however, forests were privatized by a village deciding to divide up its common forests, then the new property was also in the names of the women whose houses the lands were attached to.

More important than these formal changes have been the changes in management. Even in the traditional system, women's ancestral property was managed by an uncle or brother. The direct role of the maternal uncle or brother remained even after the men married into other clans, since marriages often took place within the same village. But more so it is husbands who are effectively managing land, including forest land. More than the land itself, it is capital that has become the key economic resource. And this capital as 'self-acquired' property is passed on from father to son. With the rise of the timber industry this has enabled men as husbands to take control of the family's economy. Women's ownership of land is no longer the determining feature of the Khasi property system, but has been reduced to a vestigial right which, however, does enable women to have a better position than if they had been completely propertyless.

Among landless families, who are tenants, women do not own even the houseplot. The main source of cash income was wages from logging, which was earned and controlled by men. In such landless Khasi families there was clear and very strong male-domination. When discussing the problems of men demanding money for liquor, women said that if they did not hand it over they would be beaten, and even thrown out of the house. Being thrown out of the house is something that a house-owning Khasi woman is not likely to be subjected to. Propertylessness has led to a strong form of male-domination among the landless Khasi, since the women do not even have claims to land or the house with which to bargain.

The Nagas have patrilineal communities, with women having no inheritance rights over property. But men have played a very minimal role in production. Men's social role was centred around war and fighting. Headhunting and bloody village feuds have disappeared, but in most Naga areas there is a continued insurgency against Indian rule. Men who remain in the villages, however, now have a lot of spare time. Other than in land preparation, men only play secondary and occasional roles in agriculture.

Besides agriculture the other main economic activity is the weaving of shawls. Such weaving by women is the main source of cash. In Ukhrul district of the Northeast Indian State of Manipur, there are numerous restrictions on the harvesting and sale of NTFPs. While there is no restriction on the extraction of NTFPs for self-consumption, sale outside the village is only permitted to monopoly traders, who secure their monopoly rights in periodic auctions. The low village gate prices of NTFPs resulting from the restrictions on sale has meant that the collection and sale of NTFPs is not a very lucrative occupation. Consequently the main source of cash income is the shawls woven by the Naga women.

Allied with women's important role in agricultural production, their sole role in the sale of agricultural commodities and their monopoly of cash earnings through shawl weaving resulted in them controlling the domestic economy of the Naga. This formed the basis of their position in Naga society, despite the warlike system of the Nagas.

The timber trade, which began mainly in the 1970s with the construction of roads for the Indian army, however, placed substantial amounts of cash in the hands of men. So much of this cash was spent on consumption of liquor that, all Naga regions have witnessed widespread women's movements for banning the sale of liquor. But, in one way or the other, the growth of the timber trade strengthened men's control over the domestic economy, which earlier had been almost the sole domain of women.

The more recent introduction of formalized village management of the economy, the setting aside of earlier fallow as village-reserved forests, and the associated flow of funds into the village through projects, like the IFAD-funded Northeast India Natural Resource Management Project, has also served to increase men's control over the domestic economy. Though their knowledge of the local economy is very limited, since they neither play much of a role in production nor in marketing of agricultural produce, their role as community managers enables them to exclude women from community level decision-making about natural resource management, including the management of forests.

But among the Nagas where men do not own any significant amount of property, when they are for instance only swiddeners with almost no, or very few, rice terraces, there, women's position seems comparatively stronger. The women tend to decide on family consumption and production matters on their own. On the other hand, among the better off families where property is important, there the women have less of a say in household economic matters. This is the opposite of the situation observed among the Khasi where propertyless women are far more at the mercy of their husbands.

The processing observed in the villages is still almost entirely manual. But it is likely that mechanization of the processing of bamboo or some other NTFP, will have to be introduced in order to both increase the volumes of material that can be supplied to the factories and in order to increase the labour-absorption and thus income earned by the farmers. Such mechanization, however, has usually displaced women. 'There is a general pattern of women being displaced by men when new labour-saving technologies for NTFP processing are introduced' (Neumann and Hirsch 2000: 33).

The above leads to three important requirements to strengthen women's position: enabling women to be the source of household funds in new economic ventures; women's equal participation in community-based schemes, for example, various projects that are increasingly becoming the norm for development funds to reach the village community; and women's access to new technologies, including mechanized or semi-mechanized processing of NTFPs.

COLLECTIVE ACTION INSTITUTIONS

Privatization of forest ownership does not mean the complete collapse of collective action institutions. Of course, even among the matrilineal Khasi, where land including forests is traditionally owned by women, the village institutions are all-male affairs. What is privatized is the economic operations of the household. Some villages do maintain sacred groves and village forests, which are used to maintain the church, support destitutes, etc. These sacred groves and village forests are both small, shrinking and deteriorating in quality. Further, in a number of cases, enclosure of the commons by the powerful was resisted by insisting on a division of the forests among all families. This occurred both in the Khasi Hills and among the Nagas in Manipur. Thus, though collective action was not able to change the direction of privatization, it was able to take some action to maintain forest quality for local environmental services and to reduce class-differentiation. Collective action, however, is not only a matter of maintaining or rebuilding collective institutions. It is also one of agreeing on new norms and rules, even if they are about private access and production.

References and Select Bibliography

Burling, Robbins. *Rengsanggri: Family and Keinship in a Garo Village*. Philadelphia: University of Pennsylvania Press, 1963. 2nd ed., Tura, Meghalaya, India: Tura Book Room, 1998.

Chakravarty, Sanat. 'Impact of Logging Ban in Khasi Hills.' Manuscript. Bangkok: Asian Institute of Technology (AIT), 2000.

Diegues, Antonio Carlos. 'Social Movements and the Remaking of the Commons in the Brazilian Amazon.' In *Privatizing Nature: Political Struggle for the Global Commons*, edited by Michael Goldman. London: Pluto Press in association with Transnational Institute, 1998.

Dutta, B. B. and M. N. Karna. *Land Relations in North East India*. New Delhi: People's Publishing House, 1987.

Government of Meghalaya. *Meghalaya Land and Revenue Manual*. Shillong, 1989.

———. *Meghalaya Land Transfer (Regulation) Act, 1978*. Shillong.

———. Report of the *Land Reforms Commission for the Khasi Hills*. Shillong, 1974.

Homma, A. K. O., 'Modernisation and Technological Dualism in the Extractive Economy in Amazonia.' In *Current Issues in Non-Timber Forest Products Research*, edited by M. Ruiz Perez and J. E. M. Arnold. Bogor: Centre for International Forestry Research (CIFOR), 1996.

Mukhim, Patricia. Gender Assessment of IFAD Project in West Khasi Hills. Manuscript, 2000.

Neumann, Roderick and Eric Hirsch. *Commercialisation of Non-Timber Forest Products: Review and Analysis of Research*. Bogor: CIFOR, 2000.

Nathan, Dev. 'Timber in Meghalaya.' *Economic and Political Weekly* 35, no. 5 (22–28 January 2000).

Nongbri, Tiplut. 'Effect of Logging Ban in North-east India: The Case of Meghalaya.' *Economic and Political Weekly* 36, no. 31 (3 August 2001).

———. Culture and Biodiversity: Myths, Legends and the Conservation of Nature in the Hills of North-east India. Manuscript, 2002.

Olsen, C. Smith. 1997. 'A Qualitative Assessment of the Sustainability of Non-Timber Forest Product Collection in Nepal.' In *Commercialisation of Non-Timber Forest Products: Review and Analysis of Research* by Roderick Neumann and Eric Hirsch. Bogor: CIFOR, 2000.

Padoch, Christine and Miguel Pinedo-Vasquez. 'Smallholder Forest Management: Looking Beyond Non-timber Forest Products.' In *Current Issues in Non-Timber Forest Products Research*, edited by M. Ruiz Perez and J. E. M. Arnold. Bogor: CIFOR, 1996.

Peters, Charles M. *Sustainable Harvest of Non-Timber Plant Resources in Tropical Moist Forest: An Ecological Primer*. Washington D.C.: Biodiversity Support Program, USAID, 1994.

Sarin, Madhu. 'Who is Gaining? Who Is Losing? Gender and Equity Concerns in Joint Forest Management.' Working paper by the Gender and Equity Sub-group, National Support Group for JFM, Society for Wasteland Development, New Delhi, 1996.

Saxena, N. C. *Rural Poverty in Meghalaya: It's Nature, Dimensions and Possible Options*. Rome: International Fund for Agricultural Development (IFAD), 2001.

Sen, A. K. 'Isolation, Assurance and the Social Rate of Discount'. In *Resources, Values and Development*, by A. K. Sen. New Delhi: Oxford University Press, 1984.

Tiwari, B. K. 'Non-Timber Forest Produce of North East India.' *Journal of Human Ecology* 10 (2000).

8

TOURISM AND FOREST MANAGEMENT AMONG THE HANI IN XISHUANGBANNA, CHINA

Pierre Walter

THE SETTING

In the centuries before the founding of the People's Republic of China in 1949, Xishuangbanna was ruled by Dai rulers in towns or fiefdoms (*meng*) occupying the lowland rice-growing valleys, while the vast mountain forests were the domain of Hani people and other migratory farming peoples practicing shifting cultivation. Much in the same way that the Dai paid allegiance to their nominal Chinese overlords, the Hani were historically under the authority of local Dai leaders, whose stilted wooden houses, settled villages and terraced rice fields they eventually came to emulate. In the early 1950s, the new Chinese people's government, under the twin policies of 'all nationalities being equal' and 'all land and forest belonging to the people', encouraged Hani people to move down from the highlands to work the wet, rice-growing valleys alongside the Dai, reinforcing a continuing Hani movement away from migratory, slash and burn agriculture and towards the more sedentary villages and agricultural practices of their Dai neighbours. Like many of the Hani villages now sharing lowland valleys with Dai villages, to the untrained eye, Manmo's Dai-style stilted wooden houses and irrigated paddy fields make it difficult to distinguish from a Dai village, and in fact it is mistaken as such by the thousands of Chinese tourists who visit the village each year.

The location of the village is both idyllic and practical, sitting as it does atop a small mountain ridge shaded by a wall of lush green forest in the rear, with easy access to village rice paddies terraced along the river banks below and to swidden fields across the river and along the main road. Cut out in great swaths from the thick tropical rain forest covering the facing mountain slope, these fields are cropped in rice, rubber, pineapple, corn, passion fruit and a multitude of other minor crops. Forested land (at about 600–1000 metres) in front of and behind the village, beyond that belonging to Manmo village, is state forest land in the Menglun National Protected Area, itself part of the larger Xishuangbanna National Nature Protected Area established in 1987.

Until about the early 1980s, the valley in which Manmo is located was heavily forested, with only a footpath following the Nanka River as it snaked its way through the mountains on its way to join the larger Lancang (Mekong) River downstream. Sightings of tigers, elephants, monkeys, wild boar, deer and other wild animals were common and gave some indication of the extent and biodiversity of the tropical forests in the local area at the time. However, in 1983–84, a new asphalt highway from Jinhong City to nearby Menglun Town and the Xishuangbanna Tropical Botanical Gardens was constructed, running only a couple hundred metres away from Manmo. This new road helped to launch a decade of rapid economic growth and development in the local area, giving Manmo easy access to markets and urban areas, and bringing the outside world into Manmo. Tourism, based on the natural beauty and cultural diversity of Xishuangbanna, is today by far the area's fastest growing industry (Berman 1998), and some 600,000 tourists now pass Manmo along the road to the Botanical Gardens each year.

The present study was conducted in June of 1999 to investigate the impact of forest devolution policies on local people's livelihood, forest conditions and gender relations.[1] Manmo Village was chosen because of its community ecotourism initiative, easy access to new markets and tourists, and the comparatively low presence of state forestry policy and regulation. In the context of state policy reforms, explosive growth in tourism and the 'frontier capitalism' prevailing in the region, what kind of local space has the community of Manmo been able to create in managing the forests? Further, what has been the impact of forestry devolution and the influx of mass tourism on Hani women's economic roles in particular? Finally, what prospects do these market

[1] My thanks to staff of the Xishuangbanna Tropical Botanical Gardens and Yunnan Academy of Social Sciences for facilitating field research for this study, and especially to Xu Youkai, Yu Xiaogang, Dev Nathan and Govind Kelkar.

changes have in balancing community livelihood and local forest preservation in the future?

FOREST CONDITIONS AND MANAGEMENT

Although the condition of much of Manmo's forest has deteriorated since the early 1980s, those areas of forest which have cultural, material and environmental value for villagers have remained relatively stable and will likely be the last to be degraded. These forests include the village community forest which encompasses Manmo Nature Reserve (the village's ecotourism initiative) and the environmental forest behind Manmo, which provides a wide range of environmental services to the village including shade, erosion control and shelter from winds. Both types of community forest also offer a host of material and economic benefits to villagers: *sharen* (a traditional Chinese medicinal root) is harvested for sale, Non-Timber Forest Products (NTFPs) are collected in these forests for both subsistence and sale, and income is generated by tourist visits. Sacred community forest is valued by villagers mostly for its cultural significance, but also because it provides numerous environmental services to the village and material benefits as well. Forest land managed by households outside the boundaries of the community forest, by contrast, shows the highest incidence of degradation, as individual households try to maximize income and minimize risk in a complex system of subsistence and cash cropping(described later in this chapter).

Forest land which is not in the swidden system managed by households, is collectively managed by the village. There are three types of collective village forest: (*a*) community forest; (*b*) environmental forest; and (*c*) sacred forest, each with traditional rules of access and use. Facing the village proper, Manmo's community forest is a large area of old growth forest on the slopes behind swiddens cut along the road. Currently this is 'surplus' forest land reserved for future generations and not now farmed by anyone in the village. It is by village custom closed to all logging and to cutting of swiddens, but open to gathering of NTFPs. However, some of the very large Toona trees (*chun shu*) in this forest have in fact been cut for coffins, following a Hani funeral tradition which requires a tree large enough to carve a coffin from a single block of wood. In addition, because the boundaries of community forest are not fixed with any certainty, household swiddens have begun to 'nibble' around the edges of this forest, which gradually diminishes in size by small 'bites' each year.

Manmo also counts as community forest the land that belongs to the Manmo Nature Reserve. Forest here consists largely of small and mid-sized trees, with the natural understory culled out to grow *sharen* along the streams. Although this is community forest land, since 1997, management of the reserve has been the responsibility of the single household which places the highest bid to the village. In return, they receive the right to collect income from tourists visiting the reserve. Partly as a result of this household management system, portions of the original reserve forest land have been converted to household swidden fields, which have slowly made their way in across reserve boundaries. What remains of forested land in the reserve is a substantial strip of thick vegetation and trees embracing its paths and streams and allowing visitors to feel they are still deep within the tropical forest. This strip of forest not only sustains ecotourism in the reserve, but also protects Manmo's water source, a stream-fed cistern located halfway into the reserve and connected to the village by a long metal supply pipe.

In addition to community forest, Manmo villagers recognize 'environmental forest' as a second type of village forest. Manmo's environmental forest is located on the steeply sloping mountainside behind the village. Village elders say they preserve this forest because it provides shade to the village, it is cool and beautiful, it shelters the village from strong winds and helps to protect paddy fields from soil erosion and collapse from flooding during the rainy season. With memories of the upheaval of the Cultural Revolution and the need at times to flee from violence or dislocation, elders also see this forest as a refuge for villagers should the need to hide arise again. *Sharen* is planted in the understory of this forest, and harvesting of NTFPs and timber for housing construction is also allowed.

Two kinds of sacred forest comprise the third type of collective village forest in Manmo. The first, is an area of 'holy forest' adjacent to the environmental forest. This forest houses the Manmo burial grounds. Here, cutting of trees is expressly forbidden by tradition, and in fact the common belief is that even visiting the forest will disturb its spirits. As such, Manmo villagers enter the holy forest only for burial ceremonies, which may occur only once every two or three years. The forest's location above village rice paddies also gives it the function of preventing erosion and controlling floods, although this is not the primary reason why villagers preserve it. The second kind of sacred forest in Manmo is 'spirit forest' located in a patch of woods occupying a bend in the river just upstream from the village. Within this stand of tall trees sits a salt water spring, thought to harbour a spirit which can cure illnesses, particularly leg injuries and numbness associated with old age. In this spirit forest, it is permissible to gather plants and other NTFPs and to hunt animals attracted by the salt, but the cutting of trees is forbidden. Large ficus trees in other locations, such as the one near the village entrance, are also thought to harbour spirits and therefore they too are not felled.

ECOTOURISM AND THE COMMUNITY NATURE RESERVE

Faced with loss of legal access to state forest reserve land in the early 1990s, Manmo villagers initiated a local alternative to government management of state forest reserve; namely, the Manmo Nature Reserve. This experiment in ecotourism would allow Manmo to balance conservation with sustainable use of the forest, provide a source of subsistence and economic livelihood for the villagers, and help preserve traditional Hani customs and culture. The rapid expansion of the local tourist trade since the early 1990s would supply visitors to the nature reserve, located on one side of the road, and to the Manmo Hani Ethnic Eco-tourism Area of Tropical Rainforest on the other.

In 1991, with the help of nearby Xishuangbanna Tropical Botanical Gardens (hereafter Botanical Gardens), Manmo village negotiated a 15-year agreement with the Jinhong County government in which Manmo village would manage a portion of the state-owned reserve in exchange for preserving the forest within it. The reserve lands were part of traditional collective village forests which Manmo villagers used to grow *sharen*, pasture water buffalo, and harvest NTFPs and wood for housing construction. As noted above, the reserve embraced the stream which was the source of Manmo's water supply and a large area of old growth tropical forest culled for *sharen* cultivation along the stream. Several interestingly shaped ficus trees and an area of cascading waterfalls further enhanced its attractiveness to tourists. The location of the reserve right along the main road and only 14 kilometres from the Botanical Gardens, the major tourist destination in the region, added to the reserve's potential for the development of ecotourism.

With fairly long-term land rights secured for village management of the reserve, in the early 1990s, the village and the Botanical Gardens, with financial support from a foundation in the USA and a Yuan 30,000 grant from the Jinhong County government, built modest tourist infrastructure for the reserve. This included a guesthouse fronting the road, a stone path along the stream, bridges, a shelter inside the forest and interpretive signs identifying various interesting trees and plants. Tourist brochures were printed and distributed to local tour agencies. These featured a location map, a short description of the reserve, and enticing photographs of the reserve and of young Hani women in traditional attire. A large display map of the nature reserve and its main attractions was set up at the entrance and a placard-style sign advertising the reserve and the Hani ethnic village was positioned along the road.

Initially, from 1991–94, two villagers, at a monthly salary of Yuan 200 per month each, were hired by the Botanical Gardens to manage and develop the reserve. By late 1994, entrance fees of Yuan 2 per person collected from tourists visiting the reserve were sufficient not only to cover salaries (now raised to Yuan 250 per month), but also to generate a surplus of about Yuan 10,000 a year for the village. This money helped to pay for electricity lines to Manmo, which were hooked into the electrical grid of the Botanical Gardens hydropower station.

In 1997, when the Botanical Gardens completed its involvement in Manmo's nature reserve, management of the reserve was trans-ferred by the village to the household level. Under this arrangement, any village household can bid for the right to manage the reserve. The family with the highest bid then has rights to keep income generated from entrance and guide fees, and fees for the guesthouse and meals supplied to tourists. In 1999, the winning bid was Yuan 15,000, and the total income from the reserve was approximately Yuan 50,000, allowing a net profit of about Yuan 35,000 to the family running the reserve. In effect, the village now manages the reserve as a kind of economic franchise restricted (for the time being) to Hani households able to afford franchise fees and provide the labour needed to run the reserve. Monies paid to the village by the family under this arrangement have most recently been spent on the pur-chase of a communal satellite television dish installed on the roof of the village school.

In some ways, the household franchise arrangement has weakened the community imperative to protect the forest in the reserve. For all families except the franchise owners, the reserve offers only a single yearly fixed sum returned to the village, to be shared out across the community. In some instances communal benefits of the reserve have accrued fairly evenly across households. This is true, for example, in the reserve's environmental function of protecting the village water supply, and in the generation of funds spent to supply electricity to the village. In other instances, like the purchase of a satellite dish, benefits mainly go to the wealthier households who can afford television sets, while the livelihood priorities of poorer families remain unaddressed. Poorer households may thus sensibly feel less restraint in harvesting timber and NTFPs from reserve lands, since they now stand less to gain in the preservation of the resources, and almost no chance at all of managing the franchise themselves in the future. At the same time, they have little hesitation marketing NTFPs and other goods to tourists attracted by the reserve.

The potential disincentives to protect forest resources in the Manmo reserve are, however, for the moment outweighed by the fact that villagers still perceive a surplus of easily accessible forest outside the reserve. This is in part because of the obvious presence of large areas of forest belonging to the Menglun Protected Area which surrounds the village. Although officially protected, villagers continue to use this forest for supplies of firewood, NTFPs and timber, as they have always done. Moreover, since geographical boundaries between village and state forest lands are imprecise, it is also fairly easy to justify cultivation of Protected Area lands on the basis that they belong to the village.

Because forests are still quite extensive in reserve areas near the village, it has become the practice to leave old growth forest along ridges and slopes most visible from the road, and to cut swiddens behind this facade. The forest in these 'buffer zones' near the village remains uncultivated only because of the close proximity of other forest lands which can be cultivated instead. Likewise, in Manmo Nature Reserve, the forest nearest the path is well-preserved in part to maintain its aesthetic value to tourists, while forest obscured from view is partially converted to swiddens. Notably, this aesthetic 'buffering' is also the practice of the Jinhong County government, which has reportedly planted trees along the road to enhance the image of a tropical forest for tourists passing by.

A new element related to the presence of adjacent state protected areas which will no doubt soon influence Manmo's forest management practices, and in particular the management and viability of the Manmo Nature Reserve, is the state-managed ecotourism reserve just 4 kilometres away from Manmo along the road to the Botanical Gardens. Managed by the Menglun National Protected Area Station (one of five such stations in the Xishuangbanna National Protected Area), this attraction will be an ecotourism initiative on a scale unmatched by Manmo, and will compete for tourists who might otherwise have supported Manmo's reserve. Thus, state-sponsored ecotourism might well undermine Manmo's community franchise very quickly. Ironically, national tourism policy, and the promotion of Xishuangbanna and the Botanical Gardens as tourist destinations in particular (the Botanical Gardens were officially recognized as a 'national tourist site' in 1991), which allowed space for the success of Manmo's ecotourism initiative in the first place, now contain the seeds of its destruction.

Table 8.1
Forestry Policy Changes and their Impact on Manmo

	Policy	Impact
1963– early 1970s	Promotion of rubber tree plantations;	• Large in-migration of Han Chinese labourers
	U.S. embargo on rubber; policy of self-reliance;	• Dai and Hani begin growing rubber
early 1980s	Devolution of forest lands; distribution to households	• More intensive cultivation of subsistence crops in multicropping systems; • conversion of rice swiddens to terracing and cultivation of rubber, passion fruit and pineapple as cash crops; • cutting of new swiddens; • expansion of irrigated paddy; • increased sales of NTFPs to tourists and others
1987	Establishment of Menglun Protected Area	• Manmo villagers negotiate establishment of Manmo Village Nature Reserve
1996	Ban on logging in Yunnan	• Little effect
1998	Ban on logging in upper reaches of Yangtze River;	• Increased cutting of and cultivation of rubber for timber;
	Hunting Ban	• villagers turn in old guns, switch to trapping
2000	Ban on the cutting of new swidden fields	• Increase in semi-permanent plantations in swidden fields; • cutting of new forest swiddens; • increases in harvesting of timber

ETHNOTOURISM AND THE 'PILFERING' OF CULTURE

Today, with tourist trade along the road expanding rapidly, a roadside store and a third building housing a karaoke lounge have been constructed across from the reserve guesthouse. On any given day, 30–40 mid-sized tour buses now stop in the parking lot here either to visit Manmo village or to tour the nature reserve or both. While the map of the reserve still stands as a rough guide to those visitors who would rather not hire a local guide, the sign announcing the 'Hani Ethnic Village' has been taken down and stowed away out of sight in the back of the karaoke lounge. In its place, young Han Chinese men can now be found along the roadside trying to flag down passing tour buses and convince them to visit Manmo—an attraction which they now present as a traditional Dai village.

The pretense of Manmo appearing as a Dai tourist village is not hard to accomplish with the cooperation of the several Manmo households involved in the arrangement: to tourists from Beijing, Shanghai or even Kunming, the houses, paddy fields, and people of Manmo in fact look and act quite like those in neighbouring Dai villages. The several hundred Han tourists rotating through the village on any given day may spend only half an hour in the village, which is only one brief stop among many on a busy tour itinerary. Thirty minutes is just long enough to be invited into an 'authentic Dai' house, be seated 'Dai-style' on the floor and served tea by an attractive young 'Dai' woman (who describes Dai life and culture in impeccable Chinese, she herself being Han Chinese or educated Hani), and asked to purchase some of silver bracelets and jewellery for which the Dai (but not Hani people) are popularly known. None the wiser, tour groups might also visit a small museum of traditional Dai tools and implements set up in one participating household, and make small purchases at their store. Here tourists are also invited to buy sweets and trinkets for village children in exchange for taking their photographs. Short-term visitors may also pay fees to visit the nature reserve and provide a ready market for various forest fruits and NTFPs collected and sold by women in the village, and mushrooms, medicinal products and other NTFPs stocked by the roadside store.

In this multilayered 'ethno-pilfering' scheme, just recently introduced by Han Chinese entrepreneurs from outside of Yunnan, both Han and Hani pretend to be Dai, adeptly adopting the cultural forms most likely to satisfy larger Han majority stereotypes of Dai nationality culture, while at the same time offering them the opportunity to purchase a piece of it. In fact, there is some surface truth to this misrepresentation of Hani culture as Dai, since Manmo villagers have widely borrowed Dai housing, agricultural and silvicultural technologies, and many, especially the young, no longer regularly wear Hani clothing, but have adopted Chinese mass-produced clothes, as have Dai youth. In this colonial ranking of ethnicities in Xishuangbanna, the Han nationality occupies the most 'civilized' top niche, Dai the middle 'younger brother' niche, and Hani and other slash and burn agriculturalists, the bottom or most 'primitive' niche. Thus, Hani pretending to be more 'civilized,' more 'culturally sophisticated' Dai can increase their cultural capital in the eyes of Han tourists and can then sell them high-priced Dai jewellery, jade carvings and other 'Dai' tourist goods. In contrast, when Manmo villagers earlier represented themselves as a 'Hani Ethnic Village,' they were tapping into the 'lower niche' stereotype of Hani as an 'exotic' and 'uncivilized' backdrop to ecotourism, with lower value cultural and symbolic capital to market to tourists. Complete with enticing images of young Hani women, and 'primitive' Hani tools and handicrafts, this first ethnotourism representation gave credence to false, but widely perpetuated notions of untouched cultures and forest, and of sexually available indigenous women, a common portrayal of indigenous peoples used in the region to market ethnotourism to outsiders (Pleumaron 1996).

As in Manmo, indigenous women and indigenous culture in other communities in Yunnan negotiating the booming ecotourism and ethnotourism trade have suffered. In an overview of the situation in Yunnan, Naxi ethnologist, Yang Fuquan (1995), warns of the deleterious cultural and environmental effects of the unchecked growth of mass ecotourism. He cites instances of ethno-pilfering of Dongba Naxi culture: where tourists illegally purchase cultural artifacts; the 'invasion of local culture' by foreign and Han cultures and lifestyles; and the commercialization and 'vulgarization' of local ethnic cultures, whereby, fake and shoddy artifacts and artworks are passed off to tourists, misrepresenting and degrading authentic cultures. Likewise, Yang writes of the eco-pilfering of indigenous ecological resources such as rare butterflies, seed plants and animals, and of scenic spots which tourists have heavily littered with garbage, including plastic bags which often choke and kill villagers' livestock, harming a major source of their livelihood. These may all be signs of the future for Manmo.

DEVOLUTION AND CHANGES IN WOMEN'S WORK

Beyond the commodification of culture and women in ethnotourism, the devolution of forest management to households, in privatizing production and providing increased income to families and to the village as a whole, has more generally begun to modify the traditional productive and reproductive roles of Manmo women. The development of village infrastructure, the movement of the agricultural system from subsistence farming toward cash cropping, and the tourist trade have all affected both the nature of the work women do and their bargaining power within households.

In the traditional subsistence economy, Manmo women's productive roles included work such as, planting and weeding of swidden fields, transplanting rice seedlings, weeding of paddy, threshing of rice, fetching water, collecting and hauling firewood, cooking, cleaning, feeding of poultry and pigs, spinning thread, weaving cloth, embroidering clothes, processing food, collecting supplementary food, medicine, fodder and other NTFPs, making handicrafts and tending of household gardens. Reproductive roles involved caring for children and disabled, ill and elderly relatives in addition to managing the household. In an earlier study in the village, Gu Fengwei (1995: 27–28), described the heavy burden of Manmo women's work as compared to men:

> The discrimination against women in the Hani nationality is very severe.... Men barely take part in [women's] activities [but] women help men to cut trees and burn fields, harvest millets, pick 'Sha Ren', dig ditches and build dams.... So long as there are women, men never cook and feed pigs. Men are more free than women. They seldom help women to weed.... Women are not worth mentioning in men's eyes. They usually say: 'Crab is not meat, women are not human beings.'

The burden of Manmo women's work has lessened in certain areas with the introduction of new technologies and market commodities in the village. Store-bought clothing has reduced women's labour in the production of cloth and clothing. Women still weave and embroider traditional Hani clothing, but it is worn only for special occasions like weddings and the Hani new year. The village system of metal water pipes delivering running water to each household has likewise eased women's labour in hauling water, bathing children and washing clothes, all of which are now conveniently done on the second floor balconies of most houses. The cultivation of fuelwood trees (*Cassia siamea Linn*), an indigenous Dai technology, has also made the collection of fuelwood more convenient, and household tractors have lessened women's labour in hauling wood and agricultural products home from the fields along the road. Large amounts of driftwood which wash up on the shores of the river in the rainy season are also a source of easily accessible fuelwood. One indication of the abundance of this driftwood is that after floods, neighbouring Dai farmers collect enough driftwood in two or three days to serve their fuelwood needs for the entire year, and even sell the surplus.

In the changes brought on by the market and the local influence of state policy, women's reproductive labour has been somewhat reduced. In part this is due to the simple fact of fewer children: family planning is common, and because households can earn more income, they need not have as many children as they did previously to secure a basic livelihood. In addition, with women spending more time in the fields, grandparents, both women and men, are increasingly called upon to take care of young children who remain at home. It is now common to see older Manmo men carrying swaddled infants on their backs, contributing their labour to reproduction while their daughters work in productive labour. State family planning policies and the availability of contraception mean that Hani women now have two to four children, while in the 1980s and early 1990s they had about three to six children, and before that five to 10 children. Policies supporting nine years of compulsory education, first at the primary school in Manmo, then in schools located in neighbouring Mengkuan and Mengha, also mean that most young Manmo villagers are fluent in Chinese and have a basic education, and thus the opportunity to continue their education and move into off-farm occupations. Currently, among educated Manmo villagers, one works in Jinhong city, another is a primary school teacher on nearby Jinou mountain, and a third is a finance official for Jinhong County government.

The emergence of large-scale cash cropping by households has, on the one hand, generated new income and eased some of the traditional work of women. On the other hand, the requirements of women's labour in intensified agricultural production has increased: not only must women perform subsistence labour in the transplanting of paddy seedlings; planting and weeding of rice swiddens; hauling of harvest down from the fields and so on; but they must now also put additional labour into cash crop cultivation. Moreover, while labour invested in subsistence rice harvests is returned directly to households as food, labour invested in cash cropping returns first to Manmo men, who customarily negotiate the sale of cash crops, and then to the household as income, where decisions about its use may or may not be controlled by women.

On top of new labour requirements created by cash cropping, the tourist trade has also stimulated demand for women's labour in collecting and marketing NTFPs and household produce. In this case, however, the income goes directly to the Manmo women who traditionally market NTFPs, as is the case for other indigenous women in Asia (Kelkar and Nathan 2003). Forest fruits, vegetables, mushrooms, honey and a multitude of other NTFPs are harvested by Manmo women in their daily trips to and from swidden fields, and by children at play or watching buffalo, and are a steady source of both supplementary food and income for the women who harvest them. One pair of local researchers has recorded 99 species of wild fruits collected by the Hani people, who use them as snacks, dietary supplements and cash crops (Chen and Tao, undated); another researcher has identified 20 varieties of edible mushrooms (Yang, undated). In Manmo, from August to October, the forest produces huge quantities of mushrooms, the spores of which are also planted in the wild. At this time of year, outside traders come to the roadside store to buy up mushrooms and other forest products from the storekeeper and others who gather in the parking lot offering NTFPs for sale. At other times of the year, it is also common for village women to sell various NTFPs directly to tourists from stands along the road or to carry them to the periodic market in neighbouring Mengkuan town.

Fuelwood is another key NTFP which the forests of Manmo still supply in abundance, yet if the barren hillsides of villages closer to Jinhong are any guide, this situation may not last much longer. Moreover, Manmo households which now cultivate fuelwood trees may soon reduce these in favour of more profitable rubber trees, as has happened in Dai communities (Henin and Flaherty 1994), likely increasing the amount of time and labour women spend collecting wood. Fuelwood and other products which rely on women's labour for collection are usually the last to be intensified (Nathan 1997), and may also be the most vulnerable to 'de-intensification' given the opportunity to convert to cash cropping of other commodities.

CONTRADICTIONS

The creation of the Manmo Nature Reserve has, at least in the short term, nominally succeeded in both enhancing the livelihood of some Manmo villagers and preserving a good section of forest reserve. The portions of the village ecotourism reserve best preserved are clearly those which provide the most environmental services and material benefits to the village: the forest protecting the water supply and streams in general; the forest along the tourist path; and that which provides shade for the growth of *sharen*, as noted above. For this reason, forest land managed by households for swidden cultivation on the borders of the reserve has been kept from overrunning the reserve, auguring well for future conservation.

Bordering state protected area forest, however, while ideally serving as a natural buffer zone to allow easier preservation of the village reserve, has in practice had the opposite effect. Because Manmo village has no official right to manage or regulate state forest bordering the reserve, decisions about its use are largely left to individual households acting on their own initiative. In the state reserve, the cutting of swidden fields and the harvesting of timber, wildlife and NTFPs is essentially unregulated by the village, and as such, traditional community-based conservation rules do not apply. The threat of local logging bans with stepped up enforcement further encourages a trend toward rapid extraction of forest resources on state reserve lands. In contrast, community forest bordering the reserve, which is officially recognized as belonging to Manmo village, is well-preserved, subject as it is to customary use rules. Manmo's environmental and sacred forests are likewise protected for the same reason. In short, household management of forests is less subject to conservation pressures than community managed forest, and a lack of rights to state forest has led to unregulated exploitation.

Although security of land tenure, along with surplus income, are clear preconditions for stopping shifting forest cultivation through the intensification of agriculture (Nathan 1997), neither factor ensures the preservation of forests. In Manmo, devolved tenure rights under the household responsibility system and increased income as a result of the free market reforms of the late 1980s and 1990s, have in fact resulted in increased deforestation even with the intensification of agriculture. Manmo's rice terracing systems, and its plantations of rubber, pineapple, *Cassia* fuelwood trees, passion fruit and *sharen* are all forms of intensified agriculture which have generated more income, yet have not provided a disincentive to cutting forests. In the state reserve, villagers perceive a surplus of cultivable and harvestable forest land. In Dai labourers and migrant Han Chinese who are now flooding into the region they see a large pool of surplus labour. Small-scale cash cropping and other economic ventures like ecotourism have given most households the capital necessary to expand agricultural production beyond their subsistence needs. Within the context of expanding local agricultural and tourism markets, land, labour and capital are thus engaged in a cycle of expansion to the detriment of forest resources.

Economic incentives for forest conservation and disincentives for forest destruction might thus be introduced by the state, following environmental accounting models now used in other parts of China (Harkness, 1998). For example, environmental services provided by Manmo's forests—storage and retention of water, erosion control, flood and storm protection, genetic diversity and aesthetic beauty—might be valued in economic terms, and those who benefit from the services made to pay for them. These users would include, above all, the many tourists who are drawn to the area specifically for its natural beauty and ecological diversity, and downstream recipients of water supplied by the Nanka River. Manmo's nature reserve is already built on this model: the environmental service provided by the forest in recreation and aesthetic pleasure taken by tourists is now valued at the cost of entrance and guide fees. Notably, the levying of 'ecological environment compensation fees' to sustain state nature reserves is already among the most promising of conservation initiatives in other parts of China (Harkness 1998).

The effect of ecotourism on gender relations in indigenous communities of the region is not promising. In the Yunnan matrilineal Mosuo community of Luoshui studied by He Zhonghua (2003), for example, the development of ecotourism around the scenic beauty of lake and mountains has changed the gender division of labour, mostly to the detriment of women. As He recounts, in the new ecotourist economy of hotels and cultural entertainment centred around Lugu lake, the gender division of labour 'has developed a new phase, in which men participate in public affairs and business, for instance, soliciting customers and loans, while women, besides housework, handle the reception of tourists' (He Zhonghua 2001: 42). Although both men and women share work in entertaining tourists through boating, horseback riding and singing and dancing performances, and men now sometimes help to collect pine needles for fuel, women take on the added burdens of guest reception, preparation of food for guests and cleaning of rooms.[2]

Growth in tourism in Luoshui has also ushered in the sex trade, drawing in women sex workers from neighbouring Sichuan province and 'seriously contaminating' the village (*ibid*.: 52). As Anita Pleumaron

---

[2] Notably, this market enlargement of women's domestic labour is true in ecotourism in other mountain communities; for instance, in the trekking business in Nepal, 'women's roles are primarily an extension of the home-manager and guest caretaker responsibility' (Brewer Lama 1999: p. 46).

(1996) notes, growth of the sex trade accompanying ecotourism is characteristic of the wider Yunnan–Northern Thailand–Burma–Laos region, where it has led to an increase not only in prostitution, but also in the trafficking of girls and women and the spread of AIDS.

The commodification of ethnicity in the village has reinforced both gender and class divisions. On the one hand, are those village households prosperous and educated enough to masquerade as Dai in the service of Han visitors. Households who have educated members who can speak good Chinese and understand Han mores and customs, who can afford the labour and space required to manage the tourist showrooms, who possess permanent Dai-style houses and the start-up capital needed to run small stores serving the tourist trade clearly benefit most from the 'Dai' tourism business. Likewise, although the nature reserve eventually brings in good annual returns, the household which runs the forest reserve must be wealthy enough to able to raise and risk the initial capital needed to bid on managing it. On the other hand, are those villagers who have less education and knowledge of Chinese language and customs, are older, dress in traditional Hani clothing, have less entrepreneurial experience, little surplus labour, space or time, live in less permanent housing and are more often women than men. At the same time, an unrecognized repository of indigenous forestry expertise is still to be found in those furthest from Han society and the market: Hani elders who best know Hani history and cultural practices related to the forest, its uses and management; Hani women healers who are experts in forest medicinal herbs, food products and other NTFPs; men hunters who intimately understand the habits and habitat of local wildlife; others who know particular species of trees and plants and their material and cultural uses in Hani society, etc. Thus, rather than relying on images of exoticized Hani ethnicity or commodified Dai ethnicity, ecotourism and ethnotourism might be built around the traditional cultural and environmental resources of the community.

In keeping with the idea of ecotourism as 'clean' development, as saving natural resources while at the same time promoting community development, the United Nations had declared 2002 as the International Year of Ecotourism (IYE). This rather uncritical promotion of ecotourism for development is now being challenged by a coalition of NGOs who call instead for an International Year of Reviewing Ecotourism (IYRE), a demand thus far little heeded by the UN Third World Network (TWN). Taking the experience of Manmo, it is clear that ecotourism is not a panacea for the preservation of forests and sustained livelihood of local communities, regardless of how fine it sounds in theory. In practice, ecotourism provides no simple 'win-win' scenario of economic benefits from forest conservation. Rather, the local complexities of government policy, market forces, forest condition, land tenure, the tourism trade, ethnicity, class and gender will decide what forest resources are preserved and who receives the benefits. In many cases, local forest environments, the indigenous forest communities which rely on them for their livelihood, and indigenous women in particular, have suffered. Pollution and deterioration of land, forest and water resources, eco-pilfering, the destruction of indigenous cultures, the sex trade and trafficking in women and children, are all among recent complaints by those critically examining the impact of ecotourism development. Taken together, these problems cry out for a review of the basic assumptions of ecotourism and development, in the interests of both environmental and cultural survival.

REFERENCES AND SELECT BIBLIOGRAPHY

Berman, M. L. *Opening the Lancang (Mekong) River in Yunnan: Problems and Prospects for Xishuangbanna.* M.A. thesis, University of Massachusetts, Amherst, 1998. http://rpcp.mit.edu/dbr/Lancang.htm.

Brewer Lama, W. 'Valuing Women as Assets to Community-based Tourism in Nepal'. *Cultural Survival Quarterly* 23, no. 2 (1999): 45–47.

Chen Jin and Tao Guoda. 'Preliminary Study of Wild Fruits of Hani in Xishuangbanna, Yunnan Province of China'. In *Proceedings of the 2nd International Congress of Ethnobotany*, by Pie et al., undated: 134–39.

Gu Wenfeng. Investigation Report: Traditional Medical and Health Care Knowledge of Dai and Hani Women in Menghan Township of Jinghong County in Xishuangbanna in Yunnan. In *Indigenous Women's Knowledge in Health Care and Water Management*. Gender and Development Studies Monograph No. 5, Bangkok, Thailand: Asian Institute of Technology, 1995: 21–32.

Harkness, J. (1998). 'Recent Trends in Forestry and Conservation of Biodiversity in China'. *China Quarterly* 156 (1998): 911–34.

He Zhonghua. Forest Management in Mosuo Matrilineal Society, Yunnan, China'. In *Gender Relations in Forest Societies in Asia: Patriarchy at Odds*, edited by Govind Kelkar, Dev Nathan and Pierre Walter. New Delhi, Thousand Oaks, London: Sage Publications, 2003.

Henin, B. 'Ethnic Minority Integration in China: Transformation of Akha Society'. *Journal of Contemporary Asia* 26, no. 2 (1996): 180–200.

Henin, B. and M. Flaherty, 'Ethnicity, Culture, and Natural Resource Use: Forces of Change in Dai Society, Xishuangbanna, Southwest China'. *Journal of Developing Societies* 2 (1994): 220–35.

Kelkar, Govind and Dev Nathan. 'Introduction—Forest Societies in Asia: Gender Relations and Change'. In *Gender Relations in Forest Societies in Asia:*

Patriarchy at Odds, edited by Govind Kelkar, Dev Nathan and Pierre Walter. New Delhi, Thousand Oaks, London: Sage Publications, 2003.

Nathan, D. Strategies of Shifting Cultivators in the Intensification Process. Unpublished Manuscript, 1997.

Pleumaron, A. 'Eco-tourism: A New 'Green Revolution' in the Third World'. *Questioning Development* edited by G. Koehler et al.. Marburg, Germany: Metropolis: 1996: 427–48.

Yang Fuquan. 'Eco-tourism and the Protection of Yunnan's Tourist Resources'. *Yunnan Shehui Kexue (Yunnan Social Science)* 1, (1995): 52–58. Translated by Merrick L. Berman. http://rpcp.mit.edu/dbr/Lancang.htm..

Yang Zhuliang. 'A Preliminary Ethnomycological Study on Wild Edible Mushrooms Consumed by Ethnic Groups in Xishuangbanna, Yunnan, China. *Proceedings of the 2nd International Congress of Ethnobotany,* by Pei et al.. Undated: 100–03.

Zou Shouqing. 'A Preliminary Study of Traditional Agroforestry by Dai People in Xishuangbanna'. *Proceedings of the 2nd International Congress of Ethnobotany* by Pei et al.. Undated: 142–45.

9

TOURISM AND GENDER RELATIONS IN LIJIANG, CHINA

Govind Kelkar

Research on the indigenous societies that are likely to be impacted by tourism has tended to focus on economic development. Only a few mention the role of women or pay attention to gender relations. (Kelkar and Nathan 1991; Kelkar, Nathan and Walter 2003; Bosu Mullick 2000; Sarin 2003; Bolles 1997; Kinnaird, Kothari and Hall 1994). This invisibility compounds patriarchy as the invisible mediator in reproducing idealized images of the past, and conceals the unequal benefits to be enjoyed from many tourism endeavours. This paper explores changes in gender relations as a result of economic development through tourism. I look at changes in gender relations in indigenous societies of the matrilineal Mosuo and patrilineal Naxi and the current situation of development of tourism as a leading industry, where women play a significant role as workers and local managers, but their social, economic and political position has come under increasing stress.

Since 1993, I have made regular visits to Lugu lake and Lashi lake in Yunnan, China. This study is based on our fieldwork in Luoshui Village in Ninglang County, Lugu lake and several visits to Naxi villages around Lashi lake, 8 kilometres away from Lijiang Dayan town. These visits were related to my collaborative work with Chinese scholars[1]

---

[1] Along with Dev Nathan, often accompanied by our daughter, Pallavi Govindnathan, who over time became an enthusiastic participant in the discussions.

(He Zhonghua, Yang Fuquan, Yu Xiaogang and Xi Yuhua) on tourism, resource development and gender relations in matrilineal Mosuo and patrilineal Naxi. Focussed group discussions and individual interviews were the main methods of data-collection, supplemented by local government data. The 1–2 hour interviews were largely structured around questions designed to elicit information from women and men respondents on matters related to their work/contributions, Chinese and foreign visitors to the area, and their changing relationship with the state, the family and the community.

These interviews were conducted to address the following major questions: How do gender relations within and outside the household affect resource management and the tourism industry? What is the extent of women's centrality in provision of livelihood, through an analysis of their role and status in management of tourism? Does the structure of gender relations within the household and in the community change as members respond to broad religio-cultural, social and economic restructuring of the indigenous societies, largely as a result of tourism?

DEVELOPMENT OF TOURISM

The Lugu lake area in the scenic Yongning plateau in Yunnan, is inhabited by the matrilineal Mosuo people. For purposes of development of tourism, this area is called 'the Kingdom of Daughters'. Lashi lake, with biological resources in the wetlands, is adjacent to the Yangtze valley and Lanchang (upper Mekong) valley. Lashi lake is inhabited by the Naxi and Yi and is 8 kilometres away from Lijiang Dayan town, which is a World Cultural Heritage site. These two are now the most popular tourist destinations in southwestern China.

People come here not just because of the area's scenic beauty, but also to acquaint themselves, in howsoever limited a fashion, with different cultures. This is what makes the mountain cultures, the matrilineal cultures of the Mosuo in Yunnan, for instance, something interesting to see and observe. The result is that the music, dance and other performances of these people have got new functions, as they are staged for tourists to see or participate in. Every minority nationality in Yunnan now stages these shows as tourist attractions.

Luoshui village is located on Lugu lake to the southeast of the Yongning plateau, 20 kilometres away from the seat of district government. It is part of the larger Luoshui Administrative village. The village is divided into two parts, the Upper village and the Lower village. The former is situated on the mountain slopes, and its inhabitants are mostly Pumi. The latter is located near the lake, and its inhabitants are mostly Mosuo. According to late 1998 statistics, there were 76 households comprising of 485 people in both the Upper and Lower villages, of which the Mosuo made up 33 households and Pumi 21 households. The rest were Han and the Bai. During my investigation in the Lower village in 1993 and 1996, I found that of the 33 Mosuo households, 31 (94 per cent) were matrilineal families. Pumi in the Upper village also commonly followed the *axia* (the visiting husbands) practices of the Lower village Mosuo.

With the development of tourism, drastic changes have taken place in transportation, communications, housing and other local infrastructure. The way of life and the mode of thinking have also undergone important change. Now the former dirt highway to the district seat is asphalt. Once impassable, the road around the lake can today reach Yanyuan County town in the dry season. Thirty-two out of 33 households have built new wooden houses and telephones, refrigerators, washing machines and television sets and small appliances are increasingly popular. Each family has a flush toilet, and some households even have water heated with solar energy equipment. However, they still retain their matrilineal system, *axia*, funeral customs, and sacrificial rites. 'In fact, they have even further consolidated these practices, not for themselves, but as tourist attractions' (He Zhonghua 2001: 42).

After the economic reforms in China men's domination of political life in the villages was further consolidated. In the former Village People's Committee of Luoshui village, the ratio of women among the committee members was 6 to 0, without a seat for a woman committee director. In April 1999, it began to offer a woman director's seat, but the ratio was still 8 men to 1 woman. Women are always considered as lacking in ability or to be less educated, incapable of participating in political affairs. In reality, women are no less qualified than men, yet the seats of village heads or officials are always for those said to be abler (i.e., the men).

The power of men is now being consolidated and strengthened. Although of equal labour value, women's activities and capacity in management of resources are not valued or recognized. They have fewer opportunities to join in scientific and technological training in the development projects of village communities.

Besides, the development of tourism has ushered in the trade in women's bodies. Beginning in 1997, some people from outside the community opened beauty parlours and set up sex trade joints, which seriously disturbed the village. In 1998, these beauty parlours were ordered to close their doors in the community. As a result, they moved to the administrative district about 1 kilometre away and continued their trade. This is something that is being ignored.

CULTURE AND WOMEN'S ROLE IN THE TOURISM INDUSTRY

Studies that have followed the growth of the tourism industry, have focussed upon the motivations of tourists. Relatively little attention has been paid to human institutions and understanding of gender relations in the communities that receive tourists. For women of the receiving communities, economics of tourism is seen in sex tourism, that 'female bodies are a tourist commodity' (Bolles 1997: 78). While sex tourism is an emerging phenomenon in Yunnan and needs to be subjected to examination to check the growing trade in the women's bodies; it is, however, only one of many roles women play in the tourism industry. The tourism industry has also provided various decent livelihood opportunities for women. In addition to having the sole responsibility for rearing and financially supporting their children and other dependents, Mosuo and Naxi women have the function of hosts, tourist workers, house keepers, boat rowers, craft and snack vendors, small entrepreneurs and managers of cottages, guest houses, night clubs, etc.

Tourism means a higher level of income, though not necessarily for all. The satisfaction of needs through consumption is possible because of the higher income. A new system of production, like tourism 'means disruption, but it also means survival and much more' (Goody 1998: 197). Survival, not only at the material level but also on a cultural level, as cultural practices become the means of earning an income.

'The becoming cultural of the economic, and the becoming economic of the cultural, has often been identified as one of the features that characterize what is now widely known as post-modernity' (Jameson 2001: 60). If the cultural practices and artifacts of the mainstream cultures can become economic sectors then what about the cultural practices and artifacts of the minority nationalities of China? Tourism has provided an avenue for the continuation of cultural practices (e.g., tea ceremonies of the Bai) or cultural products (hand printed, embroidered or woven cloth) that were in danger of extinction in the face of their seeming irrelevance or economic competition from mill-made cloth.

Besides, some of the idioms of the mountain peoples also establish themselves as artistic practices, perhaps with esoteric value, if not on par with those of the plains' peoples. In China, as a result of tourism, Naxi traditional orchestras have been revived. Having almost died out (only a handful of men in their sixties and seventies kept its embers flickering), now after a gap of more than 30 years, they not only perform regularly, but have also produced cassettes and CDs of their music. There are many similar examples among the handicrafts, etc.

The Naxi pictographic writing, which was also in danger of extinction (only a handful of old Dongba priests existed who could read it) has now made its presence felt as an idiom in painting and sculpture. These are new and different functions to be sure, but the alternative to extinction is to be able to use one's heritage in changed circumstances. Tourism does give some scope for such expressions of local culture.

CULTURE AND COMMODITY

Long looked down upon as inferior to the cultural performances of the plains, the songs, dances, handicrafts, etc., of the mountain peoples have gained an international acceptance, something that has grown with tourism. While in earlier times the music and cultural performances of the mountain peoples were facing extinction under the onslaught of the 'superior' plains' products, or were preserved in hothouse fashion with heavy-handed state patronage, the growth of tourism has led to new roles for these cultural creations.

Tourism transforms and recreates locality in a new way, a new way even for the local people. There is a selective picking of what is of value in the global system. Further, to the local people too, the cultural products or practices cease to have the old, participatory or religious values. The commoditization of these products and practices means that their value now lies only in the money they can bring in exchange. The products and practices are also influenced by changing tastes. Thus, Hani villagers in Yunnan have no qualms about dressing up and pretending to be Dai, since that is what the unknowing foreign or Han tourists expect of them. This interaction is itself the medium of expression of the circuits that create wealth and thus of domination of use value by exchange value. Cultural products that have use value may still continue to exist; but the global circuits are dominated by those that have exchange value. That is the price of cultural existence in the globalized market system, symbolized in this case by mass tourism.

It is necessary to understand the ways in which the local of the indigenous people interacts with the global in order to be able to change the terms of that interaction. In a world dominated by the commodity form, the existence of an object as a commodity does give it some value. Its non-existence as a commodity does not save it from appropriation by others—whether in the case of African sculptures or forests' environmental services, both of which have been forcibly extracted. Gaining the status of commodities these products would then have an acknowledgement of their authorship and would enable the terms of the earlier forcible and free exchange to be improved in favour of the local producers.

Of course, this does not provide a full solution to the problem of the integrity of artistic endeavour or of the value of the environment. The commodity form is ultimately inadequate for both of these concerns. Commodifying ethnicity is not a way to integrally promote culture, as only those practices are maintained that have commodity value (Pierre Walter in this book). The spread or generalization of commodity relations has its effect on all forms of human relations, including sexuality, with the spread of commercial sex. How and when an overcoming of these commodity forms can be carried out, is something that humanity has yet to come to grips with.

It is important to note that cultures are not static, something given for all time. They change and the sources of change may be varied. Many changes originate in ideas gained from other cultures, from inter-cultural discussion and communication. But whether particular ideas originate from an intra-cultural critique or from inter-cultural discussion, the ideas change the existing cultural practice of the group or community concerned. It is this changing cultural practice, resulting from intra-cultural critique and inter-cultural exchange, that forms the basis for the recognition of new human rights.

> Human rights clearly have become part of a much wider, globalized, cultural network of perspectives. This does not mean, however, that they simply constitute an influx of alien meaning or cultural form which enters into a vacuum or inscribes itself on 'a cultural tabula rasa'. They enter into various kinds of interactions with already existing meanings and meaningful forms; in this case particular conceptions of... men and women, for instance (Preis 1996: 307).

The need for various forms of public or collective decisions extends to many aspects of social life. The preservation of cultural heritage is one of them, but this does not mean the preservation of negative cultural practices. Cultural heritage has value not merely as tourist attractions, but is important for its various non-commercial use values. While tourism may provide a valuable source of income for the preservation of cultural sites, their overall development depends on a combination of private and public decisions, combining commercial and non-commercial use values and non-use values. Enshrining commercial values as the only values will not only lead to problems of equity, but will also seriously affect the supply of various public goods, including cultural heritage.

Of course, women's commercial production is still regarded as tourist souvenirs, not as genuine artistic products. That requires a change not only in the attitude of the users/consumers of these products but also in development perception of work and in particular the recognition of women's 'reproductive work' as work. It is only after the rise of the feminist movement in the West that women's decorative embroidery or quilt-making is being recognized as art. The feminist artist Miriam Schapiro coined the term 'femmage' to show the close connection between women and the making of collages. That women's decorative motifs are a basis for abstraction in art was recognized, for instance, by Wassily Kandinsky. There, however, is still a strong tendency to dismiss such domestic work as 'mere decoration' and 'not art'. The shift from such artistic work being a domestic function of women to becoming a commodity in the art world, even if it is a mass souvenir, could help in changing opinions about the artistic function of women art producers.

INCOME FROM TOURISM

The structure of the tourist trade largely determines the distribution of returns to various actors along the chain. It often happens that the mountain economy acquires relatively limited benefits from externally developed 'package tourism', with the majority of local participation being restricted merely to supplying cheap labour for menial jobs, and only a few with capital being able to move into more lucrative sections of the tourist trade.

When a substantial portion of the benefits accrue to the mountain economies, as seems to be the case in Switzerland, tourism does have the potential to create an important avenue for local absorption of labour, and thus reverse the out-migration that is otherwise a feature of mountain economies. In turn, the ability of the Swiss cantons to acquire a substantial portion of the income from tourism could be related to the strong political position of the cantons, which, among other things, enabled the rural cantons to use water revenues to develop infrastructure.

In a microcosm I saw a similar situation in the Mosuo village, Luoshui on Lugu lake, in Yunnan, China, where the guest houses in which tourists stay are all owned, most wholly and a few partially, by local villagers. The poorer villagers whose houses were not located on the lake shore have not benefitted as much, but they supply most of the other amenities, like horse and boat riding, that tourists require.

In Luoshui village by 1996, tourism had replaced farming as the leading industry of the village and was the main source of income for most households. In 1996, annual per capita income was Yuan 2,000, and the collective village income from boating, renting horses and other tourist activities alone came to Yuan 100,000. Luoshui is now known far and wide as a relatively wealthy tourist village and is, in fact, one of the 10 richest villages in Lijiang prefecture. (He Zhonghua 2001: 41)

Not only have incomes gone up there are also new types of jobs. In a purely agricultural economy, out-migration of the educated is a strong feature. Traditional agriculture does not need their type of education. But with the development of tourism many new kinds of jobs are generated that require education. Travel agencies and guides are some of them. As restaurants develop, specialized cooks also become necessary. Musicians and other entertainers also get new scope.

All of this leads to more of the educated staying back in the village. This is visible both in Lugu lake, Lijiang and in Jing Hong, Xishuangbanna. In some cases, e.g., in the village of Nanjie, Henan, there are even instances of computer operators and chefs returning to the village from Beijing or other cities. Tourism has helped to promote a reversal of the drain of the educated from the villages.

PROMOTING ENTREPRENEURS

Due to a historically self-consumption based production system the mountain communities usually have a paucity of entrepreneurial experience. Consequently when an opportunity does arise it is often identified and taken advantage of by outsiders. These opportunities may range from relatively simple matters, like operating pedicabs to setting up plants for refining medicinal herbs. In Tibet, for instance, each of the above was first taken up by outsiders. Now Tibetans own many pedicabs as also greenhouses for vegetable production.

While there is learning by imitation by the local communities from entrepreneurial initiatives by outsiders, there are also other examples where mountain communities have insisted that outside investors enter into partnership with local investors in order to invest. The Mosuo village on Lugu lake, which is now a major tourist attraction in Yunnan, has a regulation that any outside investor has to take a local partner, and that the outside investor can only remain for a period of 10 years, after which the full ownership can be bought over by the local investor.

Given the paucity of entrepreneurial ability, the mountain communities could also adopt collectively owned enterprises as a way of advancing into new fields. The township village enterprises (TVEs) of China are good examples of collectively owned enterprises. Some of the most prosperous villages in China also have collective ownership of all their enterprises. For instance, there is the village of Liuminying, which is now famous, having been named an 'ecological village' by United Nations Environment Programme (UNEP). Besides entrepreneurship such collective enterprises also require strong internal management systems in order to stimulate productivity and should not have the prop of a 'soft budget constraint'.

WHO IS BETTER ABLE TO TAKE ADVANTAGE?

The changes in the economic system have been accompanied by changes in thinking. There are ethnic, class and gender factors in determining who is able to take advantage of globalization and the growth of trade, particularly long distance trade. Taking the ethnic factor first, it is related to the differential exposure of different communities to trade and their acquisition of the capabilities that are needed to take advantage of the growing sectors. For instance, in the tourism county of Lijiang, the valley-dwelling and more urbanized and better educated Naxi have benefitted much more from the growth of tourism than the Yi or Lisu, who both live on the upper slopes and are less urbanized and educated. As in other rural–urban migrations, connections count in getting urban jobs. Besides, in the case of China, there is the difficulty of legal urban residence for those who do not have relatives in the cities, putting the less urbanized Yi and Lisu at a disadvantage.

Within trades too there are lesser and more profitable ones and the ability to enter one or the other is not just a matter of the amount of capital needed. The Dai village of Man Gue, Xishuangbanna, Yunnan, has a large daily tourist trade. In the market place there are two distinct kinds of trades—the sale of local trinkets and food stuffs and the sale of jade. The jade trade is completely dominated by the Han traders, who have come from outside the area and set up shop to take advantage of the tourist influx. The lower return sale of trinkets and food stuffs is in the hands of the Dai. There are a few Dai women (women handle business among the Dai) who have accumulated enough capital to be able to go into the jade trade. But, as one of them explained, there is a specialized knowledge that is needed to be able to enter the jade trade, and this the Han traders have.

While women often carry out small-scale, or micro-trade among the indigenous communities, when it comes to larger-scale or long-distance trade it tends to be taken over by men. In long–distance trade there are the factors of the difficulty women face in being away from home for long periods of time as it is they who are responsible for care of children, and their generally lesser knowledge of the mainstream, national languages. Of course, this is not a universal pattern and there are communities where the women being more involved in the market, even if it is local, have a better knowledge of the market language than men. This is so in some communities in Jharkhand, India. But on the whole, the long distance trade does tend to disadvantage and displace women.

At the class level, there is the obvious factor that those households with education, labour, space and start-up capital, as Pierre Walter (in this book) points out in the study of the Hani village, are able to better take advantage of the growing market opportunities. Even as mere sellers of gathered products, there is a difference in the price realized by those from surplus and those from food insecure households. Those from food insecure households are forced into sales in interlinked markets (for instance, combining sale of the product along with purchase of daily necessities, rather than dealing with the sale and purchase as separate transactions) and lose a portion of the price of the product, a portion that may be higher than the interest on borrowed capital.

Those who depend more on non-natural resource-based sources of income, like tourism or wage employment, also tend to favour the conservation of natural resources and the promotion of their ecological service functions, as compared to those who depend on transforming these natural resources into income, like those who collect fuelwood for sale. Restrictions to conserve these natural resources, e.g., not harvesting the forests on the hills around Lugu lake, benefit those who get their income from tourism, but have a negative impact on those who depend on these natural resources. The poorer sections of the village get less, while those with the privileges of external contacts and/or location get more of the benefits from the new sources of tourist income. The initial position of these sections is itself worse than that of those with more land, etc., and tends to further deteriorate.

In distributing the benefits from the new sources of income, the more equal distribution of land, and related resources, education, etc., are important. Inequalities will nevertheless develop, but the base level of income on which inequalities develop would be higher.

GROWING MASCULINE DOMINATION AND CHALLENGES

In one way or the other, with the growth of markets, external economic relations dominate domestic relations of production, although, the domestic sphere, contributed to and controlled by women, remains an important coping structure in times of economic crisis (as happened during the Asian crisis, see Nathan and Kelkar 1999). Funds for accumulation are increasingly obtained through banks or government sources. Men's role in managing the family's external affairs easily extends into such economic matters. In the matrilineal, even matrifocal Mosuo, the growth of tourism on Lugu lake has increased the say of men, who secure the finance for constructing guest houses, etc.

> At the same time, with the expansion of ties between Mosuo households and the larger society, men who traditionally had a larger role in the social arena, are enabled to give full play to their superiority in this sphere, thus expanding their power, whereas the women, whose traditional work is confined to household labour, find it difficult to step up in the same arena. The presence of men from other ethnic nationalities, brought up in the atmosphere of patriarchal systems and possessing strong business ability and economic skills, are naturally and imperceptibly remolding Mosuo traditional culture, which constitutes a crisis for Mosuo culture (He Zhonghua 2001: 43).

The increase in men's say in family economic matters is coupled with their continuing control over village and other community affairs. While earlier men's monopoly in village and community affairs was counterbalanced by women's role over the economic and domestic sphere, with the growth of the market and the growing domination of external economic relations over the domestic economy, women lose their countervailing power. All hierarchies are step by step controlled by men.

The change to male-domination is as much a patriarchal change as any of the others we have discussed here. The first phase of this change which establishes men's monopoly over the spiritual and material management of community affairs predates the spread of the market. But the second phase of this civilizational change, in which men use their domination of external relations to establish control over economic affairs, is very much the product of the spread of market-processes in which the external economy dominates the domestic sphere.

To illustrate this point we will again take the example of the Mosuo. Before the contemporary period, men's external role was limited to long distance trade and the monkhood in pre-Liberation China. Long distance trade along the 'Silk Route' was a chancy affair, and did not yield a regular income. The monkhood, of course, was a way of using surpluses, rather than of accumulating. With Liberation, men's roles changed to taking up education and political affairs. Till the growth of the market system, these roles too did not yield any substantial income. But with the growth of the market and the rise of the tourist trade, these external connections are now crucial in securing bank loans and other sources of finance. Women's management of domestic affairs has now turned more into drudgery. Though accumulation and inheritance are in the female line, it is men who are increasing their roles in families' strategic decision-making.

The new norms of masculine domination are the product of two processes. On the one hand, there is the 'learning' from other communities and the state. On the other hand, there is also the internal struggle between the genders within these communities. The civilizational change we see is neither merely imposed from outside, nor is it entirely the result of internal conflicts. Both the internal and the external work together to bring about this change.

Simultaneously, and sometimes often in the same communities, there are also struggles to overcome these new, patriarchal norms. Taking account of gender relations is not something that develops by itself. The large-scale entry of women into managing the tourist sector, for instance, among the Dai in Xishuangbanna, has reinforced their earlier domestic control. The main cash income is now also earned through women's activities and controlled by them. Even if the communities already had a practice of household cash being handled by women, the advance of women as the main cash earners does seem to make a difference to the say that women have in the use of household income.

The change in men–women relations with regard to control over household income among the Mosuo, however, have occurred largely in relations between brothers and sisters. Brothers, who are often the source of new investment funds now have more influence than formerly on household spending. But since husbands and wives still continue to live and work with their mothers, there is no change in the economic relationship of wives and husbands. Even in matters of childcare, it is uncles who spend more time with their sisters' children, than do husbands with their own children.

There were attempts, for instance during the Cultural Revolution, to force husbands and wives to live together. But soon after, with the market opening, this 'nuclear family' approach was abandoned and women and men returned to their mothers' homes. As He Zhonghua points out, this form of family relationship has got an added boost through its exotic value for tourists (He Zhonghua 2001).

TOURISM AND EFFECTS ON FOREST USE

In contrast to the transformations in Luoshui village where tourism has emerged as the main source of income, the Mosuo village of Zhengbo, Yongning Township, Lijiang County, has been largely unable to participate in this development. The village retains its traditional agricultural structure with animal husbandry as a sideline activity. But one-crop farming and animal husbandry do not produce much income. In some households, people migrate to take up odd jobs to earn some money. They also sell some of their grain, livestock, mushrooms and medicinal herbs in order to buy daily necessities, such as woven bamboo articles, brooms and butter. Villagers commonly keep a dozen pigs, and four or five horses for home consumption or use, but seldom sell them. At most they may sell a few chickens or piglets, and in case of urgent need a horse or cow may be sold. People still rely on the natural economy for self-sufficiency.

Farming as a single-product economy, may solve the problem of obtaining food, but it is incapable of improving the living standards of villages to any great extent. Until now, only three households own a washing machine or telephone, and the whole village has only one truck to haul wood and it is not in use. Sixty per cent of the households do not have television sets (*ibid.* 2001).

The provision of firewood is an urgent problem in the village of Zhengbo. Firewood is in very short supply because there are no trees around the village. People go into the state forests to collect firewood. Besides only one type of fuel is used here. Other than firewood, a small quantity of sunflower stems and corn cores are also used as fuel. However, the consumption of firewood is very high, as very few improved stoves are used.

Fierce floods also pose a problem for Zhengbo, located as it is in the lower valley of two large rivers. Deforestation of the upper valley causes floods in the lower valley every year. The old people can recall a time when the rivers rose in summer, but it was clean water, and there were no floods at all. Now, floods with mud and sand cascade downward, inundating the houses and fields, and there is no water fit to drink.

While in general it may be true that the stability of forest ownership and policy are closely related to the benefits available to the villagers, the Mosuo village of Luoshui is an exception. Although the ownership of the forest was taken back by the state, the villagers receive a rich return from the ecological effect of the forest because the village is situated in the natural protection zone. These ecological functions, including the scenery the forested hillside provides, is important to the village's main economic activity, i.e., tourism. Therefore, the division of ownership, the fact of non-ownership by the village community, has little to do with their fundamental interest. As a result of this it is not difficult to manage the state forest and enforce the rules for its use.

On the other hand, in the nearby village of Zhengbo, there is a great dependence on forest products, like firewood, for the economy of the village. At the same time there is a large area of state forest. Deforestation has spread over both the collective and the state forests.

This relationship between forest use and the development of non-farm sources of income has two aspects to it. On the one hand, there is less reliance on the direct transformation of natural resources, as in agriculture or animal husbandry, for earning an income. Agricultural products are inputs into, for instance, cooking for tourists; but there is a substantial value addition in the process. The raw material is increasingly a smaller part of the total value of the meal supplied.

The second aspect is that since it is women who are largely involved in the tourist sector, as managers of small businesses, running restaurants, and so on, there is an increase in the opportunity cost of their labour. This promotes the adoption of labour-saving equipment, like improved stoves, which also simultaneously consume less fuel, and therefore require less wood. In contrast in villages where such non-farm income for women has not developed, there is very little adoption of labour-saving domestic equipment, like improved stoves (For a review of the relevant Asian experience in this regard see Nathan and Kelkar 1997).

Besides the comparison of the two Mosuo villages given above, there is a similar strong contrast between the adoption of improved stoves in tourism-dominated Dai villages and non-tourist related Dai villages in Xishuangbanna, with the former showing a universal adoption of labour-saving equipment, not only improved stoves but also piped water, and the latter continuing with the traditional three-stone or tripod fireplaces. As one might expect, the growth of women's cash earning activities, leads to a saving of the time they spend in domestic labour, like fetching fuelwood and water.

There is also a shift from household-based collection of fuelwood from forests to either cultivation of firewood trees in the home garden or even the purchase of firewood. In general the development of tourism, means a shift from an all-round to a specialized economy. Such development of specialized economic activities need not lead to a loss of sustainability. In fact, specialized commercialization may actually promote sustainability. Take the case of fuelwood. Where fuelwood is collected from common land, often through women's labour, given the very low opportunity cost of this labour, there is an overuse of labour in the collection of fuelwood and a lack of measures to increase the area-wise productivity of the product. But as commercial activities which involve the use of women's labour develop, then that community or village may cease to collect fuelwood and instead purchase it.

The development of tourism itself requires some direct attention to forest condition as part of the scenery that attracts tourists. The Hani village of Manmo has preserved its own forest in order to provide a 'walk in the rain forest'. Cutting of trees or even collecting branches is not allowed in this forest. While this has meant some move to growing of fuelwood trees, perhaps by those directly involved in the tourist trade, there has also been a shift in the area of wood extraction. The 'other side of the hill', not visible to tourists has been denuded. Thus, there could also be a displacement of the problem.

There may be either a simple displacement of the problem, with extraction shifted elsewhere; or an intensification of production, with a saving in the use of land and labour. The crucial factor in this case is the shortage of labour. As long as labour is available and has a low opportunity cost, extensive methods of collecting fuelwood continue.

But when the opportunity cost of labour, in particular the opportunity cost of women's labour, goes up then there is a movement to reduce the labour cost of collecting fuelwood. From gathering fuelwood the move is made to cultivating fuelwood, which is more sustainable than collection.

The environmental service functions of forests, as scenery or recreational value, becomes more important than their direct income value. This holds true even in the case of what are state-owned forests. The tourist village of Luoshui is very mindful of the condition of the state forest on the hills above. It is important to protect the road leading into the village and as part of the attractive scenery around the lake. Thus, unlike in many other parts of China or Asia, the villagers do not make a distinction between this state-owned and other village-owned forest, protecting the latter and denuding the former. As a result it is not difficult to enforce the state forest rules for its protection.

Displacement of the costs of tourism can occur in other ways too. The old town of Lijiang Dayan, is in an old Chinese architectural style, with the added attraction of canals flowing by the side of streets, through most of the old town. One can still see people washing clothes or vegetables in these canals. The water for these canals comes from Lashi lake, about 50 kilometres away. The water-bearing capacity of the lake has been increased so that enough water is supplied to the town throughout the year. This has meant the flooding of former fields, depriving Naxi farm families on the banks of the lake of some of their incomes. They are paid some compensation per mu^2 of land flooded. But, as is to be expected, the compensation is much lower than the income loss.

As in the larger case of loss of timber income following the ban on logging, the assignment of property rights over the lake water to the villages around the lake would enable them to sell the water that is crucial to Lijiang town. We would mention that Swiss mountain cantons have for long had and continue to have the right to sell water to downstream, power companies. This right has enabled the otherwise-neglected uplands to share in the overall national development, and, perhaps, even provided the capital for investment in mountain tourist facilities. A similar right of local communities over, say, water would more widely spread the benefits of power development, instead of making the upland communities bear only the costs, as they now do.

---

[2] A *mu* is a Chinese measure of land—5 *mu* is roughly equal to 1 hectare.

A factor that affects the environment is the density of tourist traffic. With the high incomes generated by tourism there is a tendency to keep pushing the tourist traffic to such an extent that it strains the 'carrying capacity' of the area. It may be difficult to clearly specify a concept like 'tourist carrying capacity', but that should not be a reason for ignoring this factor. People walking around grasslands, obviously affect the state of the grass. To keep increasing the number of people who can go up to and walk around Alpine meadows would affect the very meadow itself.

The Naxi 'Suicide Meadow' overlooking 'Jade Dragon Mountain' is a place visited by tourists to Lijiang. The place has great significance in Naxi history. In 1993 when we first visited Lijiang, one could only go up on horseback, the ride was managed by young women and men, organized in a cooperative. Now there is a cable car ride up the mountain. The numbers who visit have increased from maybe 100 per day to a few thousand each day. Such large numbers tramping on the grasslands would completely destroy the meadow in a short time. The local authorities have responded very well to this problem—they have set up a slightly raised fenced boardwalk on which one must walk to go around the meadow. This allows large numbers to go up the mountain without destroying the meadow. What this means is that, as in other things too, a new combination of private and public decisions and investment is needed in order for tourist development to be sustainable.

Addressing the Concerns

With the increase of income-earning opportunities as a consequence of tourism, and technological change women have been freed from the hard life of collecting and selling firewood. The example of the tourist village of Luoshui shows that when people have other channels of earning incomes, they demand less of local forests as a direct source of livelihood, which is obviously advantageous to the protection of forests, and in turn promotes the development of the ecological service function of forests, However, it is also true that demands for firewood and timber can be merely displaced to other, non-local forests, just as tourism-related social ills, such as women in commercial sex, may be displaced to areas outside the local community. At the same time, those households that have not benefitted as much from the new sources of income have greater difficulty in meeting their fuel and other timber needs, as they are restrained from gathering wood from the nearby forests. The overall ban on logging, instituted in 1998, has also led to a fall in income of forest-dependent communities (more so the Lisu and Yi than the Mosuo and Naxi).

Liberalization of social relations as a consequence of economic reform policies and tourism, however, is much less seen in the case of gender relations. Men have taken over the social position of women in Naxi and Mosuo society, and women have now put their ecological wisdom and energy into services related to the entertainment of tourists and family affairs. In our interviews, men acknowledge that women-managed forest plots do better than those managed by men. However, women's representation in forest management committees or in political governance, whether at the village or higher levels, is usually non-existent. There is a growing tendency for men, even in matrilineal Mosuo society, to dominate important functions and positions of power.

The embedded violence of trade of women's bodies does raise the question: what has been done to change women's gender identity of subordination, including that of sexual subordination? Have the progressive, gender sensitive policies attempted to use the threat point to dismantle patriarchal powers and structures that deny poor, rural and indigenous women control over their lives?

The women's movements in the south as well as the north seem to be divided over the issue of sex work and the sex trade. I do not wish to discuss these positions of concern here. I, however, would like to say that the only way to understand this particular form of trade in women's bodies is to understand this practice as an aspect of masculine domination. The masculine domination legitimates a relationship of domination by embedding entitlement to women's sexual services in the biological nature of man. We know by now, largely as a result of feminist analysis, that the instituting of such a masculinity in men's bodies is a social construction. We are faced with the challenge to institutionalize strategies that efface masculine power and 'turn the strength of the strong against them' (Bourdieu 2001: 32).

What this means is that we have to take account of just and equality-based gender relations in policies and practices of economic development. This calls attention to halting the emerging patriarchy through the tourism industry in both Mosuo and Naxi societies, through measures like: (a) women's adequate representation in governance of their communities and resources; (b) development of capabilities (i.e., education, management and negotiating skills) of rural, poor women to manage resources and the tourism industry at management and higher levels; and (c) redefining of gender roles with a positive analysis of cultural systems. What is required is to check the monopoly over access to knowledge and management of resources. The concept of male headship of the household is to be replaced with the policy and concept of a dual-headed household system with joint ownership and management responsibility of all the household resources.

References

Bolles Lynn A. 'Women as a Category of Analysis in Scholarship on Tourism: l Jamaican Women and Tourism Employment.' In Erve Chambers ed. *Tourism and Culture, An Applied Perspective*, edited by Erve Chambers. State University of New York Press, 1997.

Bosu Mullick, Samar. 'Gender Relations and Witches among the Indigenous Communities of Jharkhand, India.' *Gender, Technology and Development* 4, no. 3 (2000): 333–58.

Bourdieu, Pierre. *Masculine Domination*: Stanford: Stanford University Press, 2001.

Goody, Jack. *Food and Love: A Cultural History of East and West*. London: Verso Press, 1998.

He Zhonghua 'Forest Management in Mosuo Matrilineal Society, Yunnan, China.' *Gender, Technology and Development* 5, no. 1 (2001).

Jameson, Frederick. 'Philosophy of Globalization'. In *Cultures of Globalization*, edited by Frederick Jameson and Masahi. Duke University Press, 2001.

Kelkar, Govind and Dev Nathan. *Gender and Tribe: Women, Land and Forests in Jharkhand*. New Delhi: Kali for Women and London: Zed Press, 1991.

Kelkar, Govind, Dev Nathan and Pierre Walter, eds. *Gender Relations in Forest Societies in Asia: Patriarchy at Odds*. New Delhi, Thousand Oaks, London: Sage Publications, 2003.

Kinnaird, Vivan, Uma Kothari and Derek Hall. 'Tourism: Gender Perspectives.' In *Tourism a Gender Analysis*, edited by V. Kinnaird and D. Hall. Chichester, UK: Wiley Publishers, 1994: 1–34.

Nathan, Dev and Govind Kelkar. 'Wood Energy: The Role of Women's Unpaid Labour.' *Gender, Technology and Development* 1, no. 2 (1997).

Nathan, Dev and Govind Kelkar. 'Agrarian Involution, Domestic Economy and Women: Rural Dimensions of the Asian Crisis'. *Economic and Political Weekly* 34, no. 19 (May 1999).

Preis, Ann-Belinda. S. 'Human Rights as Cultural Practice: An Anthropological Critique.' *Human Rights Quarterly* 18 (1996).

Sarin, Madhu, Neera M. Singh, Nandini Sunder and Ram K. Bhogal. 'Devolution as a Threat to Democratic Decision-Making? Findings from Three States in India'. In *Local Forest Management: The Impacts of Devolution Policies*, edited by David Edmunds and Eva Wollenberg. London: Earthscan, 2003.

10

CRAFTING AN ALTERNATIVE

LEASEHOLD FORESTRY FOR LIVELIHOODS OF THE POOR IN NEPAL

Dev Nathan and Girija Shrestha

INTRODUCTION

The movement away from state forestry has been in two directions: community forestry and market-based leases. Community forestry has tended to have a favourable environmental impact in increasing forest cover. But it has a limited impact on livelihoods, particularly of the poorest among the forest-dependent populations. The agenda of community forestry, whether in its full form as community-managed forestry or in its 'semi' form as Joint Forest Management (JFM) has been dominated by the forest departments, in both of their current agendas of forest regeneration and regeneration of timber stands. The study of devolution of forestry in three major Asian countries of China, India and the Philippines reached the conclusion that it had limited positive impact on livelihoods of the forest households (Edmunds et al. 2003). It is those who are less dependent on forests for livelihoods among the forest dwellers who support such initiatives. While, among forest households poor women who depend on forests either for supply of fuelwood and fodder, since they do not have sufficient private lands to provide these necessaries, or who have even to depend on sales of fuelwood (head-loading as it is called in South Asia) are the most hard hit by community-imposed restrictions on harvests from forests (Madhu Sarin 2001).

Studies of community forestry in Nepal have reached similar conclusions about the limited impact of the scheme on livelihoods. 'Overall, the community forestry intervention has had limited positive impact on the livelihood of rural households. The evidence suggests that some households, especially the poorer ones, have been affected negatively' (Malla 2000).

Thus, community forestry has tended to be iniquitous; biased against the poorest who depend on direct use of forest resources for livelihoods and against women, who have the responsibility of providing fuelwood and fodder, and even for food security among these households. Further, in a situation where many ethnic communities live together in multi-ethnic regions, if not multi-ethnic villages, it is the ethnic communities that are poorer and who have less urban contacts, i.e., the indigenous peoples who populate the upper slopes, who benefit the least from such community forestry schemes and from the investment of income from community-owned forests. This was seen in the case of the development of tourism in Lijiang, China (Dev Nathan and Yu Xiaogang, this volume). The use of forest incomes for tourist development benefitted more the valley-based Naxi, who were also more educated and had better urban contacts, than the Yi or Lisu, who inhabit the upper slopes, who are on the whole poorer, with less education and fewer urban contacts. How to devise schemes of community-based forestry that would benefit the poorest or poorer sections, the indigenous peoples and the land-poor among them, seems an open question.

Community forestry has another problem. Since these are common property systems, there are inevitably problems of dealing with incentives to investment and controlling 'free riding'. It is possible to control 'free riding', provided, the community is well organized; but this is often not the case. Particularly in very degraded and currently unproductive areas, which require substantial investment, there have been problems with community forestry schemes (Karki and Chalise 1995).

One solution to finding sufficient investment resources for degraded lands has been that of allocating them to corporations, as has been done in parts of India, or even of auctioning them to the highest bidder, as frequently occurs in China. But such leasing to the highest bidder displaces the low income and low productivity users, for instance those who continue to depend on the degraded lands for fuel collection and grazing. In one such case at Lashe lake, Yunnan, China, the leased lands were taken over for higher-productivity orchards, but this meant that the poorer Yi villagers could no more graze their animals in this area, and they were not given any alternative for this purpose (Nathan and Yu Xiaogang, this volume). Elisabeth Grinspoon (2001) details the conflicts between the lease-holders and the rest of the community in some other cases in this leasing process in China.

The auctioning of resources to the highest bidder is in line with the current thinking of neo-liberal globalization, where resources should be put to their most productive uses, which means that those who are unable to match that productivity would lose access to such resources. Traditional welfare economics asks if the gain to those who get the lease is more than the loss to those who lose use of the resource, which would mean that the winners could compensate the losers for their loss. It is quite likely that the gain is more than the loss. But there are no such compensation schemes in practice. Further the comparison of gains and losses ignores the fact that the marginal utility of the lost income is higher than the marginal utility of the gained income, since marginal utility declines with an increase in income. The important point, however, is that there are no such compensation schemes in practice.

That resources should be taken over by those who are able to put them to the most productive use, is an old concept of the rights of property that goes back at least to Locke, and was used to justify imperial rights of colonization over the access of hunter-gatherers or even cultivators, who did not produce as much exchange value as 'improving' landowners. This was used to justify colonization of Native American lands and to treat the lands of hunter-gatherers as 'wastelands' subject to *res nullius*, or the absence of property rights.[1] It is now used to demand a level playing field for capital to compete for resources anywhere. The nature of such a so-called level playing field was aptly expressed by the poet Blake: 'One law for the lamb and the lion is not justice'.

Yet another problem in the allocation of resources is that to the extent it is done, as in most land reforms, it is confined to distribution to men, supposedly as heads of households. The effects of the exclusion of women from land or productive resource ownership, have been discussed in a number of places (e.g., Bina Agarwal 1994 and Kelkar and Nathan 2001) and need not be elaborated on here. But the twin issues of equity for the poor and for women, are not

---

[1] See Ellen Meiksins Wood (2003), for a new discussion of this question in the context of the current globalization.

addressed in the usual community forestry and market-based lease systems. In designing an alternative to market-based allocation of access to productive resources these are issues that need to be addressed.

LEASEHOLD FORESTRY

An attempt to do this is the Leasehold Forestry System in Nepal. Originally tried out as a project funded by IFAD, the government of Nepal, with support from the Netherlands government and Food and Agriculture Organization of the United Nations (FAO), it is now in the process of being adopted as a general, nationwide programme, or sub-programmme within community forestry schemes. It was tried out as a project in villages in 10 districts of Nepal (Ramechap, Dolakha, Sindhupalchowk, Kavrepalanchowk, Dahding, Gorkha, Chitwan, Tanahu, Makawanpur and Sindhuli) and is now expected to be taken up on a nationwide scale.

The leasehold forestry system is based on the allocation of a portion of community forest, generally degraded forest, to groups of poor, including women, for them to develop as sites for supporting their livelihoods. In choosing the group members there is both a selection and a self-targeting mechanism. In the first place it is the households that are identified as the poorest within the villages, falling below a target level of ownership of 0.5 hectare of cultivated land and with an income of less than Nepali Rs 2,500 per year.

The self-targeting mechanism works in that access is dependent on performance of labour in the forest patch. Thus, a family that has alternate income possibilities higher than what can be realized from the forest, would leave the forest group.

Almost invariably these poorer households are not from the various caste Hindu groups, rather they are largely from among Tibeto-Burman langugage speaking indigenous peoples (like Tamang and Praja), and the lowest castes. Consequently, without making membership of these communities a condition for membership of the group, these forest lease groups were inevitably dominated by those belonging to the indigenous peoples and the lowest castes.

Initially the husband–wife partnership unit was taken as the basis for membership in the group, the idea being that this would enhance women's participation. At the same time, priority was given to single women households (or female-headed households), recognizing the high rate of male out-migration in the concerned districts.

Securing User Rights

The Nepal Forest Act of 1993 provides for the possibility of leasehold forestry. Article 32 allows for the possibility of leasing the forest to any corporate body. 'Any corporate body, industry or community established under the prevailing by law which to take the Leasehold Forest (etc).' But it also allowed for the possibility of using the system for poverty alleviation. 'His Majesty's Government may prepare project[s] for the communities living below the poverty line and hand the Leasehold Forest to the beneficiaries of such project[s]' (quoted in Ohler 2002).

Handing over such forest patches to the leasehold groups required the consent of the village, or the community forest user groups. A factor that could have made this consent easier to obtain was the fact that leasehold forestry was confined to the most degraded areas. These areas did not yield any income and required substantial investment before they could yield income. Thus, in a sense, they cost the community relatively little.

The relative ease in securing such forests to the poor lessee groups should be contrasted with the difficulty in securing such rights for poor fishers in lakes and ponds in Bangladesh. These lakes and ponds are quite productive and thus there were always attempts by the richer, former leaseholders, who would formerly secure leases through auction, to resist the handover of these lakes and ponds to poor fishers: men and women.[2] The factor of the difference in existing productivity of the lakes/ponds in Bangladesh and the degraded forests in Nepal certainly played a role in making one transfer difficult, and the other transfer relatively easy. It remains to be seen whether, the degraded lands having been restored and their productivity increased by the leasehold groups, there are subsequent attempts by the 'community' to take back these lands into community control. Legally, however, the forest patches have been transferred to the poor lessee groups for 40 years, through a 20-year lease renewable for a second 20 years. But, of course, legal rights though necessary, are not everything.

Difference From Community Forestry

The project had the twin objectives of raising the incomes of families in the hills who are below the poverty line, and contributing to

---

[2] On the experience of IFAD's Oxbow Lakes Project, see various papers in

improving the ecological conditions of the hills. These objectives were achieved through leasing blocks of degraded forest land to groups of poor households. The vegetative cover of the leased land was regenerated and improved, mainly as a result of improved management (control of livestock grazing and fire, as well as enrichment planting of grasses and trees). This management process allotted a resource area for the exclusive use of the poorest households who were given land on lease. With assured access to additional fodder production from the leased land, the families were expected to increase their income from livestock production and other activities. This was reinforced through loans to increase production on private land and other income generating activities. In the hills of Nepal, livestock raising is important not only in itself, but also for the manure it provides to terrace agriculture. Manure is often the critical resource in expanding cultivation, while the main limiting factor on raising livestock was the labour involved in grazing the animals (Ben Campbell 2000: 106). Leasehold forestry, prohibited grazing and forced a move to cutting and carrying of fodder, and that too from a limited area; thus reducing the labour cost of raising animals.

The project included components such as: (a) regeneration of degraded forest lands; (b) on-farm fodder and fuelwood development; (c) livestock development; (d) off-farm income-generating activities; (e) terrace improvement; (f) cooking stove improvement; (g) construction or improvement of access trails and foot-bridges.

The regeneration of the degraded lands was achieved through a combination of halting all grazing and control of fires, followed by enrichment planting with grasses and leguminous forage species as well as multipurpose tree species, including fruit trees. With the control of grazing, the natural vegetation also regenerated, recreating the multi-storied forest. The jobs required for the above were all carried out by the group members collectively.

Members from the poorer village sections would be unable to carry out these time-consuming tasks without some direct remuneration for doing them. They usually spend all available time in trying to earn some income, or economize on the use of inputs. Project finance becomes necessary in order to provide some income to the members to carry out the above tasks. Thus, there is a cost involved in the regeneration process; it is not only income foregone from immediate use, but also the cost of paying for the various jobs involved in

Middendorp, Thompson and Pomeroy (1998) and Dev Nathan and Niaz Ahmed Apu (1998 and 2002).

regeneration. Consequently, there is a cost, which can be higher on a per capita basis than that of community forestry (Ohler 2002), which does not involve the above replanting and related tasks.

This cost of replanting and related tasks would exist even in the case of investment by a private corporation. The difference is that while the corporation would be able to gain access to funds, groups of the poor would not have similar access to funds. Lacking their own savings, there is no other way but to provide public money for investment by groups of the poor. Of course, such provision of public funds is not for direct consumption, but for investment. Thus, it is not a recurring expenditure, as would be the case of direct social security or food security measures. It is an investment that increases the productive base of the poor. It is an asset-forming redistribution, though based on government revenues.

In a sense, there is a parallel with what is done in famine-relief works in India. From an early emphasis on mere provision of work, the emphasis shifted to increasing the productive base of the economy. But there have been schemes to utilize these 'food for work' programmes to target low productive lands of the poor and thus increase their productive base. Leasehold forestry represents such a targeting of the improved productive base directly at the poor, while community forestry is more like the food for work programmes that are confined to general infrastructure like roads, schools, etc.

In the case of community forestry, the user groups tend to be quite large, more than 100 households. They thus have to function through executive committees. It is reported (Ohler 2002) that farmers usually refer to 'committee' rather than community forests, referring to the important role that the committee performs. On the other hand, in leasehold forestry the groups are quite small, not more than 10 members. This enables direct decision-making and functioning of the group as a whole. The smallness of the group and the usually close proximity in which they stay (within the same hamlet of the village) enables group members to be quite aware of the work done and benefits gained by each member. This makes monitoring of each other's activities relatively easy, and thus checks 'free riding'. Olson (1963) had very early on pointed out the importance of group size in enabling collective action. Here, the factor of close residential proximity adds to the advantage of small group size in making continued collective action possible.

The manner in which the output/income from forestry can be used differs between community and leasehold forestry. In the former, the members of the community only have limited rights to collect firewood, and all income has to be used either for community development or for forest development. This has resulted in use of income for building schools and bridges. Such infrastructure benefits the whole community, but benefits the better off more. Bridges, for instance, are more important for those who have tradable goods. Their benefit goes up with the volume of tradable goods. Such infrastructure reduces the costs of marketing and thus increases net income. But, of course, the extent to which farmers benefit from this depends on the volume of goods they trade.

In leasehold forestry, on the other hand, income derived from the forest can be used directly by members. The main products of leasehold forestry are fodder and fuel, but also include small quantities of medicinal plants, spices, vegetables, broom grass and fruits. Fodder, in particular, is important in enabling the landless to increase their holdings of animals. The land constraint, which operates in household holdings of animals, is somewhat overcome by leasehold forestry.

CHANGES IN WELL-BEING

Thus, the products of leasehold forestry have directly contributed to increasing household income. Surveys indicate that leasehold forestry households increased the average period of food self-sufficiency from 7.8 months in 1996 to 8.4 months in 1999, even while household size increased from 6.6 to 7.1 persons. This amounts to a 16 per cent increase in food self-sufficiency per household; which should be contrasted with the 4 per cent decrease in person–months of food self-sufficiency for non-leasehold households in the same period (Thompson 2000 quoted in Ohler 2002).

There was a diversification of livelihood sources. From the earlier almost exclusive reliance on local and migratory wage labour, livestock became a means of earning an income. A study of 1,500 leasehold groups showed that the extent of diversification of sources of income increased steadily with the increase in the number of years after group formation (Ohler 2002). The growing sources of income were from sale of goats, buffalo milk and fodder; all related to the increased availability of fodder in the leasehold forest. A recent evaluation found that leasehold members had increased their holdings of goats from 4.4 on average in 1999 to more than 5 per household in March 2003 (IFAD 2003).

Members also changed the types of animals they raised, moving from low input requiring, and low productivity animals to higher input requiring but more productive animals—for instance, from cows to buffalos for milk production. But this change was quite limited and probably possible only in lowland areas with better water supply. Overall the ownership of buffaloes by leasehold members remained constant over the life of the project (IFAD 2003).

The increase in local food security was probably reflected in a decline in migration, which is a critical coping strategy to deal with the lack of food security. While 6 per cent of leasehold households reported a return of migrated members, there was no such report of returns of migrants from non-leasehold households. Migration, including the movement of girls and young women into the sex trade in Mumbai, India and of boys to Nepali Capital Kathmandu's restaurants and carpet factories (Campbell 2000: 116), is quite high in this area. Improving the economic condition of the indigenous peoples of this region is then an important contribution to increasing their livelihood options.

Along with the direct income effect of the increased resource for raising animals or even selling fodder, there were also indirect effects due to the decrease in women's time spent in fodder and fuel collection. Before the leasehold project, women, as is usual in the Nepal mountains, spent many hours in gathering fuelwood from forests. In fact, the closure of community forests often meant that women had to walk even further into distant state forests to collect fuelwood.[3] With leasehold forestry, women could now collect fuelwood and fodder close by, when the leasehold forest started yielding sufficient outputs of wood and fodder.

In the Nepal mountains, fodder collection which is women's work, is particularly arduous. With leasehold forestry, the time spent on collecting fodder decreased from an average of 3.9 hours per day to just 1.4 hours per day. This is a difference of 2.5 hours per day in the space of just five years (Ohler 2002).

If there had been no alternate way in which to use the time saved, this saving of time would not have had any other than direct health effect on women and their households. But the reduction in time spent on these activities meant that women could now use the time saved in other income-earning activities. It could be used to raise more animals, given that time spent in fodder collection was earlier a constraint in increasing the holding of animals. It could also be used

---

[3] Such an effect of the community closure of forests is reported in India too (Sarin 2003).

for taking up other income-earning activities, for which training was provided: 'Through my training, I have started cultivating vegetables and weaving wool. I have developed a [business] relationship with the vendor and conduct my own business. My income has gone a long way towards our children's education', said Purna Maya, a member of a leasehold group (IFAD 2001: 10). Other women also pointed out that they had taken up new, or expanded existing, economic activities—like cultivating tomatoes, sewing or tailoring for cash, etc. (ibid.: 7). The IFAD evaluation found that the time saved in collecting fodder and fuelwood collection was invested in livestock rearing, agricultural production, work in the kitchen garden, and even in some rest. 'Rest periods may have been included within the longer time required for household chores in the "before project" situation. However, it is a revealing aspect of their changed perceptions that respondents decided to single out 'rest' as a separate activity' (IFAD 2003: 17).

Initially, a number of women were not keen on taking up leasehold forestry, thinking that it would increase their already excessive workload. But the decrease in time spent in collecting fuelwood and fodder, because of the possibility of collecting these close by, convinced a number of women of the benefits of this scheme. Saving of labour time in collecting fuelwood and fodder was reflected in greater involvement in cash-earning activities.

Gender Relations

Initially, the project dealt with households, both men and women. But as is to be expected this led to men taking the leading positions within the groups and to their position within households also getting consolidated. Many of the Tibeto-Burman communities generally have more equal gender relations than those existing among Hindu communities. But this equality had been eroded over time, due to a number of factors including the influence of the higher status and ruling Hindu groups (Subba and Babbar 2002).

Given that care of livestock, including fodder and fuelwood collection were both generally in the women's domain, the high out-migration of males from the area, and the greater responsibility of women in food security,[4] the project, sometime in mid-course, introduced a greater focus on women's individual membership and even

---

[4] In a manner repeated across indigenous communities in India, women's greater responsibility for food security, was accompanied by men's greater abuse of alcohol.

on the formation of women-only groups for leasehold forestry. Along with the formation of a gender focal point at the project level, this led to greater involvement of women in all project activities.

In effect, since women were the ones who performed most of the relevant labour, training was now geared towards them. The formation of women's groups and greater women's representation in groups as a whole and among officer bearers, increased the role of women in the management of the leasehold forestry. This was a big change from the usual pattern of women's exclusion from management of community forest resources, a pattern invariably repeated even across indigenous Asia (Kelkar and Nathan 2003).

Women were also provided credit and were possibly able to gain greater control over household income and its manner of use. Women reported that they had acquired some more say over household expenses than earlier. Along with this they also had a greater extent of self-esteem, now that they were earning substantial amounts of cash: 'Women are now able to have a constructive discussion for household development at home with their family .... Even I used to think that only husbands must earn. When I think about this now, I feel guilty' Saili Tamang (IFAD 2001: 9).

There was greater participation of women in public activities and increased self-confidence. 'My participation in management and nursery training, and the observations I made on my tours of various land-use practices have given me confidence. I can earn on my own' Maili Tamang (IFAD 2001: 9).

Women were even confident about their ability to retain the forest after the end of the project: 'I am assured that this is my forest whether the project is phased out or not. We are no longer "mukh takne" (dependent on others)' anonymous (IFAD 2001: 12).

Or, in the event of being abandoned by their husbands: 'We used to rely entirely on men. Today, women have developed enough skills, knowledge and vision so that we can develop ourselves independently. We now feel secure that even if our husbands abandon us for a new wife, we will be okay' (Shashi Kala) (IFAD 2001: 10).

Women's direct access to productive resources, rather than mediated access through their relationship with men, is a critical factor in promoting independence and the confidence of self-reliance.

The greater role of women in group-based management of leasehold forests, which inevitably required a greater amount of time spent away from the household, and women's greater earning of cash, has had an additional beneficial effect of inducing a number of men to share some childcare and other household work (Gurung and Lama 2002).

A reduction of the time spent by women in collecting fuel and fodder has made possible a direct increase in the opportunity cost of women's labour, and also promoted a change in gender relations, with a greater sharing of household labour between women and men.

ECOLOGICAL BENEFITS

One of the first measures taken to improve the ecological condition of the degraded forests was that of stopping all grazing. This enabled a natural regeneration of grass and shrubs. This was accompanied by enrichment planting of improved grasses, shrubs and trees. Even after grasses were regenerated, grazing remained prohibited. Rather, only the cutting and carrying of fodder was allowed. Within a few years, the ecological condition was much improved, both in terms of the density of cover and of diversity of species. The infamous *alang alang* or *imperata cylindrical* grass, which tends to takeover degraded lands, was reduced and even disappeared (Ohler 2002). The shift from grazing to cutting of fodder was a particularly important shift from an extensive to an intensive system of land-use, made possible by the higher productivity of the regenerated grasses and shrubs.

Even the nature of fuelwood collection changed. Since the relatively small group 'owned' the trees, there was a monitored shift to pruning and thinning of trees, rather than competitive and destructive over-harvesting of fuelwood. The small size of the groups and the possibility of monitoring by the group members, enabled the cultivation of fuelwood, rather than its mere collection and natural regeneration, thus making it intensive as in home gardens or other privately-owned land.

A study by the International Forestry Resource Institute (IFRI) found that in two leasehold forestry areas the number of species had increased by 57 per cent and 84 per cent. The structure of the vegetation had also improved with an increase in the number of trees with stem diameter in excess of 10 centimentres and the reduction in the ground cover of *imperata cylindrical* (IFAD 2003: 20).

LIMITATIONS

The leasehold forestry system has been confined to degraded forest lands. The forest lands in better condition still remain within the system of community forestry. Further the benefits of the leasehold forestry have been seen to vary between locations. 'The measurable impact of the project was greatest in well-watered lowland sites close to markets and least in high-altitude sites with steep slopes and scarcity of groundwater, and remote from markets and government service centers' (IFAD 2003: 9). This is not an unexpected limitation, which means that the problems of high-altitude sites with steep slopes and the scarcity of groundwater will perhaps have to be looked at in terms other than the increase of income from forests.

DIRECTIONS

Preliminary evaluations of leasehold forestry show that there has been an improvement in the condition of the forest, both in terms of forest cover and of species diversity. The forests have also become more productive, yielding higher amounts of fuel and fodder. There has been a shift from an extensive to intensive use of forest land. All this has led to a higher income for the poor families and also diversified their sources of income. At the same time, the substantial involvement of women in various aspects of leasehold forestry activity, including as primary members of the groups, has contributed to women's increased self-confidence and self-esteem. Given that women continue to have primary responsibility for food security, and that women are known to spend more of the income they control on family well-being, the higher income under their control is also likely to have improved their households' well-being more than if the income had remained under men's control.

The scheme of leasehold forestry has been successful in assuring the poor and women of access to a critical livelihood resource. If and when their incomes and productivity in other sectors goes up, the current members are likely to reduce their involvement in leasehold forestry. At that time the community, or persons and groups within it, could well take up the next stage of developing forest-based industries.

What has been carried out in leasehold forestry is in effect a land reform. Instead of the usual transition from state to community forestry, we have a transition from state to a kind of private forestry for a group of the poor, including women. This is a form of privatization, but it is a privatization dedicated to assuring non-market access to productive resources for the poorest and most disadvantaged. It has the further merit of being a privatization that leads to a higher investment of capital and labour by the members, with capital being provided through international public mediation.

Were this measure to be carried out a national scale,

> Even with the most conservative figures, if we leased out 0.5 million hectares of such land to say 0.5 million households in the hills at the rate of 1 ha per household, this could turn out to be the most revolutionary land reform programme in the country [....] it would greatly improve the income levels of the poor, control soil erosion in mountain watersheds and significantly improve the ecology. This would have long-term positive impact on the conservation of natural resources and bio-diversity (Yadav and Dhakal 2000).

Such a measure would be a way of assuring non-market lease of critical natural resources to the landless and other poor. Maintaining the condition of non-marketability of the asset (forest) or of membership, the stress would be placed on the stream of sustainable benefits it can provide.

REFERENCES

Agarwal, Bina. *A Field of One's Own: Gender and Land Rights in South Asia*. Cambridge: Cambridge University Press, 1994.

Campbell, Ben. 'Properties of Identity: Gender, Agency and Livelihoods in Central Nepal.' In *Gender Agency and Change: Anthropological Perspectives*, edited by Victoria Ana Goddard. London and New York: Routledge, 2000.

Middendorp, Hans A. J., Paul M. Thompson, and Robert S. Pomeroy. *Sustainable Inland Fisheries Management in Bangladesh*, Makati: The International Center for Living Resources Management (ICLARM), Danish International Development Assistance (DANIDA), Ford Foundation, 1998.

Edmunds, David, Eva Wollenberg, Antonio P. Contreras, Liu Dachang, Govind Kelkar, Dev Nathan, Madhu Sarin and Neera M. Singh. 'Conclusion'. In *Local Forest Management: The Impacts of Devolution Policies*, edited by David Edmunds and Eva Wollenberg. London: Earthscan, 2003.

Grinspoon, Elisabeth. 'Socialist Wasteland Auctions: Emerging Conflicts over Collective Forestland in China's Transitional Economy'. Paper presented at Forestry Impacts of China's Reforms: Lessons for China and the World, 20–23 June 2001, Dujiangyan, Sichuan, China.

Gurung, Jeanette with Kanchan Lama. Empowered Women and the Men behind Them: A Study of Change within the HMG/IFAD Hills Leasehold Forestry and Forage Development Project in Nepal. Rome: IFAD, 2002.

IFAD. *Voices from the Field: Women's Access to Land and Other Natural Resources in Nepal*, Rome: IFAD, 2001.

—————. *Assessment of Rural Poverty: Asia and the Pacific*. Rome: IFAD, 2002.

—————. *Hills Leasehold Forestry and Forage Development Project in Nepal: Interim Evaluation*, Draft. Rome: IFAD, 2003.

Karki, Madhav and S. R. Chalise. 'Local forest user groups and rehabilitation of degraded forest lands'. In *Challenges in Mountain Resource Management in Nepal: Processes, Trends and Dynamics in Middle Mountain Watersheds*, edited by H. Schrier, P. B. Shah and S. Brown. Proceedings of Workshop: Kathmandu: ICIMOD/IDRC/UBC, 1995.

Kelkar, Govind and Dev Nathan. 'Forest Societies in Asia: Gender Relations and Change.' In *Gender Relations in Forest Societies in Asia: Patriarchy at Odds*, edited by Govind Kelkar, Dev Nathan and Pierre Walter. New Delhi: Sage, 2003.

Malla, Y. B. 'Impact of Community Forestry Policy on Rural Livelihoods and Food Security in Nepal'. *Unasylva 202*, 51 (2000). Quoted in Ohler, 2002.

Nathan, Dev and Niaz Ahmed Apu. 'Women's Independent Access to Productive Resources: Fish Ponds in the Oxbow Lakes Project'. *Gender, Technology and Development* 2, no. 3 (September–December 1998).

———. 'Securing Women's Property Rights: Problems of Good Governance and Establishing Norms of Economic Functioning'. *Gender, Technology and Development* 6, no. 3 (September–December 2002).

Ohler, Frits M. J. *Impact of Leasehold Forestry on Livelihoods and Environment in Nepal*. Rome: FAO, 2002.

Olson, Mancur. *The Logic of Collective Action*, Cambridge, Mass.: Harvard University Press, 1963.

Sarin, Madhu. 'Empowerment and Disempowerment of Women in Uttarakhand'. In *Gender Relations in Forest Societies in Asia: Patriarchy at Odds*. New Delhi: Sage, 2003.

Subba, Suman and Aneela Z. Babar. 'Strengthening Gender Initiatives: Case Study of Hills Leasehold Forest and Forage Development Project in Nepal'. Rome: IFAD, 2002.

Thompson, R. H. *Assessment of the Impact of HLFFDP on Participating Households from the Household Survey Data 1994–1999*. Rome: FAO, 2000. Quoted in Ohler, 2002.

Wood, Ellen Meiksins. *The Empire of Capital*. New Delhi: LeftWord, 2003.

Yadav, R. P. and A. Dhakal, A. *Leasehold Forestry for Poor: An Innovative Pro-Poor Programme in the Hills of Nepal*, Policy Outlook Series No. 6, HMG Ministry of Agriculture/Winrock International, 2000.

11

EXTERNAL TRADE AND DEVELOPMENT OF UPLAND PEOPLES IN THE HIMALAYA-HINDUKUSH

Dev Nathan and N. S. Jodha

INTRODUCTION

The two major avenues of globalization are the market and state (national) or international management policies. State and international policy, as related to the management of forests in the uplands and the creation of markets for environmental services, are discussed in the paper by Nathan (this volume).

This paper concentrates on external trade and trade-related processes. The role of 'niche' production in enabling mountain communities to benefit from globalization is discussed. This is followed by a discussion of the factors determining who benefits in the rise of entrepreneurial systems of livelihood and the consequences of commercialization for intensification of production.

We first need to take up the question whether it is, in fact, possible to utilize comparative advantage to increase export earnings. In India there is a strong (still very strong) body of economic thinking that holds that this is not possible.

From Mahalanobis to current globo-phobes, the inflexibility of export earnings is taken for granted. Exports of primary goods, with secular fall in terms of trade vis-à-vis manufactures, provides the scenario for ruling out the possibility of increasing export earnings. This, however, is specific to exports of primary goods or resource-based goods, where under-pricing of environmental services and neglect of reproduction and management costs in commons means that only collection costs are taken into account in the price of forest products—these two factors lead to subsidies for sales, including exports. Fortunately, East and Southeast Asia have not been infected by export pessimism. The successes of East and Southeast Asia, in increasing export earnings through targeted entry into lower- and middle-level manufacturing, shows that, overall, export pessimism is misplaced.

On the other hand, failure to utilize external markets will mean restricting the rate of local investment to that made possible by the growth of agriculture. This would not allow the intensification of various types of production. For instance, the domestication of different tree products, would be very narrow without external markets. Further, the needs of the upland peoples have gone beyond what can be produced locally, making trade essential to social reproduction.

Dealing with external markets, whether national, regional or global, necessarily means utilizing comparative advantage, which is based on the relative supplies of the various factors of production; chiefly labour, capital and natural resources and the productivity of their use. With increasing free trade, countries have to pay attention to productivity even in the case of goods produced entirely for the domestic market since they could be ousted by cheaper goods from outside; and to the extent that indigenous peoples and households carry on some trade, their incomes are affected by trends in global productivity of their traded goods. But indigenous people face serious price problems in their exports, with social costs being lower than prices and thus leading to a subsidy by the producers.

PRICING PROBLEMS IN EXPORTS

The social cost of a commodity is higher than its private cost because of uncompensated externalities. Why does that happen and what would be the appropriate policy in that condition?

In this chapter dealing with environmental services, Nathan showed that the values of various environmental services are not included in the pricing of products. The resulting subsidy is paid by the forest communities in terms of the value of environmental services lost because of, say, deforestation. The valuation of environmental services to external users, as proposed, will have the effect of introducing such valuation into prices.

There is yet another factor in the low relative prices of forest products—the costs of planting or replanting and other management of forests needed to sustain forest production are not included in the prices of forest products, which are collected from the commons. It is virtually only the costs of gathering that are reflected in their prices. As a result exports from the forest are at prices that are below social costs.

As argued in Chichilinsky (1994) the lack of property rights in the 'South' simultaneous with well-developed property rights in the 'North' leads to an unequal exchange between the 'South' and 'North'. In this case forest products are under-priced and thus forest producers are subject to an unequal exchange with the rest of the world. The base of the low price of forest products lies in the inadequate framework of decaying commons institutions that cannot relate to production for maximization of income. A change in the institutions governing forest management then becomes necessary to address the question of unequal exchange.

When tree products are no longer collected from the 'forest' but from domesticated trees in the home garden, the producers would necessarily take account of the costs of planting and of management of the trees in their decisions of production and sale. If existing prices are too low to cover these costs, they will not domesticate these trees or will reduce their production of its products. As more and more of these tree products are produced from home gardens their prices will better reflect costs of planting and management.

There is yet a third factor that can lead to a divergence between social costs and private incomes. This is the presence of food insecurity, which in the absence of well-developed credit markets, could lead to interlinking of markets, whether for export products and food or exports and labour.

FOOD SECURITY AND THE TERMS OF EXCHANGE

The indigenous people trade many of their products, e.g., Non-Timber Forest Products (NTFPs), with the rest of the world. They also supply wage labour, both locally and as migrants. One factor that is noticed in many projects among indigenous peoples is that, when they get the ability to invest in livelihood options, in additional crops and so on, they tend to concentrate on increasing their production of food staples. 'Among the Scheduled Tribes [in India], the food-insecure perceived that their "subjective" strategy of food self-sufficiency was a better bet than the largely theoretical prospect of selling perennials and buying food' (Greeley 1999). Is this an irrational, subjective fear of the market or is there a good basis for the insistence on first increasing food security before increasing their involvement in other markets?

A farm family that does not have sufficient food to meet its annual/seasonal needs, will be forced onto the market to secure needed food. It will have to sell either labour power or products that it collects. Food deficit families often enter into advance contracts for sale of labour power. For instance, in the hills of Chhattisgarh, agents of traders and landlords come up during the height of the lean season (i.e., the period between sowing and harvest of upland rice) and contract the sale of labour in the period after the harvest. Advancing some grain for the ongoing lean period, they fix the rates at which the labourers would work in the post-harvest period. Such advance contracting is only done by the food insecure. Those families who are food secure, but do not have the irrigated land for a second crop, also migrate to the lowlands for work after the rice harvest. But they do not contract their labour in advance; instead they acquire work at the then-current wage rates.

In this case the food insecure get credit, in real not financial means, and the price of this credit is advance sale of labour at prices lower than those that would prevail at the time of performing the labour. Those who are food secure are able to avoid this interlinking of credit and labour markets. When watershed management activities increased and stabilized the productivity of the monsoon crop, one immediate effect was the fall in advance contracting of labour.

Where there are forest resources available, the response to the lean season food deficit is to collect forest products for sale. Some are valuable nuts, like *chironji*. But in the market for such nuts, as for labour, two prices simultaneously prevail. The food insecure trade it with local shopkeepers, who give them various food stuffs, including grain, lentils, cooking oil and salt, in exchange. The collector does not sell the nuts and buy household requirements. Rather, the operation is simultaneous in both product and consumption markets. In this interlinked market transaction, the forest product collector does not even know the price he/she is getting for their product.

Those who are food secure do not sell in the above interlinked fashion. They sell their products at a given price and then buy what they need. Food security allows them to operate separately in product and consumption markets; while food insecurity leads to interlinked markets.

One might say that if there were well-functioning credit (the first case) and product markets (second case) then there would not be the observed interlinked transactions and the sellers would get a better return. But, one should turn the analysis around and point out that food insecurity plays a critical role in there not being well-functioning markets. With enhanced food security households would not be forced into interlinked transactions and better functioning markets would become the norm. But depending on the level of food insecurity, markets would continue to be interlinked to the detriment of the producers of forest products and the sellers of wage labour.

Globalization increases the options of using markets to secure income. But the extent to which various sections of indigenous peoples benefit from the expanding markets depends on their level of food security.

The above three factors—uncompensated externalities in the form of environmental service costs, unaccounted costs of replanting and management, and the presence of food insecurity, all together lead to a social cost higher than the private return from an exported product. What is the appropriate policy in this case? Following the analysis of Bhagwati and Ramaswamy (1973), since the distortion is in domestic markets (or the absence of markets) it can be treated by appropriate domestic institutional reforms. The analysis put forward earlier of creating markets for environmental services, and domesticating forest products in order to take into account costs of replanting, management and related costs that are missed in the commons— these two measures would both bring private costs more into line with social costs. The third factor, that of food security in order to enable sellers to realize a higher price, is usually neglected in trade analysis. But as we saw above, the absence of food security would force sellers to accept a lower price than is otherwise available on the market.

Institutional reform is needed to deal with the first two externalities. A strengthening of the livelihood situation is needed to deal with the third factor. Together these three interventions would increase the price realization from indigenous peoples' exports.

There, however, may be yet another distortion that results in prices lower than social costs—that is the presence of distortion in the product, or external, market. In this case, while a lot of attention has been paid to product distortion caused by monopoly of the country or its firms in the sellers' market, not so much attention has been paid to the distortion caused by monopsony in the buyers' market, i.e., the presence of just one or a handful of buyers in the market for the product, one which may be produced by a large number of small producers, as is typical for forest products.

LIBERALIZATION OF TRADE

Often these trading monopolies are created by state policy. Very common in Indian states is the granting of monopsony rights to buy certain products from mountain farmers. To take one such example, in the hill districts of Manipur, the farmers are recognized as having ownership rights over all NTFPs. But this is so only for use within the village. For any transport of the product outside village boundaries, the farmers will have to sell it only to the trader (*mahaldar*) who has acquired the monopsony right through auction.

Such legally created monopsonies not only seriously reduce the returns to farmers but also impede the development of the product. The extent to which labour, land and management will be devoted to the product depends on the expected return from the product. The lower the return the less likely will be the investment of labour, in management and in intensifying production. Removing the restraints, on the other hand, is likely to increase income and be reflected in the adoption of superior land-use and management techniques.

The removal of constraints on internal trade, in conjunction with measures to improve food security for the producers and to form producers' associations to improve their market strength, would improve the returns of indigenous people from their collection and sale of NTFPs. The increased returns from this activity would in turn foster steps to increase the investment of labour, land and management in the production of these commodities. It would also enable these mountain farmers to take advantage of global markets for their products.

But besides local monopolies, created by state fiat, there are also international trade monopolies. Many commodities are bought by just a handful of international corporations. In the coffee trade, which is very much a product of upland cultivation, two brokers, Neumann and Volcafe, alone account for 25 per cent of world coffee exports (Silver 2003). There are monopolies on a smaller scale. For instance, a handful of Thai traders, themselves owners of retail outlets in Thailand, buy all of the woven and embroidered cloth produced by Lao women in the border district of Sayaboury. Dealing with such global and local monopolies is essential to be able to increase price realization for the products of indigenous peoples. As will be discussed in more detail below, the indigenous producers of these various export commodities will need to form producers' organizations in order to strengthen their market position.

Comparative Advantage and Niche Products

Some of the crops cultivated for purely commercial reasons have been developed from existing upland agricultural systems. Various fruits, which formerly existed only in home gardens in order to provide variety in the diet, have now been extended into whole orchards. Others have been introduced from outside in order to take advantage of mountain conditions. Tea in the Himalayan mountains, coffee in the Andes, potatoes in the Hunza Valley, Pakistan, apples in Himachal Pradesh, India, are examples of such niche products, as also narcotic drugs in Highland Southeast Asia and the Pakistan–Afghanistan border region. They are all niche products in the sense that they exploit the ecological niches of the uplands, with their unique combinations of slope, precipitation, temperature and solar radiation (Funnel and Parish 2001).

Besides the ecological niches of the mountains, the specificities of mountain environments in relation to the external economy, also play a role in influencing comparative advantage (Jodha 2002a). The high cost of transport and the necessary longer period of transport, mean that comparative advantage will lie in commodities that are high-value but low-volume/weight; and also with those commodities that are not perishable or have a longer life. Large cardamom has been identified as one such commodity with a clear comparative advantage. It is exclusively cultivated and found in the Himalaya–Hindukush region. It is a low-volume, high-value, non-perishable crop, with a lower labour requirement than other cash crops. It has the further advantages of growing only as an understorey with shade trees. From earlier diversified agricultural systems cultivated with the objective of meeting most household requirements, for the purposes of commercial production, certain portions of the existing agricultural systems have been selectively developed, depending on the diversity and resource limitations of mountain agriculture (Jodha 1990; and 1997). But mountain specificities also limit the scope for large-scale operation (Jodha 2002a).

Market prices determine which among the various niche products will be developed. The commodities mentioned above, whether developed from existing mountain agriculture or from outside, have all been quite important in the development of mountain economies. But as new markets develop so too are there new opportunities. One such developing market is that for organic agricultural products through export to developed country markets like North America, Europe and Japan. Whether for health or out of worldwide ecological concerns, consumers there have shown a willingness to pay a premium for organic foods, a premium that, however, is reported to be fast disappearing.[1] In 1999 the International Trade Centre (ITC) of United Nations Conference on Trade and Development (UNCTAD) and World Trade Organization (WTO) published a market survey of organic food and beverage markets in Europe, which concluded that demand for such organic products is growing rapidly, and that insufficient supply rather than demand is the problem in these markets (Kortbech-Olsen 2000: 1).

Mountain peasant agriculture is basically organic agriculture, depending on a nutrient recycling relation with the forests, a mix of crops to provide various types of nutrients and integrated systems of pest management. If the organic products of swidden agriculture can be sold for higher prices than they now receive in the local markets, where they do not command a premium, the incomes of the uplands would increase and sustainable organic systems would get a boost.

Developing export markets for mountain products, however, requires a number of steps, in which the uplands do not have any specific advantage, on the contrary, they may face the disadvantages of remoteness and higher cost transport. The first step needed is to set up the organizations and procedures for certification. Some countries, like China and India, already have some such institutions in place. Nevertheless, at the local level, too it is necessary to set up community-based certification systems, otherwise poor producers could be excluded by costly certification procedures.

Second, the legal transition to organic agriculture takes some time. It takes two to three years in the case of formerly inorganic-based agriculture (Nadia Scialabba 2000a: 12). It should be less in the case of already organic agriculture, as is mostly present in the uplands. But declines in yields due to a fall in ecosystem services provided by forests (e.g., reduction in density of forest cover leading to reduced nutrient and water recycling) have in many places led to some use of inorganic chemical inputs. There would consequently be some transition period during which products cannot be sold as organic. The required absence of inorganic fertilizers and pesticides might lead to an initial loss of yield. This would require some compensation during the transition, and maybe even during the initial years of exportable output, for certified organic agriculture to be profitable to small producers.

---

[1] Alison Griffith, personal communication.

Third, local, traditional knowledge of natural processes needs to be consolidated and extended. In swidden systems women are the chief producers in the swidden fields and the home gardens, choosing micro-locations, deciding on seeds, combining various plants together, weeding out the undesired plants, and so on. Women's knowledge of multi-storey, multi-crop agriculture needs to be built upon 'through selective introduction of results of modern science in areas such as energy flows and bio-geochemical cycles, biotic and abiotic factors, which regulate plant development, renewable energy technologies, and management techniques' (Scialabba 2000a: 14).

The enhancement of organic agriculture does not need costly investments in irrigation, energy and external inputs. On the contrary what is needed are investments in capacity-building and related research. 'This would entail a shift of capital investments from hard to soft technologies—that is from agricultural inputs (private goods) to knowledge building (public goods)' (Scialabba 2000b: 12).

Fourth, farmers need security of tenure to undertake changes that would take some years to yield results. Along with this, access to markets is also necessary. This involves removal of any internal monopsonistic restrictions and opening of developed country markets (North America, Europe and Japan) to imports of organic products from developed countries, and removal of subsidies for organic and other agriculture in the developed countries.

But, even with the opening up of developed country markets, upland communities will not be able to remain safe in their 'niche' production. Not only in the developed countries, but even in the developing countries too, plains' producers can easily learn and duplicate organic agriculture. Once the transition period has been crossed and marketing networks set up, the better-connected plains might be able to undertake lower cost supply of organic products. The only way in which the mountain communities could protect their 'niche' markets is through developing further knowledge in this area, and innovating to build on comparative advantage.

Moving Up the Value Chain

The notion of comparative advantage is a static notion, based as it is on the relative supplies of the factors of production. Competition between different sources supplying the same commodity is then restricted to the productivity-related cheapness of the factors of production. Lower wages is one of the principal ways to compete in a comparative advantage framework. Advantage based on low cost labour, however, can always be undermined by cheaper labour elsewhere. This holds true even for 'niche products' for which there are often more than one producer, and closely competing products.

One way of responding to price competition is to reduce wages and environmental standards, a race to the bottom, so to speak. The use of child labour in carpet production is an example of such a negative use of cheap labour. Another and more positive way is to respond by increasing the value of one's product, by technological change to increase productivity, product differentiation and thus advancing from comparative advantage, based on resource endowments, to what Michael Porter calls 'competitive advantage', which can be achieved through innovation (Porter 1998: 164). Of course, innovations can always be copied, so the only way to retain competitive advantage is to upgrade it.

What kind of policy is needed to build competitive advantage? The first is that there should be sufficient, even intense internal competition.

> The presence of domestic competitors automatically cancels the types of advantages that come from simply being in a particular nation—factor costs, access to or preference in the home market, or costs to foreign competitors who import into the market. Companies are forced to move beyond them, and as a result, gain more substantial advantages (*ibid*.: 181–82).

This type of competition promotes efficiency in firms.

Domestic firms need to have sufficient control over marketing channels. With foreign control of marketing channels, the gains even from technological innovations that reduce costs, will flow out of the concerned economy.

Along with the above, government policies need to be geared to developing the specific kinds of specialized assets and skills required. Universities and training institutions need to be geared to develop the specialized skills needed by the industry or cluster concerned. And, particularly in a situation where small and medium-sized firms dominate the market, this also requires that associations of firms take up some common, scale-sensitive activities, say, in areas of marketing and research. Successful competition at the global level thus requires some forms of cooperation at the domestic, cluster level.

> In the Netherlands, for example, grower cooperatives built the specialized auction and handling facilities that constitute one of the Dutch

flower cluster's greatest competitive advantages. The Dutch Flower Council and the Dutch Flower Growers Research Groups, in which most growers participate, have taken on other functions as well, such as marketing and applied research (Porter 1998: 259).

In the rapidly emerging alternative flower centre of Kunming, China, the state itself has taken up the task of setting up the necessary auction and handling facilities. Given that Yunnan Province, of which Kunming is the capital, is a major supplier of cut flowers, one should not be surprised if it soon becomes a serious competitor to Amsterdam in the global flower market. This advance should be contrasted with the failure of Thailand, which despite being a major exporter of orchids and other cut flowers, but not having built higher-level processing and handling facilities, did not emerge as a hub in the global flower market.

The point of advancing from resource-based comparative advantage to knowledge-based advantage holds true in general for all sectors of economic activity that produce tradable goods. The mountain communities have been trading in their raw materials and natural products with very little of the crucial processing, and manufacturing, that add value to the product. Forest products, whether timber or NTFPs, are the best example of the above. Soft wood and bamboo are turned into paper and other products in the plains of, say, Assam, in India, while the mountain communities remain at the level of raw material suppliers, with processing only being confined to that which is needed to facilitate transportation. Timber is supplied as round wood, logs or at best planks by the mountain communities, while the manufacture of furniture or other products is carried out in the plains. The same holds true for NTFPs, where very often the mountain suppliers do not even know the uses to which their products are put.

The terms of trade of primary producers are subject to cyclical and even secular deterioration in the terms of trade. Within the global price system those commodities that are relatively close to natural resource origins tend to have a lower price than those commodities further removed from natural resource origins. The neglect of environmental services in the pricing of natural resources, and the neglect of costs other than that of collection in unregulated commons, together mean that the social costs of production are higher than private costs, and there is a subsidy on the basis of non-valuation of environmental resources, which are production resources for the indigenous people. But along with the earlier discussed institutional reforms to value environmental services and domesticate production of forest products, there is the need to move higher up the chain of production, and not remain at the sale of barely-processed natural resources.

The movement from selling raw materials to processing and then manufacturing final products is a relatively straightforward, if not a simple one. It is hindered by some factors of global trade policy, like the developed countries' levying higher import duties on processed rather than unprocessed or semi-processed goods. Oranges are more easily exported than, say, orange juice, affecting the possibility of moving up the value chain.

Then, again, as mentioned above there are trade monopolies in various commodities. Increasing price realization will only be possible by building countervailing market power. This, for instance, has been done by the shea growers in Burkina Faso. While the country accounts for 25 per cent of the world production of shea butter, used in cosmetics and as a cocoa substitute, it was only when the women organized in a producers' consortium that they could enter into direct deals with cosmetic manufacturers and secure in 2000 a price that was three times the price in 1998 (UNDP 2003: 153).

But moving up the value chain also requires being able to build new types of advantage. How this can be done can be illustrated with the example of wood-based products of a Mexican *ejido*, which, as usual, began by exporting wood from forests that it owned, managed and cultivated. From there it moved to setting up sawmills and exporting sawn and cut wood. With growing competition, it faced a fall in prices in the export of semi-processed wood. Instead of attempting to meet competition on the price level, the *ejido* decided to move into the manufacture of furniture and special wood products. It set up the necessary plant and strict quality controls needed for exporting high quality woods, where it now competes on global markets (Land Tenure Center and Institute for Environmental Studies 1995).

The role of processing and manufacture in the development of mountain communities can be illustrated by the example of bamboo-tiles in Suinyin County, Hunnan Province, China and more generally in China. Until a plant for manufacturing bamboo-tiles and panels as a substitute for wood-tiles and panels, was set up in the county headquarters, there was no value addition in bamboo. But with this manufacture of bamboo industrial products, villagers who earlier merely supplied bamboo, now also undertook early processing of bamboo into strips, resulting in a substantial increase in labour absorption in bamboo processing. The higher-level manufacturing facility was critical to the increase in mountain communities' bamboo-related income. At the cluster level it was the shift to a new product, a knowledge-based innovation that made the overall increase in income possible.

CLUSTERS

These examples are of individual enterprises upgrading themselves into a higher quality market. But it is more likely that such a move is made not at individual enterprise itself, but at the level of a cluster. A cluster differs from an agglomeration in that it relates not just to the geographic concentration of firms in the same industry, but relates to the various related lines that together form a whole, with not just various backward and forward linkages, but also feedback loops (Porter 1998).[2]

The supply of higher quality woods requires a higher investment of labour in the management of forests, which in turn is related to the price of wood. At the same time, with poor quality woods, producers of finished goods cannot move to higher quality products. Substantial improvement in quality would be possible only through simultaneous changes in various operations, logging, sawmill processing, standard wood classification and so on. 'Such linkages can be recognized and captured more easily within clusters than among dispersed participants' (ibid.: 218).

Clusters of various densities exist in economies that have a minimum of market orientation. In mountain communities most clusters are natural resource based, for instance, wood or bamboo clusters, medicinal and other herbal clusters. These clusters may be domestically quite shallow, as are most of the natural resource based clusters mentioned above, with their linkages to the outside world more than domestic linkages. They may be somewhat deeper, as is the tourism cluster, which includes not only hotels, travel and related tourist sectors, but also handicrafts, textiles, carpets and various other products sold to tourists.

What difference does the recognition of a cluster, rather than just an industry, as in the usual standard industrial classification, make to policy?[3] The first point is to recognize that knowledge and networks are important to the development of a cluster. Within clusters there is a strong flow of information, strong supply of specialized labour, and movement of specialized persons between organizations.

---

[2] See Michael Porter, 'Clusters and Competition', in Porter (1998).

[3] This discussion of clusters is largely based on Porter (1998).

Networking, a free flow of information and social relations are all important. Trade associations are important in a cluster of small and medium-sized firms to perform scale-sensitive functions. From the side of the government it is necessary to set up higher educational institutions to provide the specialized professionals, and not just provide general higher education and thus link higher education with the needs of the cluster. Industry and government policy need to encourage local suppliers.

Some questions of copying of mountain products can be countered by using certificates of origin—the Appellation d'Origine Controlle to provide protection for high quality mountain products. Using this, the cheese producers of the Beaufort Valley, France, developed their own micro-market (Funnell and Parish 2001: 355). But this again can be of benefit for only a limited period of time; imitations will come up and possibly be cheaper, like the various 'sparkling wines' from around the world that now compete with the original 'champagne', even if they cannot use that name, or the various long-grain rice varieties that compete with 'basmati', which itself has lost its original hill rice connotation to the plains of the Punjabs of India and Pakistan.

The linking of higher education with the needs of cluster development is particularly important in knowledge-intensive sectors like medicinal and aromatic plants. The mountain communities possess a fund of indigenous knowledge of the medicinal and other useful properties of various herbs and plants. But most of this knowledge is simply captured by foreign pharmaceutical and related manufacturers, usually without any royalty or other acknowledgement of the indigenous sources of the innovation or knowledge.

While it is necessary to insist on recognition of the sources of the original innovation and knowledge, and to secure payment of royalties for their use, it is also important to set goals that go beyond merely living off knowledge inherited from ancestors. That knowledge has to be translated into products that can be a part of the modern world. This requires setting up specialized institutions to undertake research and development of these products. Of course, not all the steps of this chain can be so easily indigenized. Costa Rica, in its agreement with Merck, for example, has taken a measure whereby its local specialists are trained as para-botanists and so on. In Nepal, at a lower level, Dabur has trained farmers to grow medicinal herbs and plants. These are first steps. Other steps would require institutes of higher education and research, and regional centres would be needed, oriented to meet the development needs of the tourism, medicinal plants, flowers and organic products clusters, for instance.

SPECIALIZATION, INTENSIFICATION AND ALTERNATIVES TO MONOCULTURE

Growth based on comparative advantage will inevitably mean a shift from a relatively all-round to a more specialized economy. Such development of specialized economic activities need not lead to a loss of sustainability. In fact, specialized commercialization may actually promote sustainability. Take the case of fuelwood. Where fuelwood is collected from common land, often through women's labour, given the very low opportunity cost of this labour, there is an overuse of labour in the collection of fuelwood and a lack of measures to increase the area-wise productivity of the product. But as commercial activities that involve the use of women's labour develop, then that community or village may cease to collect fuelwood and instead purchase it.

There may be either a simple displacement of the problem, with extraction shifted elsewhere; or an intensification of production, with a saving in the use of land and labour. The crucial factor in this case is the shortage of labour. So long as labour is available and has a low opportunity cost, extensive methods of collecting fuelwood continue. But when the opportunity cost of labour, in particular the opportunity cost of women's labour, goes up then there is a movement to reduce the labour cost of collecting fuelwood. From gathering fuelwood the move is made to cultivating fuelwood.

As mentioned earlier, agricultural production among the indigenous peoples is often centred on the swidden system, whether of longer 'forest fallows' or shorter 'bush fallows', to use the terms introduced by Boserup (1965). For individual shifting cultivators to be able to change their fallow system in the direction of more intensive land and labour use, a surplus over current consumption demands is needed. Those shifting cultivators who do not have such a surplus are unable to change their production system.

The cutting of terraces and the introduction of agro-forestry both require material inputs, which would mean a diversion from current consumption. At the level of the individual farm family this would require that '... the consumption value of the amount intended for production appears in the eyes of the family to be less than its value for production' (Chayanov 1966: 11). But we would further add that below a minimum level of consumption the family would not assess the production value for even a substantially more productive asset like terraces to be more than its present consumption value.

Thus, an individual family would require some non-shifting cultivation source of income/product to be able to undertake investments in terrace cutting or agro-forestry. The elite within these communities can use their political positions and/or external connections to gather these resources for intensification. Those who have to depend only on shifting cultivation are unable to gather such resources. Among such families, however, larger families would be in position to gather such resources. Where polygamy exists, the same elite men may have more than one wife, and thus would be able to bring more land under shifting cultivation and thus acquire resources for investing in other productive assets.[4]

Globalization enhances two possibilities for increased income needed for transformation of swidden systems. First, it allows the introduction of higher-value plants into the swidden system or increases the value of existing plants and trees, allowing for a higher-value of output. These are the niche products of the mountain and hill areas (Jodha 2002b). Second, it creates new opportunities for wage employment, whether locally or in the plains. Both of these increase the numbers of families that can utilize these external incomes to invest in the transformation of their swidden system, as compared to the earlier situation where only the few with existing surpluses from rice terraces or monopolizing the few external contacts, could carry out such transformation.

Many examples of the above transformation in parts of China, Lao PDR, Thailand and India are noted in a paper on this topic (UNOPS 1997). Here we mention just a couple of such examples. The indigenous people of Andhra Pradesh, India, were able to substantially increase their income from sale of *gum karaya* in international markets. With an improvement in quality the price realized went up from Rs 5 per kilogram to as much Rs 40 or 50 per kilogram, a ten-fold increase. This itself transformed the way the farmers looked at the *gum karaya* trees—from earlier having been left to rot, now they were carefully preserved, some even initiated plantation of these trees.

In Yunnan, China, many valuable medicinal plants have been introduced into the swidden system. The rapid growth in the global demand for Chinese medicines has enabled farmers in Yunnan to earn higher incomes and transform their fallow systems. The Ilam district of Nepal has been transformed by the development of tea, ginger and other export crops.

---

[4] For a detailed analysis of the nature of transformation of swidden cultivation systems see UNOPS, 1997.

But it is a seemingly inevitable feature of such intensification that it leads to a specialization in production and thus reduces the range of local production. In the Himalaya-Hindukush region, it is reported that families that used to produce and consume over 20 different varieties of food items; consequent upon commercialization now consume only five (Nagpal 1999).

Such commercialization of products has often, even usually, been accompanied by monoculture of the products. Tea, rubber, potatoes and a host of other upland crops are often grown in plantation monocultures. But the traditional upland cultivation system, both of swidden agriculture and the home garden, is based on multi-species, multi-storey cultivation. Dedicated monocultures would destroy an important part of the value of the uplands, both to the mountain communities themselves, and to the world at large, as biodiversity is an important global public good produced in the uplands.

Work done at a number of upland research institutes, like the Institute of Botany and the Institute of Ecology both in Yunnan (Xie Jiwu 1993), has developed models of human-made communities of trees and vegetation that could mimic the diversity of the home gardens. Choosing the combination of trees and crops, with an eye both to their commercial possibilities and to their use value for the farmers, could yield an overall value that is higher than that of single stand plantations.

New developments in the market also promote such diverse stands even with commercialization. For instance, there is now a growing market for 'shade grown coffee' as against the traditional 'sun coffee', which involved the cutting of huge areas of forests to turn them into coffee plantations. Similarly, in the Himalayan uplands too, different tree and annual crops and grass are being simultaneously cultivated in farmers' plots. In Meghalaya, India, farmers plant bay leaf trees and broom grass in the same plots. In other areas large cardamom is grown in the forest. In Kunming, China, there are experiments to grow vanilla, a high-value aromatic crop, in the natural shade of forests, rather than in greenhouses, as is currently done in the Caribbean islands.

What this shows is that commercialization and intensification of production need not necessarily lead to monoculture plantations. Under what conditions will one or the other occur? This needs further investigation and analysis. But a few preliminary points can be made. Where there is a known synergy between different components of the agro ecosystem, for instance bay leaf trees and hill broom grass, and both or all components have commercial value, then farmers are likely to take up the simultaneous cultivation of more than one plant/ tree.

Further, where the farmers undertaking the commercial production are locally resident farmers and not distant corporations, then the farmers are also likely to respond to the use values of other components of the agro-ecosystem that do not have commercial value, but can have various uses for the farmers. On the other hand, distant corporations, concerned with their commercial profits will see these other plants or trees as weeds and seek the single minded maximization of production of the commercial crop in which they are interested. Thus, the value of shade trees in tea plantations is zero to the tea corporations. But where farmers grow tea, they seek to fulfil the shade requirements with plants/trees that might also have commercial or use value. Even if this might reduce the output of tea alone from its possible maximum, the combination of the reduced value of the tea along with the new value of the other tree/plant (e.g., arhar pulse grown for shade by tea farmers in Meghalaya, or combinations of tea, rubber, spices, vegetables, etc., by farmers in Yunnan) might yield an overall higher income. While farmers would have a multi-valued function, including even use values in their assessment, corporations have a single-valued function, based on the maximization of the commercial income from what they sell.

ACCESS AND INFORMATION

A problem in the functioning of markets and the distribution of benefits from trade is the asymmetry of information. Asymmetry of information becomes more of a problem the further the location is from the market. Mountains are especially distant from the markets for the goods they produce. Poor transport networks are reinforced by poor communications systems. But if the development of mountain communities is accepted as an international public good, then there is a good case for subsidizing the construction of the needed infrastructure.

One factor of technological development, the new computer and telecommunications based, Information and Communication Technology (ICT) can both reduce the costs of connectivity and increase its benefits. But the reduction of costs, for instance, by using wireless rather than wired, land-based systems, may not be enough to remove the need for subsidies in wiring the mountain communities.

The benefits of being wired to the Internet and other forms of international communication can be substantial for the mountain communities. They will be able to check on prices in different markets and decide where to sell their products. They can set up Internet web sites to promote community-based tourism (as has been done by some communities in the hills around Mae Hong Son in Northern Thailand and is being carried out for Dayak villages in Kalimantan). They can check on possible markets for their handicrafts. Overall, the problems of accessibility due to transport difficulties could be overcome, in the area of market information, through being wired.

Further, with a sufficiently high level of education and that too in international languages like English (something that mountain communities have picked up because of the importance of tourism), the educated in the mountain communities could even go on develop what are called IT-enabled services, like call centres, back-office work and medical transcription. Once there is Internet connectivity and sufficient bandwidth, then physical distance does not count for various such services. In fact, distance, in terms of time, is an advantage, since one could take advantage of the different working hours to perform 'back-office' functions that can be carried out while the main offices are closed.

For the vast majority of mountain farmers, the benefits of Internet connectivity would largely be those of improved market information, something that can be quite important in improving price realization.

Allied with the above, and even independently, associations of mountain farmers could benefit the farmers in reducing marketing costs. This could even be done by specialized commercial organizations, as in the case of youth in some Himachal Pradesh, India, districts, who act as forwarding agents for the vegetable growers. In this way, the small growers marketing costs are reduced (H. R. Sharma 2001: 5).

Who Is Better Able to Take Advantage of Globalization?

Globalization leads to a generalization of commodity production, i.e., it makes production for sale, rather than production for self-consumption the norm. Within the mountain communities themselves who is better able to take advantage of this process?

In the chapter by Kelkar (this volume) it has been noted that due to a historically self-consumption based economic system indigenous peoples usually have a paucity of entrepreneurial experience. Consequently, when an opportunity does arise it is often identified and taken advantage of by outsiders. Tashi (2001) points out that in Tibet outsiders first took up even simple new economic ventures, like operating pedicabs, leave alone more complex operations like refining medicinal herbs. But, after a while, the locals imitated them (ibid.).

Some communities, like the Mosuo in Yunnan, China, have insisted on villagers being partners in any investment by outsiders. But when no such regulation, local or otherwise, exists, as in the Swat region of Pakistan, there the tourist industry is dominated by outsiders.

In such a process the local community is reduced to the position of merely being workers in these enterprises. They learn neither management nor entrepreneurship. If such processes of exclusion continue, they will lead to the local communities being confined to only some of the newly emerging classes, basically only to the lower-levels of the working class, since even skilled workers could be brought in from outside. Such an exclusion of the mountain communities from the new classes of entrepreneurs or managers will only exacerbate ethnic divisions and lead to ethnic conflicts.

Coming from a history of non-entrepreneurial activity, there are a number of problems in developing entrepreneurs. Knowledge and risk-taking ability may be more important than availability of capital. Collectively-owned enterprises could utilize the limited knowledge available for the benefit of the community and, simultaneously, spread risks over the community. Such collective enterprises, however, need strong management systems to overcome 'free rider' problems and should not have the prop of a 'soft budget' constraint.

In Meghalaya, we could distinguish two different types of producers, in terms of their relationship to the market. First, those who largely produced cereals and some other goods for self-consumption and exchanged on the market only some portion of their output in order to procure those goods, like clothes, tools, etc., that they did not themselves produce. These used to be the majority of the Khasi and Jaintia communities. But along the steep slopes bordering Bangladesh, the War area as it locally called, there never was much capacity to produce cereals. For as long as is known, the people in the War cultivated betel nuts and leaves, and later citrus fruits. Their production was basically all for sale, the self-consumed portion of the outputs being quite insignificant.

Thus the War families, belonging to the same ethnic communities as those on the plateau, have over generations become used to dealing with the market. They now have a reputation in Meghalaya of being especially shrewd in the ways of the market. They are in touch with the trends in the market and are quick to spot opportunities, or to react to the closure of certain windows. They have to produce that which will sell on the market, even in order to acquire basic foodstuffs.

Another group of mountain people who have become very used to dealing with the market are those of Himachal Pradesh.

> The farmers in Shimla, Solan and Kulu districts have been traditionally growing cash crops and are in touch with the market outside the states. They have developed a spirit of innovativeness and are always ready to experiment with any new crop/enterprise that promises high economic returns. Thus when the potato seed ceased to be a cash crop due to falling yields, high incidence of diseases and falling demand, they switched over to cauliflower and subsequently to other vegetables. The leading farmers remain in touch with research institutes and other sources of seed supply. They introduce a new crop and it immediately spreads to other farmers in the area (H. R. Sharma 2001: 4).

Farmers and other producers will then have to be alert to changes in the market and be willing to change production as the market changes. This is not a quality that is easily developed, particularly for those who have been used to continuing lines of production in basically the same manner or with only incremental changes. Which is not to say that mountain farmers and other producers are not innovative. But they are not used to switching whole lines of production. The ability to do this is something that the farmers of Himachal Pradesh have developed over time. Other mountain farmers will also have to develop such abilities of reacting to the market and changing lines of production.

In terms of outlook what this flexibility requires is to view any production line, not as production of a particular good, but in purely instrumental terms as production of value. In this general term what is of consequence is not the particular good produced but the amount of value. This is a flexibility that comes with working with the domination of the commodity form of production.

With globalization there is always the threat of established products being undercut by lower cost production developed at some point or the other. This can have two kinds of effects. First, it could result in some producers being unable to compete on the market. Second, even for producers who only sell a small share of their output on the market in order to buy their requirements that they do not produce, a fall in price due to an increase in productivity somewhere in the global system, would mean a fall in real income. In order to purchase their requirements they would now have to sell more of their own production.

The above factors can also affect what seem to be 'niche' products. Natural conditions can be duplicated and new sources can come up to compete in niche products. Himachal Pradesh producers, who were comfortable with their niche product of off-season vegetables, are now suddenly faced with cheaper production from greenhouses in the plains of Punjab and Haryana. Similarly having ruled the protected Indian market, Himachal Pradesh apples are now faced with competition from overseas producers. So far the imports have only been in the much higher-priced categories and thus have not affected Himachal apples. The imported apples sell for above Rs 100 per kilogram, while the Indian apples are about Rs 40 per kilogram. But soon, with China's entry into the WTO, Himachal apples will certainly face price competition from Chinese apples. Then, Himachal Pradesh's very low productivity, only one-seventh to one-ninth that of international levels (D. K. Sharma 2001: 15), will be a serious weakness in competing in the market.

What globalization means is that producers will have to pay attention to productivity levels elsewhere on the globe. Earlier on, such attention had to be paid only to those within the country, now competition can come from any other country. Questions of quality and productivity will both become paramount in retaining one's position in the market. If the market signals are correctly responded to, then globalization can be a factor improving both quality and productivity. As one observer pointed out,

> ...the import of apple has also made a favourable impact [on growers in Himachal Pradesh]. The growers have become acutely aware of the importance of supplying quality produce and proper grading and packaging. In fact, there has been a substantial improvement in the packaging and grading of apples in the post WTO period (H. R. Sharma 2001: 5).

The growers of Kinnaur have even been exporting their high quality apples. If quality and productivity can be improved, rather than being threatened in their own Indian market, the growers of Himachal could even export their apples.

What the above shows is that globalization will increase the pressure to improve quality and productivity. This is not a negative, rather it is a positive development. But responding to these pressures will require that growers and their associations, as also research organizations, be alert and continuously attempt improvements. Subsidies continued for too long or of the wrong type (for instance, those which do not encourage renovation of the rootstock, as is the case in Himachal Pradesh) will not increase competitive ability in the market. Resting on one's past achievements will spell doom as new producers come up with quality and productivity improvements. The new globalization privileges 'knowledge-based workers over non knowledge-based workers' (Hutton 2000: 25). Of course, all workers are knowledge-based, but the important distinction here is in the extent of knowledge workers embody.

The importance of enhancing 'knowledge-based workers' exists even in the case of products in which the uplands now have clear advantages. A large, though steadily decreasing, part of agriculture in the uplands, is organic. With the currently growing market for organics, it is possible for upland communities to export their products. But there is no absolute advantage in these matters. Duplication in greenhouses, whether in Europe or elsewhere, is very much possible, and it is only a matter of costs, including transport costs, in different parts of the world. Right now the advantage the upland communities have is their knowledge of organic agricultural processes. But this advantage will not last very long. Nevertheless, the exports of organic products could play a key role in increasing incomes from upland agriculture.

The chapters by Walter and Kelkar (both in this volume) show that there are ethnic, class and gender factors in determining who is able to take advantage of globalization and the growth of trade, particularly long-distance trade. Taking the ethnic factor first, it is related to the differential exposure of different communities to trade and their acquisition of the capabilities that are needed to take advantage of the growing sectors. For instance, in the tourism county of Lijiang, the valley dwelling and more urbanized and better-educated Naxi have benefitted much more from the growth of tourism than the Yi or Lisu, who both live on the upper slopes and are less urbanized and educated.

Within trades too there are lesser and more profitable ones and the ability to enter one or the other is not just a matter of the amount of capital needed. The Dai village of Man Gue, Xishuangbanna, Yunnan, has a large daily tourist trade. In the market place there are two distinct kinds of trades—the sale of local trinkets and foodstuffs and the sale of jade. The jade trade is completely dominated by the Han traders, who have come from outside the area and set up shop to take advantage of the tourist influx. The lower return sale of trinkets and foodstuffs is in the hands of the Dai. There are some Dai women (women handle business among the Dai) who have accumulated enough capital to be able to go into the jade trade. But, as one of them explained, there is a specialized knowledge that is needed to be able to enter the jade trade, and this the Han traders have.

While women often carry out small-scale, or micro-trade among the indigenous communities, when it comes to larger-scale or long-distance trade it tends to be taken over by men. In long–distance trade there are the factors of the difficulty of women, who are responsible for childcare, face in being away from home for long periods of time, and their generally lesser knowledge of the mainstream, national languages. Of course, this is not a universal pattern and there are communities where the women being more involved in the market, even if it is local, have a better knowledge of the market language than men. This is so in some communities in Jharkhand, India. But on the whole, the long distance trade does tend to disadvantage and displace women.

This points to the need for specific gender initiatives to enable women to participate in external trade, either as individual sellers or even through organizations of producers.

At the class level, there is the obvious factor that it is those house-holds with education, labour, space and start-up capital, as Pierre Walter (this volume) points out in his study of a Hani village, who are better able to take advantage of the growing market opportunities.

GRADUALISM

The necessity of taking affirmative measures to encourage entrepre-neurial and managerial development among indigenous peoples, leads to the point of strategy to be followed in opening up the upland economies to globalization. This is a question of policy, but of policy related to market processes. Should opening up be done in a 'big bang' approach, or should it be one of gradualism?

Even in the case of large, sub-continental economies, like China and India, it is accepted that a gradualist approach is better than a 'big-bang' approach, because it would enable national entrepreneurs to prepare for global competition. Globalization does not mean the end of 'infant industry' type protection. What it does mean is that such protection should be temporary, and be phased out when production matures and that it should not become a crutch that inhibits productivity and quality development. The Indian apple industry is a good case in point. After many decades of operating in the sheltered Indian market it surely should be able to compete with international producers. As pointed out earlier, the post-WTO period that has now exposed this industry to international competition has seen improvements in grading and quality consciousness. The 'infant industry' argument thus lays the ground for one kind of gradualism, i.e., in not fully opening commodity markets to competition.

Another type of gradualism is that in opening up capital markets. Particularly after the late 1990s Asian and other subsequent financial crises, it is now also quite widely accepted that developing countries need to keep in place various checks on capital movements, ranging from Chile-type sequestration of foreign invested funds, to the restricted capital account convertibility allowed in India or China.

A third type of gradualism is with respect to the economies of the indigenous peoples, the hill-forest or mountain economies that we discuss in this book. These are productive systems that have largely been geared towards sustenance. Moving from such an economy to one dominated by the creation of value involves numerous changes. At one level, it is the creation of a money hoard that can function as capital. At another it is separation of producers from the means of production, and thus the creation of a class of wage labourers. At yet another level, it is the substitution of the creation of value as the aim of production, in the place of largely self-consumed production.

All of these are momentous, changes. They involve disruptions of production patterns, the separation of access to productive resources from membership of the community, and the denial of traditional forms of reciprocity that function as mechanisms of social welfare in an economy of largely simple reproduction. They constitute what is called the 'primary accumulation of capital'—the stamping of the commodity form on social relations including relations of production (van der Pijl 2001: 3).

In this primary accumulation of capital the communities concerned clearly have a poorly developed entrepreneurial capacity. Although some sections among them, those who have been more attuned to producing value for the market, may be more entrepreneurial, on the whole, entrepreneurship is alien to their ways of life. If their markets for commodities, for capital (their savings), or land were to be opened up to others from the states within which they are enclosed, leave alone to global capital, they would in quick time lose their ownership of productive assets and large numbers would be turned into landless and even refugees. It is in this condition that there is a strong case for support for developing entrepreneurs, sequestration of local savings and restrictions on the land market in economies in the process of original accumulation.

The upland economies have to deal with a capital problem, not that of sudden movements of large amounts of capital, but the regular drain of savings through the banking system. The credit/deposit ratios in the mountain areas are uniformly lower than in the plains, leave alone the metropolitan, industrial and financial centres. For instance in the mountain state of Uttaranchal, India, the credit/deposit ratio is just 26.32 as against the all-India ratio of 46.00 (Papola 2001). Raising the credit/deposit ratios in the uplands is necessary to enable local accumulation in the uplands.

How can this savings drain from rural to urban areas be reversed? It is necessary to identify a system of regional/rural banks that could help the process of local accumulation in poor areas. As discussed in Nathan and Yu (this volume), a system of regional/rural banks could help in the localization of accumulation and related economic processes.

We now turn to the nature of markets for environmental services.

TYPES OF MARKETS FOR ENVIRONMENTAL SERVICES

Different types of markets have come into existence for provision of water and related forest-protection services. They fall into three broad categories (Johnson, White and Perrot-Maitre 2001):

1. Self-organized Private Deals: In France, the mineral water bottling company, Perrier, pays upstream dairy farmers and forest landholders for providing quality drinking water. In Costa Rica hydroelectric utilities pay upstream landowners to finance reforestation so as to ensure regularity of flow for hydroelectricity generation. In Colombia, the Association of Irrigators' pays upstream forestland owners in order to improve base flows and reduce sedimentation in irrigation canals.

2. Trading Schemes: In the United States marketable nutrient reduction credits are traded among agricultural and industrial
   units to maintain discharges into water within certain limits.
   Similarly, in Australia water transpiration credits earned by State
   Forests for reforestation are sold to irrigators, with the objective
   of reducing water salinity.
3. Public Payment Schemes: The best known of public payment
   schemes is that of the New York City to various upstream landowners with the objective of purifying the city's water supply.
   Upstream landowners are paid to undertake various measures,
   financed by taxes on water users. In the State of Parana, Brazil,
   municipalities are provided additional funds on the basis of the
   watersheds they protect. Again in Columbia there is an Eco-tax
   on industrial water users, which is transferred to private landowners and municipalities, which ensure both a regularity in
   water supply for industrial uses and water of required purity for
   drinking purposes.

In Asia such schemes are relatively new and all in China. The city
of Xian pays the Qinling forest governments for maintaining its water
supply. Again, in Guanxi, upland forest governments are paid a 'water
source regulation fee' (Harkness 1998). After the 1998 logging ban in
China, governments in upland regions of Yunnan, demanded compensation for additional forestlands that they would protect (Nathan and
Yu Xiaogang in this book).

In Nepal two new water supply schemes propose to pay mountain
communities for the supply of water. The Kushadevi Village Development Committee will be paid Nepali Rupees (NRs) 2,000,000 in the
first year and NRs 200,000 in each subsequent year to deliver water
of specified quantity and quality to the Dhulikhel Municipality.[5] Similarly, in the Melanchi project to bring water into the Kathmandu valley
negotiations are on with various mountain communities for supply
of water. It is also reported that in some parts of Nepal there have been
long-standing systems of payments in kind to mountain communities,
for instance, the Angali command area pays paddy to the upstream
communities.[6]

In Andhra Pradesh, India, Self Help Groups (SHGs) of indigenous
women in the district of Adilabad are being organized into Federations

---

[5] Personal communication, S. K. Upadhyaya.
[6] Both of these sentences are personal communications from Binayak Bhadra.

and, in conjunction with Forest Protection Committees, they are being organized to be able to take up sale of carbon sequestration capabilities (Community Forestry International 2002). The Gond indigenous peoples of the village of Powerguda in Adilabad district, Andhra Pradesh, took the initiative of replacing diesel fuel with natural oil extracted from the seeds of *pongmaia pinnata* (*karanj*) found in the adjoining forests. With this switch they were able to sell 900 tonnes of carbon dioxide emission reduction in 10 years for a price of USD 4,164 to an environmental group in Germany; beginning the process of carbon trading by indigenous communities in India (D'Silva 2003: 55). More generally The International Fund for Agricultural Development (IFAD) is working with International Center for Research in Agroforestry (ICRAF) to develop ways for upland communities in Asia to be rewarded for the environmental services they provide (World Agroforestry Centre 2002).

Issues in Markets for Environmental Services

Recent international instruments, including the Global Environment Fund (GEF), the Kyoto Protocol and the Clean Development Mechanism (CDM) have all begun the process of establishing international markets for some of the global environmental services that forests can provide. These instruments are not restricted to forests alone, but forest-based activities can also qualify under them, as for instance, in carbon sequestration or reduction of carbon emissions.

Some of the environmental services provided from forests are goods that have clear markets. Water is a good example of one such good for which there is an established market. The price of water and quantity to be supplied can then be easily incorporated into local communities' forest-use decisions. Of course, their right to sell this commodity first needs to be accepted by the relevant authorities. Goods that can be extracted from the forests, like water, are amenable to trade through markets (Wilson, Moura Costa and Stuart 1999: 5). But services that are the result of conservation activities, like carbon sequestration, are not as amenable to be dealt with through markets. For such environmental services transfer payments are more in order.

Markets for environmental services will certainly not solve all the problems of adequate provisioning of these environmental services. It will involve numerous conflicts in setting scales at which these services should be provided globally and in pricing of these services. But it would have the merit of providing income incentives for those who are surely among the poorest people in Asia, the forest communities. Particularly in the light of the failure of state policies of exclusion in providing these services, and the transformation of the forests into effective 'open access' resources, property rights, including the right to sell environmental services deriving from forests, could be tried out to increase the supply of these environmental services, while providing improved livelihoods for the providers. It would also be an important step in changing the balance of power between upland forest-based and lowland peoples, which has for a long time, at least since the formation of states, been in favour of the lowland peoples.

Markets for environmental services, by valuing different aspects of forest use, give the local community greater flexibility in its land-use, as emphasized by Smith, Mulongoy, Persson and Sayer (1999). It will not suddenly transform the management picture or the livelihood conditions of the forest communities, but it will increase the options they have and could provide incomes for a transformation of forest-based production systems.

The international conventions are based on the concept of 'additionality' in both costs and effects. To qualify under the CDM the carbon sequestration must be additional to what already exists. Similarly the GEF uses mutually agreed 'incremental costs'. Thus, as Fearnside (1997: 65) points out, no value is given to stocks or flows per se, 'But only to deliberately caused changes in flows' (ibid.). In a sense, both stocks and flows per se are the result not of current labour, but of the accumulation of past labour. Current labour comes into the picture in causing changes in these flows.

This distinction can be used to devise ways of allocating the income to be derived from the sale of environmental services. The incremental costs, whether of labour or of damage to existing production like agricultural lands that get submerged, can be paid to individuals on the basis of labour and actually incurred costs. Any money earned by the community on the basis of stocks can then be allocated to community use. This could be used to build infrastructure, educational and health facilities, all of which are very poor in forest areas. By reserving stock payments one might overcome the moral hazard that might exist in 'hand-outs'. On this basis, payments made in China on the basis of area of forests maintained in that condition, rather than being distributed as income among the community, can be retained by the villages for collective expenditures.

Along with the above, establishment of markets for environmental services provided by forests would increase the prices of agricultural commodities, in whose pricing such costs do not now enter. This would reduce, if not end, the underpricing of commodities dependent on environmental services; an underpricing that increases with increased dependence on unvalued environmental services. Thus, the pricing of environmental services would promote more efficient use of agricultural and other commodities dependent on these services.

GLOBAL TRADE REGIME

We have dealt here with the various changes that are needed for indigenous peoples to take advantage of the opportunities for global trade. The changes we have discussed, whether in property systems, food security and so on, are mainly at the level of the indigenous peoples' economies. While it is true that export pessimism as a whole is a misguided notion, based on the idea of an inelastic market for export products, it is also true that there are various obstacles in the way of increasing the trade possibilities of indigenous peoples. The export commodities of the indigenous peoples are mainly primary commodities, notorious for their secular trend of falling terms of trade and vast cyclical price movements. Whether it is in the sphere of organic products or other foodstuffs, they are up against the barrier of the huge subsidies paid by most Organization for Economic Co-operation Development (OECD) economies, the USA, the European Union (EU), Japan and South Korea, to their own farm producers. It does not matter whether the subsidies are classified in one coloured box or the other, blue box or green box, whether they are tied to levels of production and prices, or straightforward household income subsidies, their net result is to promote exports from these countries below their cost of production. This both depresses world prices and makes it difficult for developing country producers to enter these export markets. The prices of rice, corn or cotton are all depressed by subsidies by the USA and the EU. Consequently, one important enabling measure is needed at the global level—that is the elimination of subsidies in the OECD countries and the removal of tariff and other barriers to the exports of agricultural commodities from the developing world.

Other measures to counter cyclical trends in primary product prices, as proposed for instance by Keynes at the Bretton Woods conference, are also needed to provide needed support to developing country producers. Right now coffee, largely produced by indigenous peoples in the uplands, is in the midst of a steep fall in prices. Providing prices adequate for a reasonable standard of human capability is only possible with global action. As Keynes pointed out,

> Proper economic prices should be fixed not at the lowest possible level, but at the level sufficient to provide producers with proper nutritional and other standards in the conditions in which they live...and it is in the interests of all producers alike that the price of a commodity should not be depressed below this level, and consumers are not entitled to expect that it should (Keynes: 1946).

REFERENCES

Bhagwati, Jagdish and V. K. Ramaswamy. 'Domestic Distortions, Tariffs and the Theory of Optimal Subsidy'. *The Journal of Political Economy* 71 (1973): 44–50.

Boserup, Ester. *The Conditions of Agricultural Growth: The Economics of Agrarian Change under Population Pressure*. Chicago: Aldine Publishing, 1965.

Chayanov, A. V. *The Theory of Peasant Economy*, Homewood. ILL: Richard D. Irwin, 1956.

Chichilnisky, Graciela. 'North-South Trade and the Global Environment.' *The American Economic Review* 84, no. 4 (1994): 851–74.

Community Forestry International. *Environmental Service-Based Funding: Participatory Approaches to Forest Carbon Projects*. Report, 2002.

D'Silva, Emmanuel. '*Pongamia* Power Enables Adilabad Villagers to Export Carbon Credits to Germany'. In *Down To Earth*. New Delhi: SCE (15 July 2003): 55.

Fearnside, Philip. 'Environmental Services as a Strategy for Sustainable Development in Rural Amazonia'. *Environmental Economics* 20 (1997): 53–70.

Funnell, Don and Romola Parish. *Mountain Environments and Communities*. London, New York: Routledge, 2001.

Greely, Martin. 'Environmental and Food Security Objectives in Rural Project Design'. *IDS Bulletin* 22, no. 3 (1999): 35–42.

Harkness, James. 'Recent Trends in Forestry and Conservation of Biodiversity in China'. *China Quarterly*, no. 156 (December 1998).

Hutton, Will. 'Introduction'. In *Global Capitalism*, edited by Will Hutton and Anthony Giddens. New York: The New Press, 2000.

Jodha, N. S. 'Mountain Agriculture: The Search for Sustainability'. *Journal of Farming Systems Research Extension* 1 (1990): 55–75.

——————. 'Mountain Agriculture'. In *Mountains of the World: A Global Priority*, edited by B. Messerli and J. Ives. Carnforth: Parthenon, 1997.

——————. 'Policies for Sustainable Mountain Development: An Indicative Framework and Evidence'. Paper presented at Asia High Summit, ICIMOD, Kathmandu, 2002a.

——————. 'Globalization and Impacts on Upland Poor'. Paper presented at IFAD, South Asia Portfolio Review, Paro, Bhutan, 22–26 May 2002b.

Johnson, Nels, Andy White and Daniele Perrot-Maitre. *Developing Markets For Water Services From Forests: Issues And Lessons For Innovators*, Washington

D.C.: Forest Trends, World Resources Institute and the Katoomba Group, 2001.

Keynes, J. M. 'The Control of Raw Material Prices'. Reprinted in *The Collected Works of John Maynard Keynes*, Vol. XXVII. London: Macmillan, 1946.

Kortbech-Olsen, Rudy. *Export Opportunities of Organic Food from Developing Countries*, Geneva: International Trade Centre of UNCTAD/WTO, 2000.

Land Tenure Center, and Institute for Environmental Studies. 'Case Studies of Community-Based Forestry Enterprises in the Americas'. Presented at the symposium, Forestry in the Americas: Community-Based Management and Sustainability. University of Wisconsin-Madison, 3–4 February 1995.

Mountain Agenda. *An Appeal for Mountains*, Berne: Mountain Agenda, 1992. Quoted in Funnell and Parish, 2001.

Nagpal, S. 'Food Security in the Hindukush—Himalaya'. *Economic and Political Weekly* 34, no. 36 (25 September 1999).

Papola, T. S. 'Poverty in Mountain Areas'. Kathmandu: ICIMOD, 2001.

Porter, Michael E. *On Competition*. Cambridge: Harvard Business Review Book, 1998.

Scialabba, Nadia. *Opportunities and Constraints of Organic Agriculture: A Socio-ecological Analysis*. Summer Course of the Socrates Programme. Viterbo: Universiti Degli Studi Della Tuscia, 2000a.

——— *Factors Influencing Organic Agriculture Policies with a Focus on Developing Countries*. Rome: FAO, 2000b.

Sharma, P. 'Sustainable Tourism in the Hindukush–Himalaya: Issues and Approaches'. In *Sustainability in Mountain Tourism: Perspectives for the Himalayan Countries*, edited by P. East, K. Luger and K. Inmann. New Delhi: Faith Books and Innsbruck: Studienverlag, 1998. Quoted in Funnell and Parish, 2001.

Sharma, D. K. 'Rapid Globalization Process and its Repercussions for Mountain Areas with Special Reference to Himachal Pradesh'. Kathmandu: ICIMOD, 2001.

Sharma, H. R. 'Mountain Agriculture and Globalization: Micro-evidence from Himachal Pradesh'. Kathmandu: ICIMOD, 2001.

Silver, Sara. 'Coffee' in *The Financial Times*, London, 14 May 2003.

Smith, Joyotee, Kalemani Mulongoy, Reidar Peterson and Jeffrey Sayer. *Harnessing Carbon Market for Tropical Forest Conservation: Towards A More Realistic Assessment*. Bogor: CIFOR, 1999.

Tashi, Nymi. 'Economic Globalization: Process, Response and its Impact on Tibetan Socio-economic Development'. Kathmandu: ICIMOD, 2001.

UNDP. *Making Global Trade Work for People*. London: Earthscan Publications, 2003.

UNOPS. 'Factors in Intensification of Upland Agriculture'. Kuala Lumpur: Asia Office, UNOPs, 1997.

van der Pijl, Kees. 'International Relations and Capitalist Discipline'. In *Phases of Capitalist Development: Booms, Crises and Globalizations*, edited by Robert Albritton, Makoto Itoh, Richard Westra and Alan Zuege. New York: Palgrave, 2001.

Wilson, Charlie, Pedro Moura Costa and Marc Stuart. *Transfer Payments for Environmental Services to Local Communities: A Local—Regional Approach*. Rome: IFAD, FAO and IUCN, 1999.

World Agroforestry Centre (ICRAF). *Developing Mechanisms to Reward the Upland Poor for the Environmental Services That They Provide (RUPES)*, Inception and Progress Report, Bogor, Indonesia, 2002.

Xie Jiwu. *The Principles and Ways in the Design of Man-Made Ecological Systems and Their Application to the Multiple Development of Mountain Areas*. Kunming: Institute of Ecology, 1993.

Conclusion

Civilizational Change: Markets and Privatization among Indigenous Peoples

Dev Nathan and Govind Kelkar

Introduction

Consequent upon the integration of the social and economic systems of indigenous peoples into the global economy through market-driven processes, there are changes in the nature of their overall economic and social system. From one aiming at the stability of the social system to one based on accumulation. From production for self-consumption to production for sale in the market. This fosters privatization of the access to productive resources, chiefly land. Membership of the community is no longer synonymous with access to critical productive resources. Privatization is accompanied by the growing dominance of men in economic affairs. There is also a decline in earlier forms of reciprocity as social welfare. This set of changes can justifiably be called a civilizational change, so deep and broad is its scope, changing all earlier forms of social, economic and gender relations.

After discussing the features of this process of civilizational change, this essay then goes on to consider its historical role in the development of the economic and social system. While a system of accumulation does not necessarily have to be based on private property and there can be collective forms of accumulating systems, the demise of twentieth-century attempts at creating alternatives makes it difficult, if not impossible, to envisage a direct movement from kinship-based and subsistence-oriented collectivities to citizen-based and accumulation-oriented collectivities. The experience of private accumulation has its positive, even liberating effects, even while it increases inequality and leads to various kinds of social stress. This contradictory experience of modernity as privatization reveals both the negativities of privatization and also the limits of the domination of commodity forms. The cost, among other things, is a loss of guaranteed access to productive resources. The way forward is to create welfare systems based on taxes and new forms of community organization. The emerging global community of producers needs to become the reference point even for the articulation of human rights within capitalism, leave alone the overcoming of commodity production.

MARKETS AND PRIVATIZATION

Globalization comes down to local communities largely through the market. New goods may be seen on the television or come to be known through other ways. But it is through the market that they become available to be consumed or used by people. It is also through the market that producers come to know what they can sell. Often they may not know the uses to which their products are put. For instance, only recently, after the logging ban imposed by the Indian Supreme Court, indigenous women in the North-eastern state of Meghalaya, India, began selling the bark of some trees, but had no idea at all of the uses of that bark (Nathan, this volume). The indigenous people of Andhra Pradesh, India, had for decades been collecting and selling gum *karaya* without any idea of its use in making dentures. These are not isolated instances and sellers are often totally unaware of the uses of the products they sell, particularly when these products do not have local uses.

The market, of course, is not new to indigenous peoples. The fabled 'Silk Routes', for instance, passed through indigenous people's areas in the Himalaya–Hindukush Mountains. But for the indigenous peoples trade was carried on in order to obtain alien or exotic products, salt, iron, etc. With the incorporation of these mountain communities into plains-based states, and later with Western colonialism, the regular trading networks extended up into the hills and mountains. The states also more directly extracted various forest products, like timber. But with globalization there is a great increase in the scope of the market. Virtually any product can be traded on the market. And, unlike with production for self-consumption, which is necessarily limited by the extent of local consumption, production for sale on the market is not similarly locally limited, of course, when the aim of trade is no longer to incorporate exotic products into a subsistence system, but becomes part of a process of accumulation.

This growth of the market has led to a process of privatization of formerly communal land, of devolution of ownership, at least *de facto* if not also *de jure*, from supra-village and community or clan to the family. The market for timber and NTFPs grew in the colonial or immediate postcolonial periods. To that extent they certainly pre-date the 1990s, which is generally regarded as the era of globalization, with the growth of global financial markets. But the process of privatization through market-induced transformation is a feature that has become even stronger in the current era. Consequently an analysis of the privatization process, even if it pre-dates the 1990s, can tell us a lot about the effects of the growth of global markets on what were formerly relatively self-contained, subsistence-based economies.

A detailed case study of this process in Northeast India looked at this process of privatization through pressures emanating from the development of the market, timber and NTFPs, where, unlike in most of the rest of India, the communities retained ownership of the forests in the colonial and postcolonial periods. While the analysis was concentrated on the Khasi of Meghalaya, a state which is better connected than other Northeast Indian states with the rest of India and thus with the markets for timber and NTFPs, it also used material, mainly from other communities and countries of the Hindukush–Himalayan region (Nathan, this volume).

The growth of the market led to a process of privatization of formerly communal land, of devolution of ownership, at least *de facto* if not also *de jure*, from supra-village and community or clan to the family. The following are the features of this process:

- The rise of big men or big families and their links to the external world.
- The decline of earlier forms of reciprocity that inhibited accumulation.
- The separation of the objective conditions of labour (chiefly, land) from labour itself, leading to the creation of what Marx termed 'not-land-ownership' (Marx 1973: 498).
- The growing domination of men in economic matters.
- The breakdown of norms of collecting forest products only for self-consumption and in regulating collection for sale.
- The gradual or rapid decline of NTFPs in the unregulated commons and the domestication and shift of valuable NTFP species into the home gardens or privately-owned fields.

Norms Inhibiting Accumulation and Their Costs

Social norms or sanctions that inhibited accumulation or kept it within narrow limits are of different kinds. One of them is the feasting undertaken by big men or chiefs, for instance, among the various Naga communities. This feasting redistributed any surplus and prevented accumulation. With the advent of Christianity such feasting was denounced as being 'pagan' and its decline opened the way for accumulation. Simultaneously, norms of reciprocity also changed and step-by-step generalized reciprocity gave way to annual cash contributions of a portion of income.

Among the Khasi, pre-Christian accumulation was restricted to the families of the chiefs (*syiems*) and priests (*lyngdohs*). Any other family that accumulated wealth were likely to be denounced as worshippers of *u thlen* (the evil snake spirit) and forced to abandon their wealth. 'The *thlen* attaches itself to the property of the keeper and gets transferred along with it to his/her heir. The keeper can rid himself of the demon only by renouncing all his possessions' (Nongbri 2002: 4). But this does not destroy or dissipate the property; rather it is centralized with the chief or priest, since 'only the *Syiem* (chief) and the *Lyngdoh* (priest) can receive the property of *thlen* keepers without the possibility of inheriting the demon' (*ibid.*).

The Dai of Xishuangbanna, China, a Tai-speaking people, who had a well-developed chieftain (*tusi*) system also had a mechanism to inhibit accumulation outside of the families of the chiefs or their representatives, the village headman. Any prosperous family, known as a family with a 'silver plough' or that had found a 'silver box/spoon', was likely to be denounced as *pippa*, or keepers of the tiger spirit, which like the Khasi *thlen*, caused harm to people and spread sickness. Such families were driven away from the village and their lands and other property seized by the village headman or chief.[1]

Among the Munda of Jharkhand there has been a more egalitarian system of redistribution, which altogether inhibited accumulation, rather than centralized it. There any family that accumulated any wealth was subject to *hisinga* or envy.[2] Such a family or person would be denounced for having accumulated wealth through communion with evil spirits and asked to atone for the same. The atonement was

---

[1] See Nathan, Kelkar and Yu Xiaogang (1998) for a detailed account of the above.

[2] The following is based on discussions with Sanjay Bosu-Mullick.

a feast for the whole village, which left the rising family even worse off than the rest of the village.

The above norms and actions inhibited accumulation and actively promoted the redistribution of surpluses. Whether through denunciation as 'pagan' rites or through the growing scope for such persons to escape redistributive measures through urban migration,[3] these measures of redistribution have lost their earlier force. Along with them day-to-day measures of reciprocity, like the substantial provision of village or clan labour to maintain families in need (those without adults or with adults who are unable to work), have been replaced, for instance among the Nagas, by annual cash subscriptions of a percentage of family income.[4] This contribution is more like a tax, and since the proportion is fixed for all families, rich or poor alike, it is in fact regressive, i.e., its burden on poorer families is more. Such a tax, unlike the earlier potentially unlimited contribution of labour and grain, does not inhibit accumulation.

In extreme crisis situations, as during the collapse of urban incomes and remittances during the late 1990s Asian crisis, among the indigenous peoples in Thailand, there was a continuation of kinship and community relations. Returning migrants who had no immediate family could stay with relatives, or if they had no close relatives, in the Buddhist temple. In a different manner, the small patches of village forest in Meghalaya that went to support the church, could also supply timber for the houseless. These means of kinship or community entitlement during extreme crisis, were exceptional measures, they do show that the community has not been completely eroded. But they are merely remnants of what used to be the regular and normal organizing principles of these societies.

The social security systems had a high cost in terms of 'dynamic efficiency, because of their disincentive effects on work and investment efforts' (Platteau 1991: 161). Of course, incentive effects on work and investment were not concerns on which those economic systems were fashioned. But they are now becoming concerns of indigenous people and this leads to changes in their economic systems. In sum what we are witnessing is a historical change from a social system that produced sustenance for its members and the community to one that produces value or is dominated by the commodity form, from one

---

[3] The role of urban migration in escaping from the social sanctions meted out to supposed *thlen* worshippers was pointed out by Tiplut Nongbri in a personal communication.

[4] For details see Nathan (this volume).

mainly concerned about maintaining its social continuity to a system driven by the logic of accumulation and wealth creation.

CHANGE IN PRODUCTION ORIENTATION

The change in production systems is not confined to accumulation at the top, as it were. There is an overall change in the approach to production, from one based on the satisfaction of needs, relatively fixed needs, to one based on the maximization of income.

In the subsistence-oriented, 'full belly' type of production the objective was that of meeting a fixed desired level of consumption, while minimizing work or maximizing leisure (Das Gupta 2002: 3556). The desired level of consumption may be that needed for meeting household nutrition needs over the year while fulfilling social and ceremonial obligations. This leads to a maximization of leisure, after meeting consumption needs, in what Sahlins termed 'the original affluent society'. As Malabika Das Gupta points out, reports of the behaviour of Tripura swiddeners show that they acted on a basis that could be characterized by the 'full belly' model. In 1879–80 when there was a bumper harvest of rice, the swiddeners only carried home the quantity required for consumption, the surplus being left to be eaten by wild beasts. Of course, besides the limited consumption needs of the swiddeners, there was also the factor of poor communication, which made it impossible for the surplus to be exchanged with traders from the plains for anything else.

This was the nature of subsistence production. But with the growth of communication and the creation of new needs, the nature of the production objective has changed.

Since consumerism has spread among them even the remote areas...becoming to some extent a part of the global village, in making their production decisions the jhumias [swiddeners]...seem to want to maximize their utility subject to a minimum consumption and a maximum labour constraint today' (Das Gupta 2002: 3559).

What this means is that from a subsistence-oriented system of production a more surplus and accumulation oriented, maximization of utility (income) subject to a labour constraint has become the norm of peasant production. This is a big shift from subsistence to surplus production.

Of course, given the inevitable inequalities in this process, with a combination of state exclusion and unequal access to land and other productive resources, not many swiddeners make it to accumulation. But what is important is the change in the orientation towards production.

This changed orientation also seems to be unevenly developed among the swiddeners. As repeatedly noticed, the scope for hunting as a serious production activity is almost zero. Yet there are still many such communities where men go out with hunting rifles while women work in the swidden fields. If even that semblance of production, which is in fact leisure, is not there, then there is a frequent recourse by men to alcohol consumption as a leisure activity.

Women, on the other hand, try to maximize the income they can earn, going down the line to low-return activities, like collecting, carrying and selling head loads of fuelwood. The compelling factor is the gender division of responsibilities, where household food security is very much in the women's domain. Failure to provide food can even lead to women being victims of men's domestic violence, besides being socially stigmatized. As a reaction to men's alcoholic violence and the threat it brings to household food security, women across many indigenous communities of India (in Andhra Pradesh, Maharashtra and Nagaland, for instance) have responded with mass movements to ban alcohol consumption.

Inadequacy of Older Norms Governing Production

With a shift in production systems to maximize incomes, unlike with production for self-consumption, which is necessarily limited by the extent of local consumption, production for sale on the market is not similarly locally limited. Consequently, the growth of external markets for various forest products, e.g., Non-Timber Forest Products (NTFPs), has often been accompanied by the rapid depletion, even disappearance, of these products.

As discussed by Nathan (this volume), there are two processes leading to the depletion of NTFPs in common properties, even if access to the resource is controlled. The first is competitive over-harvesting and the second is the paucity of investment in sustaining the productivity of the resource.

The usual response of families and communities to the above problems has been to bring the trees into the home garden or privately-owned orchards. A study of Meghalaya showed that most NTFPs sold in the market come from gardens and not from the forests as such (Tiwari: 2000). With the disappearance or very restricted availability of medicinal herbs, in Bastar, Madhya Pradesh, India, most of what is sold as NTFPs is actually produced in the home garden or swiddens, and not in the forest as such. Valuable trees, such as tamarind and *mahua*, are in the swiddens, home gardens or otherwise within the settlements.

The process of privatizing and domesticating NTFPs depends on the return from the NTFP. As one would expect, those NTFPs which yield a higher return are domesticated, while those with lower, including uncertain returns are not domesticated. In this process there is a difference between regions depending on the trading system, which affects the return from a particular product.

We should revert to the main point being made here—the failure of traditional management systems of NTFPs to cope with problems of regeneration and of maintaining the sustainability of the output. A change in the rules governing rates of harvesting is clearly needed, as also a system of incentives to allow for investment in enrichment planting and other forms of management to improve regeneration. The first can be done by marking trees to be harvested (or, not harvested as the case may be), or by specifying the block within which harvesting will be carried out in any period. These are the rules, as suggested in Peters (1994: 42). But more important than rules is the type of institution that can implement them.

The study of indigenous forest management ideologies in Jharkhand (Singh 2000), points out that traditional approaches to forest management do not include replanting of trees in the commons. Replanting was carried out in the privatized home gardens, while forest regeneration in the commons was the result of leaving the plot fallow to natural regeneration. Even where there was replanting in the commons [see the study of forest management practices in Kalimantan by Padoch 1995] such planting activity led to the establishment of individual/family rights over the tree and/or its fruits. Such an individualized right resulting from the labour of planting trees is common in many indigenous communities [see, for example, the study of the Rungus of Sabah (Porodong 2003), or the Khasis of Meghalaya (Nathan 2001)]. What this means is that traditional approaches are insufficient for maintaining productivity in commercially exploited common forests, which require replanting. This would also strengthen the point that one cannot expect an automatic transition from a subsistence-oriented to a commercially-oriented collective management of common forests.

On the other hand, the study of the evolution of forest management approaches among the Naxi in Yunnan, China (Guo Dalie 2000), does show the development of 'regular public planting of trees... near the end of the Yuan and the beginning of the Ming dynasty'. But this was not the action of the communities themselves, rather it was the system instituted by the centralized Chinese state. This does raise the question: does public planting come up only with the formation of or taking over by a state?

While the system of public planting has continued to this day (Guo Dalie 2000) there has been a change in the method of ensuring its success. Initially and, perhaps until recently, it was only a matter of forbidding cutting of such trees planted on public land. But more recently the Naxi villages (Yang Fuquan and Xi Yuhua 2001), have started giving incentives for promoting the survival of planted saplings. Households are paid for this. This is a form of privatized incentive for preserving saplings planted on public land.

At another level, new types of individual investment can only yield adequate returns if social practices change. For instance, with continuing uncontrolled grazing, plantation can only be taken up by those who can afford to fence their plantation areas. A shift to controlled grazing, however, can open the scope for many more families to undertake investment in plantation. Backed up by sanctions for not conforming to the new rules, 'social fencing' can reduce the cost of plantation, and thus enable many more to participate in the intensification of forest-based production.

Thus it is not only in the case of collective forms of management, as in common property systems, that enabling social conditions are needed. Such enabling social conditions are also needed to institute new forms of private investment.

AN ADVANCED MODE OF ACTIVITY

The new productive forces mean a higher level of income, though not necessarily for all. In India, which has a rich tradition of women's domestic crafts, the export earnings from handicraft production have increased from about USD 50 million in 1990 to about USD 400 million in 2000 (Raj and Kapoor 2002). From a historical situation of handicrafts being destroyed for and by British mill-made products, the export markets for handicrafts have played a substantial role in the revival of handicrafts in India and across Asia.

Does the development of new forces of production represent an 'advanced mode of self-activity of the individuals' (Marx 1970)? This was always how Marx understood the meaning of more developed productive forces—as more developed forms of labour. In the example discussed above, the shift from collection of wild plant materials to the domestication of these plants, certainly represents a higher form of labour. The knowledge of plants needed for domestication is higher than in collection.

In another example, the shift of weaving from being a domestic activity of women in Laos[5] to being the main source of income—in that too there is a considerable advance in the forms of labour. From relatively fixed designs, specific to a particular community, women now learn to weave or embroider any design that is given to them, viz., any design demanded by the market. In the process there is a generalization of the capacity to weave or embroider. There is even some local development of the capacity to innovate and make new designs, a capacity largely concentrated among the local weaver–traders who over time become specialized trader–designers and also older, more experienced women, who are able to make new designs and set up looms, etc.[6]

These are all definite advances in the modes of labour, the modes of activity of the producers. While the older, ancient form of production gave satisfaction from a limited standpoint, the modern seems to give no satisfaction, following as it does the dictates of the market. But there is a higher human content in the labour, only with the capitalist form it appears as alienation, as sacrifice of the human end to the external end of income or wealth, to paraphrase Marx (1973: 487–88). But as Marx repeatedly insisted (1973: 515) this is also a movement in the dissolution of the limited presupposition of existing

---

[5] Nathan (2003).

[6] This observation is somewhat different from that of Ella Bhatt and Renana Jhabvala, who find a staticity in women artisans' work:

Their traditions provide them with knowledge about local conditions and materials and about problems specific to their techniques. But this know-how is neither built into a wider knowledge system nor taught as part of it: so, over time, there is a danger of parts getting lost in transmission. To avoid that, workers are taught to regard each step in the process—whether ritualistically or actually productive—as being sacrosanct; no explanation is given about its necessity. This creates a mind-set which venerates the past and distrusts the change. This is particularly true of women who, much more than men, are supposed to be the keepers and not the questioners of family traditions [quoted in Raj and Kapoor 2002: 11].

The difference might be due to the greater role of ritual in caste India as compared to post-monarchy Laos.

production. Something clearly visible in the transformation of decorative embroidery and weaving from being a subsidiary domestic activity of women into a commercial art production and even the main income source of women and their families.

Culture and Commodity

One of the features of the postmodern condition is identified as the becoming economic of the cultural (Jameson 2000). Is commoditization of cultural products or of major global flows, like environmental services, good or bad? Those who idealize the pristine beauty of the original cultural products, fail to note that they are both continually changing and even in danger of dying out. Commoditization, on the other hand, does enable them to exist. Even more important it enables the artists who produce these works, to exist and continue to produce such works. What is needed is for the works of these artists to not just be part of the 'exotic' that tourists buy as souvenirs, not in the margins, but as parts of the global artistic idiom. That would require a change in the terms of the interaction of the local with the global, as proposed in the artistic realm by Navjot (1998).

It is necessary to understand the ways in which the local of the indigenous peoples interacts with the global in order to be able to change the terms of that interaction. This is so for cultural products as for environmental services. In both cases there has been a forcible and free extraction, without acknowledgement of original authorship of compensation. African sculptures became part of the global artistic scene, via Matisse and Picasso, among others, but the original African sculptors remained basically unknown and even the African influences on these modern works quite unappreciated by the general audience.[7] They did not become individualized works in the global art scene.

---

[7] See the note in a standard work on the history of Western Art, of the early Fauvist works of Matisse 'based in part on...exposure to non-Western sources, such as the art of black Africa' in Arnason and Prather (1998: 131). Or that for Picasso, working on his path-breaking Les Demoiselles d'Avignon, exposure to examples of African and Oceanic sculpture and masks, provoked a 'shock', he said. 'It was at this time that he altered the faces...from the "Iberian" countenances to violently distorted, depersonalized masks' (ibid.: 187). Picasso once said that African sculptures were 'the most powerful and the most beautiful of all the products of the human imagination' (ibid.: 287). It was exposure to sculptures of Africa and Oceania that enabled Western painting and sculpture to break with the natural representation of body and muscular structure.

Gaining the status of commodities these products would then have an acknowledgement of their authorship and this would enable the terms of the earlier forcible and free exchange to be improved in favour of the local producers. This is the improvement in the current terms of exchange between the global and the local that we are advocating. It is a non-trivial change. For those who have been kept outside the sphere of commodities, though their products have been appropriated by other, forcible means, entry into acknowledged commodity production is a step forward, even a liberation from a very unequal exchange.

SOME PROBLEMS MARKETS SOLVE

Although the focus is on privatization as a consequence of the spread of markets, it is useful to take a brief look at the benefits of the spread of markets.

In the example of the leaving of surplus products on the ground for wild animals as it were in Tripura during the bumper harvest of 1879–80, one factor in this wasteful use of human labour was the absence of markets in which these surplus products could be exchanged, either for other useful products or even for stores of value, like gold or other precious metals. The spread of markets makes it possible to overcome such wasteful use of human labour and other resources.

Further, with the existing low level of local demand for various products, like timber or other forest products, there is not much scope for the intensification of resource use in their production. Extensive methods of production, dependent on use of large forest areas and relying on natural methods of regeneration are quite sufficient for meeting local needs. With the growth of external demand there is a pressure to produce more from smaller areas and with lesser use of labour. There is an intensification of production, for instance the shift from extensive collection in forests to intensive production in home gardens. This occurs even with regard to products like fuelwood, when the increase in the opportunity cost of women's labour time leads to the necessity of reducing women's labour in domestic activities.[8]

The market, with its associated privatization, does solve some existing problems in indigenous people's economies. It allows for surplus production to be sold on the market and not just be left in

---

[8] For a fuller analysis of this phenomenon see Nathan and Kelkar (1997).

the ground. In this manner it reduces inefficiency in resource use. The growth of extra-local market demand means that intensification of resource use can be carried out beyond that possible when confined to the local market.[9]

FROM ADVENTURE TO ROUTINE

We have seen that among indigenous peoples new social relations are needed to develop productive forces, the chief of which is labour, and in order to set up citizen-based systems of social welfare. There is a shift from simple reproduction to extended reproduction and accumulation. New needs are created, along with cosmopolitan consumption and production systems, taking local products to the far corners of the world and bringing new goods into local consumption. The mass media, in particular, has been a key instrument in this development of new needs and forms of consumption. A new combination of private and collective or community systems becomes necessary.

But there is also the experience of individualized hunger and deprivation. Producers often do not know why or for whom they produce what they produce. Everything seems to obey the dictates of an impersonal market.

In moving in new directions, however, people also rely on their own experience. For one who has always lived in the domestic drudgery of patriarchal domination, as young women in the North of Thailand, wage employment, however alienated and even low-paid in the garment factories of Bangkok, seems and is a real advance. Its limitations come up only later in experience. Did this movement of women as employees into light industry or commerce bring benefits to the women concerned? Did it benefit them economically and socially? Did it weaken the grip of patriarchy or merely function within the confines of old familial relations? These questions have been discussed elsewhere, notably in Kabeer (2001) with reference to the similar movement of young women in Bangladesh into garment factories in Dhaka.

Sen's (1993) capability approach allows us to see that many things have changed: choices have increased, income and consumption have increased, women's status in the family and society has improved. Young women must have some minimal education in order to get jobs

---

[9] See Johnson and Earle (2000), for a similar discussion of the problems solved by the market.

in the garment industry. Is this the factor behind Bangladesh's recent better performance in education for girls than India's? All of this constitutes substantial change in women's familial and social relations, constituting a weakening of patriarchy, if we are willing to recognize that social transformation may not necessarily occur as 'a single discrete moment of rupture with the past, but as a gradual diffusion of new possibilities' (Kabeer 2001: 192). There are discrete moments of rupture with the past, and there is also the gradual diffusion of new possibilities, expanding the capabilities of persons and changing set rules. For the individual women it is certainly a substantial rupture when they move from being unpaid family workers to being even poorly paid factory workers.

To use the analysis of Marshal Berman, modernity starts out as adventure and then turns into routine (1982: 243–48). But the transformation of adventure into deadening routine requires the experience of modernity. This time of experience, perhaps, is a necessary factor in making alternative projects feasible.

Of course the time of experience is not strictly calendar time. Singular moments can reveal social contradictions that would otherwise not be obvious in more placid situations. Further, those who have gone through such experiences (for instance, people in Euro-America and Japan who have for more than a century lived under the sway of capital, or the urban classes in the developing countries) and seen all its negative consequences for life, are understandably impatient with those for whom the freedom of wage employment seems a liberation and consumption by choice a valuable freedom.

It is no use pointing out that the choice of brands in a supermarket is a tawdry choice, of not much consequence, that consumerism is a curse in making people slaves of the endless change of commercial fashions. For one who only buys a pair of shoes when the older one is unwearable, the choice of being able to buy something not because you absolutely need it, but because you like it – this choice seems and is a higher level of living.[10]

A consumption statement is a limited kind of statement; it is not usually a statement of creativity, of production. But for people whose consumption is severely circumscribed by poverty, the ability to buy something, even when it is not absolutely needed, is a valuable

---

[10] An NGO worker, Md. Sultan then of BRAC in Bangladesh, when told about the fads of consumerism, remarked, 'How nice it must be to buy something even when you do not absolutely need it.'

choice, a type of freedom. Here, however, we need to distinguish between two kinds of choices—choice between, say, flavours of ice cream and choice in being able to buy an ice cream at all. The first is a relatively trivial choice, while the second is non-trivial and reflects the difference between necessity and choice—as freedom to enjoy a satisfaction above a minimum level of necessary consumption.

The contradiction in this development of commodity-based consumption, however, cannot be revealed in its absence. In order to 'rise above the din of the market place' (Kumar Shahani quoted in Geeta Kapur 1998) there must first be a market place. And in a sense, one must be in the market place and go through the market place in order to realize its contradictions and thus rise above it.

DEALING WITH THE NEGATIVE

Among indigenous people, the destruction of indigenous welfare systems of reciprocity and the rupture of access to productive resources, push destitute women, with their continuing responsibilities for household food security, into selling their bodies for sexual services.

This is in our view, a clear negative effect of the development of market relations. However, this effect of market relations must be seen in conjunction with the establishment of masculine domination and its sexual contract, whereby men are enabled to have access to women's sexual services, when they can pay the price for their sexual services. Dealing with it is to deal with patriarchy, its forms of masculinity and the 'sexual contract' (Pateman 1988); not to acquiese in it as an inevitable phenomenon accompanying the spread of the market. On the other hand, it is also to deal with the vulnerability of women, who continue to have responsibility for food security, while suffering from the decline of earlier forms of reciprocity and the loss of assured access to productive resources.

MASCULINE DOMINATION IN ECONOMIC AFFAIRS

Whether formally or informally, openly or covertly, establishing new norms is the result of political struggle. Forest-based communities have gone through, and in some there are still occurring, protracted struggles to establish patriarchal norms. As analyzed in detail elsewhere (Kelkar and Nathan 1991; and Nathan, Kelkar and Yu Xiaogang

1998) the demonization of women, often in the form of persecution for practicing malevolent witchcraft, is one form that the struggle takes through which men excluded women from the spiritual and material management of community affairs.

With the growth of the market, however, what we see is men taking charge of economic affairs too. While small-scale and localized sale of NTFPs remains in women's hands, the more important timber sale is controlled by men. Even in formally matrilineal communities like the Khasi of Northeast India, this has meant a big shift in control over household income. Not only is the control over income in men's hands, the growing proportion of so-called 'self-acquired', as against ancestral property, resulting through accumulation from timber income, means that property too is increasingly controlled by men.

In one way or the other, in the chapter by Kelkar (this volume), it was seen that with the growth of markets, external economic relations dominate domestic relations of production, although the domestic sphere, contributed to and controlled by women, remains an important coping structure in times of economic crisis [as happened during the Asian crisis, see Nathan and Kelkar (1999)]. Funds for accumulation are increasingly obtained through banks or government sources. Men's role in managing the family's external affairs easily extends into such economic matters. In the matrilineal, even matrifocal Mosuo of Yunnan, China, the growth of tourism on Lugu lake has increased the say of men, who secure the finance for constructing guest houses, etc.

The increase in men's say in family economic matters is coupled with their continuing control over village and other community affairs. While earlier men's monopoly in village and community affairs was counter-balanced by women's role over the economic and domestic sphere, with the growth of the market and the growing domination of external economic relations over the domestic economy, women lose their countervailing power. All hierarchies are step-by-step being controlled by men.

The change to men's domination is as much a civilizational change as any of the others we have discussed here. The first phase of this change which establishes men's monopoly over the spiritual and material management of community affairs predates the spread of the market. But the second phase of this civilizational change, in which men use their domination of external relations to establish control over economic affairs, is very much the product of the spread of market-processes in which the external economy dominates the domestic sphere.

To illustrate this point we will again take the example of the Mosuo. Before the contemporary period, men's external role was limited to long-distance trade and the monkhood in pre-Liberation China. Long-distance trade along the 'Silk Route' was a chancy affair, and did not yield a regular income. The monkhood, of course, was a way of using surpluses, rather than of accumulating. With Liberation, men's roles changed to taking up education and political affairs. Till the growth of the market system, these roles too did not yield any substantial income. But with the growth of the market and the rise of the tourist trade, these external connections are now crucial in securing bank loans and other sources of finance. Women's management of domestic affairs has now turned more into drudgery. Though accumulation and inheritance are in the female line, it is men who are increasing their roles in families' strategic decision-making.

The new norms of masculine domination are the product of two processes. On the one hand, there is the 'learning' from other communities and the state. On the other hand, there is also the internal struggle between the genders within these communities. The civilizational change we see is neither merely imposed from outside, nor is it entirely the result of internal conflicts. Both the internal and the external work together to bring about this change.

Simultaneously, and sometimes often in the same communities, there are also struggles to overcome these new, patriarchal norms. 'Taking account' of gender relations is not something that develops by itself. The inclusion of women in management committees also results from political struggle of various kinds. The difference in these gender struggles is often that external agencies too have a substantial role to play. For instance, external project rules requiring the inclusion of women in committees, or legislation on the same matter, are important factors in bringing about the changes in gender relations. Here too, what is necessary to note is the dialectical relation between internal struggles and external enabling rules and decisions. Each one feeds into the other.

Is Masculine Domination Inevitable?

We saw that with the growth of the market there is a shift from men's domination of the spiritual and political realm to domination in the economic system, including the unravelling of matriliny. But is it inevitable that there be masculine domination? In a way this question is parallel to the one posed later: is privatization inevitable with market-based growth. Our answer there was: no, but the transition from a kinship-based collectivity for subsistence to a citizenship-based collectivity for accumulation seems impossible, given the lack of adequate social structures (social capital) for such a direct transition.

In the arena of masculine domination, however, the situation is somewhat different. Even while there has been a spread of masculine domination among indigenous peoples with relatively more equal gender systems, there has also been a counter-movement of women's resistance to gender inequalities. These movements of resistance to gender inequalities make it more possible that inheritance and property systems will not mirror those in the plains' societies, with their millennia-long history of strong patriarchy.

To illustrate the above. Among the Munda in Jharkhand, India, the produce of swidden is understood to be more the domain of women. But rice is exclusively the men's province. Women cannot take rice out from the storage bin; not even for household food needs. If the man is absent women will borrow rice from neighbours but not touch the household rice bin. Wet rice is then quintessentially a man's domain, and a strengthening of masculine domination is historically associated with the spread of wet rice cultivation.

Does this mean that any spread of wet rice cultivation must necessarily lead to masculine domination? In the absence of any other intervention, it is likely that this will happen. But nowadays states themselves have laws for equal land rights, e.g., Chhattisgarh in India, among others. In China too there are some land rights for women in the 'household responsibility system'. These rights are not easily secured, but their existence does make it possible for women's mobilization to succeed in realizing these rights.

The point is, unlike in the case of privatization, there is no incentive or productivity case for men's sole ownership of property. If anything, the incentive case works on the other side—women's ownership of land and other productive resources would increase their incentive to labour more, better, and more productively and also use and develop their own knowledge of production systems.[11]

Similarly, the laws for women's representation in village councils have had their effect in changing the formerly male-dominated village assemblies. Equality of voting rights as citizens has led to village

---

[11] A few examples in Africa do show that there is a clear difference in women's efforts in weeding, leading to significant productivity differences, on their own farms and on their husbands' farms (IFAD 2002).

assemblies in Munda villages no longer distinguishing between senior (*khuntkatti*) and junior (*praja*)[12] lineages, or even between women and men.

Privatization in the present situation can go along with the assertion of relatively more-equal gender rights, and even with measures of democracy, based on equality before the law. Privatization and the intensification of production today do not have to mimic Bronze Age transitions to strongly patriarchal systems.

Is Privatization Inevitable?

There is no *a priori* reason why globalization through the market must lead to privatization. The introduction or all-pervasiveness of the market does dissolve the old system of clan or kinship-based access to productive resources. But whatever new system comes up in its place, depends not on the factor of trade itself, but on the nature of the older system of production relations.

In the examples given above the basic economic activities are carried out not at that of the level of the community but at the individual household, with a lesser, more enabling role for community-organized labour. For instance, there may be community-organized labour in clearing forest for cultivation, but all the other aspects of cultivation are organized by the household, with forms of labour exchange. The higher level of community organization does exist in setting norms for distribution of land, keeping certain portions as community reserves, and so on. The higher level also exists in rituals, a level that has been replaced in most of Northeast India by the church. Naga villages, for instance, have built magnificent churches with communal labour, but their economic activities are organized at the level of the household.[13] Whatever trade was carried out before the large-scale intrusion of trade, was also at the level of the household. In such a situation of a largely household-based economic production system, it is no surprise that large-scale trade led to privatization.

On the other hand, we should note counter-examples in Yunnan Province of China, where the market has not led to privatization of

---

[12] The *praja* are the families of women with in-marrying husbands, *ghar jamai*.

[13] 'It is not cooperation in wealth-producing labour by means of which the commune member reproduces himself, but rather cooperation in labour for the communal interests (imaginary and real), for the upholding of the association inwardly and outwardly' (Marx 1973: 476).

forests. While in China as a whole the introduction of the 'household responsibility system' was followed by the distribution of collective (but not state-owned) forests to individual households, the various indigenous peoples of Lijiang County, Yunnan, other than in the locations close to the town, did not distribute their forests to the households. They argued that they had long traditions of collective management of forests, with well-established norms for regulating access to and use of forests, and did not want to divide up their forests among households. When these operative units, what are called administrative villages and used to be work teams in the old commune system, received permission to carry out logging, they did this collectively. Of course, logging wages were individual. But the residual income, after paying state taxes and all other costs, went to the administrative villages, which used this income for a variety of infrastructure, educational and welfare functions.[14]

Some Mexican *ejidos* have also similarly developed collective logging enterprises. Further, faced with the threat of competition due to the opening up of the Mexican market, they have also moved up the value chain to selling not logs or even cut wood, but manufacturing furniture of good quality (Land Tenure Centre and Institute for Environmental Studies 1995).

What is needed for such a collective response to the market? The villages must be well organized, in the sense of being able to establish and implement norms of access to and use of the forests, along with sanctions for breaking those norms. In particular the harvesting of timber needs to be decided upon and carried out collectively—a system of collective ownership with individual harvesting will soon degenerate into an unregulated commons and be subject to competitive over-harvesting [as was the experience with some 'public mountains' in Lijiang, where harvesting of timber was legally not allowed, (see Yang Fuquan and Xi Yuhua 2003; and He Zhonghua 2003)]. To put it briefly, the collective institution must be able to overcome the 'free rider' problem and institute norms of common property functioning. For such well-functioning collective systems to be sustained in the market system, it is also necessary that there be a basic agreement within the community and between the leaders and the rest on the goals of economic development.

In a sense, what is needed is a 'developmental state' at the micro-level, with a corresponding trust based on an agreement on goals.

---

[14] See Nathan and Yu Xiaogang, in this book, for details.

There are richer and poorer in these villages [and also in the few other collective villages in China, e.g., those studied in Nathan and Kelkar (2001)]. But what is common to all of them is that the poorest also gain a substantial measure of the benefits from the villages' economic enterprises, whether in logging or industry.

The factors of internal organization of the community to overcome 'free rider' problems and of trust, based on shared development goals, are then necessary if village communities are to evolve as collective institutions within a market system. Can such collective institutions develop without having experienced the negative consequences of privatization?

Marx in his notes on the 'Russian road'[15] mentioned the possibility of a direct transition from the traditional Russian commune to socialism, without an intervening period of capitalism.[16] One of the factors on which this possibility rested was the worldwide condition of the socialist movement. More than a century after Marx, at the beginning of the twenty-first century, with the collapse of twentieth-century, public sector, statist attempts at constructing socialism, the contours of an alternative to capitalism have yet to be re-established, even if there are signs of a growing dissatisfaction with capitalist market fundamentalism in the developed capitalist countries, often seen as opposition to 'globalization'.

Our analysis above points to another and more fundamental factor which makes unlikely such a direct transition from traditional communal forms of organization to a post-capitalist alternative—that is the difference between subsistence oriented management of production for use and one centred on accumulation, driven by production for gain, between simple and expanded reproduction, and the different management norms needed for the two.

There is then the further empirical question of the extent to which the collective system of regulating production has disintegrated. In none of the areas studied do we find a collective production. While

---

[15] 'But does this mean that the development of the "land commune" must necessarily follow the same lines under all circumstances? Certainly not. Its constitutive form allows the following alternative: either the element of private property implied in it gains the upper over the collective element, or vice versa/ Everything depends upon the historical background in which it finds itself.... Both these solutions are possible *a priori*, but both obviously require entirely different historical environments' (Marx 1881, in 1970, 3, p. 156).

[16] One of the authors of this paper had earlier taken the cue from Marx's analysis in arguing for a similar possibility for Jharkhand. See Nathan (1987) 'The Future of Jharkhand.'

land ownership may be acknowledged to be that of the clan or community, production has for as long as we know, been basically organized by the family or household. Even the periodic redistributions of land have long since ceased. 'Once these redistributions lapse of themselves or in virtue of a special decree, you have a village of peasant small-holders' (Engels 1894 in1969: 402).

What kept the village together as a community were the systems of reciprocity and redistribution (Polanyi 1944: 47). In the Northeast India case study we have seen how the systems of reciprocity and redistribution declined and enabled the rise of individual accumulation.

LAISSEZ FAIRE OR 'NEO-LIBERAL' TRANSITION

In one way or the other, it is a big step from management that is based on simple reproduction to one that aims at accumulation and at expanded reproduction. How the new norms are established, the struggles of conflicting sections of the society for or against these norms, the ways in which new practices are set up—these are all important issues for study.

In this 'Great Transformation' (Polanyi 1944), or 'civilizational change', old norms are falling apart or are clearly inadequate for the new kind of behaviour. New norms are not yet in place. This process is proceeding in a *laissez faire* manner. In this original accumulation, it is the poor, including women, who possess much less of economic and political resources, who particularly suffer. In the usual manner of *laissez faire* economics and politics, market-induced privatization would end with its benefits going disproportionately to the more powerful, who become the new rich. But to the extent that ownership of land and allied resources is widespread, to that extent the benefits of privatization of the commons would be also more widespread.

Some new institutional set up and new norms are needed in order that the benefits are spread more widely. 'Contrary to what was supposed by theorists of the original contract, only a contract can free a group from the contract-less constraint of social mechanisms that is sanctioned by *laissez faire*' (Bourdieu 1990: 111). In the first place, measures are needed to enable the orderly distribution of lands for private use, along with setting up nested public decision institutions to bring under local common management, the areas of 'critical natural capital', whether they be forests, watersheds and so on. Along with that, the growing inequalities in access to productive resources and masculine domination need to be addressed.

In any situation there are always those who benefit from the existing norms or from the *laissez faire* situation following the breakdown of those norms. Those who benefit from the existing norms (or lack of norms as the case may be) will oppose the setting up of new norms. This resistance will need to be overcome by struggle/mobilization of those who are likely to benefit or expect that they will benefit from the new norms. If the new norms are necessary for building the capability of the community to deal with its internal forest and other management problems, then we can say that political struggle is necessary for setting up new norms, or in moving from a *laissez faire* situation to one of accepted norms as the case may be.

ALTERNATIVES IN GLOBALIZATION: NORMS OF NON-MARKET ACCESS TO PRODUCTIVE RESOURCES

Take the situation in the Khasi areas of Meghalaya. In some villages, when the village headmen (*sirdars*) or other village notable men and their families were grabbing community forests and registering them as their own, or more often their wives', private lands, the poorer sections of the community, who were being left out of this process, mobilized themselves and forced a change in the rule regarding community forests—the community forests were then divided up more or less equally among all members of the village community. This village-level mobilization instituted new forms of ownership and control of former community forests, which led to more care of the forests, management practices of various kinds and even enrichment planting, all of which increased the community's capability to efficiently manage its forests.

This changes the usual pattern of enclosure being a 'revolution of the rich against the poor' (Polanyi 1944: 34). Instead we get a more egalitarian distribution of community assets. Of course, in both cases, there is a productivity enhancing effect. We saw above in the Khasi case that enclosure of the commons through distribution led to improved management practices. Polanyi too points out that enclosures in England increased the yield of the land (*ibid.*). What these results show is that the change in norms led to an increase in productivity, something that the indigenous peoples certainly need.

The spontaneous solution of privatization, which would be more sustainable than what now exists, is the *laissez faire* trend that is at work. But privatization works against those who don't have any land or have less land. Access to common forests is important for the poorest, particularly for single women, i.e., widows or divorced women. Privatization is inevitably inequitable.

The other attempted solution, as in various Joint Forest Management (JFM) experiments in India, is to institute village-level control over access to NTFPs. But with varying levels of dependence on forest products this is difficult to implement and also leads to inequity. The better off sections and those relying less on forest resources for income, very easily decide to set aside areas of forest for regeneration. As repeatedly pointed out by Sarin (e.g., 1996; and 2003), with regard to women who collect fuelwood for use or sale, such restrictions go against the poorest, usually single women.

A more viable solution to the problem might be to organize at the level of producer or user groups. Given that there are many alternate uses of forest resources, and many different types of users, this would not be easy to implement. But it has been tried out in two types of cases. The first, which is quite frequent in China, is the lease of the land to the highest bidder for developing orchards, with the condition that it cannot be used for agriculture. With this privatization of formerly common land, investment and regeneration can follow. But the poor are left out of this process of enclosure of the commons. This solution is also often discussed in India in the context of so-called wasteland development.

Another approach is to lease the degraded forestland, not to the highest bidder, but to the poorest sections of the village, those who depend on common lands more than others in the village. This has been tried out in at least one case, the Inernational Fund for Agricultural Development (IFAD) project of Leasehold Forestry in Nepal (Nathan and Shreshta, this volume). In this project, as opposed to the usual community forestry project, the (degraded) forestland is leased out to groups of the poor to be developed as their common resource. Such a relatively homogenous group can both set up rules about labour contribution and sharing of income/resources, monitor the observance of the rules and impose sanctions for breaking accepted rules. Since the returns from the enrichment planting and other investment measures, accrue to the group itself, there is a connection between investment and returns.

Yet another approach could be to combine group access with family labour. While certain tasks, like guarding or 'social fencing', through control of grazing, may be carried out at a group level, the major labour of tending plots and extracting products could be family based. This would have the advantage that group organization could be used to establish user rights, while family labour would be the basis of income distribution. Credit could also be group based, with individual liability. The level of social organization needed to make such a system function may be less than with the full-fledged group or collective system.

The 'Extractive Reserves' system implemented in a number of South American countries is just such a combination of collective and family labour. 'The extractive reserves are administered communally. Although not allocated in individual plots, families have the right to exploit the resources along their traditional tapping routes (the *colocacoes*) within the reserve' (Diegues 1998: 73). The restriction of families to specific resources for tapping can ensure that the producers take care of regeneration in the course of tapping and invest sufficient labour for regeneration of the trees in their areas.

In the context of developing production of NTFPs, what is important is to end the largely prevalent current situation of no link between investment and returns, because of which investment, whether of labour or other resources, is not forthcoming in the development of production and leads to depletion of the resource. Problems of excludability and subtractability are not adequately addressed by the existing management systems, creating what are effectively open access conditions. Further, it is also necessary to address these problems in such a manner that the poorest do not lose access to resources. This can be achieved by combining the elements of common management, as mentioned above in fencing, etc., with family-based direct labour inputs.

The old forms of social capital of these indigenous peoples were based on reciprocity and non-accumulation, as discussed previously. These forms of social capital are no longer functional and can be clearly be seen to be breaking down in the face of changes in the nature of economic activities from largely self-production for subsistence to market-oriented production for accumulation. New forms of social capital are needed. These new forms of social capital may not be related to the older ones and may well also require some prior experience with market-based, individualized systems for their formulation. There may be no easy, leave alone automatic, transition from kinship-based collectivities to newer citizen-based collectivities.

RESTRICTIONS ON PROPERTY RIGHTS

There, however, is need to have certain restrictions on the property rights set up for forests. The first right, those over residual incomes, should accrue to the forest-communities. The right to sell the environmental goods provided from forests would link labour and other investment in their supply with income from this supply. Thus, this right that is likely to lead to an increase in the supply of various environmental goods, or environmental services. At the same time, it is clear, from the Northeast India case studies (Nathan this volume; and Nongbri, this volume) , that complete or virtually private owner-ship of forests leads to an undersupply of local environmental ser-vices. This means that in certain forest areas, crucial for the maintenance of 'critical natural resources', there should be a community ownership of the relevant forests. Full private ownership tends to undersupply environmental goods and to oversupply environmental bads.

Further, absentee ownership (whether by individuals in the process of migrating as in Northeast India or by local governments that are dominated by lowland communities in Lijiang, China) leads to an over-harvesting of forest products in order to transfer the residual income to urban accumulation. If forests are not to be rapidly de-pleted by such a process, there needs to be a restriction on the right to earn an income from forests. There should be an obligation on the owner to use the forests himself/herself in order to claim the residual income. Such an owner–manager was seen to be more interested in maintaining the longer-term supply of forests than absentee owners or those with leases (Nathan 2000). Forests should then be a means to use labour, and not otherwise a source of income. This is the type of restriction found in the 1867 Homestead Act of the USA, under which a person could not 'own' a piece of land unless he worked on it (Roemer 1998: 223). Similarly, the land system instituted after the Mexican Revolution allowed land rights only to those who tilled the land.

Absentee ownership usually goes along with the right to sell the asset (forests), and leads to a 'forest as real estate' situation, with the neglect of both local and other environmental services. The restriction to sell land only to those within the community does not really serve to restrict such sale of land as real estate, as seen in Northeast India (Nathan this volume). This type of problem can be reduced, if not eliminated, by removing the right to sell the asset. This is linked with the necessity of oneself working on forests in order to own it, or claim a share of residual income from it. Analyses of the evolution of land rights in Africa also leads some to advocate the non-transferability of agricultural land titles (Platteau 1996: fn. 52). Such restrictions are particularly important in a situation where there are few alternatives to farming, and, as argued above, to enhance the environmental service functions of forests.

The destructive effect of the right to sell, that is speculate in land, on the provision of natural, i.e., environmental services, was pointed out by Polanyi in *The Great Transformation*. More recently Roemer (1998) has introduced the necessity of attenuating the right to sell an asset as a necessary condition to link equity with efficiency. Our proposal is in line with this thinking that would eliminate the right to sell forests as assets. This, of course, goes against the grain of current neo-liberal thinking on globalization, which would demand a level playing field for capital to compete for resources anywhere. The nature of such a so-called level playing field was aptly expressed by the poet Blake, 'One law for the lamb and the lion is not justice'.

A lower order of right is that to sell membership of forest committees. In Uttarakhand the sale of individualized rights by migrants has become an obstacle to residents to meet their needs. In JFM committees in West Bengal those who have migrated still continue in the lists of members. (Both points from Madhu Sarin, personal communication). As pointed out earlier, migrants have very short time horizons with regard to forests as assets. In another sense the continuation of migrants in local forest management committees violates the essential localness, or local embeddedness of the forest management decisions. In order to preserve the space for local forest management, such migrated interests need to be eliminated from the forest management committees. Local residence plus labour contribution should guide allocation of returns from forest management.

The type of property rights reform suggested in this study is an asset transfer, and not the more usual income transfer. There are many proposals to tax buyers of forest products and redistribute the incomes to forest communities as a means of bringing the prices of these products more in line with their full costs of production. Such income redistribution may have little or no effect on productive efficiency. It, for instance, would not improve micro-management of the forests. But redistribution of assets, as also argued by Bowles and Gintis (1998), would link income with labour and investment in producing the necessary environmental and other forest goods for sale. This is an egalitarian or equality enhancing measure that is asset and not income based. It is likely to be both more just and to also increase productivity.

LIMITS TO THE MARKET AND COMMODITIZATION

In the analysis of environmental services and goods we have advocated the use of prices of environmental services and other income-transfer methods for compensating the forest communities who produce these services and goods. At the end it needs to be clarified that this is not an argument for using the market and price mechanisms to determine the scale on which these public goods are to be provided. The provision of these goods is an explicitly political matter, whether at the local, global or regional levels. Thus, it is clearly outside the market.

How is this public decision to be transmitted to the forest-dwellers who provide these environmental goods? For local public goods, since the costs and benefits are both local, i.e., the same group of persons both bears the costs and gains the benefits, there is no need for any other compensation mechanism. But in the case of externally provided goods, where the local beneficiaries are only a small part of the total beneficiaries but the local providers bear the full costs of such provision, there is a strong case for compensating the providers for the costs they bear. In a sense it is no different from saying that those who work to perform various public services should not have to do so free of any charge or compensation. Even in the field of cultural production, public decisions would be taken on providing these practices over and above that which is paid for directly in the market. But in every such case the artists who produce these works (e.g., public sculptures or symphony orchestras) are paid for their work out of public funds. It is at this level of transmission of political decisions on the provision of public goods that we are arguing for a role of the market (price) and other compensatory mechanisms.

We are not arguing for market or quasi-market valuations of public goods, as, for instance, in the following, 'Physical accounts are useful in answering ecological questions of interest and in linking environment to the economy.... However, physical accounts are limited because they lack a common unit of measurement and it is not possible to gauge their relative importance to each other and non-environmental goods and services' (Pearce, Barbier and Markandaya, in O'Neill 2001:1867).

The non-commensurability of those goods and services that have use value, but cannot be exchanged, cannot be expressed by monetary values. These values, the local-use values, we have seen in the empirical studies in this book, are integrated by various rules of thumb into local environmental management. At higher levels too such rule of thumb will inevitably prevail and be subject to political processes of decision-making. The market only comes into the picture after this political process in efficiently securing the supply of environmental goods and services at the desired level. This combination of political decision and market processes is necessary to combine an adequate level of supply of pubic goods along with adequate incentives for their production.

ALTERNATIVES IN GLOBALIZATION: RECREATING THE COMMUNITY

Accepting the necessity of the market system for the intensification of production, accumulation and the increase of incomes, does this have to be done in a *laissez faire*, or as it is nowadays called, a neo-liberal (leave it all to the market) type of system? We have already seen that in the cases of provision of public goods, like local environmental services, and the preservation of cultural heritage beyond the commoditization of ethnicity, various forms of public intervention would be needed. Similarly in the matter of food security too, various new forms of public intervention would be needed to deal with the limitations of the market.

At the economic level it is not necessary that integration into the market necessarily erode and destroy all forms of community inter-action. Of course, the market is likely to destroy the traditional com-munity. With conscious intervention, however, the community can be recreated. But the nature of the interaction would have to change, from the earlier kinship-based reciprocity and redistribution welfare systems to a new form of citizen-based social welfare system, com-bining state and community-based mechanisms. Forms of collective functioning are also needed for maintaining critical natural resources. Forms of collective entrepreneurship could also be developed. The relatively more equal gender relations of the indigenous peoples are certainly being eroded, but more productive technologies and market systems do not have to necessarily enshrine patriarchy.

Even within the capitalist market there can be enterprises with a variety of internal relations—contrast the 'hire and fire' method of American capitalism with the until-recently 'life-long employment' of Japanese capitalism (at least for its core of male, permanent workers), and also the fairly elaborate social welfare systems of the collective villages and collective enterprises of China. Technology and the market do not dictate even the full form of enterprise. But the extent to which they are able to institute different and more welfare oriented forms of internal relations, depends crucially on the productivity, and be-cause of globalization, even comparative productivity of these enter-prises. With the decade-long stagnation in Japanese productivity and thus with the loss of these firms' advantage over their competitors,

Japanese firms are being forced to abandon the more expensive system of life-long employment.

Developing citizen-based collectivities for public action on food security would need to move from 'reciprocity' to taxes in order to provide 'safety nets'. As food itself becomes less of a problem, it is necessary to intervene in public provision of education and health care. This requires that local communities have unequivocal rights over portions of tax revenues. The Chinese devolution of certain taxes to the local level (the agricultural products tax, for instance) has been seen to have beneficial effects on local accumulation. It is for local communities and their authorities to also use these revenues to fashion new forms of human welfare.

Productivity may make certain levels of welfare expenditures possible, but it does not necessarily have to occur. Whether or not more people-friendly welfare systems are instituted will depend on the extent of struggle for such systems, a struggle that now, however, switches from the formerly national scale to the new global scale. Let alone relatively weak indigenous peoples, even strong states are losing their ability to meet their former welfare commitments. With the loss of autonomy with regard to interest, inflation and exchange rates, the one arena of competition among states is to reduce costs by cutting welfare expenditures. As a result it is a race to the bottom with regard to welfare commitments even in developed countries, negating commitments that were gained after long battles in the last century.

In a system of potentially unrestrained movement of capital, with equal treatment for capitals, irrespective of their origin, there is no escaping the conclusion that a global working people's response, a global New Deal, or a global social contract (Castells 2000: 253) can be the only alternative to a race to the bottom. This will surely be difficult to achieve. But the creation of alternatives in globalization need not stop with the creation of 'safety nets', which after all are ways of aiding those who have fallen below. A more equal distribution of former community lands would mean doing away with, for instance, the grabbing of land by the politically influential, as now happens. Land reform, in one way or the other, is a necessary part of a more democratic alternative in globalization. This could itself be fashioned at a local level, in villages or groups of villages.[17] What this means is that unlike in the neo-liberal doctrine, there should be a non-market access to land (or forests) as a critical productive resource. And this

---

[17] See the proposals in Nathan (2001) carried over into Saxena (2001).

access should be not for the 'household' or the 'family' but for the individual adult, woman or man.

While land reform would enable a more equal distribution of income from land, more and more it is education that becomes a crucial factor in inequality. Income from land may enable a more equal access to land but may not in itself be enough. This can be observed, for instance, in Yunnan, China, where inequalities in land distribution are not as high as in access to higher education and thus to non-farm incomes. The removal of the earlier state-based access to education and its replacement by various forms of fee payment have increased inequality in access to education beyond the compulsory primary level. The ban on logging itself led to higher dropout rates among children of upland Yi versus valley-bottom Naxi communities. Among the Hani in Xishuangbanna too the necessity of private payment of fees led to a higher dropout rate among the already-poorer sections of the villages. Of course, given the prevalence of son preference there was a clear bias against girls in school dropouts.

Promoting higher education, however, requires more than just state support. It also requires the creation of job opportunities; otherwise the result would only be the frustation of educated unemployment. This is where the promotion of non-agricultural employment, as in tourism or cultural products, or new forms of agriculture and agricultural processing would have a beneficial effect in promoting employment for the educated. At the level of public action, however, it also requires a change in the approach to high school education—primary education and literacy are now accepted as public goods whose consumption cannot be restricted by private, household decision. In a globalizing world it is necessary to move up the ladder to high school education as a first step.

Similarly, in the contemporary situation heavy medical expenses are often the route to falling into poverty. In a situation where health care costs are privatized, they become a major factor in the near-poor falling into the category of the poor.

Indigenous peoples, areas are characterized by low levels of state-provided social welfare expenses. Their road systems too have historically been designed for extraction of timber and other products. The levels of education and health infrastructure available in the hills are significantly lower than in the plains. Increasing the health and education infrastructure in the hills requires greater public investment in the above, something that the allocation of tax revenues on timber and other forest products to the indigenous peoples' governments is likely to promote.

Thus, we see a necessity of intervening in the privatization process in a number of ways—public decision for locally needed environmental services, combined with market-based provision of environmental services for external needs; public decision for preservation of cultural heritage, beyond the limits of that promoted by the commoditization of culture; land reform to enable a more equal distribution of land-based income; restrictions on the saleability of forests and agricultural land; mobilization and intervention to create more equal gender relations; higher public provision of education and health care needs. All of these change privatization from a straightforward *laissez faire* or neo-liberal system to one that is less unequal. They are, however, alternatives in globalization—not an alternative to globalization.[18]

The civilizational transformation of indigenous peoples' economies and societies is occurring at a time when the increased stratification that historically accompanied intensification carries with it some factors for overcoming this stratification.[19] In the contemporary world, as compared to that of urban civilizations after the Bronze Age, there is not just elite, specialized consumption. Mass-production carries with it mass-consumption and mass culture. The power of the mass media in this regard is increased by the growth of universal literacy, as against the earlier creation of a literate elite. Adult franchise means that the economically marginalized cannot just be ignored. Gender relations and family systems, too, are not of the kind that just reproduce earlier forms of patriarchy but are tending in the direction of more equal gender relations. Finally, forms of civil society, bringing together the indigenous peoples all over the world, and linking them with other global civil society organizations are now the order of the day. All of this makes possible a greater spread of benefits, if not also a quicker overcoming of limits.

REFERENCES

Arnason, Harvard H. and Marla F. Prather. *History of Modern Art*, fourth Edition. New Jersey: Prentice Hall and Henry N. Abrams, 1998.

---

[18] The scheme put forward here has a lot in common with that proposed by MacEwan (2000) for a more equal and democratic form of market economy and Jean Dreze and Amartya Sen's notion of 'participatory development'(2002).

[19] This passage owes much to Johnson and Earle (2000: 387).

Berman, Marshall. *All That Is Solid Melts Into Air: The Experience Of Modernity*. New York. London: Penguin Books, 1982.

Bourdieu, Pierre. *The Logic of Practice*. Cambridge: Polity Press, 1990.

Bowles, Samuel and Herbert Gintis. *Recasting Egalitarianism: New Rules for Communities, States and Markets*, edited by Erik Olin Wright. London, New York: Verso, 1998.

Castells, Manuel. *The Network Society*. Oxford: Blackwell Publishers, 2000.

Das Gupta, Malabika. 'Objective Function in Economic Models of Decisions on Production: Evidence from Swiddeners in Tripura'. *Economic and Political Weekly* 37, no. 34 (24 August 2002).

Diegues, Antonio Carlos. 'Social Movements in the Remaking of the Commons in the Brazilian Amazon'. In *Privatizing Nature: Political Struggle for the Global Commons*, edited by Michael Goldman. London: Pluto Press, 1998.

Dreze, Jean and Amartya Sen. *India: Development and Participation*. New Delhi: Oxford University Press, 2002.

Engels, Frederick. 'On Social Relations in Russia'. In *Karl Marx and Frederick Engels, Selected Works in Three Volumes, Volume Two*. Moscow: Progress Publishers, 1894 in 1969.

Guo Dalie. 'A History of Naxi Forest Ecology and Management'. Manuscript, 2000.

He Zhonghua. 'Forest Management in Mosou Matrilineal Society, Yunnan, China'. In *Gender Relations in Forest Societies in Asia: Patriarchy at Odds*, edited by Govind Kelkar, Dev Nathan and Pierre Walter. New Delhi, Thousand Oaks, London: Sage Publications, 2003.

International Fund for Agricultural Development (IFAD). *Assessment of Rural Poverty: West and Central Africa*. Rome: IFAD, 2002.

Jameson, Frederic. 'Philosophy of Globalization'. In *The Cultures of Globalization*, edited by Frederic Jameson and Masao Miyoshi. Durham: Duke University Press, 2000.

Johnson, Allen W. and Timothy Earle. *The Evolution of Human Societies*, Second Edition. Stanford: California University Press, 2000.

Kabeer, Naila. *Bangladesh Women Workers and Labour Market Decisions: The Power to Choose*. New Delhi: Vistaar Publications, 2001.

Kapur, Geeta. 'Navigating the Void'. In *The Cultures of Globalization*, edited by Frederic Jameson and Masao Miyoshi. Durham: Duke University Press, 1998.

Kelkar, Govind and Dev Nathan. *Gender and Tribe: Women, Land and Forests in Jharkhand*. New Delhi: Kali for Women, and London: Zed Press, 1991.

Land Tenure Center and Institute for Environmental Studies. 'Case Studies of Community-Based Forestry Enterprises in the Americas'. Paper presented at the Symposium on Forestry in the Americas: Community-Based Management and Sustainability. University of Wisconsin, Madison, 3–4 February, 1995.

MacEwan, Arthur. *Neo-Liberalism or Democracy?* Dhaka: The University Press Limited, 2000.

Marx, Karl. *Grundrisse*. Translated by Martin Nicolaus. Harmondsworth: Penguin Books, 1973.

——. 'First Draft of the Reply to V. I. Zasulich's Letter'. *Karl Marx and Frederick Engels, Selected Works in Three Volumes, Volume Three*. Moscow: Progress Publishers, 1881 in 1970.

Marx, Karl and Frederick Engels. 'Feurbach: Opposition of Materialistic and Idealistic Outlook'. In *Selected Works*, Vol. 1. Moscow: Foreign Languages Publishing House, 1845–46 in 1970.

Nathan Dev. 'The Future of Jharkhand'. *Economic and Political Weekly* 24, no. 6 (13 February 1987).

—————. 'Timber in Meghalaya'. *Economic and Political Weekly* 15, no. 4 (22 January 2000): 182–86.

—————. 'Land Systems in Meghalaya'. A Study for the Asia Division. Rome: IFAD, 2001.

—————. 'Responding to Globalization: Women, Poverty Reduction and Livelihoods Diversification on the Lao-Thai Border'. A Study for the IFAD Gender Mainstreaming in Asia Project. New Delhi, 2003.

Nathan, Dev and Govind Kelkar. 'Woodfuel: The Role of Women's Labour'. *Gender, Technology and Development* 1, no. 2 (1997).

—————. 'Rural Dimensions of the Asian Crisis: Agrarian Involution, Domestic Economy and Women'. *Economic and Political Weekly* 34, no. 19 (8–14 May 1999).

—————. *Collective Villages in the Chinese Market*. Delhi: Rainbow Publishers, 2001.

Nathan, Dev, Govind Kelkar and Yu Xiaogang. 'Women as Witches: Struggles to Change Gender Relations'. *Economic and Political Weekly* 33, no. 44 (31 October–6 November 1988).

Navjot Altaf. 'Discursive Invisibility'. Paper read at Asian Institute of Technology, Bangkok, 1998.

Nongbri, Tiplut. 'Culture and Biodiversity: Myths, Legends and the Conservation of Nature in the Hills of North-east India'. Manuscript, 2002.

O'Neill, John. 'Markets and the Environment: The Solution Is the Problem'. *Economic and Political Weekly* (26 May 2001): 1865–73.

Padoch, Christine. 'Creating the Forest: Dayak Resource Management in Kalimantan'. In *Society and Non-Timber Forest Products in Tropical Asia*, edited by Jefferson Fox. Honolulu: East-West Centre, 1995.

Pateman, Carole. *The Sexual Contract*. London: Polity Press, 1998.

Peters, Charles. *Sustainable Harvest of Non-timber Plant Resources in Tropical Moist Forests: An Ecological Primer*. Washington: Biodiversity Support Program, USAID, 1994.

Platteau, Jean-Philippe. 'Traditional Systems of Social Security and Hunger Insurance: Past Achievements and Modern Challenges'. In *Social Security in Developing Countries*, edited by Ehitsham Ahmed, Jean Dreze, John Hills and Amartya Sen. New Delhi: Oxford University Press, 1991.

—————. 'The Evolutionary Theory of land Rights as Applied to Sub Saharan Africa: A Critical Assessment'. *Development and Change* 27 (1996): 29–86.

Polanyi, Karl. *The Great Transformation*. Boston: Beacon Press, 1944.

Porodong, Paul. 'Bobolizan, Forests and Gender Relations'. In *Gender Relations in Forest Societies in Asia: Patriarchy at Odds*, edited by Govind Kelkar, Dev Nathan and Pierre Walter. New Delhi: Thousand Oaks, London: Sage Publications, 2003.

Raj, Ashok and Rakesh Kapoor. 'Globalising Handicraft Market and the Marginalisation of Women Craft-workers'. Paper presented at UNIFEM and

SEWA Bharat Workshop on Globalization and Its Impact on Women Workers in Informal Economy, New Delhi, 4–5 December 2002.

Roemer, Paul. 'The Limits of Private-property-based Egalitarianism'. In *Recasting Egalitarianism: New Rules for Communities, States and Markets*, by Samuel Bowles and Herbert Gintis, edited by Erik Olin Wright. London, New York: Verso, 1998.

Sarin, Madhu. 'Who is Gaining? Who is Losing? Gender and Equity Concerns in Joint Forest Management'. Working paper by the Gender and Equity Sub-group, National Support Group for JFM, Society for Wasteland Development, New Delhi, 1996.

————. 'Empowerment and Disempowerment of Forest Women in Uttarakhand, India'. In *Gender Relations in Forest Societies in Asia: Patriarchy at Odds*, edited by Govind Kelkar, Dev Nathan and Pierre Walter. New Delhi: Sage, 2003.

Saxena, N. C. 'Poverty in Meghalaya'. A Study for the Asia Division. Rome: IFAD, 2001.

Sen, Amartya Kumar. 'Capability and Well-being'. In *The Quality of Life,* edited by Martha Nussbaum and Amartya Kumar Sen. New Delhi: Oxford University Press, 1993.

Singh, K. S. 'Changing Attitude to Forest and Nature: A Historical Review with Focus on Jharkhand'. Manuscript, 2000.

Tiwari, B. K. 'Non-Timber Forest Produce of North East India'. *Journal of Human Ecology* 10 (2000).

Yang Fuquan and Xi Yuhua 'Naxi Women: Protection and Management of Forests in Lijiang, China'. In *Gender Relations in Forest Societies in Asia: Patriarchy at Odds*, edited by Govind Kelkar, Dev Nathan and Pierre Walter. New Delhi: Sage, 2003.

About the Editors and Contributors

Editors

Dev Nathan, an economist by training, is, Senior Visiting Fellow, Institute for Human Development, New Delhi. He is also a columnist and a regular contributor to the *Economic and Political Weekly*. Dr Nathan has previously co-authored *Gender and Tribe: Women, Land and Forests* (1991), *Assessment of Rural Poverty in Asia and the Pacific* (2002), edited *From Tribe to Caste* (1997), and co-edited *Gender Relations in Forest Societies in Asia: Patriarchy at Odds* (2003). Dr Nathan frequently serves as a consultant to IFAD, Rome, several UN organizations and ICIMOD, Kathmandu, on issues of rural poverty and the development of indigenous peoples.

Govind Kelkar is Coordinator, IFAD–UNIFEM Gender Mainstreaming Programme in Asia, New Delhi, and the founding Editor of the journal *Gender, Technology and Development*. She has previously taught at Delhi University, the Indian Institute of Technology, Mumbai, and the Asian Institute of Technology (AIT), Bangkok, Thailand where she also founded the graduate programme in Gender and Development Studies. Dr Kelkar has previously co-authored *Gender and Tribe: Women, Land and Forests* (1991), and co-edited *Feminist Challenges in the Information Age* (2002), and *Gender Relations in Forest Societies in Asia: Patriarchy at Odds* (2003). Dr Kelkar is a frequent consultant to IFAD, Rome, UNIFEM, New Delhi and other UN organizations on mainstreaming gender in development besides being a keynote speaker at many related conferences.

Pierre Walter is Assistant Professor, Department of Educational Studies, University of British Columbia, Vancouver, Canada. Dr Walter's research interests include literacy, immigrant and extension education, comparative education and policy studies, alternative education, Asian studies and gender and development. He has contributed numerous articles to leading scholarly journals, besides serving as an Assistant Editor of *Gender, Technology and Development*. He has co-edited *Gender Relations in Forest Societies in Asia: Patriarchy at Odds* (2003).

CONTRIBUTORS

N. S. Jodha is Senior Policy Analyst, International Centre for Mountain Area Development (ICIMOD), Kathmandu, Nepal.

Sanjay Kumar is Conservator of Forests, Ranchi, India, and Special Officer at the Ministry of Environment, New Delhi, India.

Tiplut Nongbri is Associate Professor, Anthropology, School of Social Sciences, Jawaharlal Nehru University, New Delhi, India, and currently Professor of Sociology, North-Eastern Hill University (NEHU), Shillong, India.

Girija Shrestha is Program Officer, Urban Management Program, Gender and Development Studies, Asian Institute of Technology, Bangkok, Thailand.

Wang Qinghua is Director, Institute of Ethnology, Yunnan Academy of Social Sciences, Kunming, China.

Yu Xiaogang is Associate Professor, Institute of Ethnology, Yunnan Academy of Social Sciences, Kunming, China and a Doctoral Candidate in Gender and Development Studies, Asian Institute of Technology, Bangkok, Thailand.

Index